EUROPE
AFTER WYCLIF

FORDHAM SERIES IN MEDIEVAL STUDIES

Mary C. Erler and Franklin T. Harkins, series editors

EUROPE
AFTER WYCLIF

J. PATRICK HORNBECK II
AND MICHAEL VAN DUSSEN

Editors

FORDHAM UNIVERSITY PRESS

New York   2017

Fordham University Press has no responsibility for
the persistence or accuracy of URLs for external
or third-party Internet websites referred to in this
publication and does not guarantee that any content
on such websites is, or will remain, accurate or
appropriate.

Fordham University Press also publishes its books
in a variety of electronic formats. Some content that
appears in print may not be available in electronic
books.

Visit us online at www.fordhampress.com.

Library of Congress Cataloging-in-Publication Data
available online at http://catalog.loc.gov.

Printed in the United States of America

19 18 17   5 4 3 2 1

First edition

CONTENTS

EUROPE
AFTER WYCLIF

INTRODUCTION: THE EUROPE OF WYCLIFFISM

J. Patrick Hornbeck II and Michael Van Dussen

[T]here have remained [in England] not a few shoots of this heresy which, unless they are quickly rooted out, will continue thus to grow high; so that there is great doubt whether England (may God in His mercy prevent it) may not come to the same fate as Bohemia. Even if no indications appeared in former times, it has been detected more evidently in recent days, when in different parts of England, many heretics have been detected and captured. A rumor reports, and it is very likely, that they have many associates and a great number of allies who (as daily it comes to pass), infecting and seducing others to the destruction of the entire realm, will increase and become more abundant, until this heresy thrives in Bohemia. Similarly, we have been informed by a trustworthy source (and you certainly ought to have perceived) that frequently messengers of the Wycliffites, hiding in England, set out for Bohemia, to encourage [the Hussites] in their faithlessness and provide them with hope of assistance and support.

—Pope Martin V[1]

Writing in the 1420s, Thomas Netter (ca. 1374–1430) introduces his *Doctrinale antiquitatum fidei ecclesiae catholicae* as the latest in a venerable tradition of defenses "by the ancient Church against heretical novelties from the time of the apostles," before he eventually reveals the Wycliffite heresy to be his primary subject.[2] From an English domestic perspective, Netter's massive Latin treatise would seem to have been out of touch with the times, something that might have been useful, perhaps, in countering Wycliffite heresy earlier in the century, but too blustery (and directed at the wrong audience) for the 1420s. Even Netter recognized the belatedness of his polemic, as if he would have preferred to present it during Wyclif's lifetime.[3] Earlier, the so-called Oldcastle Rising of 1414 had arguably foreclosed any chance of official support for Wycliffism in England, at least in any ostentatious sense, and before that, in the writings of Richard Wyche and William Thorpe, we can discern the entrenchment of academic Wycliffism in its last stand.[4] Perhaps Peter Payne fled England for Bohemia around 1414 for similar reasons.

Of course, we should not overstate the case: Wycliffite ideas, in one form or another, continued to circulate and generate new texts and affiliations throughout much of the fifteenth century in England, particularly in the vernacular, and this despite Archbishop Thomas Arundel's best efforts to thwart such activity through his *Constitutiones* (1407/09).[5] The Wycliffite Bible would become the most widely copied Middle English text ever to be produced. Copies were even commissioned and purchased by prominent patrons; some of them, contrary to the stereotype of Wycliffites as purveyors of only plain texts, contained illustrations that Kathleen Kennedy investigates in her essay in this volume.[6] Wyclif's own writings continued to circulate and find homes in libraries. Lollard "conventicles" (the disparaging term used to describe more or less formal lollard teaching and learning communities) continued to gather, and concern over a more widespread, nonacademic brand of Wycliffism clearly exercised bishops in several dioceses into the sixteenth century.[7] It is less clear, however, if learned, *Latinate* discourse surrounding Wyclif's doctrines continued in England in such a way as to warrant a systematic response like Netter's. Reginald Pecock's vernacular treatises directed at the "lay party"—his ambiguous designation for a group that identified in some way with Wycliffite positions—give the impression that the campaign for the souls of the Wycliffites had moved *extra muros*, beyond the specifically Latinate discursive environment of the academy.

To reiterate, then, Netter produced the most sustained, systematic counter-argument to Wycliffite positions ever to be written, at a time when Wycliffism as an academic, Latinate phenomenon seems to have been a thing of the past—at least in England.[8] But Netter was not addressing an exclusively, or even principally, English domestic audience, or a specifically English heresy. If from an insular perspective it is hard to account for the *Doctrinale*, the view from the continent places the project in better company. Netter took a markedly *European* view of Wycliffism, one that was sensitive to the place of Wycliffite thinking in a broader cultural and geographical context.[9] Few of Netter's English contemporaries shared the breadth of his perspective, despite the embarrassment that their self-imposed blinders had caused for them before the Council of Constance and in the years that followed.[10] The chastising letter from Pope Martin V excerpted in the epigraph to this introduction is but one example of the censures directed from the continent toward England, from which the new heresy had sprung.

Netter dedicated his treatise to Pope Martin V, the pope who had been elected at Constance to help resolve the Great Schism, and who would become a leading figure in the crusades and other campaigns against the Hussites (to whom, as Pavel Soukup's essay here shows, many referred as "Wyclefistae"). Netter's knowledge of the situation in Bohemia was remarkably detailed. Recent work has suggested that he attended Constance, and we know that he acted as a diplomat to Poland, where he joined a delegation to negotiate a peace treaty between the Polish King, the Duke of Lithuania, and the Teutonic Knights; perhaps he passed through Bohemia during that trip. He also knew of Peter Payne, who by the 1420s had become a leading spokesman for the Hussites in Bohemia and who was one of the last remaining partisans of Wyclif in that region (there is an account of Payne delighting over a copy of Netter's text during a break in sessions at the Council of Basel, though by that time Netter was already dead).[11] For all his defenses of English rigor in combatting heresy, Netter was in a position to see that English insularity presented a stumbling block in the campaign against what he and others regarded as the crisis of Wycliffism, which had by that time reached European proportions.

Netter's response to Wycliffite heresy represents a belated recognition of what had been developing for decades. The reach of Wycliffite ideas outside of England began at a very early date, not least because Wyclif and the first generation of Wycliffite academics were part of a European network of scholars and universities that was kept vibrant by the *peregrinatio academica* of both students and masters. Many of Wyclif's initial interventions with regard to logic and philosophy were responses to prevailing theories and methodologies that pervaded university life throughout Europe: for an intellectual of Wyclif's stature, it is hard to speak in terms of English regionalism. Soon Wyclif's controversial teachings were being discussed in Paris and Prague. In Prague the Czech masters found in Wyclif's writings a robust intellectual framework that some felt to be consistent with existing

Bohemian reform agendas. As Ota Pavlíček's essay shows, men like Jerome of Prague sought out more of Wyclif's writings, and soon Wycliffite realism was being used to challenge the prevailing nominalism of the German masters at the university. Eventually, in 1409, the controversy over Wycliffism in Prague (which extended, of course, to more than just Wyclif's doctrines) led to the exodus of most of the German masters, who left to establish a new university at Leipzig. These controversies would continue to attract the attention of church and secular officials in Rome, Paris, and elsewhere, making otherwise regional Bohemian developments to be of continental concern. Eventually Hus and Jerome of Prague would be summoned to Constance, where they would be required to answer for a number of articles allegedly drawn from Wyclif's writings. The post-humous condemnation of Wyclif in May 1415 was followed immediately by Hus's own trial and execution, and then Jerome's the following year. So while the most obvious place to look for the reach of Wycliffism outside of England is clearly Bohemia, the phenomenon cannot be limited to Anglo-Bohemian communication. Further, as Ian Christopher Levy's essay ex-emplifies with regard to the sacrament of the eucharist, nearly all major concerns in Latin Christendom eventually passed through the councils of Constance and later Basel,[12] so regional English and Bohemian emphases and developments were never separable from more centralizing forces in the world of Latin Christianity—what its leaders considered to be the uni-versal church.

Not unlike Thomas Netter—yet with a dramatically different end in sight—the present volume insists upon a similarly comprehensive approach to the study of Wycliffism. Our method might be termed *lateral* (as op-posed to regional or teleological), in as much as it is concerned with the geographical and cultural reach of the Wycliffite controversies in their own time and with the cultural interplay of their period in medieval Europe, rather than with teleological trajectories determined by regional or confes-sional preoccupations. Indeed, one could take a similar approach to any number of figures, texts, regional phenomena, or movements from the later medieval period (or, for that matter, any period). Recent scholarship has begun to do precisely this, not only with regard to the place of Wyclif and his teachings in the Europe of the so-called long fifteenth century, but also to the interplay of regional and interregional currents in the lives of other groups elsewhere on the continent.[13] John Van Engen has emphasized, here as well as elsewhere, the availability of what he has called multiple, competing options, a lively mix of overlapping interests that were never able to preclude one another completely during this period.[14] Others have begun to work against the persisting view of an older Protestant historiography that values Wyclif only insofar as he prefigured Protestantism, modernity, or English (and even German) national identity. Anne Hudson's celebrated monograph, *The Premature Reformation* (1988), represents the first sustained attempt to understand Wyclif and the English contemporaries influenced by him on their own terms. Many others—too numerous to name here—have followed her lead and explored various dimensions of the archive of Wycliffite and anti-Wycliffite sources from late medieval England.[15] Ian Christopher Levy and Stephen Lahey have repeatedly emphasized Wyclif's embeddedness in broader medieval philosophical, theological, and sacramental currents, including the developments in Bohemia.[16] Kantik Ghosh has asked if it might be more appropriate to regard Wycliffism not as "a discrete phenomenon in English religious history," but as participating in "a much more complex and extensive international network of religious, intellectual, and institutional conflicts and synergies."[17] From a central European perspective, detailed studies of the place of Wyclif's thinking in Bohemian reformist circles have been around for some time, though this work has made noticeable inroads into Anglophone scholarship relatively recently.[18]

The past three decades have witnessed a series of revolutions in the study of religion, politics, writing, and culture in late medieval Europe. These revolutions have led scholars to question much received wisdom about the ways in which medieval Europeans—clergy as well as laypeople—approached religious questions, and about how the events of the later Middle Ages are to be related to those of the religious reformations of the sixteenth century. Scholars have begun to cross both disciplinary and geographical boundaries in their work on late medieval religion.[19] Historians, theologians, and literary scholars are now borrowing more often than ever before from one another's methodologies and findings.

In the wake of these developments, the time is now ripe for scholars across the range of disciplinary perspectives and national affiliations to come together to share their findings, collectively assess the state of the field, and identify future opportunities for scholarly engagement. *Europe After Wyclif* provides one such forum, taking as its goal to broaden significantly the boundaries of scholarship on Wyclif, Wycliffism, Lollardy, Hussitism, and cognate topics in order to consider more holistically both the pan-European context in which these movements were situated and the categories that contemporary scholars use to describe and contest them. The volume therefore builds on recent discussions of religious controversy in late medieval England that have increasingly adopted a continental scope. Here, essays by John Van Engen, Pavlína Cermanová, and Luigi Campi, among others, extend this trajectory in their studies of topics ranging from apocalyptic thinking to philosophical disputes about free will. At the same time, the international scope of recent scholarship on English and European religious controversy has also been enriched by interdisciplinary crosscurrents. The essays by Fiona Somerset, Mishtooni Bose, Jennifer Illig, and Louisa Z. Foroughi demonstrate the continued vitality of approaches that defy modern categories that separate the literary, theological, legal, and diplomatic spheres. As Somerset and Bose especially show, what was formerly perceived as a fixed boundary between Latinity and vernacularity is now treated as porous and contested.

The shifts within and between academic disciplines that we have been tracing call for a reevaluation of the categories and academic forums that mediate the study of religious controversy in the later Middle Ages. Do longstanding discussions of Lollardy and Wycliffism adequately capture the transnational realities of cultural exchange in late medieval Europe? Are the labels we employ too restrictive as we attempt to gather the most innovative new scholarship on medieval religious controversy at conferences and in collected volumes? And importantly, has the study of religious controversy in England become too insular and therefore unrepresentative of medieval realities? *Europe After Wyclif* seeks to approach questions like these as well, coupling discussion of cultural and material intersections in late medieval Europe with deliberate assessment of the venues presently available to scholars for the exchange of ideas. Many of the essays that follow—such as Illig's, Foroughi's, and Mary Raschko's—retain a core emphasis on Wycliffism and English religious controversy, but the volume as a whole does not regard Wycliffism as its sole raison d'être, and several essays take the continent as a starting point. Indeed, our authors have been encouraged to explore intersections—the points at which Wycliffism and

English religiosity meet with broader social, cultural, historical, literary, and material issues of European significance.

The essays collected here therefore reflect a string of recent developments in the study of late medieval religion, but they also point to the volume of work that remains to be done. Boundaries—disciplinary as well as linguistic and geographical—continue to stand in the way of the holistic approach to medieval religious controversy that this volume seeks to champion. For instance, texts such as *Opus arduum valde*, explored here by Cermanová, remain unedited, and we still await full canonical analysis of the "religion" (*religio*) of the laity and clergy that serves as the basis for part of Van Engen's trenchant argument. Some work on English religious controversy still remains indebted to strict binaries between Lollardy and orthodoxy, binaries that many essays here show are artificial at best. And many Anglophone scholars are not yet as familiar with Bohemian texts and religious history as are their central European counterparts—a gap we seek to bridge here with the inclusion in this collection of three essays written by scholars from the Czech Republic.

Thomas Netter believed that Wycliffism was a European problem. Today, far fewer people than in Netter's time are willing to treat as problematic, much less diabolical, a competing religious system, but many of us could benefit from elements of the geographically and temporally sweeping perspective through which Netter saw his opponents. *Europe After Wyclif* seeks to show some of what may be possible if scholars broaden the set of lenses through which we look at the religious controversies of the later Middle Ages. It is our hope that this volume will accomplish more than simply to present twelve studies of the world of the Wycliffites and Hussites. We also hope that it will reveal what more can be seen when specialists step back to consider as a whole the bustling stage on which their subjects moved.

NOTES

1. Pope Martin V in a letter to officials of the Church of England on 9 October 1428: "[R]emanserunt ibidem hujus haeresis non parvi surculi, qui nisi celeriter extirpentur, adhuc ita exurgent in altum, quod valde dubitandum est ne Anglia (quod Deus per suam misericordiam avertat) adveniat quemadmodum & Bohemia: quod & si superiori tempore nonnulla indicia apparuerunt, a paucis citra diebus evidentius detectum est; cum in diversis Angliae partibus multi

reperti sunt & capti haeretici, quos & fama refert, & valde verisimile est, multos habere participes & magnum sociorum numerum, qui, ut quotidie fieri solet, inficientes & seducentes alios in perniciem totius regni crescent & abundabunt magis, quamdiu vigebit in Bohemia haec haeresis. Et a fide dignis accepimus, & vos certius intellexisse debetis, quod saepenumero a Wicklefistis in Anglia latentibus, in Bohemiam proficiscuntur nuncio, illos in sua perfidia confortantes, & praebentes eisdem auxilii & subsidii spem." The Latin text of the complete letter is printed in Gratius Ortwinus, *Fasciculus rerum expetendarum et fugiendarum*, ed. Edward Brown, 2 vols. (London: Bassani, 1690; repr. Tucson, AZ: Audax, 1967), 2:616–617.

2. Thomas Netter, *Doctrinale antiquitatum fidei catholicae ecclesiae*, ed. B. Blanciotti, 3 vols. (Venice, 1757–1759; repr. Farnborough, England: Gregg International, 1967), 1:2: "contra novitates haereticas antiqua ecclesia a temporibus apostolorum." Netter certainly completed his work by 1430, the year of his death, though it is unclear how much earlier he began its composition. See Anne Hudson, *The Premature Reformation* (Oxford: Oxford University Press, 1988), 50–55.

3. *Doctrinale*, 3:578–579.

4. For the notion of Lollardy as a "failed revolution," see Rita Copeland, *Pedagogy, Intellectuals, and Dissent in the Later Middle Ages: Lollardy and Ideas of Learning* (Cambridge: Cambridge University Press, 2001), 200.

5. For revisionist approaches to the hitherto prevailing claim that Arundel's constitutions devastated vernacular theological writing and activity in England, see Vincent Gillespie and Kantik Ghosh, eds., *After Arundel: Religious Writing in Fifteenth-Century England* (Turnhout, Belgium: Brepols, 2011).

6. For a first entry to the subject of its circulation, see also Kathleen E. Kennedy, *The Courtly and Commercial Art of the Wycliffite Bible* (Turnhout, Belgium: Brepols, 2014), passim.

7. See Norman P. Tanner, *Heresy Trials in the Diocese of Norwich* (London: Royal Historical Society, 1977); and Shannon McSheffrey, *Gender and Heresy: Women and Men in Lollard Communities, 1420–1530* (Philadelphia: University of Pennsylvania Press, 1995). A useful list of heresy trials in fifteenth- and sixteenth-century England is found in J. Patrick Hornbeck II, *What Is a Lollard? Dissent and Belief in Late Medieval England* (Oxford: Oxford University Press, 2010), 205–214.

8. Other Carmelites, perhaps with Netter's contribution, likewise remained mobilized against the perceived Wycliffite threat. See *Fasciculi zizaniorum*, a Carmelite collection of mainly anti-Wycliffite material from the mid-fifteenth century (ca. 1439 in its present form). Sections of the manuscript—now Oxford, Bodleian Library, MS e Musaeo 86—are edited by W. W. Shirley as *Fasciculi zizaniorum Magistri Johannis Wyclif cum tritico* (London, 1858).

9. For studies of Netter and his work from the last few decades, see especially

Kantik Ghosh, *The Wycliffite Heresy: Authority and the Interpretation of Texts* (Cambridge: Cambridge University Press, 2002), 174–208; Johan Bergström-Allen and Richard Copsey, eds., *Thomas Netter of Walden: Carmelite, Diplomat and Theologian (c. 1372–1430)* (Rome: Edizioni Carmelitane, 2009); and Kevin J. Alban, *The Teaching and Impact of the "Doctrinale" of Thomas Netter of Walden (c. 1374–1430)* (Turnhout, Belgium: Brepols, 2010). By the 1420s, and after Hus's execution at Constance in 1415, few in Bohemia paid much attention to Wyclif's writings, an exception being the Englishman Peter Payne.

10. We find exceptions in the encyclopedic collections of John Whethamstede and Thomas Gascoigne, but seldom anywhere else. For English embarrassment at Constance, see Van Dussen, *From England to Bohemia: Heresy and Communication in the Later Middle Ages* (Cambridge: Cambridge University Press, 2012), chap. 4.

11. *Monumenta conciliorum seculi decimi quinti, concilium Basiliense scriptorium* (Vienna, 1858), 1:307.

12. See John Van Engen, "Multiple Options: The World of the Fifteenth-Century Church," *Church History* 77 (2008): 262–263.

13. See, for example, Michael Van Dussen and Pavel Soukup, eds., *Religious Controversy in Europe, 1378–1536: Textual Transmission and Networks of Readership* (Turnhout, Belgium: Brepols, 2013).

14. Van Engen, "Multiple Options."

15. For an overview of the historiography of English Wycliffism, see J. Patrick Hornbeck II, *A Companion to Lollardy* (Leiden, Netherlands: Brill, 2016).

16. In *From England to Bohemia*, Michael Van Dussen has also discussed the development of Wycliffite communication with the Hussites in terms of broader religio-political developments of the late fourteenth and fifteenth centuries.

17. "Wycliffite 'Affiliations': Some Intellectual-Historical Perspectives," in Mishtooni Bose and J. Patrick Hornbeck II, eds., *Wycliffite Controversies* (Turnhout, Belgium: Brepols, 2011), 32. A number of recent studies, not all of them taking Wycliffism as their primary subject, highlight broader European cultural developments in which the Wycliffites participated. See especially Kathryn Kerby-Fulton, *Books Under Suspicion: Censorship and Tolerance of Revelatory Writing in Late Medieval England* (South Bend, IN: University of Notre Dame Press, 2006); John Van Engen, *Sisters and Brothers of the Common Life: The Devotio Moderna and the World of the Later Middle Ages* (Philadelphia: University of Pennsylvania Press, 2008); Daniel Hobbins, *Authorship and Publicity before Print: Jean Gerson and the Transformation of Late Medieval Learning* (Philadelphia: University of Pennsylvania Press, 2009); and Michael Van Dussen, *From England to Bohemia*.

18. However, several Anglophone studies appeared in the middle decades of the last century that remain of lasting value. See, for example, R. W. Seton-Watson, ed., *Prague Essays* (Oxford: Clarendon Press, 1949); and R. R. Betts, *Essays in*

Czech History (London: Athlone Press, 1969). There is also a distinguished tradition of scholarship on Wycliffite manuscripts in Bohemia; see especially the work of Williel R. Thomson and Anne Hudson. For Czech and German studies of the place of Wyclif's thought in the Bohemian Reformation, see the extensive bibliography in the essay by Ota Pavlíček in this volume.

19. This work of course has been made increasingly possible after the fall of the Iron Curtain, which has led to a gradual deepening of contact between scholarly communities.

CHAPTER ONE

A WORLD ASTIR: EUROPE AND RELIGION IN THE EARLY FIFTEENTH CENTURY

John Van Engen

In the early to mid-1430s, a young boy named Egbert walked through a public square in the market town of Deventer bearing a plate of food, eyes down, clothing and hair cut distinctively. Son of a nearby gentry family, he had been sent to the local Latin school, widely regarded as the best in the region (where Erasmus would go fifty years later), in hopes of securing him an advantageous clerical career. Once in Deventer he encountered a newish group of "Brothers" living a "Common Life." They drew him toward another option, to choose spiritual rigor rather than careerist ambition. On this day he chanced to encounter a female relative in the square. When he did not lift his eyes to greet her, she knocked the plate out of his hand and exclaimed, "What for a lollard is this who goes walking about like that?"[1] Here was a teenage relative of good family and fine education walking through town in a hyperreligious manner, as she saw it, lacking the courtesy even to greet kin, possibly harboring suspect views. The slur this woman reached for was "lollard." It came from a Dutch word meaning "to mumble" and had originated as a dismissive gesture toward extraordinarily religious persons who spent their time, as it appeared, mumbling prayers, much as the word *beguine* sprang from a French word of more or less the same meaning. She might instead have used *beghaert*, a word suggesting someone "puffed up," especially about religion. These words would accumulate multiple meanings over time: a slur directed at anyone accounted hyperreligious, the accepted slang for groups living specially religious lives outside formal religious orders, a tag for individuals with dubious spiritual views or practices, sometimes all three working at once—which would then, confusingly, also become true in historians' subsequent use of these terms.[2] The word *lollard* seemingly migrated across the Channel, doubtless from seaport to seaport, from the Low Countries to England (though some have also suggested a native English origin).

What should we make of calling someone a lollard in the mid-1430s at Deventer?[3] Had the term moved back to continental Europe freighted with new meaning in the wake of Master John Wyclif? Had lollards become the talk of seaport towns? It's hard to say. This slur might echo Wyclif's condemnation at the Council of Constance, *lollard* thus taking on tones not only of the hyperreligious and suspicious but of the seriously heretical. No allusions to Wyclif or lollards as such appeared however in the flurry around the Sisters and Brothers of the Common Life, though they were themselves pursued early by an inquisitor and then a decade or so later by a hostile Dominican. On the continent Hussites loomed larger in popular rumor and worry. These were people sustaining open rebellion against church and emperor and threatening Prague, the capital of the empire and the home to central Europe's earliest university, and sometimes outside Bohemia they were labeled *Wycliffites*. *Hussite* also occasionally appears as a general slur in early fifteenth-century Europe, though likewise nearly never applied to the Sisters and Brothers of the Common Life.

Traditional accounts of medieval heresy have framed lollards and Hussites as national heresies. This label mirrored the nineteenth century's preoccupation with the nation-state as well as romantic notions of national character, even as it echoed and perpetuated inherited protestant genealogies for the Reformation. What we make of this story of young Egbert—or, on a grander scale how we position lollards and Hussites in late medieval society and culture—hinges upon how we frame religious stirring broadly in fifteenth-century European society. One temptation is to make religion and especially religious upheaval nearly the whole story, another to treat such dissenting groups largely apart from European society and religion more generally. Since the 1980s John Wyclif, together with those writings and teachings in English and Latin deemed "lollard," have awakened intense scholarly inquiry on the part of intellectual historians and theologians but especially among scholars of Middle English literature. Indeed, lollard writing for a time nearly came to dominate a literary canon or anticanon otherwise given over to Chaucer and Langland or Julian and Margery. To a historian, lollards can appear to have become a wholly owned subsidiary of English departments, the libeled or apotheosized lollards assuming center stage—an ironic inversion which other scholars have in turn disputed, denied, or ignored. Recently we seem to have entered a season of reflection and indeed of moving on, an *after* phase, evident in a widely noted conference "After Arundel" and in this volume's "Europe after Wyclif."[4] Many scholarly questions, old and new, persist: the exact connections between Master Wyclif and lollards, the degree to which Hussite positions and debates bore the mark of Wyclif's writings, the possible relation of lollard writing to something called *vernacular theology*, the extent to which Arundel's intervention remolded religious culture or language, any ripple effects of lollards on devotion and devotional writing more broadly, the character of the "lollard" Bible, what writings should be called lollard, and so on.

I readily acknowledge the continuing importance of these questions and the learning that has gone into them this last while. I come to this from another angle, however, as a historian of religious movements in the high and later Middle Ages, mostly on the continent, especially the Low Countries and German lands. I seek richer accounts of the culture and religion of the fourteenth and fifteenth centuries, more variegated storylines and cultural paradigms not stuck inside rigid and antiquated notions of humanists versus scholastics, Latin versus vernacular, churchmen versus people, inquisitors versus mystics, priests versus women, orthodox versus heretical, and so on. Tensions there were in late medieval religious culture, sometimes awful ones, at times murderous ones. Still, lines were not always so simple, clear, or clean. Tensions proved creative as well as destructive, and crossovers and intersections often surprise.[5] To overstate the point, and perhaps unfairly, if we insist on seeing this world entirely through a narrow version of Eamon Duffy's thriving "traditional religion," or just as entirely through the tight focus of heroic "dissenting lollards," we effectively create the obverse and reverse of one and the same false coin. Moreover, the notion of "Europe after Wyclif" is itself ambiguous, perhaps intentionally so, implying both a question and an assumption, about ripples of change across Europe. The focus here will not be upon ripples of influence as such, real, imagined, or feared. Such work rests on detailed reception studies which claim considerable scholarly attention in Bohemia just now, careful and technical manuscript work that is both admirable and important. Here my question is about historical positioning, how we imagine a Europe in which lollards and Hussites in some sense fit in, not just as the paradigm for subversion or as a rebellious anomaly, but as players in a late medieval Europe all astir.

Ever since the sixteenth century, humanist and reformist punditry, sometimes allied now with reductionist approaches to social or cultural power, have conspired to turn our storylines into binaries, even among scholars who piously foreswear all binaries. We must be careful. Jean Gerson could shake his head at the visionary claims of Birgitta of Sweden but defend those of Joan of Arc, write in French or Latin as it suited, as did too Hus (Czech) and Grote (Dutch) and countless other contemporary figures. Master Gerson could act to condemn masters Wyclif and Hus, while defending the Sisters and Brothers of the Common Life against a Dominican inquisitor whom he condemned. He could expound on ecclesiastical power at length, and also lead the Council of Constance into declaring conciliar authority ancient, authentic, and binding under the Holy Spirit. He could attack simony as eating away at the integrity of the church, and yet defend the ranked enjoyment of the accoutrements of office and its privileges as essential to the dignity of those estates. Gerson was undoubtedly an exceptional personality, but his paradoxes were not so exceptional. Religious rhetoric and spiritual claims could be shrill, even unrelenting, and the more so as they moved past the complexities of all social or religious reality. In a world of amazing contrarieties, late medieval religious practice steadily complicated, layered, and nuanced the meaning and working out of these pronouncements. We must imagine people finding ways to live with such contrariety, as too those who insisted on very particular visions of what religion was or should be.

For people in the fifteenth century too, this could all prove quite bewildering. In 1383, five years into the papal schism, Master Geert Grote, founder of the Devotio Moderna, wrote a long canonistic exposition for a close friend, also a Parisian-trained cleric, answering an agonized call for advice on the rival popes. In the end Master Geert characterized his words as disordered outpourings of mind and heart which came to no clean legal resolution favoring either pope. He talked instead of overcoming his own "interior schism," and moving in love to "gather" (*congregare*) a few around him into a sheepfold of Christ.[6] A shorter letter to this same friend at that same time noted the "fall" and "ruin" of the church as marks of the end time, and recommended that they no longer pursue the inherited ways of worldly and worldly-wise clergymen but rather the books and truth of clergy—moving themselves to act as preachers and teachers of that bookish truth (both were deacons, not priests).[7] In this same atmosphere of uncertainty Cardinal Pierre d'Ailly, along with not a few others among the learned, turned for help to prophetic revelation,[8] even as they pored over

law and scripture and wrote learned tractates and entered into tough negotiations, all to bring some order and understanding to a European church
they found, even beyond the trying matter of papal schism, in disarray.
Catherine of Siena with her followers in Tuscany and beyond vigorously
backed the Roman pope, while Friar Vincent Ferrer, a preacher active in
Iberia and France, firmly backed the Avignon pope, both reformers renowned for the power of their rhetoric in their native tongues.

CANON LAWYERS ON THE SHAPE OF RELIGION

If we stand back a little from literal readings of the angry or the pious
pronouncements of single-minded reformers and prophets, we may seek a
more panoramic view of the late medieval church, and for that we turn to
lawyers. By the late fourteenth century law and lawyers, not theologians,
had dominated the church and its business for over two centuries.[9] This is
precisely why they were so fiercely (and ineffectively) impugned by theologians, who always remained distinctly in the minority and rarely gained
powerful posts (thus Wyclif and Luther, and many already before them).
To grasp what these church lawyers took for granted and tried to account
for, we must begin with what they presumed. Remember that in medieval
society nearly all persons (small communities of Jews or Muslims excepted)
were christened as babies, and by virtue of the invisible and ineradicable
mark of the Lord Christ imprinted on their forehead were joined at birth
to Christendom, and hereby also obligated from childhood to religious
duties at once cultic, moral, and faithful. This meant church jurisdiction
over dimensions of their lives we might account social—thus marriage,
wills, tithes, land-bearing church claims, and more. This took in over
90 percent of Europeans (indeed down to the Reformation or the Revolution). Beyond them a smallish minority, highly privileged in religion and
often in social status as well, bound themselves to a more particular rule of
life by vow, and these people professed to religion had long since co-opted
the word (*religio*) for their status and life, indeed were commonly referred
to as "the religious."

Accordingly, the term *apostate* referred most commonly in this era to
renegade monks or nuns or friars and only occasionally to those relative
few in the later Middle Ages who repudiated their baptism to join a community of Jews or Muslims. The jurisdictional claim that came with baptism

could in principle still order apostates of either sort back to their previous estates, though actual practice on this account was more nuanced and varied.

Those deemed heretics too continued to fall under the church's jurisdiction by virtue of their christening. Here coercive power was intended in principle not to torture or kill but to turn errant souls back to keeping the church's law. Condemnation followed properly only on the persistent refusal of such persons to acknowledge the authority implicit in that baptismal mark and obediently to recant errant views or practices pointed out to them by churchmen.[10] In Latin and all later medieval languages this "law" enfolded layers of meaning stretching from Scripture itself to items of belief and practice as well as its broader inherent sense of obligation—a point that masters Wyclif and Hus fully shared with the larger community, even if the term was employed by them more specifically to drive their conception of that community. Ecclesiology, how one understood the makeup of the church (though, remarkably, not yet an explicit part of Peter Lombard's *Sentences* in the 1150s and hence of the required formal teaching of theologians) underlay any coherent articulation of how medieval European society and religion conjoined and indeed how the community itself was constituted. This too was a point that both Wyclif and Hus intuitively grasped (whence the importance of works on this subject in their oeuvre), as had theologians and canonists more explicitly since the battles between mendicants and seculars and then the showdown between Pope Boniface VIII (a smart canon lawyer) and King Louis the Fair (counseled by his lawyers). Still, in some sense it all rested on baptism, indeed the baptism of infants. In the eleventh and twelfth centuries several dissident groups had explicitly challenged this foundation, calling for a conscious or chosen adult baptism or blessing. Notably, too, the consecrated vows of those called religious had long since accounted in monastic spirituality as a second baptism. All this, interestingly and intriguingly, the fundamentals of christening and community, Wyclif, Hus, and other reformers and dissidents from around the year 1400 left untouched as such.

Given these presumptions, then, canonists offered a scheme that parsed the social and religious state of a Europe-wide church in a layered definition of religion. The scheme summarized here comes from Johannes Andreae (ca. 1270–1348), a Bolognese professor of law, by way of Archbishop Antoninus of Florence (1446–1459). Master Johannes, notably, had been married and spawned children inside and outside of marriage, including a daughter ("Novella") said to help him in copying his lectures, while Friar Antoninus, an Observant Dominican in the middle of Medici Florence, authored a *summa* of law and theology subsequently dubbed *moralis* since he focused more on matters of practice than doctrine, more on jurisdiction in the internal court (confession and the like) than the external (ecclesiastical property and personnel). According to this scheme,[11] widely echoed, religion referred, first and most broadly, to all who offered up that cult or worship owed the true God, thus all the christened (*totam christianitatem*), also called simply the *religio christiana*. This is a term that both Gerson and Wyclif also invoked for their own distinct purposes: Gerson especially to establish the religion of the parish (not the cloister) as basic,[12] Wyclif (and Hus) to highlight his vision of a "true" parish or "congregation" as foundational.[13]

Second, *religio* referred more specially, these lawyers say, to those who acted upon their christening in virtue, thus all good Christians (*uniuersitatem bonorum christianorum*). These, we might say, are the people Duffy lifted out for us, their presence real enough, those laity zealous in deed and devotion, while his account in effect silently passed over the spectrum of less zealous folk in the lawyers' first inclusive typology. "Good Christians" are the people Wyclif and Hus have in mind too, their "goodness" somewhat differently framed (as other reformers did each in their own way); these true, zealous, or devout whom they aimed to define, foster, or set apart from that larger more amorphous body embracing all the christened. That broader group of all the christened often appear as the apt targets of reproachful preachers and confessors (and, of course, of the "good" who needed reminding). These were people who appeared, or perhaps were, relatively indifferent to church attendance, from time to time unscrupulous in work, unfaithful in marriage, miserly in prayer or alms-giving, foggy about the creed, and easily resentful of clergy. They were not heretics—those judged to have taken an alternative way in belief or practice—and certainly not infidels (meaning, unbaptized). Nor indeed did they see themselves as anything like those smaller groups of the true, illumined, or zealous, while the latter in turn regularly distinguished themselves from this reputedly negligent horde of the christened, as lollards or Hussites did as well. We might say that this broad category was intended to embrace people christened at birth who as adults drifted into, or quietly sorted out

for themselves, a level of practice that might suit, just which duties and de-
votions to fulfill and how intently and reverently to take guidance and instruction from clergymen. Our expositions often overlook these more
"ordinary" cases, though they were held so firmly in the eye of preachers—
drawn as our interests often are to the special or more "interesting" cases
of the religiously animated. Importantly, we have no real way to construe
in what percentages these two typologies coexisted among the later medieval laity. As for those rightly or wrongly called lollards, beyond their
possibly taking a striking stance toward one or another common practice
or belief, it was doubtless their earnestness that stood out, their determined
zeal which verged toward religion in the stricter set-apart sense of the
religious.

Third, and more specially still, *religio* referred, these lawyers suggested,
to the clerical estate, those persons dedicated to the maintenance and
carrying out of religious cult and practice, the tonsured in effect, all those
in the "secular" clergy from minor orders to the vicar of St. Peter. In some
later medieval ecclesiologies those positioned theologically or politically at
the opposite end of conciliarists defined church more exclusively or em-
blematically as the clergy or the bishops or simply the cardinals and pope,
for they bore and sustained the whole cult of religion.

Lastly, and most strictly (*strictissimo*), these lawyers say, the term *religio*
referred to those who had submitted by vow to a superior and dedicated
their entire lives wholly to God alone, coming thereby personally to inhabit
the estate of religion (*status religionis*). Master John Wyclif was well aware
of all these distinctions, or ones like them. He would himself in time
repudiate altogether any exclusive claim to religion by those whom he
called, by a key and deliberate inversion, the "private religious," meaning
especially friars but also propertied monks. He echoed a virulent antifra-
ternal mood growing since the thirteenth century, especially among secular masters and priests (he was both, as were Hus and Gerson). Friars and
their churches operated at the center of every town of any size, rivaling
local parish pastors, such that resentment of these "privileged religious"
became widespread in late medieval Europe, this often mirrored to comic
effect in vernacular satire—along with, one must also add, equal admiration
for and attraction to the friars as learnedly and actively working among the
people. In terms of our typologies we might also say that masters Wyclif
and Hus, and in a more restrained way Gerson, each of them a secular

priest and thus of the third category, were upending the more exclusive claims to religious status of the fourth, though their critique in its particulars could also reach well beyond that.

These lawyerly typologies corresponded to intelligible socio-cultural perceptions of Europe's religion of the christened in the high and later Middle Ages, and as such would be commonly and broadly understood even by many in the "out" groups. *Religion* referred collectively to all the baptized, whatever their degree of practice and however minimal their knowledge or devotion, then more particularly to those laity accounted zealous and virtuous in actual deed; more narrowly still it referred to the secular clergy, the bearers of cultic religion and moral authority among the people, and then most particularly to the consecrated professed, religion's embodiment and exemplars. The first two groups, lay, were subject to local civil law in all matters except those touching the oversight of the church and churchmen; the last two, the clerical and the professed, were subject in principle exclusively to ecclesiastical jurisdiction, the oft-resented benefit of clergy, that sacral and juridical autonomy for which Thomas Becket had given his life a good two centuries earlier, founding thereby the best-known and most widely visited pilgrimage site in England and one of the best-known in Europe.

Not everyone, reserving heretics and apostates for now, fit neatly into these categories, and those who did not have also tended to capture more scholarly interest, as they did to some degree in their own time. For such extraordinary types, however, precedents and even quasi-legal forms of recognition also emerged. Already in the thirteenth century the distinguished canonist Cardinal Hostiensis recognized that some laypeople lived more religiously (*arctiorem et sanctiorem*) than others, meaning not just more virtuously but in forms of life identified as more religion-like, for instance, as hospitalers, recluses, hermits, or pious widows, types all visible in thirteenth-century Italian towns. These too, he opined, might be called religious in an extended sense (*largo modo dicitur religiosus*). While this position never gained full traction—it does not appear, unless I am mistaken, in Friar Archbishop Antontinus's exposition, for instance—it regularly was invoked in legal rulings as well as practical settlements worked out with local communities over the next two centuries—until this was all shut down by the Council of Trent.[14] In the fifteenth century Friar Johannes Nider (ca. 1380–1438), likewise a key figure among Observant

Dominicans, himself in attendance at both major councils and a player in interactions with Hussites, wrote two still-unedited works on "laity living as religious," as he called them. The works remain unedited in part because they are so densely packed with canon law, hence not easily recognized by scholars of religious life for what they are: his attempt to sort out the status of some nine socioreligious groups, overwhelmingly but not exclusively women (beguines, secular canonesses, recluses, and so on) who had all assumed a large presence in his world, especially the Rhineland and South German cities, and who also fell disproportionately to the care of friars. These were zealously religious people who looked and acted in ways or forms neither clearly lay nor clearly clerical or religious, who also in part did not know how to position their own form of life within the church. Nider, though tough-minded about church matters, aimed mostly to defend these groups as legitimately or plausibly religious and to interpret their way of life as protected—presuming they did not overstep certain trip wires that might suggest disobedience or heresy.[15]

DISSIDENT GROUPS, THEIR SELF-REGARD, AND THEIR LABELS

Friar Johannes Nider hardly approved of Wyclif—he aimed to refute Hussites, though also to converse and negotiate with them. Yet Master John Wyclif held to some views little different on this point from Friar Nider: namely, that a Christian keeping to the perfection of the gospel outside the cloister was not to be called worldly or lay (*observans perfeccionem evangelii extra claustrum corporale non dicitur secularis*), for Christ and the apostles had lived that way too, and for that matter the "imperfect" might live as well inside as outside a cloister.[16] Wyclif's voice here may be indignant, defensive, or even prospective. But the Oxford master and parish rector could imagine, indeed more and more, Christian or religious people who observed Gospel perfection outside a cloister, and hence were not to be dismissed merely as "in the world." Obviously some of these would come to be called lollards. Because the lay among them were often married—the poor preachers looked more like austere friars outside formal orders—they did not resemble so obviously those varied groups of celibate quasi-religious (beguines, recluses, and so on). Were they then a novel and improved form of the zealous laity? Or, under their "Abbot Christ," with their poor priests and preachers, were they in fact a good deal like Nider's "laity practicing religion," in this case "true religion"? To certain authorities they manifestly looked quite otherwise: people who had broken in belief or practice with their compact at christening (one way of articulating heresy) and hence in dire need of being brought back round by teaching, inquisition, or coercion before their spiritual disease be allowed to infect the larger body.

But what of their own self-regard?[17] Lollards and Hussites certainly did not see themselves as breaking with their christening, rather as fulfilling it, and they never challenged infant baptism. They saw themselves more as a faithful remnant, the true and zealous, first of all over against all the indifferent and errant but equally over against errant clergy. They called on people to make a turn back to the true ways of the Law of Christ. In a sermon preached in 1406 at St. Paul's Cross, William Taylor urged people to recognize, first, that the whole church, priests and people, had fallen away from the love and especially the "law" of God, that nearly all the baptized were hypocrites, which he found evidenced for instance in their sham fasting.[18] The need was for the "true people" to "gather," and for these true to separate out as a group of law-keepers.[19] Still others among these "true" would accuse the majority of late medieval churchgoers of rampant idolatry for their reliance on images in worship or their turning bread (the reserved host) into an object of worship. Still, we must be careful not to isolate certain charges out of context, as earlier protestant pundits did. We must situate these charges and countercharges in a larger world of religion astir.

One recurrent difficulty in approaching this religious stirring with a less over-determined narrative language springs from the labels they then and we still wield. Terms like *lollard*, *Beguine*, or *Beghard* suffer now, and suffered then, from acquired interpretive associations, also true for Cathars and Waldensians as well as Free Spirits. In a pioneering dissertation forty years ago, Robert Lerner concluded that there were in fact no Free Spirits; the sect, at least in the sense of identifiable people adhering to an intentional sect of religious libertines, was a concoction rather of the papal ruling *Ad nostrum*. More recently Mark Pegg, now followed by R. I. Moore, has argued that there were no Cathars, at least in the sense of a distinct religious community with a self-conscious dualist cosmology or theology; there were rather *boni homines* zealously pursuing religion in varied ways, only some of which may have moved into a fully dualist cosmology, such a theology constructed as much, or possibly more, by adversaries and inquisitors.[20]

Modern Devout, English lollards, and Czech Hussites there certainly were, Waldensians too, and people whom others pointed to as Cathars or Free Spirits. At the same time, not every rumor of unusual religious practice or belief yields evidence of heroic religious dissenters. A good deal of what we can detect on the ground falls somewhere in between, the lives of individuals or groups that often played out very locally.[21] Hence we have problems, as scholars increasingly see, deciding what should count as, say, lollard or Free Spirit in teachings or writings.[22] Too often scholars fail to perceive or determine how freely or suspiciously or even ordinarily such works or people circulated among other parishioners or alongside those more extraordinarily religious, with works of all sorts also often found in the same codex.

I am not wholly persuaded myself by those who see charges of heresy as mainly manufactured in order to bolster an ecclesiastical establishment on the march; among other possible objections this vision tends to rob the religious aspirants themselves of their humanity and singular spiritual energies. At the same time, I readily concede that the pursuit and categorization of persons as heterodox could generate its own realities and drive people moreover toward adopting new positions in society and religion. And in a society where religion and social power came so thoroughly intertwined, acts in one sphere nearly always had consequences for the other. Rumors spun about the oddly or extraordinarily religious could acquire a proverbial life outrunning the more mundane or complex realities, while measures taken against such groups or individuals could well drive them to the fringe or into resistance and new forms of coalescence. But what they actually were, what they were rumored to be, and the ways that rumors and charges in turn created their own realities—these still confront historians with puzzles not easy to untangle. Ian Forrest, if I read him correctly, laid out more by way of methods for finding heresy or warning of it, as well as for dealing with rumors and reports of it, than instances of heresy as such.[23] While a narrative of people making their own communities and finding their own religious way, only to be confronted by an arrogant new university-trained intellectual elite, has generated wide resonance, it masks more conflicted complexities on the ground, including instances and attitudes of practical tolerance. It also confers on these clerical inquisitors a degree of power, as well as a stickman quality, that also does not necessarily bear out in realities on the ground.[24]

Master John Wyclif, a priest with a living, died quietly in bed in 1384, reportedly after hearing mass, exiled from Oxford with certain teachings under censure to be sure, but writing furiously nearly to the end. That same year Master Geert Grote died of the plague in Deventer while appealing to Rome against the bishop of Utrecht's withdrawal of his license to preach, a right he had secured as a deacon and exercised vigorously for three or four years around the diocese. In fall 1383, as an honor, he was invited to preach to the annual diocesan synod, and took this occasion to lambast its assembled clergy for their female companions, hearth-mates or hearth-girls as slang had it (*focarista*)—and he loudly called upon laypeople to shun their masses.[25] Still, most secular clergy, most parishioners too, were easy with an ancient custom whereby 25 to 65 percent of local parish priests may have had companions.[26] We must not draw our lines too simply. So too for the first decade and more, Master Jan Hus's local battle in Prague was grounded not only in his preaching and in strife within the theological faculty at Prague, but concretely in local legal actions disputing his leading a highly successful preaching church independent of a parish; in this matter, reigning law, though fungible, was mostly not on Hus's side—an act that could look too much like what friars had done.[27]

As with Master Geert each side immediately tried to wield canon law to their advantage, all the way up to Rome in appeals. This had long since become standard operating procedure in the late medieval church for those who had the learning and access as well as time and money. Between late 1414 and early 1418 these actions shifted to Constance and were now dealt with in council. At Constance, Birgitta would be critiqued and approved and later critiqued again, with Gerson's intervention on the matter circulating in over one hundred extant manuscripts. If we focus only on Wyclif or Arundel, with little sense of the push and shove that could be church business as usual in this period and with a storyline already implicitly in hand, we overlook striking anomalies. This Oxford master was not personally condemned (as distinct from a selection of his teachings in 1382) until thirty years after his death and burial in a country churchyard fifty miles north of Oxford in 1384. His bones were dug up and burned only in 1428, thirteen years after the condemnation in May 1415 at Constance. Consider too that after more than a generation of bloody warfare between splintered Hussites and imperial and ecclesiastical forces, both sides additionally riven by social partisanship, a face-saving solution was proffered in offering communion in both kinds, an issue not part of Master Hus's original reform agenda.

LOCALITY AND CENTRALITY IN LATER MEDIEVAL
RELIGIOUS HISTORY, A REVERSED DYNAMIC

Europe around the year 1400 had emerged as an increasingly networked whole while still built essentially upon deeply local societies. From the mid-twelfth to the mid-fourteenth centuries the driving forces in culture and religion had tended toward invading those customary worlds, even to pulling people out of them. I speak here not so much of Bartlett's conquest moving outward from a northwest heartland to far-flung peripheries, a conquest driven by military force as well as expanding ecclesiastical power—this vision in part an inflection of the Anglo-Norman conquest of Ireland in the 1170s.[28] I have in mind varied distinct impulses that reached into local societies multiply: a common law for the christened (canon law) working its way out from a monarchical papacy and from masters of law in Bologna and elsewhere into every diocese and potentially every parish; an ever more philosophically inflected understanding of the arts and of the Christian faith as "theology" radiating out from masters in Paris, Oxford, and mendicant *studia*; ever more common literary motifs traveling from court to court and town to town across every vernacular literature; ever more centrally institutionalized religious orders with friars commanding a strong presence in nearly every town; ever more common patterns of devotion planted by those friars in sermons, confessional guides, and meditational practices; ever more common expectations for pastoral care after Lateran Council IV spread by way of episcopal synods and pastoral manuals. All this tended slowly but surely to undo an older cultural and religious order. It also generated local resentments, famously toward friars, but also inquisitors and canon lawyers. Yet the momentum never halted, even during the papacy's residence in Avignon. Figures like Wyclif and Hus and Grote and Gerson and D'Ailly might critique various aspects of all this themselves, even vigorously; still, paradoxically, their own careers and work and writing wholly presumed and shared in this larger networked world.

From about the 1370s, however—whether owing to papal schism, or the deepening devastation of plague, or the disruptions of economic boom and bust, or the planting of universities now across Europe, or the appointing of more permanent regional inquisitors, or the energies of newly emerging religious groups, or indeed the deepening of Christian religious culture at lower social levels—this centralizing momentum was confronted with equally strong forces originating locally and regionally. I lift out only a few aspects relevant here. Consider the character of a newer leadership, in three broad types. We have Master John Wyclif alongside Master Geert Grote, Master Jan Hus and Master John Gerson, also Sister Birgitta and Sister Catherina of Siena, and further Friar Vincent Ferrer, Friar Johannes Nider, Friar Bernardino—with many more like them. After three generations of dominance by friar-theologians, secular masters of theology assumed real leadership again, all of them masters who also had an eye now on the state of parishes. Women visionaries and prophets in turn were gathering communities around them to a degree not seen since Hildegard of Bingen, however expansive the role of quasi-religious women's communities had been in the intervening years. Friars and monks hardly disappeared. Crucial, however, was the emergence among them of Observants, ardent reformist minorities within virtually all orders from the 1370s or so, often quite embattled internally, mostly in the end splitting off to form their own houses and networks, as with the Colettines among the Clares. These Observants easily paired in purpose and worldview with the new urbanized Carthusians, and the one or two new orders that emerged in this era such as the Brigittines or the Windesheim canons and canonesses (the professed branch of the Devotio Moderna).

They all saw themselves as a faithful core in a church or within orders overrun with corruption, privilege, and indifference. Failing to bring the larger whole with them, they focused upon gathering the likeminded around themselves, normally without wholly repudiating the church as such, however fiercely and relentlessly they critiqued it. Indeed, they soon came to count on its privileges and support for their own favor, as they did on wealthy lay patrons. These reformers, especially its leaders, but often adherents too, worked across Latin and the vernacular, back and forth, according to need and purpose. Ambidextrous writers and preachers, they actively promoted a new spiritual intensity and in effect a new spiritual order, in both languages—preaching with the pen, as the Carthusians said—their views often articulated with a rigorous if not extremist edge. These groups too proved mostly relaxed about mixing status or rank differences, be it clerical with lay or elite with common, associating in ways that ventured beyond reigning custom in either secular or ecclesiastical society, often incurring critique here too from those accustomed to more status-conscious inherited patterns of religious life. They also presumed liturgical worship and resolved to practice it, be it that of an order or in private exercise such as the Little Hours of the Virgin; but they focused most intently on meditational regimes, more and more of them self-designed. Those regimens commonly presumed both reading and writing as well as the use of song, ballad, hymn, or verse.

Allow me to illustrate briefly with a little-known figure on whom I am currently at work. Alijt Bake of Utrecht and Ghent (1413–1455) would eventually become a canoness and then prioress for ten years, at Galilee, a new Windesheim house founded in Ghent, the largest city in the Low Countries. Already as a laywoman in Utrecht she had tried out various religious options including that of urban recluse, and would weigh joining the Franciscan Colettines. She suffered in despair through an extended vocational crisis without losing her questing spirit, determined that she must become a nun inwardly, as she put it, before becoming one outwardly—all this later written up in a searing account she entitled *My Beginnings and Progress*.[29] Among other exercises she undertook, self-imposed while still a lay postulant, she worked daily through her own form of passion exercises. Here I offer a small recollection, penned in her own tongue, of what she did: "time in, time out, I stayed with it, not only the talking but also the meditating and learning inwardly what I should be doing to that end. What I learned in this way, I wrote all out so I would not forget it. Thus I spent my whole time: ever talking and pondering and learning and writing and scratching out and writing yet again, such that I forgot about all my other scattered thoughts."[30] That is to say, amidst these meditational exercises she took as well to talking aloud and writing down what she intended and experienced and learned as ways of honing her mental focus, making her a nun "inwardly" while still a layperson. Reading and writing and exercising and self-reflection were all of a piece. Forms of this may be found scattered across nearly the whole spectrum of adherents to these new religious circles, whether in the vernacular (as here in Middle Dutch) or in Latin. At the heart of it lay the working assumption that these texts or regimens could be adjusted or fine-tuned or even individually invented, written down, or compiled as needed. University and devout circles are not exactly the same, but we find interestingly in both similar patterns of textual transmission and of community or group formation around those transmitted texts. These texts, and acts of reading and writing, were very much at the center of this era, and their proliferation was famously fostered by the crisscrossing of texts at the councils, then further facilitated locally by regional networks which might form in turn their own focal point as local communities.[31]

Consider for a moment the story of the fifteenth century's most successful text, Thomas of Kempen's *Imitation of Christ*, penned in the early 1420s, and surviving still in nearly nine hundred manuscripts.[32] This too is a story both of locality and multiple networks, one which scholars have yet fully to work out. What came to be accounted as one book titled *De imitatione Christi* began as four distinct pamphlets circulating as singles and clusters, eventually more often three together. In Thomas's own autograph copy of 1441 they appear in fact (in slightly different order) as the first four of thirteen such pamphlets—but we have notably more than a dozen manuscripts containing one or another of the four books dating prior to 1441. The inciting moment for penning the first two pamphlets, we think, was Thomas's term as novice master in a new house of Windesheim canons regular outside Zwolle in the early 1420s, hence his call to pursue an inner life (the kingdom of God within you) and ultimately to dedicate oneself to religious life as such (overt at the end of the present Book I). The teachings come to us, however, in part from remembered collations which Thomas had heard delivered by Brothers of the Common Life in Deventer when he was a teenage schoolboy there, destined like Egbert for a clerical job. These "talks" were delivered to any and all comers. Their "points" or "sayings" (*dicta*) were remembered, or eventually written down, as aphorisms or spiritual proverbs, sentence by sentence, memorable lines conceived in part as antidotes to the earthy proverbs that governed lay life. Like Egbert in our opening scene, Thomas had come to live for a time in the Brothers' house. Later as a canon regular, from notes or memory, in his thirties and in a cloister, he turned these sayings, some no doubt also of his own making now as novice master, into assonant Latin, gathered in themed units as chapters and little books—without wholly losing their contact with the street and young clerics and lay life.

Such were the origins as best we can surmise. But its transmission was broad and almost instant through multiple networks still to be sorted out, a kind of map to fifteenth-century religious life. Already by mid-century and in Thomas's own lifetime three of its books went into English, probably at Sheen, even earlier into Dutch for a house of Sisters, likewise very early into Low German, also quite soon in Latin reaching all the way to reformist Benedictines in Italy, and so on. It traveled both anonymously and under several different names, most prominently, strikingly, that of Jean Gerson. For the next three generations the "book" (in one form or another) circulated widely in Observant circles across many orders, especially the more monastic, as well as among the Carthusians, but no less among women Franciscan tertiaries. Then in the sixteenth century it became required reading for Jesuits, though Reformation protestants also avidly appropriated it after making some necessary modifications—an "interior life" for them, yes, but no "monastic life."[33] All the same, we must not be misled by those nine hundred manuscripts. The great majority of people in Deventer—people like the aunt who had dismissed her schoolboy nephew as a "lollard"—did not attend these Sunday afternoon conferences. Transmission, as it now reaches us, inevitably favors religious or semireligious houses and obscures lay ownership except in high court circles; so we do not know how many of these sayings traveled in little individual quires. At the same time many lay people remained chary of these solemn calls to a special interior life or a separatist religious circle, just as parish priests and a Dominican inquisitor worried that these Brothers were in effect setting up their own parish by taking preaching and spiritual guidance into their own hands—as in many ways they were, along with the lollards and Hus.

The *De imitatio Christi* was not alone in its rooted locality and simultaneous spread across intersecting regional or transregional networks. This is what we find for many religious texts in the fifteenth century, quite especially—at least with surviving books—among Observant houses, some of the most spectacular producers and gatherers of books. Observant movements in the fifteenth century could never take over whole orders, or even come close, in good part owing to the self-interest of those already comfortably inhabiting convents and monasteries, abetted by the strength of the social and political connections they could call upon. Further, the majority of contemporary religious saw themselves as exercising good sensible customs for upholding religious life developed over time, not entering into the rabid new schemes of extremists.[34] In a long plaintive treatise, Johannes Nider laid out all the objections that established houses threw up to being reformed.[35] So too most parishioners were wary of reformist groups, including the lollards—not necessarily keen to suppress them, unless they threatened social unrest, but dubious about this loud call for a "true" religion that moved in ways so contrary to embedded custom, so seemingly extreme, even if it echoed common concerns and touched on widespread resentments or doubts. Historiography has commonly grouped Observants and Carthusians in one category as reformist, and Wyclif and Hus in another as dissenters or heretics—and of course there were real differences of approach and principle. At the same time, we risk thereby creating historical blinders of our own making and in effect telling our own form of a partisan story. We fail to see the range and the paradoxes: how a Master Geert could be shut out of preaching for his attack on priests keeping companions, only to be revered subsequently as the spark igniting that diocese's largest religious movement; how Friar Bernardino of Siena could become the leading popular preacher in Italy and stage a large revival of Franciscan piety in and outside orders, while also being charged with heresy for promoting the cult of the Name of Jesus by way of his imageless image (bearing symbols of the Name) held up as a key prop in his preaching.

COMMON "NODAL POINTS" AND MULTIPLE RESPONSES IN A DIVERSE RELIGIOUS CULTURE

Such binary narratives obscure concerns that cut across nearly all groups. They also fail to acknowledge the presence now of modalities in communication and text production that enabled the formation of such groups and of greater networking within and beyond them. So to round out this essay I highlight ways in which these groups, if distinct, also lived in the same world, the degree to which they presumed widely recognized simmering hot points, or *nodal points* as I call them, in the culture, even when the varied groups also took quite diverse paths in pursuing their religious ends.

This was the great age of medieval parishes. They remained for most people, and arguably more than ever, the fundamental matrix. Among nearly all those "stirred-up" about religion in this era we find the formation of separate circles, sometimes adjunct to a parish, sometimes in effect alternate or even antiparishes, in still other cases convent-like gatherings apart from vows or an order, a more exclusive or even anticloister, or a distinct community within and yet outside an order as in the case of Observants. Such initiatives appear everywhere: the group that formed around Catherine of Siena and the groups sustained by her letters (often taking the formal shape of "tertiaries");[36] the communes formed by the Sisters and Brothers of the Common Life as well as the broader gatherings for *collationes* (talks, bible studies) held in their houses Sunday or feast day afternoons; the multiple Hussite parties forming up around particular leaders or agenda points with their own chants or broadsides; not to speak of those gentry or burger laypersons with money, leisure, and zeal enough to acquire books or a spiritual guide and form their own private devotional circle. Despite all the recent research we are less clear perhaps about what lollards were (or if they were even one thing), in or out of the local parish, their own alternative or paraparochial community, or an adversarial gathering—and these realities, as with Waldensians over the generations, would have varied deeply in localities and over time.

The forming of distinct and independent religious communities was everywhere being tested and often at issue, thus prominently the case of Hus's Bethlehem. It nearly always came with charges that preaching or teaching or confessing or spiritual guidance went on inside these groups apart from parish jurisdiction or mendicant oversight. While there was a long tradition of paraparochial confraternities and tertiaries, along with guilds and side altars, this looked like a different sort of threat, to the wholeness of the parish itself, the base community of the christened, even a way of appropriating to themselves or setting up something like their own religious order. Dominican inquisitors—one in the 1390s, another at the Council of Constance—tried to charge the Brothers and Sisters with mortal sin for forming communes outside a recognized religious order, something they had undertaken in order to imitate the first community at Jerusalem, that model long since reserved for recognized religious orders. The Modern Devout had managed to bring it off by way of an ingenious use of civil law, ceding to one another mutual ownership and inheritance of all their formerly private goods.[37] But for a lay person to undertake this constituted mortal sin, even a form of murder, Friar Grabow charged, for it cut that person off from carrying out those tasks essential to their estate, namely, bearing children and caring for material needs. It made a "lay" person (*secularis*) like a "religious" (i.e., without property), an inherent contradiction. Ultimately this generated a protracted legal process, carried all the way from the local world of Utrecht to the church's center at Constance. There Masters Gerson and D'Ailly argued in a determinative *consilium* that the only religion properly speaking was the one Christ had observed, the *religio christiana*. This Christian religion (in contrast to Benedictine or Franciscan or Dominican religion) did not require the counsels of perfection as such, and could be observed perfectly apart from vows, as the apostles and disciples had done in the early church, many of whom were married or had property. It required no "added-on" or "made-up" religion (*religiones facticias*). Popes, cardinals, and prelates, they observed pointedly, could also "perfectly" observe this "Christian religion" apart from vows and while possessing property.[38]

Another Dominican inquisitor earlier had charged a group of Devout Sisters with confessing to their Martha before going off to their local priest. This Martha held that she (or people she could provide) offered deeper and better guidance than he. In many or nearly all these instances the parish of christening, of cultic and fiscal duty, and of burial would get at least partly if not wholly repudiated by a select circle claiming to speak more acutely to godly life—thus those choosing to attend sermons at Bethlehem in Prague or to gather around "poor preachers," or still others orienting their spiritual lives around the ministrations of an Observant friar or a trusted recluse. Many of the religiously animated in this period—Wyclif perhaps, Hus fairly early on, Gerson, Catherine, and countless others—sought to reconstitute a more godly community at the local level, which was in principle the parish itself, but often in effect projected new communities that partly mirrored the parish, partly supplanted it. To varying degrees, they yearned at the same time (as in some sense both Langland and Chaucer did) to project or foster or favor more godly forms of the parish priest, a figure that was commonly maligned as ignorant, bossy, immoral, and so on through a long list of charges. In the schemes of Gerson and others, the parish priest, not the bishop or pope or friar, was now for the first time accounted ideally the foundational figure in sacral office; this move came to ecclesiastical or political expression at the Council of Basel with the inclusion of parish priests, at least in theory, as possible constituent members.

So in this religious culture one nodal point is the forming of distinct godly communities, imagined increasingly as taking shape beyond the parish or the cloister and yet still very much in the image of a parish or a cloister. In all this, we are dealing, we must always remember, with the religiously zealous, whether lay or clerical, who in most instances were a tiny minority. In a town like Deventer, the Sisters might have represented 4 percent of the town's population, arguably more in some large beguine towns. Moreover, in the making and especially the expansion of some of these communities, social considerations (need, shelter, broken families) moved people to join as much as religious ones.[39]

A second nodal point has already been touched on: reading and writing, thus the producing, consuming, and distributing of books, especially in the vernacular, but also in Latin as now becoming fundamental to the promotion of religious life (which also presumed the new availability of paper). The fifteenth century generated a veritable explosion of religious prose in the vernacular and Latin alike, leaving us with more manuscripts still than from any other century. Print emerged midway through this century in part simply as a new and more efficient way to keep up with demand. In German and Dutch about three-fourths of the manuscript material is religious in nature, far outdistancing, say, romances. On the continent especially scholars have turned their focus to tracing book production within these newly emerging religious networks, thus the Modern Devout, Carthusians, or Observants.[40] Care is needed with both our tallies and our rubrics. It is too tempting to reduce these masses of spiritual prose to block categories, thus ascribing them wholesale to the Modern-Day Devout in the Low Countries, or configuring them in England as lollard, nonlollard, or antilollard. So too the label *pre-Hussite* has sadly predetermined interpretations of a whole body of textual material.[41] Copies of Richard Rolle on the Psalms, a text lollards appropriated along with many others, equal or outnumber those manuscripts distinctly lollard in character, leaving to one side the now much-studied matter of "lollard" Bibles and the degree to which they were or should be accounted as distinctively lollard. Some fifteenth-century religious writings plainly reflect distinct partisan agendas, and can be traced back in theme or emphasis to a particular religious circle. But one miscellany—and we have hundreds or thousands of them— or indeed one library list from the late Middle Ages ought to keep us from forming quick and easy conclusions. Crossover, merging, and amalgamation appear everywhere. So what in actuality do we have then? Evidence of people or communities with shared belief or simply layered intertextualities? A codex harboring some leaves with writings deemed lollard or Wycliffite and kept in a convent library proves what? Marguerite Porete's work famously, and despite the burning of both her person and her book, was read in orthodox circles, the book circulating whole or in fragments and in translations.[42] We are just at the beginning of understanding a world with distinct communities and yet also with broad interwoven interests, concerns, and contacts, as manifested for instance so strikingly in these miscellanies and in book collections.

Furthermore, while there could be trouble on occasion about reading religious books in the vernacular, the English attempt to suppress some vernacular books (which in any case appears to have been singularly ineffective) must be treated as the exception rather than the rule. Prayers and parts of the Bible and meditations had been emerging in the vernacular in many languages since the thirteenth century, and that pace accelerated dramatically after the 1370s. Likewise, while well into the thirteenth century the language of legal documentation across Europe was Latin (one of the markers of Bartlett's "colonization"), more and more property agreements or fee arrangements, varying in time and by region, began to get recorded in local languages. The reasons have only partly been explored as yet, one likely driver being enhanced roles for local magistrates and burgers in the making of these documents (and in England of course "Law French" remained its own "sacred" language for legal and administrative affairs). The very real parallel with shifts into the vernacular for religious texts as well has hardly been explored as yet. In any case, the basis of primary education remained mostly Latin for a long time, and the gold standard for stately documents remained Latin, as it did for most things ecclesiastical. Still, a shift toward the vernacular in everyday legal matters—whatever the sequence and connections, again varying by region and language—must have made the shift toward more and more religious books written and reproduced in the vernacular seem natural as well, partly to meet the needs of lay social elites (noble or burgher), partly to meet the needs of dedicated religious groups such as beguines; perhaps even disproportionately so—but not exclusively, as Grundmann first argued,[43] to meet the needs of women, who read romances or eventually kept household books in the vernacular.

The Modern Devout in Dutch towns, in the face of some hostility and of an inquisitor, vigorously and successfully defended their use of books in the vernacular in the 1390s, a defense probably intended for the Sisters and their books first of all. This apologia was written in Latin with a heavy inflection of law and authorities in order to address an inquisitor and ultimately the bishop, then made available in somewhat simpler form in Middle Dutch.[44] The Devout strategically conceded that critiqued authors like Eckhart should be avoided. In reality they and others went on reading Eckhart widely in the fifteenth century (most extant manuscripts date from then), as well as Jan Ruusbroec, whom Gerson had attacked, and of course Marguerite Porete, if not under her name. One of the striking traits of these miscellanies—lost in editions and in the singling out of a particular author, orthodox or suspect—is their range of materials, some of it common, some of it quite distinct.

Of late the term *vernacular theology* has sometimes been invoked for those aspects of this phenomenon that involve the writing and circulation of religious texts in the vernacular. The term was launched by Bernard McGinn with a different intent,[45] then expanded by Nicholas Watson explicitly for the world of English religious prose (especially Julian of Norwich), and is now increasingly invoked as well on the continent. It has sparked considerable discussion, from a historian's viewpoint carried on too exclusively inside English or literary departments.[46] Just as interpretive approaches to lollards and Hussites remain tainted still at times by their earlier confessional and nationalist framing, so this term—echoing its origins as a riff on monastic theology—comes loaded with freight. Jean Leclercq proved ingenious and also astonishingly successful in 1956 when—faced with the dominance of scholastic theology both inside the Catholic Church and in perceptions of medieval thought—he perceived and himself helped make accessible to others an explosion of innovative and refined religious writing in Latin in the eleventh and twelfth centuries led by Cistercians, Carthusians, and Premonstratensians. So he countered with his innovative notion of a distinct monastic theology, which he set against the themes, genres and purposes of scholastic theology. This term is now a commonplace in textbooks and general narratives, and one that mostly dismays scholars. It carries no precise meaning, intellectual or social, and eludes nearly every attempt at a more nuanced definition, while silently living off its originating binary tension and occluding more complex understandings of twelfth-century culture and quite especially its crossovers (Peter Abelard was a monk, and from the beginning Leclercq said that Anselm of Bec/Canterbury did not fit). To speak of a vernacular theology may, like the term *monastic theology*, represent one way to give this religious prose space and standing in our conceptions of later medieval culture. But its binary energies only blur and confuse our grasp of contemporary linguistic, cultural, and religious realities.

Another matter is whether one language or another may somehow more authentically express the intent of a person or a heart. This is an especially intriguing one for the fifteenth century, when many could to varying degrees move back and forth passively and actively between more than one language, also between, say, Latin liturgy and prayers or sermons in the vernacular. But neither Latin nor a vernacular is necessarily in itself a decisive determiner or inflector of content as such; routine or radical religious thought could appear in either language (and in the case of Meister Eckhart both). So too insistence upon *reformatio*, whether of the self or of a community or the church at large, may be found everywhere, and in all languages, as could nearly every other "hot" religious theme in this era. The determining consideration was more likely one of presumed audience. Further, all of this likewise has a distinct rhetorical dimension, going both ways. As with twelfth-century monastic authors assailing schoolmen or rival forms of monasticism, attacks on Latin learning or philosophical sophistry, or alternatively of lay unreliability in religious expression, were recognizable rhetorical tropes and carriers of group prejudice or resentment as much as substantive critiques. Sermons, arguably the dominant medium of this era, were usually vernacular outside cloister, university, or chapter settings, but sometimes nonetheless Latin in their recording, copying, or reading. Other genres, meditations for instance, similarly crossed languages easily and regularly.

If religious community is one nodal point, and the reading and writing and group-forming potential of texts another, a third was property. The medieval church was big business, very big business, collectively and locally. A parish always meant, beyond pastoral care, fiscal obligations, a parish priest's ritual services rarely being rendered apart from stole fees, a monastery never entered apart from expected gifts, and so on. This applied a fortiori at the papal court, which had grown even more dependent since Avignon on monies it harvested from appointments, judicial decisions, and curial business of every sort. For Observant reformers the enemy were the *proprietarii*, propertied monks and friars, as they labeled the vast majority of their co-religious, all those fitted out with personal funds or goods or rooms. For the Modern Devout the answer was to form a strict commune in a community of mixed laity, clerics, and priests, with only a small number ordained and chosen by internal election. Calls for disendowment among still other groups aimed to sever all links between property and religion, even if the effect of the lollard initiative would mainly have been to enrich the crown and lay lords, though the Lollard Disendowment Bill also foresaw these reclaimed monies directed to educational institutions (as Luther would later argue for). On the other hand, it was often the crown and great lay lords who with their resources significantly patronized the newly reformed or Observant or Carthusian houses, also coincidentally beguines. At the Council of Constance the clamor about property, broadly called simony, was constant, and all the solutions proposed or legislated proved makeshift and partial. God's work in parish and cathedral remained at the heart of things, and God was highly honored, most agreed, in buildings, endowments, vestments, images, and prayers—indeed, more than honored, also accessed. At Constance, churchmen railed against the ways of the papal curia, but they met first of all in order to restore the curia; one person's excessive fee was another's income. Anyone approaching the grand Carthusian houses at Pavia or Mount Grace, communities embodying the epitome of the age's spiritual ideals, would be gazing up at stone walls, a splendid gate, guesthouses, and servants. Had these visitors been allowed inside, they would have seen single luxury condos, so to speak, inhabited by learned reading and writing monk-hermits.

Beyond this unavoidable and even indivisible intersection of the spiritual and the material, to which scholars are now giving thoughtful attention, some fifteenth-century writers within the more zealous of these religious circles worried equally or even more about another kind of property, a personal self-possession, a propertied interior (*eighenheid* in Dutch)—a notion first influentially articulated by Dominicans like Eckhart and Tauler in German but central already to Marguerite Porete in French and later to Jan Ruusbroec in Dutch. Many related texts came to be accounted Free Spirit in some interpretations. For the spiritually intent the issue at stake here was all too real, a preoccupation of Alijt Bake, for instance. The more zealously religious a person became, the harder one worked at it inwardly—whether as a professed or a lay person, or as an in-between— the more such persons might also come to take ever fuller inner ownership of their religiosity, be it of their virtue or asceticism or constancy in prayer or tasting of God's sweetness. They became thus inwardly propertied with luxuriant and privileged spiritual goods. Hence their intent and language of returning to the "ground"; of the need to have this interior stripped down to nothing, willingly or unwillingly, however harsh that way in experiential practice, however long a person might find herself indeed abandoned in spiritual poverty and emptiness. These preoccupations dotted the spiritual landscape, whence a continuing readership for Eckhart and Marguerite among others (whether or not the source was known). This also opened up writers and practitioners to charges of Free Spirit heresy, even when their own speculations were mostly headed in quite different directions, and not toward any libertine freedom from religious or moral expectations.

Parish and community, reading and writing, property and spirit are only three key nodal points deeply embedded in this religious culture and so evidently at work across many or in some instances all these groups. One could mention others, for instance, a turn to the "law" or rules as the answer, whether that law be Scripture or strict adherence to a rule or a self-imposed spiritual regimen. Equally or even more central, as already noted, is the role of the material in the spiritual,[47] an attack on images amidst a world filled with ever more and ever more lifelike painted and sculpted presences of the divine, of bleeding hosts from a risen Lord, and much more we could go on naming. It is not at all my intent here, it should be said, to deny the particularity, authenticity, and creativity of distinct fifteenth-century groups such as lollards, nor indeed their locality in the first instance. Nor do I fail to recognize that some proved far more radical in word and more rejectionist in practice than others. It is to point first of all toward a common landscape alive with identifiably particular but also widespread nodal issues. These underlay distinct initiatives pursued both broadly and locally amidst a culture generating widespread stirring, and especially in matters of religion—these religious stirrings, however, always and inevitably touching on matters that were equally social and the material.

It is appropriate then to ask why some groups or movements or teachings in this era gained acceptance, while some slipped by, some found workable compromises, and some met with rejection and even bloody exclusion. There is no simple answer. This reverts to questions of locality, first of all, to the particular circumstances, personalities, and issues. Still, some religious matters were patently more dangerous to raise than others, especially as one moved out of the understood *sic et non* of university debate to take them up in such ways as to inspire distinct local communities. Yet it was hardly predictable that the bloody host at Wilsnack could eventually gain acceptance despite episcopal and theological objections, as well as the Hussites' communion in both kinds, even as Wycliffites would be singled out for their repudiating the eucharistic transformation. In principle theologians, especially those in leadership at the Council of Constance, claimed to welcome open debate. Pierre D'Ailly, in the case involving the Modern Devout, held that the subcommittee taking up this matter of *fides* should convoke all masters of theology present at the council to hold a free and open discussion, learn from one another and determine what conformed to Scripture, the matter thus to be settled not in the dark and by individuals but in the light and by all. That was how he handled "matters of faith" assigned to him at council, he claims.[48] It had hardly gone so in the condemnation of Wyclif and especially Hus, possibly something he was now ruing two years later, that also manifestly a matter of *fides*.

Again circumstances count, and not only the much studied ones surrounding Hus and the emperor and the fate of the council in its opening days. Initially, and then for two more years, the matters of *unio* and *reformatio* looked frustratingly, even dangerously, intractable. But Master John Wyclif, several of his teachings already condemned at the Blackfriars council in 1382 and long dead, seemed in a sense easy picking, thus their confirming an earlier papal denunciation and pleasing the English prelates, their denunciation of articles already deemed heretical, if now reinforced with a fuller theological apparatus. Furthermore, they appeared to be dealing with a matter of *fides* that seemingly threatened the whole community of the christened, and the capital of the empire in particular—even if their catastrophic railroading of Hus the next month only made the matter far worse in the end.

Nearly a century ago Johan Huizinga published a visionary portrait of the late medieval Low Countries imagined as in a late autumn harvest glow. He aimed, he said, to recapture the world he saw in Flemish painting. His portrait in fact derived mostly from texts, a deep and rich reading of late medieval chronicles, poetry, and court epics mostly written in French. His vision of religion in all this was by contrast strikingly spare and dour, his vision of all these late medieval religious enthusiasts and ascetics, the Modern Devout in particular, overshadowed perhaps by the stern Dutch

Calvinists among whom he lived in Groningen. Now, after generations, even centuries, of a declining late Middle Ages, scholars are looking again with fresh eyes. Imagine a portrait of later medieval religious life that captured in full measure and in all its radiant variety this explosion of religious writing in all languages including Latin. It would not be like one of those slightly staid set-pieces featuring a person or group. It would capture the spirit and texture of one of those extravagant late medieval altarpieces which presented far more three-dimensional carved or painted figures and stories than any single viewer could possibly take in at once, even if most of the individual saints or story lines were relatively common and recognizable. Such altarpieces, I suggest, come closer to the religious world I am trying to describe than do those more famous and elegant Flemish primitives. This was a world of religion all alive and astir and bursting out of its frame. Such large multidimensional altarpieces, we should also remember, stood at nearly every pillar or side chapel in some late medieval churches. That said, one must also, and paradoxically, include in our mind's eye too those ardent and influential minorities whose religious lives turned entirely away and inward and upward, some discounting altogether such altarpieces and devotion, while a few others would have simply destroyed such pieces as idolatrous.

The vision I am suggesting here has some difficulty with Berndt Hamm's influential *Frömmigkeitstheologie*, with its notion of a *Zentrierung* of religious culture during this period.[49] Mine suggests rather a vision of landscapes alive with multiple distinct and even adversarial communities, each embedded in quite particular local cultures, and yet also paradoxically linked increasingly in a broader world of shared networks and common cultural nodal points, laden with religious, cultural, and social potency: issues of religious community and property, of reading and writing in Latin and the vernaculars alike, of the divine presence in the eucharist or relics or images, of spiritual modes radically this-worldly and fleshly or alternatively radically otherworldly, not only disembodied but in a sense dispirited. This is the exuberant European religious world bursting out of its frame in multiple forms during the two or three generations following the deaths of Masters John Wyclif and Geert Grote in 1384. Yet, we must remember too, the majority of people still went on working out their religious duties and aspirations mostly within the framework of their local parish and whatever additional options (shrines, quasi-religious groups, recluses, friars) might be available to them, whether they did so routinely or indifferently or zealously. When we attempt to understand lollards or Hussites or Modern-Day Devout or Carthusians or Free Spirits or whatever else in the fifteenth century, we must try to keep all of this somehow in the frame, something contemporaries too could hardly manage.

NOTES

This essay remains close to the paper I delivered at the "Europe After Wyclif" conference. My thanks to Michael Van Dussen and Patrick Hornbeck for their invitation, and also for their patience.

1. *Vita Egberti*, ed. Gerhard Dumbar, *Analecta seu vetera aliquot scripta inedita* (Deventer, 1719), 162–165.

2. See Jennifer Kolpacoff Deane, Letha Böhringer, and Hildo van Engen, eds., *Labels and Libels: Naming Beguines in Northern Medieval Europe* (Turnhout, Belgium: Brepols, 2014), and Tanya Stabler Miller, *The Beguines of Medieval Paris: Gender, Patronage, and Spiritual Authority* (Philadelphia: University of Pennsylvania Press, 2014), both with extended bibliographies. With respect to the phenomenon of "in-between" religious types, and those claiming "third-order" Franciscan links, see Alison More, "Institutionalizing Penitential Life in Medieval and Early Modern Europe: Third Orders, Rules, and Canonical Legitimacy," *Church History* 83 (2014): 297–323, and for the enormous importance of this movement in the Netherlandish "Devotio Moderna," see Hildo van Engen, *De derde orde van Sint-Franciscus in het middeleeuwse bisdom Utrecht* (Hilversum, Netherlands: Verloren, 2006).

3. To be clear, this is when the incident would have occurred; our written account of it by disciples of Egbert, doubtless a story he told of himself, comes from ca. 1483.

4. Vincent Gillespie and Kantik Ghosh, eds., *After Arundel: Religious Writing in Fifteenth-Century England* (Turnhout, Belgium: Brepols, 2011).

5. I wrote about this, from a different angle, in "Multiple Options: The World of the Fifteenth-Century Church," *Church History* 77 (2008): 257–284, and earlier in "The Church in the Fifteenth Century," in *Handbook of European History in the Later Middle Ages, Renaissance, and Reformation*, ed. Thomas Brady Jr., Heiko Oberman, and James Tracy (Leiden, Netherlands: Brill, 1994), 305–330.

6. "utinam scirem scisma interius calcare et domesticam vitare scissuram cordis mei, et aliquos in ovile Christi per ueram caritatem que sola coniungit congregare." Gerardi Magni, *Epistolae*, n. 21, ed. Willelmus Mulder (Antwerp: Soc. Ed. Neerlandiae, 1933), 92. On the date and manuscript witnesses, see now Rudolph Th. M. van Dijk, *Prologomena ad Gerardi Magni Opera Omnia* (Turnhout, Belgium: Brepols, 2003), 498–501.

7. "maxime ad hoc, ut non sequeremur antiquitatem mundane conversacionis in clero, sed veram predicacionem et doctrinam eius non ex operibus cleri sed ex libris et ex veritate." Gerardus, *Epistola* 20, ed. Mulder, 77.

8. See, representatively for a large literature, Renate Blumenfeld-Kosinski, *Poets, Saints, and Visionaries of the Great Schism, 1378–1417* (University Park: Pennsylvania State University Press, 2006); Kathryn Kerby-Fulton, *Books under Suspicion: Censorship and Tolerance of Revelatory Writing in Late Medieval England* (Notre Dame, IN: University of Notre Dame Press, 2006); and Laura Ackerman Smoller, *History, Prophecy, and the Stars: The Christian Astrology of Pierre d'Ailly, 1350–1420* (Princeton, NJ: Princeton University Press, 1994).

9. Whence the right instinct, some matters of interpretation and its deep debt to the Czech work of Jiří Kejř aside, in Thomas A. Fudge, *The Trial of Jan Hus: Medieval Heresy and Criminal Procedure* (Oxford: Oxford University Press, 2013).

10. See, for instance, Christine Caldwell Ames, *Righteous Persecution: Inquisition, Dominicans, and Christianity in the Middle Ages* (Philadelphia: University of Pennsylvania Press, 2009); and for a stark and famous instance, my "Marguerite of Hainaut and the Medieval Low Countries," in *Marguerite Porete et le "Miroir des simples âmes": Perspectives historiques, philosophiques et littéraire,* ed. Sean Field, Robert Lerner, and Sylvain Piron (Paris: Vrin, 2013), 25–68, esp. 61–68.

11. *Sancti Antonini Summa Theologica,* vol. III, 16.1 (Verona 1740; repr. 1959), 3:843.

12. See John Van Engen, "Illicit Religion: The Case of Friar Matthew Grabow O.P.," in *Law and the Illicit in Medieval Society,* ed. Ruth Mazo Karras, Joel Kaye, and E. Ann Matter (Philadelphia: University of Pennsylvania Press, 2008), 111–112. Gerson's was a *consilium* drawn up at the Council of Constance; an imperfect text in J. D. Mansi, *Sacrorum conciliorum nova et amplissima collectio* (Graz, repr. 1960–1961), 28:391–394.

13. See my "Conversion and Conformity in the Early Fifteenth Century," in *Conversions Old and New,* ed. Anthony Grafton and Kenneth Mills (Rochester, NY: University of Rochester Press, 2003), 45–50.

14. There is a fairly large literature on this topic; the subject is also central to my *Sisters and Brothers of the Common Life: The Devotio Moderna and the World of the Later Middle Ages* (Philadelphia: University of Pennsylvania Press, 2008). In addition to Elizabeth Makowski, *"A Pernicious Sort of Woman": Quasi Religious Women and Canon Lawyers in the Later Middle Ages* (Washington, DC: Catholic University of America Press, 2005), see the work of Kasper Elm, who regarded this position as a major modification of his teacher Herbert Grundmann's claim that all religious enthusiasts ended up either in cloisters or in heresy; amidst his large bibliography a basic work: "*Vita regularis sine regula:* Bedeutung, Rechtsstellung und Selbstverständnis des mittelalterlichen und

frühneuzeitlichen Semireligiosentums," in *Häresie und vorzeitige Reformation im Spätmittelalter*, ed. František Šmahel (Munich: R. Oldenbourg, 1998), 239–273.

15. An introduction to these works is my "Friar Johannes Nyder on Laypeople Living as Religious in the World," in *Vita Religiosa im Mittelalter: Festschrift für Kaspar Elm zum 70. Geburtstag* (Berlin: Duncker and Humblot, 1999), 583–615. See also Michael Bailey, *Battling Demons: Witchcraft, Heresy, and Reform in the Late Middle Ages* (University Park: Penn State University Press, 2003): 64–74, 152.

16. "sicut est religio privata claustralis perfectorum, sic est vel potest esse religio privata secularis sive exclaustralis perfectorum. Et a pari est vel potest esse religio privata, tam claustralis quam exclaustralis imperfectorum." Wyclif, *De religione privata I* c. 8, ed. Buddensieg, 515, 516.

17. This is what Fiona Somerset has tried to get at most recently, *Feeling like Saints: Lollard Writings after Wyclif* (Ithaca, NY: Cornell University Press, 2014).

18. *Two Wycliffite Texts*, ed. Anne Hudson (Oxford: Early English Text Society, 1993): 6–7, 10–11.

19. Somerset, *Feeling like Saints,* 72. In fact, while the particularities of the Lollard emphasis upon law may distinguish them, an emphasis upon keeping to or restoring the law is common to many groups in this period, including many of the most rigorous and "orthodox." Compare my work in n. 13 supra.

20. This is a large and sometimes contentious scholarly conversation that has hardly touched as yet the discussion of Lollards and Hussites. Robert Lerner, *The Heresy of the Free Spirit in the Late Middle Ages* (Princeton, NJ: Princeton University Press, 1972); Mark Pegg, *The Corruption of Angels: The Great Inquisition of 1245–46* (Princeton, NJ: Princeton University Press, 2001); R. I. Moore, "The Cathar Middle Ages as an Historiographical Problem," in: *Christianity and Culture in the Middle Ages*, ed. L. Wolverton and D Mengel (Notre Dame, IN: University of Notre Dame Press, 2015), 58–86; Christine Caldwell Ames, "Authentic, True, and Right: Inquisition and the Study of Medieval Popular Religion," in ibid., 87–119 (both with extensive bibliographies); and R. I. Moore's new general narrative, *The War on Heresy* (Cambridge, MA: Harvard University Press, 2012).

21. Admirable for its balance in my view is the work of Peter Biller, *The Waldenses, 1170–1530: Between a Religious Order and a Church* (Burlington, VT: Ashgate, 2001).

22. Somerset, *Feeling like Saints,* acknowledges this issue at the outset and settles it by aligning "lollard" with those who echoed teachings of Wyclif. But of course only certain teachings of Master Wyclif were condemned, and in fact much that she recounts is quite similar to broad stretches of late medieval religiosity more generally. In so far her findings often confirm the broader argument of this essay rather than setting out a distinctive Lollard ethos.

23. Ian Forrest, *The Detection of Heresy in Late Medieval England* (Oxford: Oxford University Press, 2005). Ann Hudson, *The Premature Reformation: Wycliffite Texts and Lollard History* (Oxford: Oxford University Press, 1988)

already raised some of these issues, as have her many studies and editions over the past forty years.

24. Consider here the approaches taken now by Christine Caldwell Ames, *Righteous Persecution*, and Karen Sullivan, *The Inner Lives of Medieval Inquisitors* (Chicago: University of Chicago Press, 2011). For indications of local resistance or tolerance, see for instance Carol Lansing, *Power and Purity: Cathar Heresy in Medieval Italy* (New York: Oxford University Press, 1998).

25. The works generated by this controversy, and the controversy itself, are now wonderfully edited and laid out by Rijcklof Hofman, ed. *Gerardi Magni Sermo ad clerum traiectensem de focaristas*, Corpus Christianorum Continuatio Mediaevalis 235 (Turnhout, Belgium: Brepols, 2011).

26. See A. J. A. Bijsterveld, *Laverend tussen Kerk en wereld: De Pastoors in Noord-Brabant 1400–1570* (Amsterdam: VU Uitgeverij, 1993).

27. Fudge in *The Trial of Jan Hus*, 116–117, building on Kejř, presents some of this material, but too much in the shadow of what will come, as if the whole were of a single piece. This was, however, just how such conflicts were originated and initially worked out, in court and with law, always of course with matters of power and rank and religion hovering over them. And their outcome could go either way, in the case of the Modern Devout ultimately in their favor, as in my *Sisters and Brothers of the Common Life*, 84–118, and then again at the Council of Constance, "Illicit Religion," 103–116.

28. Robert Bartlett, *The Making of Europe: Conquest, Colonization, and Cultural Change* (Princeton, NJ: Princeton University Press, 1993).

29. Bernhard Spaapen, "Middeleeuwse passiemystiek III: De autobiografie van Alijt Bake," *Ons geestelijk erf* 41 (1967): 209–301, 321–350.

30. Ibid. I am nearing completion of a full reconstruction and translation of all her work.

31. See now, for instance, *Religious Controversy in Europe, 1378–1536: Textual Transmission and Networks of Readership*, ed. Michael Van Dussen and Pavel Soukup (Turnhout, Belgium: Brepols 2013), with extensive bibliographies for each article.

32. Literature on the *Imitatio Christi* is both vast and disappointing. For orientation see Uwe Neddermeyer, "*Radix studii et speculum vitae*: Verbreitung und Rezeption der 'Imitatio Christi' in Handschriften und Drucken bis zur Reformation," in: *Studien zum 15. Jahrhundert: Festschift für Erich Meuthen zum 65. Geburtstag*, ed. Johannes Helmrath, Heribert Müller, and Helmut Wolff (Munich: R. Oldenbourg 1994), 1:457–481; and the essays in *Aus dem Winkel in die Welt: Die Bücher des Thomas von Kempen und ihre Schicksale*, ed. Ulrike Bodemann and Nikolaus Staubach (Frankfurt: Peter Lang, 2006).

33. See, for instance, Maximillian von Habsburg, *Catholic and Protestant Translations of the* Imitatio Christi: *from Late Medieval Classic to Early Modern Bestseller* (Burlington, VT: Ashgate, 2011)

34. See, for instance, James Mixson, *Poverty's Proprietors: Ownership and*

Mortal Sin at the Origins of the Observant Movement (Leiden, Netherlands: Brill, 2009).

35. See Bailey, *Battling Demons*, 75–90; Van Engen, "Conversion and Conformity," 39–45.

36. See Thomas Luongo, *The Saintly Politics of Catherine of Siena* (Ithaca, NY: Cornell University Press, 2006).

37. One central theme in my *Sisters and Brothers*; see especially chap. 5.

38. See my "Illicit Religion" for more details.

39. See my *Sisters and Brothers*, 128–135.

40. Work in this area has multiplied in recent years, especially in German and Dutch, also Latin and English, somewhat less so in French and Italian. A recent fine example among a host of such new studies: Anna Dlabačova, *Literatuur en observantie: De* Spieghel der volcomenheit *van Hendrik Herp en de dynamiek van laatmiddeleeuwse tekstverspreiding* (Hilversum, Netherlands: Verloren, 2014). Beyond the recent volume edited by Van Dussen and Soukup, see, mostly for English literature and with a more inward gaze, *Devotional Culture in Late Medieval England and Europe: Diverse Imaginations of Christ's Life*, ed. Stephen Kelly and Ryan Perry (Turnhout, Belgium: Brepols, 2014).

41. Another category is sometimes a "new devotion" spreading across late medieval Europe. See the Europe-wide body of essays in *Die 'neue Frömmigkeit' in Europa im Spätmittelalter*, ed. Marek Derwich and Martial Staub (Göttingen, Germany: Vandenhoeck and Ruprecht, 2004).

42. See now the splendid essays in *Marguerite Porete et le "Miroir des simples âmes": Perspectives historiques, philosophiques et littéraire*, ed. Sean Field, Robert Lerner, Sylvain Piron (Paris: Vrin, 2013). I attempted to locate her contextually with "Marguerite of Hainaut and the Medieval Low Countries" (25–68).

43. Herbert Grundmann, *Religious Movements in the Middle Ages. The Historical Links between Heresy, the Mendicant Orders, and the Women's Religious Movement in the Twelfth and Thirteen Century, with the Historical Foundations of German Mysticism*, trans. Steven Rowan (Notre Dame, IN: University of Notre Dame Press, 1995), first argued in the 1930s that vernacular religious writing was intended for women. For critiques of his "women's thesis," see Martina Wehrli-Johns, "Voraussetzungen und Perspektiven mittelalterlicher Laienfrömmigkeit seit Innozenz III. Eine Auseinandersetzung mit Herbert Grundmanns "Religiösen Bewegungen," *Mitteilungen des Instituts für Österreichische Geschichtsforschung* 104 (1996), 286–309.

44. See Nicholas Staubach, "Gerhard Zerbolt von Zutphen und die Apologie der Laienlektüre in der Devotio moderna," in *Laienlektüre und Buchmarkt im späten Mittelalter*, ed. Thomas Kock and Rita Schlusemann (Frankfurt: Peter Lang, 1997): 221–289; Van Engen, *Sisters and Brothers*, 266–281.

45. Bernard McGinn raised questions about the language in which writers thought and articulated their experience of God, obviously women writing in the vernacular but no less trained scholastics. See especially his work on

Eckhart: *The Mystical Thought of Meister Eckhart: The Man from whom God Hid Nothing* (New York: Crossroad, 2001), where the issue is, for instance, whether Friar Eckhart could think and express certain notions by way of the German word *Grund* for which he could produce no real equivalent in Latin.

46. In what has now become a larger bibliography, see representatively, for the range of opinions, the essays in *After Arundel: Religious Writing in Fifteenth-Century England*, ed. Vincent Gillespie and Kantik Ghosh (Turnhout, Belgium: Brepols, 2011), especially Vincent Gillespie's attempt (3–42) to nuance the state of religious conflict and reform in the earlier fifteenth century, Ian Johnson's hard-hitting critique (73–88) of a notion of "vernacular theology," and Nicholas Watson's effort (563–589) to save aspects of it as at work positively in fifteenth-century religious writing. Jeremy Catto, a historian, implicitly echoing some of the broader dynamics invoked above, suggests (43–54) that the period after Arundel was more open than ever in England to international influences of all kinds.

47. This is receiving much attention of late, led in part by the works of Caroline Walker Bynum, *Wonderful Blood: Theology and Practice in Late Medieval Northern Germany and Beyond* (Philadelphia: University of Pennsylvania Press, 2007), and *Christian Materiality: An Essay on Religion in Late Medieval Europe* (New York: Zone Books, 2011). See also Sara Ritchey, *Holy Matter: Changing Perceptions of the Material World in Late Medieval Christianity* (Ithaca, NY: Cornell University Press, 2014), and Shannon Gayk and Robyn Malo, "The Sacred Object," *Journal of Medieval and Early Modern Studies* 44 (2014): 457–467.

48. Van Engen, "Illicit Religion," 390.

49. English-speaking readers now have a way into this learned and important body of work, in *The Reformation of Faith in the Context of Late Medieval Theology and Piety: Essays by Berndt Hamm* (Leiden, Netherlands: Brill, 2004).

CHAPTER TWO

COSMOPOLITAN ARTISTS, FLORENTINE INITIALS, AND THE WYCLIFFITE BIBLE

Kathleen E. Kennedy

The Wycliffite Bible was a medieval English best seller, and most of the copies that remain date to the fifteenth century. While not theologically suspect in theory, vernacular scripture translation caught the attention of followers of both John Wyclif and Jan Hus, and in this way Bible translation played a part in the debates concerning late medieval church reform explored in this present volume. Until recently the Wycliffite Bible was more frequently discussed than studied itself, and so the manuscript networks in which copies were made and decorated remained relatively unknown. Recent close examination of manuscripts has revealed copies originating in a wide range of otherwise well-attested manuscript traditions and has situated the production of many copies of the Wycliffite Bible squarely within mainstream English book production.[1] This essay describes one such production network that I argue was in close dialogue both with European cultural developments such as humanism and with the same high-level, international clerical households who took part in fifteenth-century theological debates. Manuscript evidence leaves us in little doubt that some of the Wycliffite New Testaments produced in the 1440s were decorated by an English artist familiar with both Italian art and the first English humanist scribe.[2] This scribe worked in the papal curia, and the evidence further suggests that the artist too was attached to a clerical household, and had direct experience of Florentine style as well as his native English techniques. The Wycliffite scripture decorated by this artist therefore form a particularly English segment of a truly international oeuvre. Previously understood to be a popular, though insular artist, I argue instead that this artist navigated apparent binaries such as Latin/vernacular, English/Italian, heterodox/orthodox with ease, much as Wycliffism itself did.

Today artists do not live or work in vacuums, and in the Middle Ages throughout Europe they influenced each other just as theologians did. Continental ideas inspired fifteenth-century English border artists as they did their miniaturist colleagues.[3] Whether cautiously or swiftly, throughout the course of the fifteenth century, English border and initial artists adopted (and sometimes adapted) color, motifs, and technique typical of continental styles. Among manuscripts of Wycliffite scripture this process of adaptation and adoption of European techniques and motifs can be seen especially in a group whose style derives from that of the artist known as the Corpus Master. Active from the 1410s through the 1420s, this artist executed the famous miniature of Chaucer declaiming to an audience in the Corpus Christi College copy of *Troilus and Criseyde*, and Kathleen L. Scott claims that the same artist decorated the borders of that miniature.[4] This essay significantly expands our knowledge of the European influences and clerical connections of those artists who followed the Corpus Master's style.

As the evidence for the clerical, transnational networks inside which the Corpus Master and those later artists developing his style (who I call the Followers of the Corpus Master) worked is both historical and artistic, this essay must treat both contexts. First, I will introduce the artistic technique and known patrons of the Corpus Master himself. This will allow me to compare these to the techniques and patrons of his Followers. In particular, I will associate the Followers of the Corpus Master more closely than Scott has with the French nobleman, Charles d'Orléans in the year immediately prior to his release from English captivity. Then I will explore in depth one type of humanist initial made exclusively by the Followers and connect this style to an English scribe writing in a humanist hand in the papal curia of Eugenius IV and Nicholas V. Together all of this evidence strongly suggests that the Followers of the Corpus Master, decorators of a range of Wycliffite New Testaments, were connected to very high-level clerical households and some of them may have traveled with those households in Europe during the Council of Basel and its aftermath.

THE FOLLOWERS OF THE CORPUS MASTER, CIRCA 1430–1450

While we lack biographical details for the Corpus Master, as we do for most medieval artists, his artistic style is readily identifiable. The Corpus Master favors bright, clear colors, and his colored motifs twist and curl on organically waving sprays. This technique creates a lively, mobile border design at least a decade before such a style is otherwise widely practiced in English border art. Though it is by far the best known of his works, the Corpus *Troilus* is the only literary work featuring this Corpus Master's decoration.

Scott identifies just a handful of examples of the Corpus Master's work, and she makes a strong argument that they offer unusual insight into his career as a manuscript artist for clerical patrons.[5] Aside from the *Troilus,* his art decorates scholastic works and one liturgical text. While the patrons of the *Troilus* and a missal remain unknown, in the rest of his artistic career the Master worked exclusively for high-level clerics: John Whethamstede, abbot of St. Albans (who attended the Council of Pavia): Stephen Scrope, archdeacon of Richmond, and Philip Repingdon, bishop of Lincoln.

According to Scott, in each of these roughly half-dozen extant volumes, the Corpus Master decorates only the highest-ranked art. Lesser artists complete the manuscripts. In medieval books art forms an important paratext that guides a reader through a text. Borders and initials identify important textual divisions. In volumes from an era before page numbers became common, borders or large decorated initials facilitate finding one's place within a volume. For this reason, borders and initials beginning particularly important textual divisions are finer than initials beginning smaller, less important textual units. For example, the beginning of a text might feature a large, elaborate initial and the border of the page might also feature decoration, while a paragraph or sentence might begin with a small initial, or no special initial at all. We do the same thing today when we set the title of a chapter in larger typeface than the capital beginning this sentence.

Scott underlines how the Corpus Master's particular clientele and the very few pages illuminated in each volume strongly suggest that he was not a jobbing artist, and it seems to me that he may have been clergy himself. The Corpus Master worked infrequently, painted only the most important borders, and was employed almost exclusively (and possibly solely) by churchmen.[6] These connections lead me to question Scott's assumption that the Corpus Master had a "shop."[7] I think we need to broaden our imagined activities for the Master and consider whether he may have himself been a member of the clergy, likely in one of the great clerical households. Moreover, a position in such a retine might also explain the concentration of those artists who worked in the Corpus Master's style on religious works, rather than literary or legal works.

In her landmark *Later Gothic Manuscripts,* Scott identifies one or more apprentices of the Corpus Master, and in *The Courtly and Commercial Art of the Wycliffite Bible,* I identify this style with the decoration in over a half-dozen Wycliffite New Testaments.[8] Scott calls the Corpus Master's main apprentice "the most prolific hand in English book decoration" of the later 1430s and 1440s and identifies seventeen manuscripts in his style.[9] Small but persistent stylistic differences within these manuscripts, together with their number, suggest to me a group rather than an individual, and so I refer to the Followers of the Corpus Master more frequently as a group of artists producing a style of border art than as individuals.[10] The Followers clearly specialize in decorating religious works, as only a few of their manuscripts are not religious in nature.[11] Aside from Wycliffite New Testaments, their corpus includes several books of hours and prayerbooks, psalters, and a missal, and this style also appears in the Benefactor's Book of St. Albans Abbey.[12]

Scott states categorically that the Corpus Master was trained in a French style, and it is therefore no surprise to find Anglo-French characteristics in the works of the Followers as well. The Followers typically employ light, clear colors and lively, organically curling sprays that are dotted with green lobes. The colored motifs play with three-dimensionality and use self-shading as one way to achieve this effect. The gold motifs are often finished with a flourish, itself sometimes ending in a colored lobe. The Followers frequently employ a visual signature: a short stack of circles atop a gold ball, finished with a flourish and lobe. This signature is a variation on one that Scott claims that the Corpus Master used.[13] Overall the style is light and clear, and the motifs remain nicely proportionate with their settings. Given the number of manuscripts in their style, the Followers' work seems to have sold very well.

Beyond simply extending their Master's French-influenced style, the Followers of the Corpus Master employ decidedly continental motifs that were otherwise never adopted into English border and initial art, revealing a transnational familiarity that was possible in a traveling clerical household. Both the peacock feather motif and the horned moon decorated with gold lobes that the Followers employ are continental motifs, as are the grape-like clusters of gold balls and red or blue colored lobes: none of these enter the general English repertoire outside Followers manuscripts.[14] (For examples of several of these motifs, see Figure 2-1.) Furthermore, with one exception, the only fifteenth-century English *draakjes* of which I am aware were painted by the Followers.[15] *Draakjes* are dragons that artists from late medieval Utrecht employed to infill initials.[16] In one instance, the Followers use the *draakje* in a book of hours.[17] The *draakje* also appears in at least one of the initials in the Prayerbook of Charles d'Orléans.[18] While many artists worked together to decorate this large, lavish volume, Scott attributes this particular initial to the Corpus Master.[19]

Tracing the involvement of English artists in the Prayerbook of Charles d'Orléans offers unique proof of cultural networks stretching from England to France and beyond, and extending from Latin religious texts to the Wycliffite Bible. I agree with Gilbert Ouy that the Prayerbook most likely dates to the later 1430s and therefore I believe that it does not include the Master's work at all, but that of the Followers.[20] Charles left England in late 1440, and for most of his captivity he was far too impecunious to order such a lavish manuscript as his Prayerbook. Only in the last year or so would such a financial outlay have been possible, and the haste with which this lengthy and deluxe manuscript was produced may explain why so many artists worked on it, as each decorating a few quires might have completed the project much more quickly than one or two on their own.

Even the working practices of the artists which Scott identifies in the Prayerbook suggest to me those of the Followers rather than of the Master. It would be highly unusual for the Master to execute so many initials and borders in a single volume: Scott finds no other volume in which he decorates more than a few leaves.[21] Unlike the Corpus Master, the Followers routinely decorate the entirety of their manuscripts, as they do in their Wycliffite New Testaments. Moreover, the Corpus Master's borders and initials feature a narrow range of motifs that contrasts sharply both with the wide array offered by the Followers and with the delightful assortment offered in the Prayerbook.

Scott accepts that the Master had help from one of his apprentices in executing the Prayerbook initials, but I think this assessment must be revised and that these initials in the Prayerbook should instead be identified with several members of the Followers.[22] The style of decoration that is visible in the Prayerbook matches that of other Followers' manuscripts that date to between 1435 and 1445, including a Wycliffite New Testament. We can take as an example the Prayerbook *draakje* initial, which Scott credits to the Master.[23] Its sprays feature low, rounded aroids, or lily-like flowers, much like those in one of the Followers' Wycliffite New Testaments.[24] Another of the Wycliffite New Testaments decorated by the Followers is dated 1444 and features similar, though not identical aroids.[25] A further Followers' Wycliffite New Testament is dated 1436.[26] Together, the art of all three manuscripts appears similar enough to have been produced inside the same decade. Moreover, a copy of the religious work *Donatus Devotionis* features decoration by the Followers that is also similar to that in the Prayerbook, and it contains corrections linking the volume to Charles d'Orléans and his brother Jean.[27] Like the dated New Testaments, the *Donatus Devotionis* manuscripts in England seem to date to the later 1430s or early 1440s.[28] Nevertheless, there are features in these pages of the Prayerbook that at least superficially suggest the Master's hand. The sprays illustrate several pen motifs that Scott finds characteristic of the Master: a trail of empty circles, a stack of circles ending in a flourish, and a pear-shaped motif.[29] However, each of these appears elsewhere in volumes that are certainly not by the Master.[30] In short, the style and order of work of the prince's Prayerbook fits the Followers better than the Master himself, and this suggests a later date that also fits the prince's life records better.[31] This evidence points to members of the Followers having experience with and access to the highest levels of nobility. Other evidence exists suggesting that at least one member of the Followers traced in the Master's footsteps more directly as part of the retinue of a clerical prince.

ENGLISH WHITE VINE-STEM INITIALS

The other exceptional motif that the Followers of the Corpus Master employ is the white vine-stem initial bearing English sprays, and these form unmistakable artistic proof of the transnational culture explored throughout this volume. White vine-stem is the initial design created in that cradle of the Renaissance, Florence, and white vine-stem initials are used extensively in Latin, humanist texts. Very few English artists indeed adapt this specially Florentine design in the fifteenth century, and none of these add English style sprays to the initials as is done in the illustration.[32]

The Followers' white vine-stem initials are modeled on the Italian style named for its interlacing white vines set against a gold letter and particolored

backgrounds. Jonathan Alexander highlights how these initials are as ar-
chaizing as the humanist scripts that usually accompany them: the design
evokes manuscripts several hundred years older, if not actual ancient
Roman manuscripts.[33] These initials begin quite modestly but rapidly develop inhabiting animals and plants, and in some places accrue extensions
into the margins.[34] The white vine-stem style originates in Florence and
spreads elsewhere in Italy before moving into other parts of Europe. Alexander emphasizes that even in Florence other styles continue to decorate
religious and liturgical works and that, while white vine-stem initials might
decorate any type of text, they are especially associated with humanist
texts.[35]

I believe that Oxford, Magdalen College, MS Lat. 39 offers good examples of the Followers' initials that are closest to the Florentine model, albeit
an elaborate version of it. The vines are not exclusively white created by
parchment left bare of pigment, as is usual in white vine-stem initials, but
are frequently delicately tinted with a pale hue to achieve the same effect as
bare parchment.[36] While we might view these techniques as escaping a
strict white vine-stem model, since the parchment is not left bare, the
shading enabled by this careful use of color demonstrates an interest in
three-dimensionality common to Renaissance art. An appreciation for
representations of naturalistic volume explains an apparently English tendency to pierce the letterform with the vine, simulating three-dimensional
space, rather than the two-dimensional space represented in earlier medieval art.[37] While vines also pierce the letter in some Italian examples, the
frequency of this motif in English white vine-stem initials indicates a vig-
orous adoption there. Overall, however, the Followers' initials match the
Italian standard closely, and there is no question about what the stylistic
model is: Clusters of three white dots powder the grounds; light-colored
acanthus vines form the interlace; and aroids are pointed, Italian-style,
and pale like the vines. David Rundle dates this manuscript to the late
1430s, and this early date may explain the Followers' closer adherence in
Magdalen Lat. 39 to the Florentine model than in other volumes.[38]

In Oxford, Magdalen College, MS Lat. 23 it seems to me that the Followers decorate only the Petrarchan introduction, but this small collection of
initials begins to illustrate the ways in which the Followers modify the
white vine-stem style. These initials are small, just three lines high, and
relatively basic, with grounds of red and blue but not green. The sprays are

likewise basic and consist almost exclusively of gold elements. Simpler, more routine initials can be seen elsewhere in nonhumanist works by the Followers, however, so the simplicity itself does not render this manuscript unusual.[39] Delicate self-shading in blues and roses forms the white vine-stem work here as in Magdalen Lat. 39, and instead of white vines, the interlace consists of acanthus and aroids set against the colored ground. These initials evoke the white vine-stem style but do not adopt it altogether. Despite the variation in initial execution, Magdalen Lat. 39 and Magdalen Lat. 23 may well be by the same artist, as the final initial in Magdalen Lat. 23 forms a midway point between the larger initials in Magdalen Lat. 39 and the smaller initial in Magdalen Lat. 23. This small, two-line initial uses the same pale, English acanthus-based white vine-stem style as Magdalen Lat. 23.[40] However, its sprays are like those of MS Lat. 39 and feature both gold and colored motifs in the Followers' style.

"Adapted" may offer a more precise description of the Followers' white vine-stem style than "modeled," for as we have seen, the Followers make some alterations to the Italian pattern in most cases. Clearly this is not due to inability, as the Followers exhibit consummate professionalism, even virtuosity, in such a brand new style. Dating to the early 1440s, Oxford, Bodleian Library, MS Bodley 915 emphasizes the deliberateness of this adaptation and highlights the blend of Florentine and English style (see Figure 2-1).[41] This artist seems to be the same who decorated the Magdalen College volumes, as the acanthus forms and the bulbous aroid bracts, the stiff casings out of which flowers emerge, are identical between volumes, as are the zoomorphs in Bodley 915 and Magdalen Lat. 39.[42] However, in Bodley 915 this artist inserted traditional English forms into the white vine work in a more expansive fashion than in Magdalen Lat. 23. Many of the aroids in these initials are rounded and colored yellow with orange dots in the English style, rather than the pale, carrot-shaped aroids of Florentine style.[43] In cases where the artist employs pointed aroids, these emerge from elaborate English-style ruffled bracts.[44] While some of the features added to the initials in this volume also appear in Italian models, such as zoomorphs and birds, others are more exclusively English.[45] Two initials in particular illustrate motifs used elsewhere in the English artistic lexicon, or in the Followers' style specifically. In one initial oak branches transform the white vine, and acorns sprout amidst the branches.[46] Acorns are uncommon among the Followers' manuscripts that I have examined,

Figure 2-1. Oxford, Bodleian Libraries, MS Bodley 915, fol. 100v, illustrated motifs by Poggio Bracciolini. Courtesy of The Bodleian Libraries, The University of Oxford.

as they are in fifteenth-century English art generally, but they do appear on the Followers' pages of the Prayerbook of Charles d'Orléans.[47] Even more typically English is the lion's mask with vines emerging from ears and nose that makes up the central feature of another initial.[48] No one could confuse this with Italian work, but the Florentine inspiration is clear in all cases. There is absolutely no reason such a masterful artist could not have replicated pure white vine stem style, and so we must see this adaptation as deliberate.

These humanist manuscripts feature sprays similar to those in other Followers' manuscripts of the later 1430s and 1440s, and this suggests links between their Anglo-French style and this Anglo-Italian white vine-stem style. As in their other manuscripts, the humanist manuscripts feature green lobes, or blue or red for highlighting purposes. Peacock leaves and lobed horned moons appear here, as do gold balls arrayed in sets of four or six. Stacks of balls end with flourishes, themselves tipped with lobes. The sole difference in the sprays between the Followers' white vine-stem initials and their other initials is that the motifs on the sprays are smaller in comparison to the initial than is usual in Followers' manuscripts. However, this may be a reflection of the artist's complicated adaptation, as there is some evidence that the Followers adjust the size of their motifs to the size of the initial or the dimensions of the page.[49] The style of the sprays attached to these white vine-stem initials is particularly similar to those in one of the Wycliffite New Testaments and the *Donatus Devotionis*.[50] While I hesitate to assign individual volumes to specific hands within the Followers group, these manuscripts cluster tightly in motif, execution, and, as far as it can be known, date, and so may have been the products of a single artist.

That the blend of these English and Italian features gives us a rare glimpse into the reception of artistic styles. Since luxury manuscript production was strictly a bespoke process, the existence of these manuscripts proves both the availability of English artists able to work across styles and the existence of patrons who appreciated both European and native styles. Like the Followers' other continental elements, we must consider that one of the members of this group knew that both the white vine-stem initials and the English elements would be enjoyed by his patron. Moreover, this patron must not only have appreciated these styles individually, but also the clever stylistic blending achieved by this member of the Followers of the Corpus Master. We are not just viewing one artist's complex interaction with Renaissance art here, but a book owner's complex appreciation of native and Renaissance aesthetics.

In developing an "English white vine-stem style" over the duration of several projects, the Followers of the Corpus Master were arguably taking part in a process of regionalization that Italian styles also demonstrate.

Alexander describes the effect on local styles as the white vine-stem initial swept through Italy.[51] While affordable for those humanists committed to the supremacy of the text, Alexander suggests that, in their original forms, white vine-stem was simply not luxurious enough for the princes of other Italian cities. The elites in these cities encouraged artists to add sprays or borders in local styles to white vine-stem initials, or to modify the vine letters by adding inhabitants or altering the vinework itself. This enabled the elites to highlight their patronage of a wider range of artists from their own and other Italian cities, as well as French artists from across the Alps. The patron of the Followers seems to have been doing likewise in England.

Rather than simply English, or continentally influenced, then, I wonder if we might best describe the Followers' style, and therefore their patrons' taste, as cosmopolitan. Further, I argue that other, similar cosmopolitan manuscripts offer clues to who these patrons might have been. The scribes with whom the Followers worked point in that direction. At least one later Followers' manuscript was copied originally in Middle English by a scribe who was unfamiliar with that language.[52] This manuscript was continued in the 1460s in Latin by the scribe Theodorik Werken, a Dutchman who had long served English clergy in Europe.[53] Werken joined the retinue of William Gray, eventually bishop of Ely, in the early 1440s, and together they traveled throughout Italy while Gray served as the papal proctor for the King of England.[54] Later, in the 1450s and 1460s, Richard Bole employed Werken, as he had previously himself been attached to Gray, and was by that point chaplain of Cardinal Kempe, archbishop of York. Werken seems to have joined his future masters in Cologne when Gray was studying there, and he continued in Gray's service as he moved on to study in Italy. Werken followed Bole back to England in the late 1440s.

Credited with being the first Englishman to have learned the humanist script, Thomas Candour took part in copying the manuscripts containing the Followers' white vine-stem initials discussed earlier, and moved in some of the same circles as Gray.[55] The famed humanist Poggio Bracciolini knew Candour, and called him "a most cultured man and bound to me by close acquaintance."[56] Originally from Shropshire, Candour appears to have been in Italy as early as 1437, and became a doctor of canon law in Padua in 1446, a year after Gray graduated there with his own doctorate of divinity.[57] The two men almost certainly knew each other and in addition it seems likely that Candour knew Werken and Bole. Candour appears to have spent most of the 1440s and 1450s as a papal *cubicularius,* a kind of secretary, for both Eugenius IV and Nicholas V. The scribe's association with Gray would have cemented in the later 1440s, when Gray was appointed the king's proctor in the curia. Candour returned to England at some point in the 1460s, but he continued to travel back to Rome on behalf of his employers before dying in 1476 or 1477. While most of Candour's corpus is undated, the dates that can be ascertained suggest that his English copying took place for the most part early on in his career, in the later 1430s and into the 1440s.

A. C. de la Mare wonders if Candour might have been the illuminator responsible for the white vine-stem initials in these manuscripts, and David Rundle asserts this to be the case.[58] Both scholars note the unique adaptation of the Florentine white vine-stem initial style in some of the manuscripts by Candour; these are all but *sui generis* in their style and use of English sprays. Rundle seems unaware of the Followers of the Corpus Master, or of Scott's identification of some of these initials with the Followers (published since de la Mare's work).[59] Truly it would be marvelous to find that the first English humanist scribe was also trained in a French style of illumination, while at the same time adapting an Italian style for English tastes. However, I think it unlikely that Candour decorated these manuscripts himself. It seems much more likely to me that Candour or his English contacts arranged to have these manuscripts illuminated by an English artist working in the Followers' style who was interested in Italian artistic styles, just as Candour was interested in humanist script styles. That is, I see no reason why artists might not be just as cosmopolitan as scribes.

Indeed, we know of manuscripts that were copied and decorated in two different countries, though this member of the Followers might also have worked in Italy as Candour had done. Gray had manuscripts copied in Italy, and then he had them decorated in an Italian style in England in the early 1450s.[60] While considerably different than the Followers' white vine-stem initials, and lacking sprays, the artists responsible for these initials likewise show exceptional facility with the white vine-stem technique at the same time as they explore ways to inject English motifs into this style.[61] The methods of these slightly later artists often mirror those of the Followers, and this suggests either influence or, I think more likely, a similarity of response to the challenge of adapting the foreign style. Like the Followers,

Gray's artists prefer self-shading the vine to create a three-dimensional effect, and in these initials the vine frequently pierces the letterform.

We do not know the names of many of the Followers' original patrons. A few volumes appear to have been purchased, either originally or eventually, by gentry and nobility.[62] A number of volumes are connected to clergy: John Whethamstede, abbot of St. Albans; the Weston priors of the Hospital of St. John of Jerusalem, William Brygon, canon of Salisbury; the Cluniac abbey of Bermondsey; and Cardinal Thomas Bourchier.[63] Of these, Whethamstede traveled in Italy, collected humanist manuscripts, and employed the Corpus Master as well as his Followers.[64] Further, Candour lived in the Hospice of St. Thomas in Rome while Gray's retinue was largely in charge of it. Members of Whethamstede's and Gray's circles might all be considered potential patrons.[65] These and other, yet-unidentified patrons, at least some of which must have been clerical, apparently enjoyed the blend of contemporary continental motifs with traditional English designs in which the Corpus Master and his Followers specialized.

Given this present volume's emphasis on the role of the councils in the religious controversies of the fifteenth century, and given his active interest in these issues, it is worth exploring Whethamstede's role as a patron a bit further. Two of the Candour-Followers volumes date to the late 1430s (a humanist miscellany including a life of Seneca) and early 1440s (works by Poggio including a preface by Piero Del Monte).[66] During this period the papal collector and humanist Del Monte and Whethamstede exchanged letters and Whethamstede obtained a copy of Plutarch from Del Monte.[67] In 1440, Del Monte returned to Italy. In his turn, in 1440 Whethamstede resigned the abbacy until 1452 on a sort of extended sabbatical. Whethamstede employed the Followers just prior to this date, as they decorated two leaves of the St. Albans Benefactors' book that predate 1440.[68] During the abbot's sabbatical he lived on his manor of Whethamstede and may have continued to work on his encyclopedic *Granarium*.[69] The first part of this large work was in a complete form, if not its final form, by 1440, as it includes papal documents dating to 1439.[70] Notably, the first part concentrates on the conciliar issues of the constitution of the church and heresy.[71] It is unfortunate that so little work has been done on the *Granarium*: it is known that in it Whethamstede cites Petrarch, Boccaccio, and Bruni's Plutarch obtained from Del Monte. However, it is not known if the texts copied by Candour and decorated by the Followers—Petrarch, Poggio, Virgil, and a life of Seneca, among others—are cited specifically.[72] Whether or not Whethamstede was the patron of the Candour-Followers manuscripts, his life gives a notion of the erudite, wealthy, clerical, and international milieu in which these books would have found homes.

Given a summary of the evidence, I think it likely that some of the Followers of the Corpus Master, including artists who decorated Wycliffite New Testaments, were connected to the households of higher clergy, and at least one traveled throughout Europe as a member of such a household in the era of the Council of Basel. The clerical careers of Werken and Candour, along with Bole and many others, found them crisscrossing Europe for decades while serving their clerical masters in part with scribal work. Lay princes traveled with both scribe-clerks and artist-clerks, and Scott goes so far as to wonder whether the Corpus Master's teacher might have been in Charles d'Orléans's entourage.[73] Certainly the Followers learned their unique style from the Corpus Master. But this does not entirely explain their blend of motifs: the French and Italian styles that Scott notices, coupled with the Dutch *draakje*, that she does not. London was an international hub, and it is not impossible that these manuscript artists had enough contact with European artists and manuscripts of foreign manufacture to take inspiration from them. Yet in the case of Candour's manuscripts, even this supposition falters. The English white vine-stem initials must have been based on Italian examples, and these were still very rare in England. While it is possible that one of the few illuminated humanist texts already in the country was provided to this artist as a model, the easiest explanation of the Candour-Followers manuscripts is that, like Candour, one of the Followers shuttled back and forth between England and Italy during a career spent serving clergy.

Even if this speculation, that the Followers of the Corpus Master had personal connections with high-ranking clergy, is a bridge too far, some known facts are in themselves sufficiently significant and suggestive. If not personally connected with high level clergy, these artists worked with stationers or booksellers who were, as the manuscripts they decorated land in clerical hands. Moreover, aside from the humanist texts and with one other exception among the twenty-eight volumes so far identified with their work, the Followers produced religious manuscripts exclusively.[74] Throughout this predominantly religious corpus, the Followers use markedly continental motifs, including adapting cutting-edge Florentine white vine-work for English tastes. A quarter of their known output consists of Wycliffite scripture. Through their illuminators, these copies of the Wycliffite New Testament inhabited a religious manuscript network stretching from England through Europe to Rome and an intellectual network spanning late scholasticism to humanism.

NOTES

Travel for research leading to this article was in part funded by the Pennsylvania State University Institute for the Arts and Humanities.

1. As of this writing, the most extended investigation is Kathleen E. Kennedy, *The Courtly and Commercial Art of the Wycliffite Bible* (Turnhout, Belgium: Brepols, 2014), but see also a forthcoming monograph on the Wycliffite Bible by Elizabeth Solopova and important shorter pieces in Eyal Poleg, "Wycliffite Bibles as Orthodoxy," in *Cultures of Religious Reading in the Late Middle Ages: Instructing the Soul, Feeding the Spirit, and Awakening the Passion*, ed. Sabrina Corbellini (Turnhout, Belgium: Brepols, 2013), 71–91; Matti Peikola, "Aspects of Mise-en-page in Manuscripts of the Wycliffite Bible," in *Medieval Texts in Context*, ed. Graham D. Caie and Denis Renevey (New York: Routledge, 2008), 28–67, and "The Sanctorale, Thomas of Woodstock's English Bible, and the Orthodox Appropriation of Wycliffite Tables of Lessons," in *Wycliffite Controversies*, ed. Mishtooni Bose and J. Patrick Hornbeck II (Turnhout, Belgium: Brepols, 2011), 153–174; and Elizabeth Solopova, "Manuscript Evidence for the Patronage, Ownership and Use of the Wycliffite Bible," in *Form and Function in the Late Medieval Bible*, ed. Eyal Poleg and Laura Light (Leiden, Netherlands: Brill, 2013), 333–349.

2. Though not exclusively New Testaments, this group's output of Wycliffite scripture consisted overwhelmingly of New Testaments, and so I will occasionally refer to the whole as New Testaments.

3. Kathleen L. Scott, *Later Gothic Manuscripts, 1390–1490*, 2 vols. (London: Harvey Miller, 1996), describes both miniatures and border and initial art, allowing for a direct comparison.

4. Kathleen L. Scott, "Limner-Power: A Book Artist in England c. 1420," in *Prestige, Authority, and Power in Late Medieval Manuscripts and Texts*, ed. Felicity Riddy (York: York University Press, 2000), 56–72.

5. This paragraph is derived from Scott, "Limner-Power," especially 74–75.

6. This leaves aside Scott's claim for patronage by Charles d'Orléans, a claim I rebut in this essay.

7. Scott, "Limner-Power," 75.

8. Kennedy, *Courtly and Commercial Art*, 130n11.

9. Scott, *Later Gothic Manuscripts*, 2:180.

10. Ibid.

11. Of the two that are not religious in Scott's lists, one is humanist (discussed shortly) and the other is medical; see ibid., 2:180.

12. This list is based on Scott's list in ibid., with additions at 2:189–190 and 201, together with my own additions in *Courtly and Commercial Art*, 130n11.

13. Scott, "Limner-Power," 57.

14. These motifs can be seen widely in European manuscripts but rarely or not at all in English manuscripts of this era; for some relevant examples see, Kathleen L. Scott, *Dated and Datable English Manuscript Borders c. 1395–1499* (London: British Library, 2002), 82, 90.

15. The additional *draakje* is London, British Library MS Arundel 302, a Bury St. Edmunds manuscript. Bury was known for the continental influence of its art. I do not think that the Prayerbook *draakje* and that of the book of hours are by the same hand, though both artists are Followers.

16. J. P. Gumbert, *The Dutch and Their Books in the Manuscript Age* (London: British Library, 1990), 35–38. Further examples of *draakjes* and discussion of their use in Utrecht can be found in Anne S. Korteweg, *Kriezels, aubergines en takkenbossen. Randversiering in Noordnederlandse handschriften uit de vijftiende eeuw* (Zutphen, Netherlands: Walburg Pers, 1992), 33–55.

17. Oxford, Bodleian Library, MS Liturgical 184, fol. 34v.

18. Paris, Bibliothèque Nationale de France, MS Latin 1196, fol. 14v.

19. Scott, "Limner-Power," 73, and *Later Gothic Manuscripts*, 2:180.

20. Gilbert Ouy, "Charles d'Orléans and his Brother Jean d'Angoulême in England: What Their Manuscripts Have to Tell," in *Charles d'Orléans in England, 1415–1440*, ed. Mary-Jo Arn (Woodbridge, England: D. S. Brewer, 2000), 53n9.

21. Scott, "Limner-Power," 57.

22. Scott, *Later Gothic Manuscripts*, 2:180.

23. Ibid.

24. Compare Latin 1196, fol. 7v and the lower spray on Dresden, Sächsische Landesbibliothek MS Dres. Od. 83, fol. 20v.

25. Manchester, John Rylands Library, MS English 80, fol. 165v; a similar combination of aroids can be seen on Latin 1196 fol. 240v. For other similarities compare for example the motifs of Latin 1196, fol. 194r and English 80, fol. 165v (top spray), also compare fol. 194v's initial to fol. 182v in the New Testament, which is not identical but very similar.

26. Cambridge, Magdalene College MS Pepys 15, fol. 194v.

27. Compare the work of the second Followers illuminator in Latin 1196, for example fols. 162v, 169v, and 222v, with Oxford, Bodleian Library, MS Bodley 918, fols. 3v, and 84v; note especially the similarity in the loose oakleaf and holly leaf forms, among others. On the *Donatus Devotionis*, see A. I. Doyle, "The European Circulation of Three Latin Spiritual Texts," in *Latin and Vernacular: Studies in*

Late-Medieval Texts and Manuscripts, ed. Alastair Minnis (Cambridge: Cambridge University Press, 1989), 139.

28. Bodley 918 is one of the two that contains an inscription dating the base text to 1430, and so the volume must postdate this; see Doyle, "European Circulation," 139. The art does not allow it to be much later than 1450.

29. Scott, "Limner-Power," 57.

30. See Bodley 918, fol. 84v for trails of circles (Scott identifies this manuscript as by the Followers, *Later Gothic Manuscripts*, 2:180); see London, British Library, MS Arundel 23, fol. 1r and London, British Library, MS Harley 2471, fol. 3r for pear-shaped motifs. The stack of circles is replicated in almost every volume of the Followers' work, as it was one of their signatures. If the stacks are not as long as the undoubted Corpus Master works—such as Cambridge, Corpus Christi College MS 61, fol. 1v—then they match others by the Master, such as London, British Library, MS Cotton Nero C. VI, fol. 3r and Oxford, Bodleian Library, MS Auct. F. Inf. 11, fol. 1r.

31. Moreover, the ink flourishing of these sections of the Prayerbook resembles those of the Followers manuscripts as well, though the Followers did not always pair with this rubricator. The decorative line enders and lively curling sprays on flourished initials and paragraphs of these manuscripts are all quite similar, and unlike the straight flourished sprays of such Followers manuscripts as Liturgical 184 and San Marino, Huntington Library MS HM 142. Though there has been very little work done on late medieval English flourishing, this similarity may suggest an association in the larger teams at work on these manuscripts extending beyond the pigment artists.

32. The sole exception of which I am aware is London, British Library MS Harley 2471, which is not clearly by the Followers, though it includes some similar pen motifs: I think may be by a continental artist mimicking the English style.

33. Jonathan Alexander, "The Humanistic Manuscript," in *The Cambridge Illuminations: Ten Centuries of Book Production in the Medieval West*, ed. Stella Panayotova and Paul Binski (Turnhout, Belgium: Brepols, 2005), 327–328.

34. Alexander, "Humanistic Manuscript," 327.

35. Alexander, "Humanistic Manuscript," 328, and Jonathan Alexander, "Patrons, Libraries and Illuminators in the Italian Renaissance," in *The Painted Page: Italian Renaissance Book Illumination, 1450–1550*, ed. Jonathan Alexander (New York: Prestel, 1994), 15.

36. Compare for example Oxford, Magdalen College MS Lat. 39, fols. 97r and 101r.

37. See for example Magdalen Lat. 39, fol. 24v.

38. David Rundle, "The Scribe Thomas Candour and the Making of Poggio Bracciolini's English Reputation," *English Manuscript Studies 1100–1700* 12 (2005): 15.

39. For example, London, Lambeth Palace Library, MSS 369, 547.

40. Magdalen Lat. 23, fol. 120v.

41. Rundle dates the adaption to after 1442, "Poggio," 15.

42. Bodley 915 fol. 2r, Magdalen Lat. 23, fol. 8r (bulbous aroid bracts); Bodley 915 fol. 110r, Magdalen Lat. 39 fol. 1r (zoomorph).

43. See, for example, Bodley 915, fol. 99r.

44. See, for example, Bodley 915, fol. 62r.

45. Bodley 915, fols. 110r, 139v (zoomorph), and fol.140v (bird). I have not been able to compare this bird to that in Oxford, Merton College, printed book 76 a. 6, flyleaf, noted by Rundle, "Poggio," 18.

46. Bodley 915, fol. 169r.

47. Latin 1196 fols. 162v, 222v. This artist uses other motifs similar to those of Bodley 915: for example, the pointed aroid bracts on fol. 160r and those of Bodley 915, fol. 141v.

48. Bodley 915, fol. 65v.

49. For example, Bodley 918 employs smaller spray motifs on smaller initials, and larger spray motifs on larger initials. Cambridge, Magdalene College, MSS Pepys 15, 16 are very small Followers volumes that show consequently smaller motifs, and London, British Library, MS Additional 6894 is an unusually large Followers volume that exhibits larger than usual motifs on the bar.

50. Compare the sprays of JRL English 80, fol. 132r with Bodley 918 fol. 84v. For example, see the selection of motifs on the sprays on Bodley 918, fol. 3v and Magdalen Lat. 39 fol. 120v. The acanthus throughout JRL English 80 is similar to that throughout Magdalen Lat. 39 and to a lesser extent, Bodley 915. Further, these manuscripts are similar to the yet-undated copy of John Arderne's translation of a medical treatise and possibly a roll of the genealogy of Christ: London, British Library, MS Additional 29301, fols. 3r, 55r, and Oxford, Bodleian Library, MS Barlow 53.

51. This paragraph is based on Jonathan Alexander and A. C. de la Mare, *The Italian Manuscripts in the Library of Major J. R. Abbey* (New York: Praeger, 1969), xxxvi–xxxvii.

52. HM 142: for the attribution of this manuscript to the Followers, see Scott, *Later Gothic Manuscripts*, 2:201. For the scribe of the manuscript, see H. C. Schulz, "Middle English Texts from the 'Bement' Manuscript," *Huntington Library Quarterly* 3 (1940): 443–444.

53. A. C. de la Mare, et al., *Duke Humphrey and English Humanism in the Fifteenth Century: Catalogue of an Exhibition Held in the Bodleian Library, Oxford* (Oxford: Bodleian Library, 1970), 24–25, and Daniel Wakelin, "Writing the Words," in *The Production of Books in England 1350–1500*, ed. Alexandra Gillespie and Daniel Wakelin (Cambridge: Cambridge University Press, 2011), 39.

54. The following several sentences are based on de la Mare et al., *Duke Humphrey*, 24–25.

55. This attribution is by de la Mare, in A. C. de la Mare and B. C. Barker-Benfield, eds., *Manuscripts at Oxford: An Exhibition in Memory of Richard William Hunt (1908–1979)* (Oxford: Bodleian Library, 1980), 93.

56. Margaret Harvey, *England, Rome, and the Papacy 1417–1464: The Study of a Relationship* (Manchester: Manchester University Press, 1993), 34.

57. On Candour's life, see de la Mare and Barker-Benfield, *Manuscripts at Oxford*, 95–96; Harvey, *England, Rome, and Papacy*, 34; and Rundle, "Poggio," 1–20.

58. See de la Mare et al., *Duke Humphrey*, 32 and Rundle, "Poggio," 14–18.

59. Scott, *Later Gothic Manuscripts*, 2:180, 201 identifies Bodley 915 and New College 271 with the Followers.

60. The following several sentences are based on de la Mare et al., *Duke Humphrey*, 24–25, and 28, where she describes especially Oxford, Balliol College, MS 290 that was copied in Italy by an Italian scribe but decorated in England for Gray.

61. In these initials English floral motifs in English style such as the rear-facing trilobes and cinquefoils with aroid centers appear consistently; see Oxford, Balliol College, MS 131, fol. 3r. The whorl of leaves on fol. 111v is also an English technique. For similar cinquefoils in a more complex white vine-stem style, see Balliol 290, fols. 200r and 286r.

62. Edinburgh, University Library, MS 39 (Babhams, gentry, Scott, *Later Gothic Manuscripts*, 2:236); Cambridge, Trinity College, MS B.11.11 (Anne Bourchier, Countess of Eu, and William Bourchier and their son Cardinal Thomas Bourchier, Scott, *Later Gothic Manuscripts*, 2:190). The arms in this volume are those of Anne Bourchier, who died in 1438, and this makes this volume one of the earlier datable Followers volumes.

63. London, British Library, MS Cotton Nero D. VII (Benefactor's Book of St. Albans); Cambridge, Magdalene College, MS Pepys 2073 (William Weston, fol. 351v); Oxford, New College, MS 271 (William Brygon, canon of Salisbury; de la Mare et al., *Duke Humphrey*, 35). Doyle identified Bodley 918 as belonging to Bermondsey; Doyle, "European Circulation," 139. For Bourchier, see n. 62 supra.

64. James G. Clark, "Whethamstede, John (c. 1392–1465)," in *Oxford Dictionary of National Biography*, online ed., www.oxforddnb.com/view/article/29197 (accessed September 7, 2014). For the most recent work on Whethamstede, see Alfred Hiatt, "The Reference Work in the Fifteenth Century: John Whethamstede's *Granarium*," in *Makers and Users of Medieval Books: Essays in Honour of A. S. G. Edwards*, ed. Carol M. Meale and Derek Pearsall (Woodbridge: Brewer, 2014), 13–33.

65. Harvey, *England, Rome, and Papacy*, 66–67.

66. Bodley 915 (?1442) and Magdalen Lat. 39 (?1437), dated by Rundle, "Poggio," 15.

67. On this exchange see Roberto Weiss, "Piero del Monte, John Whethamstede, and the Library of St. Albans Abbey," *English Historical Review* 60 (1945): 399–406.

68. Scott, *Later Gothic Manuscripts*, 2:180.

69. Clark, "Whethamstede."

70. Hiatt, "Reference Work," 15.

71. Ibid., 17.

72. Ibid., 14.

73. Scott, "Limner-Power," 73–74.

74. This other exception is a medical translation by John Arderne, Additional 29301. For the complete list of known Followers' works, see n. 12 supra.

CHAPTER THREE

CONSTRUCTING THE APOCALYPSE: CONNECTIONS BETWEEN ENGLISH AND BOHEMIAN APOCALYPTIC THINKING

Pavlína Cermanová

The rhetoric of apocalyptic urgency and the use of evocative apocalyptic images as instruments in disputations between Hussites and Catholics, as well as within the diversified Hussite party, were relatively common phenomena in Hussite Bohemia. This rhetoric was used to defame one's opponents and draw attention to their evils. The effort to explain current events as the fulfilment of apocalyptic prophecies was manifested not only in interpreting current events in the apocalyptic vein, but also by naming historical players in terms of apocalyptic figures—most often the Antichrist, false prophets, apocalyptic beasts or, on the contrary, Enoch and Elijah who would help renew the world in perfection.

Hussite theologians worked with materials from both biblical and nonbiblical prophecies, yet the manner in which they worked with these two groups of texts differed greatly. While they actively interpreted biblical prophecies as prefiguring present-day events, they adopted nonbiblical prophecies more casually, as supplementary material, mainly for rhetorical embellishment in texts they would use in disputations. Hildegard of Bingen's name in particular was often heard on opposite sides of conflicts, whether used by reform authors and mendicants at the end of the fourteenth century or, later, by Hussites and their opponents. The typical example was the pseudo-Hildegardian prophecy *Insurgent gentes*, originally written during the 1250s in Paris by an author from the circle of William of Saint Amour in the context of antimendicant disputations.[1] When such a prophecy was interpolated into a Hussite text, it was usually left without commentary, and attempts to link these prophecies to current events were rare. Catholic authors, on the other hand, worked with nonbiblical prophetic texts somewhat differently, as tools for accusing Hussites as heretics. The figures presented in these texts were connected directly with Hussites; older prophecies were thus updated and labelled as "De Wyclefistis" or "contra falsos Wyglefistas," among other variations. In these cases the authority of the text was aimed explicitly at Hussite opponents.[2] During the period when radical Hussite theology flourished (1419–1421), the Hussites consistently preferred to use biblical texts and exegesis, no matter how radical the interpretation. One of the Hussites' most significant inspirations for their reservoir of biblical prophecies and commentaries was Lollard apocalypticism. Indeed, the relation between Lollard and Hussite apocalyptic texts, including rhetoric and terminology, is crucial to understanding Hussite apocalypticism.[3] This essay focuses primarily on the diffusion of the Lollard treatise *Opus arduum valde* among Hussite theologians and preachers and its influence on the Hussite "reading" of events in Hussite Bohemia in terms of apocalyptic schemes of history.

If it had not been for the Hussites, *Opus arduum valde* would probably have fallen into oblivion. For whatever reason, the Hussites took a great interest in this text, presumably because it contained answers to the questions that they had already been pondering in their texts and sermons. The Hussite radical theologians read this apocalyptic commentary as a confirmation of their own views of current events. The similarity of Hussite and Lollard critical approaches to the Roman church, the shared feeling of a fatal battle, as well as the fact that *Opus arduum* was likely written by an adherent of John Wyclif (and thus the possibility that the text also represented his ideas) were all conducive to the adoption of this text in Hussite Bohemia. The text was obviously read together with other apocalyptic commentaries circulating at this time, primarily *Confiteor tibi*, combining reformist ideas and the Dominican emphasis on the centrality of preaching into an apocalyptic scheme.

The text of *Opus arduum valde* gradually became part of the Hussite textual tradition and remained part of it even after the radicals had been defeated. This can be demonstrated by the example of the apocalyptic commentary preserved in Prague, Národní knihovna, MS X.F.2, written by an anonymous Hussite author in the late 1440s. The only "radical" parts of this treatise—a text which treats the necessity of defeating the Antichrist—are quotations from *Opus arduum*.[4] Paradoxically, the Lollard commentary continued to preserve and transmit radical Hussite concepts even after the defeat of Hussite radicalism.

ECHOES OF LOLLARD APOCALYPTIC THINKING
IN BOHEMIA

But *Opus arduum valde* does not represent the only contact between Hussite and Lollard apocalyptic thinking. Strategies for using apocalyptic figures to describe contemporary situations are also found in the letters between Jan Hus and the English Wycliffite Richard Wyche.[5] For example, the idea of an open battle between Christ and Antichrist appears explicitly in these letters. Wyche and Hus's extant correspondence suggests that images and structures from the tradition of Lollard apocalyptic thought were also applicable in the Czech milieu. In a letter sent from London, dated September 1410, Wyche revealed to Hus that he had heard how the Antichrist afflicted Christ's loyal followers in Bohemia and how the red dragon of the Apocalypse was already preparing to devour the church. He called on the Bohemians to battle for the law of Christ, to aspire to knighthood for Christ, and specifically to return to the traditions of the early church fathers and the imitation of the saints of the Old and New Testaments, both in life and in death.

Wyche was a member of John Wyclif's circle, and this granted him exceptional authority in the eyes of the Czech reformers. In light of this authority, Wyche's reading of events in Bohemia through an apocalyptic lens could not go unnoticed. Indeed, his letter served both as confirmation that the time of open battle with the Antichrist was truly at hand and as a guide for how to respond. Hus attempted to represent Wyche's letter as a kind of apostolic epistle to the Bohemian reformers by translating it into Czech, reading it to an assembly of people, and presenting it as a message not only to himself personally, but also to all of Christ's believers to encourage them to preach the word of God.[6] Hus also underlined the exceptional importance of Wyche's missive in his reply, when he wrote that the letter had strengthened and comforted them so much that "even if all of the other writings were sucked into the abyss by the Antichrist, this one would suffice for the redemption of Christ's faithful."[7] In his letter, Richard Wyche (as well as Hus through his translation) articulated in condensed form the fundamental values of the reform program: a return to the life of the primitive church, the exemplarity of the biblical saints, the imitation of Christ, the struggle for his Truth, sealed by the possibility of martyrdom, the rejection of secular wealth, and a disposition to religious values.

These were all supported by apocalyptic interpretations of the present, characterizing present struggles as a battle against the Antichrist.

Hus's answer to Wyche, which he sent to England in 1411, was written in the same spirit. He cast the ecclesiological motif of the redemption of the elect in terms of events that were understood apocalyptically, which defined the essence and character of the conflict itself: Satan, writes Hus, has already arisen and the Behemoth has moved its tail; it only remains for Christ to crush the head of Antichrist. Hus says that he himself has touched that head and provoked a counterattack: "the snout opened to devour also me and my fellow brethren; it raged and with false words raised an accusation of heresy. However, the final hour of the struggle has not yet come, because the Lord, through me and my brethren, has not freed from the mouth of the Behemoth all those whom He has called before to a life in glory. [The Lord] therefore reinforced the bravery of those who preach the Gospel to torment the Behemoth's tail until he will be destroyed even with his head."[8]

In this description, Hus's definition of the church of the elect and its route to redemption is given contours defined by a radical apocalyptic symbolism: Christ's faithful, predestined-for-redemption, stand-in opposition to the Antichrist's forces, namely those who stand against Hus and his followers, their ecclesiological concepts, reformist criticism of the church, and their adherence to Wyclif's teachings (which their opponents label as heresy).[9] Hus characterizes himself and his followers as those who have weakened the Antichrist by preaching in Christ's name, and who have followed the path of the predestined to redemption. According to Hus, Christ has engaged in the struggle through his preachers, as well as through the Eucharist and prayers. From all these concepts Hus also derived his own self-conception as an imitator of Christ, even in death.[10]

The apocalyptic commentary *Opus arduum valde*, written in England in 1390 by a Wycliffite who was imprisoned for his doctrines,[11] was among the apocalyptic texts that Hussite theologians preferred and from which they extensively quoted. We know of fourteen extant manuscripts, all of Bohemian origin (no copies survive in English manuscripts), a significant indicator of the treatise's resonance in Hussite Bohemia.[12] Hussite authors adopted not only general concepts from *Opus arduum*; they quoted specific passages as well. We find traces of the Lollard text in writings by Jakoubek of Stříbro, Nicholas of Dresden, Jan Želivský, Nicholas of Pelhřimov, and others.[13] Jakoubek of Stříbro, for example, in his extensive *Exposition on the Apocalypse*, written in Czech between 1420 and 1421, followed the text and concepts of *Opus arduum* in several points.[14] Some parts of *Opus arduum* were subsequently adopted by the preeminent theologian of the Hussite radical party, Nicholas of Pelhřimov, in his Latin commentary *Expositio super Apocalypsim* (ca. 1430). As sources, Nicholas used both *Opus arduum* itself and Jakoubek's *Exposition*.[15] For instance, all three authors interpreted Revelation 11:6 in a similar way,[16] describing a connection between the plagues of Egypt and the power to cause catastrophes that was given to two apocalyptic witnesses, Enoch and Elijah. In fact, each of the texts discussed in this essay interprets these plagues as the punishment God sent down on sinners for their disobedience of the Decalogue.[17]

To express the importance that Hussite authors attributed to treatises like *Opus arduum*, we turn to Jan Želivský, a Prague priest and radical Hussite who was executed in 1422 in Prague. In a sermon preached there in 1419, he discussed the significance of vernacular Bible translations and of texts that unmask the true character of the Antichrist, both in the vernacular and in Latin. In making his argument, he draws on *Opus arduum* verbatim when he borrows a passage that compares the apocalyptic woman in the desert threatened by the red dragon and the repression of vernacular texts by opponents of their diffusion. Texts warning against the Antichrist, he claims, are more resistant than iron and stand under God's special protection.[18] Clearly he regarded *Opus arduum* as one of these texts. Quoting a long passage from *Opus arduum*'s commentary on the twelfth chapter of Revelation, Želivský compares the methods of those who prevent the spread of God's word in the vernacular (which, for Želivský, was Czech) to the activity of the Antichrist, or rather the apocalyptic dragon.[19] Želivský made only a small modification to the text, replacing the word *Anglicis* with *Bohemis*.[20] The original Lollard author himself proclaimed his treatise to have been a tool of reform of the universal church, and the Hussite preachers and theologians accepted it in precisely this sense.[21]

The image of an "evangelical preacher" put into an apocalyptic context was powerful in Lollard and Hussite milieux.[22] As they believed, these were the preachers on whose shoulders rested the burden of the reform of the entire church and the final struggle against the Antichrist. According to the author of *Opus arduum*, God shall send faithful preachers (i.e., Lollards) to spread the Gospel and to warn and fight against the Antichrist during the time of his reign and persecution: "tempore persecutionis Antichristi nihil esset magis necessarium, quam predicatio Evangelii."[23] It was the preachers who would reveal the true sense of the prophecies and of scripture in general, and through their preaching the Antichrist would be defeated.[24] In this sense, in *Opus arduum* the preacher took the place of the prophet, a parallel revealed in its commentary on Revelation 11:3: "Et prophetabunt, id est praedicabunt."[25] This prophetic status was affirmed in the prologue to *Opus arduum*, whose author compared himself, in his own persecution and in his act of interpretation, to John of Patmos's original act of authorship in exile.[26] At the same time, the author of *Opus arduum* emphasizes the necessity for preaching *clero et populo*, in both Latin and the vernacular.

To link vernacular preaching and prophecy was an element not only of Lollard apocalyptic thought as represented here by *Opus arduum*; it was also commonly employed by Hussite thinkers who used apocalyptic vocabulary to express their ideas. I have already mentioned the apocalyptic commentary written by Jakoubek of Stříbro.[27] In this text, Jakoubek interwove the matter of exegesis, based on authorities including Bede, Haimo, and Richard of St. Victor, with descriptions of current events in Bohemia, and he interpreted these events according to patterns of apocalyptic thinking. In doing so, he proceeded from the positions of Prague University and of moderate Hussite theology, characterized by nonviolent church reform and the centrality of communion *sub utraque*. Jakoubek's commentary was based on the traditional premise of medieval apocalyptic thinking, namely, that the words of Revelation are prophetic of the contemporary world and perceived to be continuous in history.

Jakoubek recognized preaching and the revelation of the real sense of the Word of God to be fundamental acts in the apocalyptic scenario. In his eyes, the understanding of the biblical message and its dissemination through fearless preachers had to be perceived as a powerful tool against the Antichrist. In this sense, he followed a concept which had been present in the Bohemian reform movement since Milíč of Kroměříž and Matěj of Janov. The fact that Jakoubek cast his apocalyptic commentary in the form of a collection of sermons that were written and delivered in Czech is a significant indicator of how highly he regarded the importance of vernacular preaching.[28] According to apocalyptic exegetes, the ability to understand the meaning of apocalyptic prophecies was something that developed over time, and it was the task of the preacher to reveal this understanding to the faithful, particularly in the dangerous end times.[29] This point was emphasized by Nicholas of Pelhřimov, who described the "apocalyptic reality"[30] of the radical Hussite community and its "saintly" preachers in terms of Enoch and Elijah.[31] In drawing this parallel, Nicholas of Pelhřimov considered Hussite preachers to be warriors against the Antichrist who reinvigorate old prophecies: "In the time of Antichrist they will prophesy, that is, renew prophecies, and expound them and affirm they are fulfilled, and so they will have great authority, standing against idolaters, just as Elijah, and against every iniquity of the Antichrist."[32] In order to fulfil this task, preachers had to be virtuous in humility and mercy and lead exemplary lives.[33]

Commenting on the verses in which the author of *Opus arduum* speaks about the role of vernacular texts and preaching, Jakoubek persuasively argues that Scripture must be interpreted correctly and that the correct meaning must be revealed at the appropriate time.[34] Lollard and Hussite apocalyptic exegetes were persuaded that anyone who wants to understand Scripture correctly must be filled with the Holy Spirit, lead a good life, be disposed to virtue, and receive God's grace.[35] In his virtues and in the grace received from God, the preacher has to possess the same spiritual gifts as a biblical prophet himself.[36] As mentioned earlier, the author of *Opus arduum* compared himself to John of Patmos. In Jakoubek's commentary on Revelation, we find a similar allusion: John, exiled to the island of Patmos, humbly and tearfully receives the sealed secret, and is then compared to the preacher who, thanks to his humility and perfect Christian life, is able to understand correctly the meaning of Scripture—in Jakoubek's case the truth about communion under both kinds and the true meaning of apocalyptic prophecy in the first place.[37]

THE BOHEMIAN "REDUCTION" OF *OPUS ARDUUM VALDE*

Several Hussite preachers and theologians drew on *Opus arduum*. In addition to the fourteen Bohemian manuscripts of the text, a fragment of a Czech translation dated to the Hussite period has been found in a manuscript in the Strahov Monastery Library in Prague.[38] Some of the extant copies also include Czech glosses. In Prague, Národní knihovna, MS V.E.3, for example, a fifteenth-century reader made small marginal glosses translating difficult words from Latin into Czech.[39] The earliest of the surviving manuscripts with a complete text of *Opus arduum* is Brno, Moravská zemská knihovna, MS Mk 28. The colophon explains that the text was pronounced (*pronuntiatum*) at Prague University by Matěj Engliš (Matthias English), and is now being written down by Martin of Verona (the Latin name for Beroun, a town near Prague) in 1415.[40] As we shall see, however, the text of *Opus arduum* was already known in Bohemia before 1415, at least among reformist masters at Prague University.

Among the copies of Bohemian origin, there are three manuscripts that contain a reduced version of the text (two of them in the Czech National Library in Prague, MSS VI.D.21 and III.G.17, and one in the Biblioteca nazionale in Naples, MS VII.A.34). Prague, Národní knihovna, MS VI.D.21, in particular, gives us an important clue for reconstructing the diffusion of *Opus arduum* in medieval Bohemia,[41] and helps us to date the first Bohemian encounters with the text to before 1415.[42]

The main text of MS VI.D.21 is the lengthy "Testamentum Novum cum expositione interlineari et marginali." This is followed by a Prologue to Revelation (*Gilberti Prologus in Apocalypsim*, fols. 759v–762v) with the incipit, "Omnes qui pie volunt." The last part of the codex (762v–769v) is comprised of mnemotechnical verses that were intended to help the reader handle the material of the New Testament easily (part of a near-identical mnemotechnical tool was added to the copy of *Opus arduum* in Vienna, Österreichische Nationalbibliothek, MS 4526; it is likely that these two copies were based on the same model).[43] Manuscript VI.D.21 includes a transcription of biblical verses, each with commentaries in the form of large interlinear or marginal glosses. The glosses to Revelation are almost completely drawn from *Opus arduum* and, when combined, may justifiably be regarded as a condensed version of the Lollard text. Since the Prague manuscript is dated to before 1413, we have proof that theologians in Prague were already working with the Lollard exposition by that time. Concerning the character of MS VI.D.21, we are probably dealing with the scholarly tool of a university student, in which commentaries read aloud were inscribed between the lines during a university lecture.[44] Such commentaries were then copied and subsequently diffused, which could explain the fact that at least two manuscripts containing this reduced version of *Opus arduum* (Prague, Národní knihovna, MS VI.D.21 and Naples, Biblioteca nazionale, MS VII.A.34) preserve the same form. The presence of mne-motechnical verses further supports the university origin for this text. The existence of the two other redactions mentioned above, both related to the reduced version in VI.D.21, allows us to presume that *Opus arduum* circulated in Bohemia not only in its genuine long version, but also in the reduced one, supplemented by new ideas by a Bohemian author.

A comparison of Prague, Národní knihovna, MS VI.D.21 with the Naples, Biblioteca nazionale, MS VII.A.34 reveals that the Prague manuscript is older and probably served as a model for the copy in Naples. A second Prague manuscript, Národní knihovna, MS III.G.17,[45] is dated to the second half of the fifteenth century and includes an even further reduced version of *Opus arduum* than the one preserved in VI.D.21; however, as VI.D.21 was probably not its direct model, we must presume an intermediate version that is now lost. One major difference between the two Prague manuscripts is that the most radical passages from VI.D.21, which were no longer relevant in the religious situation of the second half of the fifteenth century, were omitted in III.G.17. The two manuscripts also differ in their prologues, neither of which was adopted from the long version of *Opus arduum* preserved in other manuscripts of Bohemian origin. On the other hand, both prologues were included in Luther's edition of 1528. The reduced text in VI.D.21 is introduced by a prologue with the incipit, "Johannes Apostolus et Evangelista a Christo Domino electus,"[46] which corresponds with the second prologue to Luther's edition.[47] The prologue in manuscript III.G.17 (incipit: "Omnes qui pie volunt")[48] corresponds to *Prologus Gilberti*, attributed to Gilbert of Poitiers.[49] It is worth mentioning that *Prologus Gilberti* is included in MS VI.D.21 as well (fols. 759v–762r). The form of the prologue in manuscript III.G.17 clearly corresponds with the version in VI.D.2, not only in terms of the text of the prologue itself, but also the supplementary glosses. The incipit of *Opus arduum* in III.G.17 even refers to the interlinear gloss complementing the beginning of *Prologus Gilberti* in manuscript VI.D.21: "Omnes qui pie volunt. In prima parte huius prologi primo premittit Gilbertus tribulacionem ecclesie exteriorem, ut proficiat; secundo interiorem Dei consolacionem, ne deficiat; tercio utriusque revelacionem, ne timore succumbat."[50]

There is no prologue included in the Naples manuscript that could provide us with a clue as to where to place it in a stemma with the Bohemian copies, but (as mentioned above) Prague VI.D.21 probably was a model for the Neapolitan copy. The marginal gloss "hussowske" (Hussite), written by a fifteenth-century hand on fol. 81r of the Neapolitan version, gives us proof that the manuscript had a Bohemian reader before the famous preacher John Capistranus took it away to Italy.[51] The gloss is associated with the commentary on Revelation 7:14, which focuses on the blood of the lamb, namely, Christ ("Et laverunt stolas suas et dealbaverunt eas in sanguine agni").[52] This Eucharistic motif presumably encouraged its Czech reader in the second half of the fifteenth century to associate the passage with Hussite ideology, while in fact the text had been copied verbatim from *Opus arduum*. This mistake reveals a persistent association between the motif of Christ's blood and Hussite ideas, especially in Bohemia.

If we look for a possible owner or user of manuscript VI.D.21, the lead-ing radical Hussite theologian, Nicholas of Pelhřimov, is a logical choice.[53] This copy was written before 1413, at a time when Nicholas was active at the University College of Queen Hedwig in Prague. Analysis of Nicholas's own Latin Commentary on John's Apocalypse from the late 1420s clearly proves that he knew the text of *Opus arduum* and quoted it extensively (discussed shortly). The passages he used from *Opus arduum* were almost all con-tained in the reduced version as well, in the form preserved in MS VI.D.21. Further, in Nicholas's commentary on Revelation 1:1–2 we read the follow-ing: "[John] suffered greatly from the heretics attacking the nativity of Christ and from Domitian, the most impious emperor. From the sect of heretics, as Gilbert, the interpreter of this book, says in the prologue, many faults and various heresies sprouted and grew upon those churches that he, John, presided over."[54] As we know, the copy of *Opus arduum* in VI.D.21 was introduced in the prologue with the incipit, "Johannes Apostolus et Evangelista a Christo Domino electus." This version does not include quo-tations from *Prologus Gilberti*, as is the case in the later manuscript, III.G.17. As stated earlier, *Prologus Gilberti* was itself included in MS VI.D.21. Fur-ther, the passage quoted here corresponds with Gilbert's text (incipit: "Omnes qui pie volunt"), at one point alluding to it explicitly ("sicut dicit Gilbertus in prologo"), which indicates that it was probably drawn from Gilbert's text itself. We can assume there was a later copy combining the Lollard commentary and *Prologus Gilberti*, as in VI.D.21, and that this later copy was a model for the version preserved in Prague, Národní knihovna, III.G.17. But the situation is even more complicated. *Prologus Gilberti* and the prologue beginning "Johannes Apostolus et Evangelista" were also included in the apocalyptic commentary now referred to as *Confiteor tibi* (both prologues were placed after the introductory section with the incipit, "Confiteor tibi"). This text was originally written by an author from the circle of Hugh of St. Cher, probably Peter of Tarentaise, the future Pope Innocent V.[55] There are several copies of *Confiteor tibi* preserved in Bohemian libraries, the oldest dated to 1386 (Prague, Národní knihovna, MS VIII.C.25).[56] This fact is central to the process of reconstructing the influences of Hussite apocalyptic texts and thinking. It is certain that the author of the apocalyptic commentary preserved in VI.D.21 worked with both *Opus arduum* and *Confiteor tibi* as his main sources. Nicholas of Pelhřimov can also be said to have worked directly or indirectly with these two texts. When he wrote his *Expositio super Apocalypsim*, he could choose to use the text from MS VI.D.21 or work with *Confiteor tibi* and *Opus arduum valde* independently of the texts included in that manuscript (which seems to be less probable, as I will show shortly). In every case these texts belonged to one textual grouping that formed the contours of Hussite apocalyptic thinking.

The marginal and interlinear glosses to Revelation in manuscript VI.D.21 (and subsequently in Naples, Biblioteca nazionale, MS VII.A.34 and Prague, Národní knihovna, MS III.G.17) were almost completely copied from the text of *Opus arduum*. But the construction of the apocalyptic commentary was more complicated than it first appears. The text drawn from *Opus arduum* was complemented by elements that were not part of any of the preserved versions of that text. To demonstrate this fact, let us focus on the commentary on Revelation 8:1 ("Cum apperuisset sigillum septimum, factum est silentium in caelo quasi media hora") as it appears in the relevant manuscripts, a verse that was traditionally connected with the visualization of the seventh age of peace inaugurated in church history after the defeat of the Antichrist.[57]

Extant Bohemian copies of the long version of *Opus arduum* correspond in their interpretation of the opening of the seventh seal: the seventh age shall be inaugurated on earth, and its beginning is associated with the destruction of the Antichrist and his rejection by the faithful. The author of the text then adds that this age will be inaugurated at the moment when the faithful cease to worship the pope, who is, of course, the Antichrist.[58] At that point the faithful, including those who formerly adhered to the Antichrist, will be offered a chance to repent. Further, the author describes the different numbers of days or years which, on the basis of various prophecies (Ezekiel, Daniel), define the length of this age. In the end he concludes that its true duration must necessarily remain hidden from everyone.

Whereas the original long versions of *Opus arduum* comment very briefly on the silence that fell in heaven for half an hour (Revelation 8:1 "factum est silentium in celo, id est in ecclesia"[59]) and continue with the enumeration of prophecies describing the character of the seventh age and its length, the author of the commentary in VI.D.21 adds further characteristics, connecting the silence after the opening of the seventh seal with the freedom of preaching: "without being impeded or attacked, the saints shall preach freely."[60] On the other hand, MS VI.D.21 remains silent about the possibility of final repentance before the Last Judgment, which was an explicit emphasis in *Opus arduum*.

The motif of free preaching must already have been highly attractive in the pre-Hussite Bohemian reform; later it even became one of the four main points of the Hussite reform program (the Four Articles of Prague). We find this association of preaching with the seventh age in later Hussite apocalyptic commentaries by Jakoubek of Stříbro and Nicholas of Pelhřimov. Nevertheless, this emphasis on free preaching was surprisingly not of Hussite origin, adopted instead from texts belonging to the tradition of Dominican apocalyptic commentaries. The passage concerning free preaching, as found in the interpretation of Revelation 8:1 in MS VI.D.21, was borrowed from the apocalyptic commentary *Confiteor tibi*, already mentioned. The copy of *Confiteor tibi* in Prague, Národní knihovna, MS VIII.C.25 describes the seventh age in very similar terms as the reduced version of *Opus arduum* in Prague, Národní knihovna, MS VI.D.21: "There was silence, that is, peace and tranquility in heaven, that is, in the church; then the saints will be permitted to preach freely, with no one to hinder or attack them" (VIII.C.25, fol. 40v); "There was great silence, that is, peace and tranquility. In heaven, that is, in the church. Then the saints will be permitted to preach freely, with no one to hinder or attack them" (VI.D.21, fol. 599r).[61] It is safe to assume that the prologues included in VI.D.21 were likewise adopted from *Confiteor tibi*.

The reduced version of *Opus arduum* supplemented by other sources (especially *Confiteor tibi*)—as preserved in Prague, Národní knihovna, MS VI.D.21—provided the radical Hussite authors with powerful tools for shaping their apocalyptic thinking. The ideas and concepts included in this text were adopted by later Hussite apocalyptic authors in their visions and interpretations of present and future events, for example in their extensive commentaries on Revelation. One of these was by Jakoubek of Stříbro, as we already know. He wrote his exposition as a corrective alternative to radical Hussite chiliastic prophecies, which had spread throughout Bohemia since 1419, and spoke of the Day of Wrath, the flight from Babylon, the concentration of the elect, the active defense against the forces of the Antichrist, the bloody revenge on sinners, and above all the inauguration of the Kingdom of Christ on earth. On the other hand, we can understand Jakoubek's apocalyptic exposition as a Eucharistic treatise, where the correct form of communion (under both kinds) and interpretation of the Eucharist were the alpha and omega of religious life, of the fight against the Antichrist, and the way to salvation. Jakoubek knew and was inspired by *Opus arduum*. In his interpretation of Revelation 8:1 are traces of the concepts we have witnessed in the reduced version of *Opus arduum* and in commentaries by Dominican authors who were his models on certain points. Jakoubek typically associated the opening of the seventh seal with the seventh age of the church, a period that had to fill the time between the destruction of the Antichrist and the Last Judgment. In this age, there shall be a respite from various adversities and sufferings experienced during the sixth age, when the Antichrist ruled openly and powerfully. In the list of adversities that shall end in the seventh age, Jakoubek mentions "auzkosti a trápenie o článciech viery, bludové, kacířstva a roztržení [anxieties and troubles about articles of faith, errors, heresies, and discords]."[62] This reproach was directed, among others, against radical Hussites, whose chiliastic doctrine Jakoubek found unacceptable. He rejected most of the glaring points of the radical Hussite chiliastic program in his apocalyptic commentary, namely, immortality, and the absence of pain and suffering in general, which were aspects that had been attributed to the anticipated Kingdom of Christ by Hussite chiliasts since 1419.[63]

But even Jakoubek did not renounce the arguably chiliastic idea of a better age filling the time between the defeat of the Antichrist and the Last Judgment. From his perspective, the seventh age shall bring peace, freedom to preach the Word of God, and freedom in communicating the body and blood of Christ.[64] Free preaching as an attribute of the seventh age could have been adopted from earlier writings, including *Opus arduum* in its reduced version. It seems likely that *Opus arduum* belonged to the preferred lecture at Prague University when Jakoubek was active there. This emphasis on the Eucharist added a new dimension to the standard commentaries on the seventh age. The last age of church history was presented in Jakoubek's commentary as a great Eucharistic feast when the Word of God shall be freely spread. It is no coincidence that these two main characteristics of the seventh age of the church coincided with two of the four leading Hussite requirements known as the Four Articles of Prague.[65]

In his *Expositio super Apocalypsim*, Nicholas of Pelhřimov interpreted the opening of the seventh seal in a similar way as Jakoubek. He described the seventh age as a time of rest and peace after the difficult ages governed by the power of Antichrist.[66] Apparently in direct response to *Opus arduum*, the defeat of the Antichrist and the beginning of the seventh age were merged with the moment when believers diverged from the pope and his statutes that stood in open conflict with Christ.[67] We do not find this motif in the reduced version of *Opus arduum*, which makes it likely that Nicholas had the long version at his disposal as well. According to Nicholas, the seventh age shall be filled with peace of the spirit; all the faithful shall resist worldly values completely; and free preaching and listening to the word of God will be central to the Christian life (an aspect that echoes the Dominican apocalyptic commentaries and the reduced version of *Opus arduum*).[68]

THE MODEL OF THE PRIMITIVE CHURCH

The main reform concepts used by the Lollard author of *Opus arduum* were highly attractive for the Hussite theologians and accorded with their own views—for instance, in its construct of the Antichrist (even if the Hussites would use different terms to describe him). Following John Wyclif, *Opus arduum* postulated that the Roman pope was identical to the Antichrist whenever the pope opposed Christ in his life and deeds. According to *Opus arduum* and Hussite ideology, the Antichrist had corrupted and damaged the terrestrial institution of the church to such an extent that salvation was no longer available within it.[69]

Lollard and Hussite apocalyptic thinking also corresponded with regard to the idea that the primitive church was seen to be the binding model for the contemporary church. Modelling the ideals of the primitive church was an important part of the reform process, the motivation for which lay in the recognition of a deep discrepancy between the ideal of the past and the perception of a gradually degenerating situation in the present.[70] Yet despite the symbolic value of their concept of the primitive church, the Hussites did not advocate a return to apostolic standards strictly defined, as described in the biblical text, which stood at the center of their reform rhetoric and actions. They directed their efforts rather toward a fundamental reform of the existing situation, with a recognition that historical circumstances had changed since the apostolic age.

When elaborating the concept of the *ecclesia primitiva* as a model for the contemporary church and society, Hussite theologians also incorporated non-Bohemian sources including *Opus arduum valde*. As we have seen, Nicholas of Pelhřimov summarized his historiographical concepts, shaped by apocalyptic prophecy, in his *Expositio super Apocalypsim*, with *Opus arduum* as one of his sources. His radical Hussite positions were reflected in this commentary, which was written some years after the bitter end of the chiliastic movement.[71] The whole of his apocalyptic commentary forms the idea that the primitive church was renewed again in the community of the Hussite radicals, interpreted here as a society of the elect defeating the Antichrist, ridding itself of sin, and making way for its own redemption.

The religious framework into which Nicholas of Pelhřimov embedded his apocalyptic commentary was underlined by his concept of the Antichrist, in which he mixed his own views with other textual traditions, including characterizations from the *Opus arduum*. He understood the Antichrist not only as a conglomeration of enemies of the true faith but also as a personification of the evil that ruled the material world. This definition of the Antichrist also shaped Nicholas's image of a renewed *ecclesia primitiva*, which he cast in opposing terms to his concept of the Antichrist. He labeled earnest prayer, bodily oppression, and ardent preaching as the main characteristics of the apostolic ideal, revived in the Hussite present. To describe the way the church should achieve the apostolic ideal, he quoted *Opus arduum* verbatim:

> The Church is crying out, laboring in preaching, praying, and teaching, and desiring to generate sons of the Gospel, as long as it is able. It is tormented, exhausting its body, living according to the Gospel, thoroughly studying the Scripture in order to give birth and to spread the conceived teaching in the presence of everyone, the darkness of Antichrist fleeing, and so that the light of evangelical truth may be revealed to everyone.[72]

The definition of true priests and preachers was closely related to the concept of the primitive church as well. Only when all preachers fulfill the premises postulated by the ideal image of the primitive church can the church be renewed, inaugurating the last age of history in all its bliss. At this point in his argument Nicholas enumerates five characteristics that must be fulfilled: faith and knowledge, zeal and ardor, devout prayer, bodily torment, and good deeds.[73] The unity of faith and knowledge (*sciencia*) as the basic characteristic of a good preacher leading the faithful to salvation was a traditional feature of prophetic literature, and was also part of Hussite apocalyptic strategies. Jakoubek of Stříbro proceeded in a similar way when he described preachers sent by God as filled with faith, humility, and intellect.[74]

The passage quoted above leads us back to Prague, Národní knihovna, MS VI.D.21, where we find the same words on folio 609r in a marginal gloss commenting on Revelation 12:2, and forming part of the text which we already know as the reduced version of *Opus arduum valde*. This passage was added to the text of *Opus arduum* in manuscript VI.D.21 and is not a part of the original version of the Lollard commentary.[75] This fact contributes to the impression that there is a direct link between the reduced version of *Opus arduum* as recorded in Prague, Národní knihovna, MS VI.D.21 on the one hand, and Nicholas of Pelhřimov's treatises on the other. The passage that enumerates the five necessary characteristics was inserted into VI.D.21 and subsequently adopted by Nicholas of Pelhřimov. It also drew upon the Dominican *Confiteor tibi*, which has been an important source for Hussite apocalyptic texts.[76] The author of the reduced version of *Opus arduum valde* in VI.D.21 was, then, an assiduous reader of apocalyptic commentaries. These texts, written in the Dominican tradition, concentrated naturally on the position and quality of the preacher and the role of preaching in the history of salvation—an idea that was then renewed for deployment in the Hussite reform movement.

NOTES

This essay was written in the framework of a research project sponsored by the Czech State Grant Agency: "Cultural Codes and their Changes in the Hussite Era" 405/12/G148.

1. Santos Paz and José Carlos, "Insurgent gentes," in *La recepción de Hildegarde de Bingen en los siglos XIII y XIV*, ed. Santos Paz and José Carlos (Santiago

de Compostela: Universidade de Santiago de Compostela, 1998), 523–624. See also Michel-Marie Dufeil, *Guillaume de Saint-Amour et la polemique universitaire parisienne 1250–1259* (Paris: Picard 1972), 317 and 342.

2. See Pavlína Cermanová, "Waiting for Paradise—Waiting for Damnation. Concepts of Apocalyptic Time in Prophecies of the Hussite Period," in *Mittelalterliche Zukunftsgestaltung im Angesicht des Weltendes. Forming the Future Facing the End of the World in the Middle Ages*, ed. Felicitas Schmieder (Köln, Weimar, Wien: Böhlau 2015), 150–154. Hildegard's texts influenced reform thinking in England as well: see Kathryn Kerby-Fulton, "Prophecy and Suspicion: Closet Radicalism, Reformist Politics, and the Vogue for Hildegardiana in Ricardian England," *Speculum* 75 (2000): 318–341.

3. See Anne Hudson, "A Neglected Wycliffite Text," *Journal of Ecclesiastical History* 29 (1978): 257–279; Curtis V. Bostick, *The Antichrist and the Lollards: Apocalypticism in Late Medieval and Reformation England* (Leiden, Netherlands: Brill, 1998).

4. Prague, Národní knihovna, MS X.F.2, fol. 477v. See František Michálek Bartoš, "Lollardský a husitský výklad Apokalypsy," *Reformační sborník* 6 (1937): 112–114.

5. *M. Jana Husi Korespondence a dokumenty*, ed. Václav Novotný (Prague: Nákladem Komise pro Vydávání Pramenů Náboženského Hnutí Českého, 1920), Nr. 22, 75–79. See also John A. F. Thomson, *The Later Lollards, 1414–1520* (Oxford: Oxford University Press, 1965). On the correspondence of Richard Wyche see Michael Van Dussen, *From England to Bohemia: Heresy and Communication in the Later Middle Ages* (Cambridge: Cambridge University Press, 2012), 78–79.

6. *M. Jana Husi Korespondence*, Nr. 29, 92: "Habeo literas de Anglia et presertim unam bonam epistolam, quam fidelibus Christi et specialiter michi scripsit Richardus Witz, presbyter Magistri Joahnnis Wicleff, confortando nos, ut sine advertencia censure fulminacionum predicemus efficaciter verbum dei." See also *M. Jana Husi Korespondence*, Nr. 24, 83–84.

7. *M. Jana Husi Korespondence*, Nr. 24, 83: "si alia scripta singula per Antichristi consummerentur voraginem, ipsa Christi fidelibus sufficeret ad salutem." See also "si ego nullam haberem scripturam aliam, deberem me pro Christi ewangelio exponere usque ad mortem" (84).

8. *M. Jana Husi Korespondence*, Nr. 24, 85: "Ex quo consurrexit Sathanas, quia iam cauda mota est ipsius Vehemoth, et restat, ut dominus Ihesus Christus conterat caput eius. Ecce caput eius lente tetigi, et apperuit os suum, ut me cum fratribus pariter deglutiret. Furit nunc et mendaci verbo hereticat. . . . Nondum enim hora venit, quia nondum de ore suo eripuit per me et fratres meos dominus, quos ad vitam glorie preelegit; propter quos dabit fortitudinem ewangelizantibus, ut ipsum Vehemoth saltim in cauda tribulent, donec caput ipsius cum membris eius singulis totaliter conteratur."

9. For Hus's teaching on predestination, see Paul De Vooght, *L'Hérésie de Jean*

Huss (Louvain: Publications Universitaires de Louvain, 1960), 57–58; and Zdeněk Kučera, "Husova nauka o predestinaci" *Theologická revue* 71 (2000): 8–15.

10. For Hus's attitude to martyrdom, see Dušan Coufal, "Neznámý postoj Jana Husa k mučednictví v jeho Enarratio Psalmorum (ca. 1405–1407): Na cestě do kruhu zemských svatých," *Časopis Matice Moravské* 129 (2010): 241–257.

11. One of the Bohemian copies preserved in Brno, Moravská zemská knihovna, MS Mk 62, dated to 1444, states the author of the treatise to be "magister Ricardus." Anne Hudson has denied that Richard Wyche was the author of *Opus arduum*; see Hudson, "A Neglected Wycliffite Text," 270. Cf. Romolo Cegna, "L'Opus arduum valde: da Gioacchino a Guglielmo predicatore evangelico," *Annali di Scienze Religiose*, N. S. 5 (2012): 199–221.

12. Prague, Národní knihovna, MSS V.E.3, III.G.17, VI.D.21; Prague, Knihovna metropolitní kapituly, MSS A.117, A.163, B.48/1, B.48/2, B.82/2; Brno, Moravská zemská knihovna, MSS Mk 28 and Mk 62; Naples, Biblioteca nazionale, MS VII.A.34; Karlsruhe, Landesbibliothek, MS 346; Vienna, Österreichische Nationalbibliothek, MSS 4526 and 4925.

13. For the influence of *Opus arduum* on Nicholas of Dresden, see Romolo Cegna, "Ecclesia Primitiva: Dall'Opus arduum valde a Nicholaus de Drazna (de Rosa Nigra)," *Archa Verbi* 9 (2012): 66–88.

14. Jakoubek of Stříbro, *Výklad na Zjevenie sv. Jana*, ed. František Šimek, 2 vols. (Prague: Česká akademie věd a umění 1932–1933). For Jakoubek's apocalyptic approaches, see Paul De Vooght, *Jacobellus de Stříbro († 1429) premier théologien du hussitisme* (Louvain: Publications Universitaires de Louvain, 1972), 3–15; Amedeo Molnár, "Poslední věci v pohledu Jakoubka ze Stříbra," in *Směřování: pohled do badatelské a literární dílny Amedea Molnára provázený příspěvky domácích i zahraničních historiků a teologů*, ed. Noemi Rejchertová (Prague: Kalich, 1983), 61–66.

15. *Expositio super Apocalypsim*, Vienna, Österreichische Nationalbibliothek, MS 4520.

16. Anne Hudson ("A Neglected Wycliffite Text," 262) argues this part was originally a separate treatise.

17. Jakoubek of Stříbro, *Výklad*, 1:424–452; Prague, Národní knihovna, MS V.E.3, fol. 85r. See also *Expositio super Apocalypsim*, Vienna, Österreichische Nationalbibliothek, MS 4520, fol. 140r.

18. Jan Želivský, *Dochovaná kázání z roku 1419*, ed. Amedeo Molnár (Prague: Československá akademie věd, 1953), 190–191. Cf. Amedeo Molnár, "Apocalypse XII dans l'interprétation Hussite," *Revue d'histoire et de philosophie religieuses* 45 (1965): 219.

19. Želivský, *Dochovaná kázání*, 190–191: "Praeparat etiam se ad devorandum filium matris ecclesiae, id est fructum, per scripturarum studium conceptum destruere, quod iam patet quam in eo est completum per generale mandatum praelatorum, ad comburendum, destruendum, condemnandum omnes libros,

scilicet Homeliarum, Evangeliorum et Epistolarum in lingua maternal conscriptis, dicentes: Non licet vobis Bohemis laicis legem divinam habere in vestro vulgari, quod tamen Hebreis, Graecis et Latinis est commune."

20. Cf. Prague, Národní knihovna, MS V.E.8, fol. 95r. Reduced versions of *Opus arduum* preserve the term *Anglicis* as well; see Prague, Národní knihovna, MS VI.D.21, fol. 609r.

21. Bostick, *Antichrist*, 50.

22. It was preaching in the first place that the reformers considered to be a powerful tool, and in this respect they followed in the footsteps of the Dominicans. Indeed, the Dominicans had initially established a precedent for employing apocalyptic commentaries in their preaching on church reform (these were the commentaries on John's Revelation written in the circle of Hugh of St. Cher, incip. "Vidit Iacob, Aser pinguis, Confiteor tibi etc." and the apocalyptic commentary of Nicholas Gorranus). Strategies drawn from Dominican apocalyptic commentaries were now embedded in a new reformist context.

23. Prague, Národní knihovna, MS V.E.3, fol. 63v–64r.

24. Prague, Národní knihovna, MS V.E.3, fol. 81v, "Quia postquam fidelis predicator apprehendit sensum huius prophecie et aliorum contra Antichristum, id est doctrinam, vitam et mores Antichristi, non debet tantum thesaurum abscondere quacunque occasione, sed omni tergiversacione postposita ipsum docere et publice predicare clero et populo."

25. Prague, Národní knihovna, MS V E 3, fol. 84r.

26. Prague, Národní knihovna, MS V E 3, fol. 14v: "Multa sunt insuper nescio qua occulta disposicione, que alliciunt et provocant ad onus exsequendum, ut qualis fuerat huius prophecie scriptor, talis nunc in plurimis habeatur interpretes. Ille namque relegatus in insulam, que dicitur Pathmos, hanc sanctam vidit et scripsit propheciam; ego ergastulo carceris deputatus ac duplici conpede cathenatus, ad ipsius tendo interpretacionem." Cf. Bostick, *Antichrist*, 50–51; Kantik Ghosh, *The Wycliffite Heresy: Authority and the Interpretation of Texts* (Cambridge: Cambridge University Press, 2002), 142–143.

27. Jakoubek compared preachers to prophets in several places; see, for example, Jakoubek of Stříbro, *Výklad*, 1:392.

28. Jakoubek of Stříbro, *Výklad*, 1:405.

29. Prague, Národní knihovna, MS V.E.3, fol. 14v; Jakoubek of Stříbro, *Výklad*, 1:417.

30. Howard Kaminsky, "Nicholas of Pelhřimov´s Tabor: an Adventure into the Eschaton," in *Eschatologie und Hussitismus*, ed. František Šmahel and Alexander Patschovsky (Prague: Historický ústav AV ČR, 1996), 139–167.

31. Vienna, Österreichische Nationalbibliothek, MS 4520, fol. 136r.

32. Ibid.: "Et prophetabunt, id est prophecias renovabunt hoc tempore Antichristi et interpretabuntur et compleri affirmabunt, et sic erunt magne auctoritatis, instantes contra ydolatras, sicut Helias, et contra Abtichristi omnem nequiciam."

33. Vienna, Österreichische Nationalbibliothek, MS 4520, fol. 136v.

34. Jakoubek of Stříbro, *Výklad*, 1:355–356, 393.

35. Fiona Somerset, *Feeling Like Saints: Lollard Writings after Wyclif* (Ithaca, NY: Cornell University Press, 2014), 205–209.

36. For example, Jakoubek of Stříbro, *Výklad*, 1:417. Jakoubek elaborates here the parallel between a preacher and Elijah.

37. Jakoubek of Stříbro, *Výklad*, 1:228–229.

38. Bohumil Ryba, ed., "Strahovské Zjevení," *Strahovská knihovna* 1 (1966): 14–25.

39. Prague, Národní knihovna, MS V.E.3, fol. 84v.

40. Cf. Hudson, "A Neglected Wycliffite Text," 259. František Michálek Bartoš, "Husitský diplomat Matěj Engliš," *Jihočeský sborník historický* 21 (1952): 114–115.

41. Anne Hudson did not include Prague, Národní knihovna, MS VI.D.21 in her list of manuscripts; see Hudson, "A Neglected Wycliffite Text," 259–260. It was Brno MS Mk 28 (1415) that Hudson labeled as the oldest surviving copy of *Opus arduum* in Bohemia.

42. The version preserved in Prague, Národní knihovna, MS VI.D.21 probably provided Martin Luther with the basis for his edition of *Opus arduum*, printed in Wittenberg in 1528: *Commentarius in Apocalypsin ante centum annos editus*.

43. In general, mnemonic principles and techniques were used in the form of verses or auxiliary collections of words.

44. For parallels in the study of rhetoric, poetics, and composition theory and practice, cf. Marjorie Curry Woods, *Classroom Commentaries: Teaching the Poetria Nova across Medieval and Renaissance Europe* (Columbus: Ohio State University Press, 2010).

45. Prague, Národní knihovna, MS III.G.17 was put together in the second half of the fifteenth century. In addition to *Opus arduum*, the codex contains a collection of texts from the milieu of moderate Utraquists (Jan Hus, John of Příbram, Jakoubek of Stříbro, a letter addressed to John of Rokycana, who was the head of the Utraquist church, etc.).

46. Prague, Národní knihovna, MS VI.D.21, fols. 579r–580v.

47. *Commentarius in Apocalypsin*, sig. A.7.

48. Prague, Národní knihovna, MS III.G.17, fol. 1r.

49. For Guilbertus Poretta, see Friedrich Stegmüller, *Repertorium biblicum medii aevi*, 11 vols. (Madrid: Instituto de Teología Francisco Suárez, 1949–1980), 9.1:28.

50. Prague, Národní knihovna, MSS III.G.17, fol. 1r and VI.D.21, fol. 759v.

51. Cegna, "Ecclesia Primitiva," 68n12.

52. Naples, Biblioteca nazionale, MS VII.A.34, fol. 81r: "In sanguine agni. Id est in fide et imitatione passionis Christi. Sed quomodo dicit dealbaverunt, cum sanguis non est albus sed rubeus? Respondeo, hoc dicit, quia sanguis per multam decoctionem sic lac. Sicut patet in naturali generatione lactis. Et ideo, quia sanguis Christi maxime fuit decoctus igne passionis, ideo dicitur habere naturam lactis, cui est albificare."

53. *Testamentum Novum cum expositione interlineari et marginali*, Prague, Národní knihovna, MS VI.D.21, fols. 2r–759r. Without mentioning a connection to *Opus arduum*, Bohuslav Souček suggested that Nicholas of Pelhřimov owned this manuscript; see Souček, "Veritas super Omnia," *Cahiers théologiques de Křesťanská revue* 28 (1961): 81; cf. Molnár, "Apocalypse XII," 227n46 and F. M. Bartoš, "Husitský diplomat," 114–115.

54. Vienna, Österreichische Nationalbibliothek, MS 4520, fol. 1r: "Multa enim passus est ab hereticis nativitatem Christi impugnantibus et a Domiciano, principe impiissimo. De secta enim hereticorum, sicut dicit Gilbertus in prologo, qui fuit expositor huius libri, ecclesiis, quibus preerat, scilicet Johannes, multa pullulaverunt atque inoleverunt vicia diverseque hereses."

55. Cf. Robert E. Lerner, "Poverty, Preaching, and Eschatology in the Revelation Commentaries of Hugh of St. Cher," in *The Bible in the Medieval World: Essays in Memory of Beryl Smalley*, ed. Katherine Walsh and Diana Wood (Oxford: Blackwell, 1985), 157–189.

56. Another copy is in Prague, Knihovna metropolitní kapituly, MS B.46.

57. Robert E. Lerner, "'Refreshment of the Saints': The Time after Antichrist as a Station for Earthly Progress in Medieval Thought," *Traditio* 32 (1976): 97–144; Lerner, "The Medieval Return to the Thousand-Year Sabbath," in *The Apocalypse in the Middle Ages*, ed. Richard K. Emmerson and Bernard McGinn (Ithaca, NY: Cornell University Press, 1992), 51–71.

58. For example, Prague, Národní knihovna, MS V.E.3, fol. 66r: "post mortem, id est destructionem et execrationem ipsius Antichristi a cordibus fidelium . . . quia postquam fideles deserunt obedire precepta pape antichristianis."

59. Prague, Národní knihovna, MS III.E.8, fol. 66r.

60. *Testamentum Novum cum expositione*, Prague, Národní knihovna, MS VI.D.21, fol. 599r: "Tunc enim licebit sanctis predicare libere, nec aliquis astringet eos nec impugnabit." Cf. Naples, Biblioteca nazionale, MS VII.A.34, fol. 81v: "Et cum apperuisset sigillum septimum. Ostendo mihi ultimum statum ecclesie, qui erit post mortem, id est destructionem et execrationem ipsius Antichristi a cordibus fidelium. Factum est silentium. Id est pax et tranquillitas. In celo. Id est in ecclesia, tunc enim licebit sanctis predicare libere [nec] aliquis astringet eos nec impugnabit. Quasi media hora. Per quod datur intelligi, quod bonum tempus illud breve erit."

61. "Factum est silencium, id est pax et tranquillitas in celo, id est in ecclesia, tunc enim licebit sanctis predicare libere, nec aliquis astringet eos, nec impugnabit" (VIII.C.25, fol. 40v); "Factum est silentium magnum, id est pax et tranquillitas. In coelo, id est in ecclesia. Tunc enim licebit sanctis praedicare libere, nec aliquis astringet eos nec impugnabit" (VI.D.21, fol. 599r). In other copies of *Confiteor tibi* of supposedly Bohemian origin the text differs partially. For example, Prague, Knihovna metropolitní kapituly, MS B.46, fol. 126v: "factum est silentium, id est tranquillitas et pax in celo, id est in ecclesia. Tunc enim sancti libere et sine obstaculo predicabunt et annunciabunt veritatem fidei catholice, nec aliquis eos

affliget nec impugnabit." Cf. [Peter of Tarentaise], *In Apocalypsim B. Joannis Apostoli luculenta expositio*, in Albertus Magnus, *Opera omnia*, ed. A. Borgnet, 38 vols. (Paris, 1890–1899), 38:600: "Tunc enim licebit sanctis praedicare libere, nec aliquis adstringet eos, nec impugnabit."

62. Jakoubek of Stříbro, *Výklad*, 1:304.

63. Jakoubek of Stříbro, *Výklad*, 1:304–305. For chiliastic concepts in church history, see Andreas Hinz, *Zeit als Bildungsaufgabe in theologischer Perspektive* (Münster: Lit Verlag, 2003), 203–205, 305.

64. Jakoubek of Stříbro, *Výklad*, 1:305: "A bude také věrným pokoj na těle a tehdy věrní budau mieti svobodu kázati slovo Páně, přijímati tělo jeho a krev svatú."

65. For discussion of the Four Articles of Prague, see Howard Kaminsky, *A History of the Hussite Revolution* (Berkeley: University of California Press, 1967), 369–375; František Šmahel, *Die Hussitische Revolution*, 3 vols. (Hannover: Hahnsche Buchhandlung, 2002), 1:636–674.

66. *Expositio in Apocalypsim*, Vienna, Österreichische Nationalbibliothek, MS 4520, fol. 82v: "Hic iam agit de septima seu ultima etate seu statu ecclesie, qui incipit ab interitu Antichristi et durabit usque ad diem iudicii."

67. *Expositio in Apocalypsim*, Vienna, Österreichische Nationalbibliothek, MS 4520, fol. 82v; cf. Prague, Národní knihovna, MS V.E.3, fol. 66r: "Cum destructus fuerit Antichristus in suis membris potentissimus, cum fideles incipient resilire a pape statutis et ab eius mandatis, Christi legi et eius operibus contrariis. Et postquam taliter discesserint ab eo et a suo collegio, tunc iam implebitur, quod dictum est: Cum aperuisset sigillum."

68. *Expositio in Apocalypsim*, Vienna, Österreichische Nationalbibliothek, MS 4520, fol. 82v: "Sed spirituales, qui spiritualia amant, non curant multum de pace supradicta, dummodo habere pacem possunt, ut libere verbum Domini predicaretur et audiretur. . . . Factum est ergo silentium in celo, id est pax in ecclesia; tunc predicare licebit sanctis."

69. For Lollard interpretations of Antichrist, see Bostick, *Antichrist*, 76–102. The basic studies concerning the Hussite interpretation of Antichrist are: Vlastimil Kybal, "M. Matěj z Janova a M. Jakoubek ze Stříbra," *Český časopis historický* 11 (1905): 22–37; Karel Chytil, *Antikrist v naukách a umění středověku a husitské obrazné antithese* (Prague: Česká akademie císaře Františka Josefa pro vědy, slovesnost a umění, 1918); and Pavlína Cermanová, *Čechy na konci věků. Apokalyptické myšlení a vize husitské doby* (Prague: Argo, 2013), 55–67.

70. Giles Constable, *The Reformation of the Twelfth Century* (Cambridge: Cambridge University Press, 1996), 160–162.

71. Kaminsky, *History of the Hussite Revolution*, 418–433.

72. *Expositio super Apocalypsim*, Vienna, Österreichische Nationalbibliothek, MS 4520, fol. 156v: "clamat ecclesia predicando, orando, docendo parturiens, quousque potest, generare filios evangelii cupiens. Et cruciatur, carnem suam macerando, evangelice conversando, profundissime et Scripturis studendo; ut

pariat, doctrinam iam conceptam palam omnibus effundat et tenebris Antichristi effugatis quibuscumque poterit lucem aperiat evangelice veritatis." Cf. Prague, Národní knihovna, MS V.E.III, fol. 94v (or Brno, Moravská zemská knihovna, MS Mk 28, fol. 174r).

73. *Expositio super Apocalypsim*, Vienna, Österreichische Nationalbibliothek, MS 4250, fol. 156v: "Tanguntur ergo hic quinque, que sunt necessaria predicatori et prelato. Primum est concipere per fidem et scientiam. Secundum est parturire per zelum et fervorem. Tertium est clamare per devotam orationem. Quartum cruciari per carnis afflictionem. Quintum est parere per boni operis ostensionem."

74. Jakoubek of Stříbro, *Výklad*, 356.

75. Cf. Prague, Národní knihovna, MS V.E.III, fol. 94v; Brno, Moravská zemská knihovna, MS Mk 28, fol. 174r.

76. Prague, Národní knihovna, MS VIII.C.25, fol. 58r.

CHAPTER FOUR

WYCLIF'S EARLY RECEPTION IN BOHEMIA AND HIS INFLUENCE ON THE THOUGHT OF JEROME OF PRAGUE

Ota Pavlíček

In honor of Professor Zénon Kaluza on the occasion of his 80th birthday

In studying the reception of Wyclif's doctrines in Bohemia, particularly at the University of Prague, research has focused mainly on the texts of Jan Hus, who was the leader and later symbol of the Bohemian efforts to reform the church. Thus, Hus has overshadowed other Bohemian masters, including his colleague and friend Jerome of Prague. The aim of this essay is to help address this unevenness by analyzing Jerome's relation to Wyclif's doctrines on the basis of Jerome's known and extant texts (as well as other sources), and at the same time to provide background on the beginnings of the reception of Wyclif's thought in Bohemia. The first section will therefore present the initial reception of Wyclif's thought in Bohemia and its relation to the group of younger masters from the Bohemian university nation at the Prague faculty of arts, including Hus and Jerome. The second section will discuss contemporary sources related to Jerome's attitude toward Wyclif, and will show that according to Jerome's own assertions, his reception of Wyclif's thought was limited. Following from this discussion, the last section will demonstrate, on the basis of an analysis of Jerome's *quaestiones*, that although Wyclif's doctrines significantly influenced the Prague philosopher, Jerome's reception of these doctrines was indeed discriminating. Moreover, we will see that he did not rely only on Wyclif and that there are other important influences present in his *quaestiones*, for example, Plato's *Timaeus* and Calcidius's commentary on this dialogue. Since Jerome was primarily a scholastic philosopher and (with few exceptions) his extant texts are philosophical, philosophical topics are central to Jerome's engagement with Wyclif's teachings. For this reason, the final part will delve into more specialized philosophical matters.

BEGINNINGS OF THE RECEPTION OF WYCLIF'S THOUGHT IN BOHEMIA

Out of all the regions of Europe, Wyclif's texts were the most influential in Bohemia, where the Oxford master lived a kind of second life. It is unclear, however, when exactly the reception of Wyclif's thought in Bohemia began. Historians agree that Wyclif's opinions were circulating in Bohemia prior to his death in 1384, perhaps as a consequence of increased diplomatic and cultural exchange connected with the marriage of the Czech Princess Anne and King Richard II, or in the context of the regular circulation of texts and ideas between universities as well as schools of religious orders.[1]

The assumption that Wyclif's ideas were known in Bohemia at this early period is based on the dating and content of the *Sentences* commentary by the Dominican Mikuláš Biceps (d. 1390/91). According to the analyses of Włodzimierz Zega, this commentary is preserved in two versions, an A version dating to 1380–1381, and a B version to 1386–1388. We find echoes of Wyclif's teachings already in the first version, where Biceps mentions Wyclif's name and introduces opinions originating from Wyclif's treatise *De individuatione temporis* (*De tempore*) and perhaps also from the treatises *De potentia Dei productiva ad extra, De benedicta incarnatione, De eucharistia*, and one of the treatises on universals. This does not necessarily mean that Biceps had these treatises at his disposal, although we cannot exclude the possibility entirely. As Zega writes, we can be sure that Biceps had *De tempore* available as he wrote the B version.[2] Already in the A version, Biceps employed Wyclif's division of types of predication and an argument for the real existence of universals. In the B version, Biceps may also have drawn inspiration from *De veritate sacrae scripturae*, because similarly to Wyclif, he used a citation from Anselm's treatise *De incarnatione verbi* to designate those who denied the reality of universals as heretics in dialectics.[3] On the other hand, already in the A version of book IV Biceps rejected Wyclif's remanentist denial of transubstantiation in the Eucharist as heretical.[4]

The theory of such an early reception of Wyclif's thought presupposes that the *peregrinatio academica* between England and Prague occurred remarkably quickly in this case. Wyclif presented his remanentist views only at the end of his life (Thomson dates Wyclif's treatise *De eucharistia* to the second half of 1380).[5] At the same time, in his A commentary, Book III, Biceps cites the *Sentences* commentary of Peter of Candia (who would become Pope Alexander V), which was prepared in 1379–1380.[6] If Biceps's A version really dates to 1380–1381, at least echoes or fragments of Wyclif's and Peter of Candia's treatises would need to have arrived in Prague within several months of their composition, and Biceps would need to have used them nearly immediately for his own text. This speed should make us cautious, leading us to consider the possibility that Biceps's A version—the dating of which has been used to establish the *terminus ante quem* of the reception of Wyclif's thought in Bohemia—could have been written later than 1381. Although this possibility cannot be entirely excluded, Zega's arguments for 1380–1381 seem convincing. Together with Zega, we consider as decisive the colophon in Prague, Knihovna metropolitní kapituly, MS C.19, f. 223va, which dates the text to 4 October 1381. The fact that we find book I of Biceps's commentary in its B version in this manuscript, which means that manuscript C.19 originated later, perhaps even in 1390s, does not necessarily contradict the 1381 dating, as the colophon was probably copied together with the text from the exemplar for MS C.19.[7] The later origin of the *manuscript* could explain the passages "But this is a heresy which the disciples of Wyclif *still* hold [Sed hoc est haeresis, quam *adhuc* discipuli Wicleff tenant]" and "this *was* Wyclif's opinion [Et haec opinio etiam *fuit* Wicleff]," both of which appear in the text in connection with Wyclif's remanentist position. These words, however, do not necessarily imply that when Biceps's A version of book IV was composed, Wyclif was already dead.[8] One possible way to explain them is that the scribe who was acquainted with Wyclif's death could have added or changed these words on his own in the 1390s. A more probable explanation of these expressions is that Biceps's rejection of Wyclif's remanentism was not based on a direct knowledge of Wyclif's treatises, but rather on the similarly formulated Oxford condemnation of Wyclif's position, which was pronounced sometime before 10 May 1381. The condemnation could have quickly reached Bohemia. On this basis, Biceps could have considered Wyclif's doctrine of remanence as condemned and presume that Wyclif had not held, contrary to his disciples, this position any longer.[9]

One motive that could explain the initial positive reception of a part of Wyclif's philosophical realism in Bohemia is Biceps's declared effort to face the pronounced dissemination of nominalist philosophy at the University of Prague.[10] Efforts like this may have prompted an unknown author to remark that the Bohemians always searched for peculiarities (*quaesierunt specialitates*) to set themselves apart from the other university nations. Precisely for this reason, according to this author, sometime when Charles College, one of the first colleges of the university, was still "inter Iudeos" (i.e., in a house on the edge of the Old Town, near the Jewish quarter), Mařík Rvačka, a later opponent of the Hussites, allegedly journeyed to Oxford and brought back Wyclif's books.[11] The possibility of this journey finds support in *Veršované letopisy* (*Versed annals*), which also mention Rvačka in this context.[12] Since the new building underwent reconstruction from 1383 to 1386, we know that the Charles College was "inter Iudeos" until 1386.[13] In consequence, Rvačka's alleged journey would have to have taken place before 1387, which would correspond to the dating of the B version (and perhaps of the A version) of Biceps's commentary, in which Biceps benefited from a direct acquaintance with some of Wyclif's works.[14]

Further support for 1387 as the *terminus ante quem* for the direct knowledge of Wyclif's books in Prague is Jan Hus's note in the polemic *Contra Johannem Stokes* from 1411, according to which the members of the Prague University had been reading Wyclif's books for more than twenty years.[15] Although it is legitimate to suppose that Hus exaggerated,[16] it is also necessary to emphasize that Biceps's commentary, or parts of it, had long been available in the college of the Bohemian nation, and in at least four exemplars at that.[17] Hus considered Biceps to be one of the best Bohemian theologians (he called him *argumentator accutissimus*),[18] and Jiří Kejř has convincingly argued that Hus read Biceps's commentary and used it while composing his own *Sentences* commentary.[19] These facts suggest that Biceps was highly regarded by the next generations of the *natio Bohemorum* at the university. Nor can we exclude the possibility that Biceps's defense of real universals led future Wycliffites (the term applied to the group of younger masters who enthusiastically received some of Wyclif's ideas at Prague) to start looking for more of Wyclif's treatises. Before circa 1395/96, however, there was nothing but the most limited circulation of Wyclif's treatises in Prague, if indeed they circulated at all.[20] In the background, we may see the iron hand of Archbishop Jenštejn, the chancellor of the University, who in 1385 designated Wyclif as "a most wicked heresiarch."[21]

It was perhaps not purely by accident that when the archbishop's influence declined due to disputes with the king, Wyclif's reception at the university came to be more pronounced. We have evidence that in Prague the treatises *De tempore*, *De materia et forma*, *De universalibus* and *De ideis* were available in the first half of 1397. They are all in Prague, Národní knihovna, MS III.G.10, the copy of *De ideis* being finished on 29 May 1397. Since in this manuscript the treatise *De universalibus* finishes in the middle of a sentence in the ninth chapter, it is likely that the full version was still not available at the time of copying. Nevertheless, this fragment of *De universalibus* became the subject of a commentary, probably by Štěpán of Páleč, whose last sentence reveals that the fragment was studied thoroughly in Prague.[22] In September 1398 at the latest, the group of younger Bohemian masters managed to acquire the rest of *De universalibus*, which appears between three other treatises in a famous glossed copy executed by Jan Hus himself. It is striking that Hus did not have the complete treatise available when he started his copy; in fact, he used the fragment in MS III.G.10 as the exemplar for the first chapters.[23] Sometime in this period, Wyclif's *De universalibus* inspired Stanislav of Znojmo, one of the first Bohemian propagators of Wycliffite realism, to write a treatise of his own by the same name.[24]

Although certainly not all of the Bohemian masters came to advocate Wyclif's ideas, we can safely say that important parts of Wyclif's philosophical thought were warmly received by a group of Bohemian masters in the faculty of arts. As we see in Hus's glosses, Wyclif's philosophical realism became a means of setting the Bohemians apart from the German masters, and consequently contributed to the emancipation endeavors of the Bohemian university nation.[25] Probably for these reasons, the Bohemian masters were interested in broadening the available collection of Wyclif's treatises. In this respect, the scholarship established by Vojtěch Raňkův of Ježov (Adalbertus Ranconis de Ericinio) for Czech students who wanted to study at Oxford or Paris facilitated the *peregrinatio academica* that would lead to further important exchanges.[26] One of the students sent to Oxford was indeed Jerome of Prague, whose reception of Wyclif is the main topic of this essay.

JEROME OF PRAGUE AND JOHN WYCLIF

Jerome of Prague joined the group of Prague supporters of Wyclif's philosophical realism shortly after his formal matriculation at the faculty of arts.[27] Not long after gaining his bachelor's degree in 1398,[28] he set off for Oxford in 1399, probably to acquire some of Wyclif's treatises that were not yet available in Prague. He may also have made an earlier journey to Oxford, but we have no direct evidence to support that possibility.[29] According to Jerome's testimony at the Council of Constance, he brought back from Oxford Wyclif's *Dialogus* and *Trialogus*; the accusations also claim that he brought back the treatises *De corpore Christi* (*De eucharistia*) *major* and *minor, De ideis, De compositione hominis, De simonia, De morte* and *De hyppoteticis.*[30] The next accounts concerning Jerome's reception of Wyclif emerge in the context of Jerome's disputations at the University of Paris, where he became master of liberal arts in 1405, and at the Universities of Cologne and Heidelberg.[31]

Having returned to Prague from his studies before the end of 1406, Jerome significantly strengthened the Wycliffite group at the university. In 1408, after Stanislav of Znojmo and Štěpán of Páleč departed for the papal curia to answer a complaint of the German masters, Jerome became one of the leaders of the group. The controversy surrounding the Wycliffite group at the university further escalated, and on 18 October 1408, Archbishop Zdeněk Zajíc of Házmburk imposed a ban on the teaching of any of Wyclif's articles and books.[32] In this atmosphere, Jerome played an important role in the final part of the quodlibetal disputation in January 1409, where he took charge of the defense of the study of Wyclif's treatises. At the end of the disputation, Jerome delivered his *Recommendatio artium liberalium*, in which he defined his approach to Wyclif's treatises. He exhorted the Prague students to seek the "vein of truth" in Wyclif's texts. If they would find something that would contradict the faith, however, they should err on the side of the faith. He stressed that he read Wyclif's writings in the same way that he read the books of other doctors, and that he had found much that was good in them. He denied, however, that he held all he read in Wyclif's or other doctors' books as firmly as his faith. Such universal acceptance was exclusively reserved for Scripture. He noted that the books of Aristotle and other pagans contain conclusions that cannot be reconciled with the Christian faith, but nobody is prevented from maintaining nu-

merous truths from them.[33] At the end of his speech, he showed a document with a seal of the University of Oxford, which attested to Wyclif's
orthodoxy, and then he declared that Wyclif was an evangelical doctor.[34]

According to the accounts of Jerome's *Recommendatio* in the testimonies of witnesses during the Vienna trial against him, Jerome considered
Wyclif's teaching to be the path to truth (*via veritatis*). In this context, he
allegedly designated the German masters as heretics in dialectics because
they did not subscribe to Wycliffite realism. It would seem, therefore, that
Jerome's *Recommendatio* was intended to be a defense of the realism of universals considered as the only path to truth.[35] Even if this testimony were
true, it would not mean that Jerome accepted Wyclif's realism together
with its heretical consequences. In his own testimony in Vienna, Jerome
more or less confirmed his discriminating approach to Wyclif's teaching
that we have already seen in the *Recommendatio*. According to the record,
Jerome did not hold everything that Wyclif said, although Wyclif taught
many good things. Jerome also followed other doctors, he claimed, and
what they rejected, Jerome rejected as well.[36]

The records of Jerome's interrogations at the Council of Constance give
us additional details about Jerome's reception of Wyclif. Jerome admitted,
for example, that in Prague he had given lectures on *De probatione propositionum*, the second treatise of Wyclif's *Logicae continuatio*.[37] He also had
Wyclif's portrait, together with those of other philosophers, on the wall of
his dwelling in Prague. However, a diadem surrounding the head, in the
manner of saint ("in circumferentia capitis, ad modum sancti") had probably not adorned Wyclif's portrait, and Jerome had almost certainly not
adored it as the prosecution claimed,[38] although he probably enjoyed provoking the audience by declaring that Wyclif was worthy of veneration.[39]
Just as in Vienna, Jerome was accused in Constance of spreading and prais-
ing Wyclif's ideas in different places throughout Europe.[40] In his replies,
Jerome characterized his reception of Wyclif as discriminating. He stated
that he had not studied Wyclif's books in order to follow his errors, but (as
with the books of the "magnus Philosophus") to accept what was good and
reject what was bad. He also did not praise Wyclif the heretic, but Wyclif
the philosopher.[41] He had not dogmatized (*dogmatizasse*) Wyclif's errors or
heresies, or at least he had not done so intentionally.[42] It was not Jerome,
but Wyclif himself, who should be praised or condemned for what Wyclif
had written.[43] Shortly before the end of the trial, however, Jerome declared

that he did not know of anyone who could write as well or as profoundly as Wyclif. He wanted to adhere to what Wyclif had written with the exception of his remanentist position on the Eucharist.[44]

We might regard this last declaration as Jerome's effort to redress his former approval of Wyclif's condemnation by the council, which Jerome had made, according to his own words, in fear of the fire.[45] Aside from his own statements, and the accusations against him, we may also discern aspects of Wyclif's influence on Jerome through textual and doctrinal analysis. The final section of this essay is devoted, therefore, to a survey of how Wyclif influenced Jerome's *quaestiones* and the role of Wyclif in Jerome's oeuvre.[46]

WYCLIF'S PRESENCE IN JEROME'S *QUAESTIONES*

In his earliest extant text, *Quaestio de veritatibus generalibus*, which he disputed in Heidelberg, Jerome presented his views on three main topics. These were (1) divine ideas and their relation to (a) God, understood here as the first cause, and to (b) created things; (2) the manner of existence of universals and their relation to other universals and to singulars; and (3) logic. Although scholars have not yet found any certain textual borrowings from Wyclif's treatises in this *quaestio*, Jerome's solutions employed arguments and authorities that conformed to Wyclif's. Much like Wyclif, Jerome believed in ideas as eternal examples in the Divine mind, which stand in causal relation to the created and creatable things to which they symmetrically correspond.[47] Likewise, the basis of Jerome's text is the formal distinction between ideas and God, and between created genera, species, and singulars. This distinction requires the essential identity of essential components of a given entity.[48] As for created universals, these are hierarchically arranged principles and causes of less common entities.[49] Also according to Jerome, every existing thing (e.g., Socrates) is a real proposition (*propositio realis*) constituted by real, thus primary, significates (i.e., the individual components of a given existing thing). Such an ontological proposition is a prerequisite of any proposition based on signs.[50] Jerome was thus a partisan of realist logic, as Wyclif had been. For his explanation of realist logic, Jerome used slightly different vocabulary than Wyclif, however. In this case, he was possibly influenced by other supporters of realist logic, perhaps by the Prague Wycliffites Stanislav of Znojmo and Štěpán of Páleč.[51]

In the *Quaestio de veritatibus generalibus*, Jerome's reference to created and creatable things is the only trace of Wyclif's important reinterpretation of Augustine's theory of creation in two steps from *De Genesi ad litteram*. According to this reinterpretation, God created in the first instant all creatable things *in potentia* in the prime matter that corresponds (in the frame of this theory) to the analogical being (*ens analogum*). Only in the second step is the actual existence of a creature produced on the basis of prime matter in the sensible world.[52] Jerome, however, did not develop this idea in his *quaestio*. He emphasized Augustine's theory from the *quaestio De ideis* based on the dichotomy between the intelligible world of ideas in the divine mind and the sensible world. He supported his argument with additional arguments from Plato's *Timaeus*, which he could not have found in Wyclif. This side-lining is remarkable also because the *Quaestio de veritatibus generalibus* contains the highest number of conclusions and corollaries out of all of Jerome's texts, and we might therefore expect that he would say more about the *ens analogum*, the key component of Wyclif's metaphysics and theology of creation, just as he did in some of his other texts and disputations.[53]

In his second earliest extant text, Jerome discussed the double *Quaestio de formis universalibus—de universalibus extra signa*, which he gave during the process of his recognition as *magister in artibus* at the University of Prague. The *Quaestio de formis universalibus* focuses on the subject of ideas, and here we find borrowings from Wyclif, including the use of the same authorities. One of these borrowings appears at the very beginning of the *quaestio*, where Jerome refers to Grosseteste's commentary on Aristotle's *Posterior analytics*, using the expression "rerum exterarum concreatrices" (cocreators of external things, i.e., of things outside of God's mind) to designate the ideas. However, Grosseteste's original expression was "creatrices." We find the word "concreatrices" only in Wyclif's *De universalibus*, which was most likely Jerome's immediate source.[54] Some other authorities and arguments in this *quaestio* also come from Wyclif, mainly from the first chapter of *De ideis*. Jerome, however, used them to different ends.[55] In his *quaestio*, he wanted to present the subject of ideas as a necessary part of the curriculum for the faculty of arts by justifying the importance of the study of ideas by philosophers. In so doing, he argued that the Platonic school (in the sense of the Christian reinterpretation of Plato's ideas by Augustine and Eustratios of Nicea) is the only legitimate one for philosophers.[56] Only members of the Platonic school fulfill, according to Jerome, the definition of philosophers as lovers of wisdom, since wisdom is conditioned by knowledge of ideas as causes and principles of all created and creatable things—an argument that Jerome supported with quotations from Augustine's *quaestio De ideis* and Aristotle's *Physics*.[57] To substantiate this set of claims, he needed to prove in his *quaestio* that the multitude of divine ideas is eternally present in God's mind and that the ideas are necessary for the rationality of creation and the organization of the sensible world. He did so by showing an extensive set of authorities and arguments supporting this position.[58]

In the *Quaestio de universalibus extra signa*, Jerome first presented the metaphysical, hierarchically ordered organization of all created reality, at the peak of which stands the *ens analogum*, understood here as the first created, most common entity, about which he had already spoken at the end of the previous *quaestio*.[59] Although Wyclif is not mentioned here—indeed, Wyclif is mentioned rarely in Jerome's *quaestiones*[60]— Jerome borrowed the definition of *ens analogum* from Wyclif's *De dominio Divino*.[61] In the ensuing introductory passages (*notabilia*) and with slight changes, Jerome borrowed some important parts of Wyclif's theories of universals, predication, and supposition from the treatises *De universalibus* and *De logica*.[62] He also relied on some of the same authorities that Wyclif had used in *De universalibus*,[63] as well as several of the arguments, sometimes briefly developed.[64] A part of Jerome's *conclusiones* is also based on Wyclif's text.[65] Although the *Quaestio de universalibus extra signa* is nearly completely dependent on Wyclif, it is necessary to emphasize that Jerome did not mention Wyclif's more controversial extensions of his theory of real universals.[66] Jerome introduced the philosophical dimension of Wyclif's realism, focusing on the criticism of nominalism, against which, according to Jerome, many authorities have spoken, including Aristotle and Averroes.[67] From his realist interpretation of Aristotle, and following Wyclif, he rejected nominalist metaphysics and logic as unsustainable and leading to the impossibility of knowing reality, and as opposing even scriptural testimony of universals.[68] Similarly to his *Quaestio de veritatibus generalibus*, in the double *quaestio* Jerome emphasized the dichotomy between ideas and the sensible world. Here he spoke also about *ens analogum*, but he did not deal with its role in the process of creation. From these perspectives, Zénon Kaluza was right when he concluded, on the basis of his analysis of the *Quaestio de universalibus extra signa*, that Wyclif's teaching made a master of arts out of Jerome.[69]

Chronologically, the next text is the *Quaestio de convertibilitate terminorum*, which demonstrates that Jerome used Wyclif's texts as support for his own treatises on topics that were not necessarily consistent with Wyclif's original purpose. In this case, Jerome inserted long passages from Wyclif's *De dominio Divino*, such that they comprise almost half of the entire *quaestio*, including Jerome's *conclusiones*.[70] Comparison of both texts reveals that Jerome carefully selected passages that were useful for his purposes and omitted some of the more controversial theological passages, such as the claim that God created the *ens analogum* out of absolute necessity.[71] Of course, the fact that he omitted such passages does not exclude the possibility that Jerome did not share at least part of Wyclif's views on Divine dominion. On the contrary, Jerome probably accepted an important part of the metaphysical basis of Wyclif's doctrine together with his theory of creation.[72] Similarly to Wyclif, Jerome also argued that God created (*produxit*) his work (*opus*) out of purely intelligible being *ex nihilo* and preserves (*conservat*) this work in the created being (*esse creato*) over which he exercises his rule (*gubernat*).[73] He becomes *dominus* over creatures only with the act of causing the creation.[74] The first created thing, the *esse analogum*, is also, according to Jerome, the only real transcendental in the proper sense. Jerome rejects just for the present (*pro praesenti*) that the *esse analogum* would be common to God and creatures,[75] and continues with a passage concerning the necessity of a certain degree of human understanding of God in order to understand creatures.[76] Next Jerome presents the descending hierarchical scale of created things that we also find in his other texts.[77] In correspondence with Wyclif's theory of creation is the fourth conclusion of the *Quaestio de convertibilitate terminorum*, according to which the perfect cause (God) is the form of universals, mainly of those situated in *esse quidditativum*. This *esse quidditativum* cannot be augmented or diminished, and in consequence God cannot produce any other species than those that he already produced in the *esse quidditativum*. Also according to Jerome, no universal quiddity is annihilable.[78] These passages correspond to Wyclif's doctrine according to which the universals on the level of *ens analogum*, that is, *in potentia* in the prime matter, are not annihilable.[79] Taking into consideration that other passages of this *quaestio* also correspond to Wyclif's theory of creation, there is no doubt that Jerome adopted this theory in at least some of his texts. Nevertheless, it is remarkable that he inserted it into texts on topics that are so thematically distant.

The main topic of the *Quaestio de universalibus a parte rei*, Jerome's next extant text, is the harmony of the sensible world. According to Jerome, this harmony depends on the harmony of ideas in the divine mind and on created universals. Just as in the *Quaestio de formis universalibus—de universalibus extra signa*, Jerome stressed the dependence of the sensible world on the ideas. He once again dealt with the *ens analogum*, the definition of which he borrowed from *De dominio Divino*. As in the *Quaestio de universalibus extra signa*, the *ens analogum* is understood in the *Quaestio de universalibus a parte rei* as the most common created metaphysical entity standing at the peak of all created reality.[80] The passages with authorities and arguments are substantially shorter in this *quaestio*, partly corresponding to that of the *Quaestio de formis universalibus* and therefore to Wyclif's *De ideis*. As discovered by Zénon Kaluza, Jerome used the division of universals from Wyclif's *Logicae continuatio*.[81] Jerome, however, was brought to the main subject of this *quaestio* not by reading Wyclif, but by reading Calcidius's translation of and commentary on Plato's *Timaeus*. Not only do excerpts from the *Timaeus* in the final part of the *quaestio* testify to this, but so does a passage in the commentary that links analogy and harmony.[82] Besides this, Jerome considered Plato to be the king of pagan philosophers (*rex philosophorum gentilium*), and *Timaeus* as well as Calcidius's commentary were some of the most important sources for Jerome's thought.[83] Kaluza concluded that Jerome in this *quaestio* inscribed Wyclif's ontology into the Platonic scheme.[84] We can add that Jerome also employed the ontology of Robert Alyngton, from whom Jerome borrowed his harmonic division of Aristotle's categories.[85]

Jerome's defense of the importance of divine ideas and real universals in the *Quaestio de universalibus a parte rei* provoked polemical reaction, in which the older Czech master Blasius Lupus formed arguments against real universals.[86] Lupus attacked Wycliffite metaphysics skillfully, focusing on the doctrines of ideas, universals, and the analogy and simultaneous univocity of being. The polemic therefore forced Jerome to defend not only his position as presented in the *Quaestio de universalibus a parte rei,* but also more controversial components of his realism. It seems from Jerome's replies that he adhered to Wyclif's thesis of univocity and simultaneous analogy of being that is common to God and to creatures.[87] In accordance with the program presented in the *Quaestio de universalibus extra signa,* in this polemic he defended Wycliffite realism using principles he had found in Wyclif. He argued, for example, by simple supposition (*suppositio simplex*),[88] by distinctions, or by distinguishing several types of real predication comprising habitudinal (*secundum habitudinem*) and essential predication.[89] Jerome supported the latter with a reference to scholars "nourished" in the logic of Scripture. Such a "nourishing" is, according to Jerome, necessary for finding the correct meaning of the Bible (*rectus sensus*). This statement is symptomatic of Wyclif's work, inasmuch as we also find this reference in connection with the essential predication in Wyclif's treatise *De ideis.*[90] Since the dispute is conserved as a *reportatio,* Jerome probably had little time to prepare answers to Lupus's attacks beforehand, and in consequence, he had to know some arguments from Wyclif's *De universalibus* by heart.[91]

At several points, Jerome addressed Lupus's attempts to show the contradiction between Wycliffite realism and the Trinity. For our purposes, the most interesting is a passage in which Jerome admitted that God is a universal *in essendo.*[92] In doing so, he borrowed a similar idea from Wyclif, which Jerome originally developed in an image called the *Shield of Faith.* His diagram found its basis in an older *Shield of Faith* tradition, which depicted the relations in the Trinity. Jerome added to this diagram a series of common names from the created world under the Godhead and names sharing this common name under the names of the Persons. According to the explication, the relations between the created things are similar to those in the Trinity.[93] In Constance, Jerome was accused of having used the image to show that without real universals it is impossible to defend the catholic faith, which is an idea close to Wyclif. From his explication at Constance, it seems more likely, however, that he had used the image to demonstrate the functioning of real universals.[94] We can trust Jerome on this defense because if he had held the position for which he was accused in connection with the *Shield of Faith* at Constance, Lupus would certainly have mentioned it in his polemic. It may be added that a newly discovered exemplar of Jerome's *Shield of Faith* accompanying Wyclif's *De logica* in a manuscript of Czech provenance shows that scholars in Prague were aware of certain similarities in the functioning of Jerome's *Shield of Faith* and the logical square of opposition, that is, a diagram representing logical relations between propositions (see Figure 4-1).[95]

Another of Jerome's texts, the *Quaestio de potentia materiae primae*, is perhaps his most interesting work, although essentially it is a skillful compilation of implicit borrowings from a variety of sources. In it, Jerome dealt with the process by which prime matter was created, its inner structure, and its function in relation to the production of the sensible world.[96] He borrowed long passages from Wyclif's *De materia et forma* and *Trialogus*, and part of one of his arguments comes from *De universalibus*.[97] Characteristically, Jerome supported this argument (in which he argues that although prime matter is created by God, God cannot annihilate it) with a passage from Plato's *Timaeus* 41a–b:

> Materia prima licet sit a Deo creata, non tamen potest esse adnichilata. Probatur, quia Deum decet in meliorando procedere, sed anichilacio nullam bonitatem includit, non igitur potest esse opus Dei aut terminus operacionis eiusdem. *Et confirmatur per illud dictum Platonicum, quod bona racione iunctum est atque modulatum[,] dissolvi velle non est Dei.*[98]

> [Although the prime matter is created by God, it cannot be annihilated. This is demonstrated, because for God it is proper to proceed in the way of making better, whereas annihilation does not include any goodness. Consequently, annihilation cannot be a work of God or the end of his activity. *And this is confirmed by the Platonic maxim that it does not pertain to God to wish to destroy something that was assembled and harmonized by a good rational principle.*]

In fact, the whole *quaestio* is a reinterpretation of Wyclif's double creation theory. Jerome adopted a substantial part of Wyclif's theory, adding to it several components from the *Timaeus* and mainly from Calcidius's commentary on that text. Besides these long and carefully selected passages, he joined to the mosaic implicit borrowings from Aristotle, Honorius of Autun, Isidore of Seville, and Augustine.[99] Thus, he harmonized Platonic and Neoplatonic theories of the world's creation with Wyclif's theory. At the same time, he removed from his citations from Wyclif some of the more

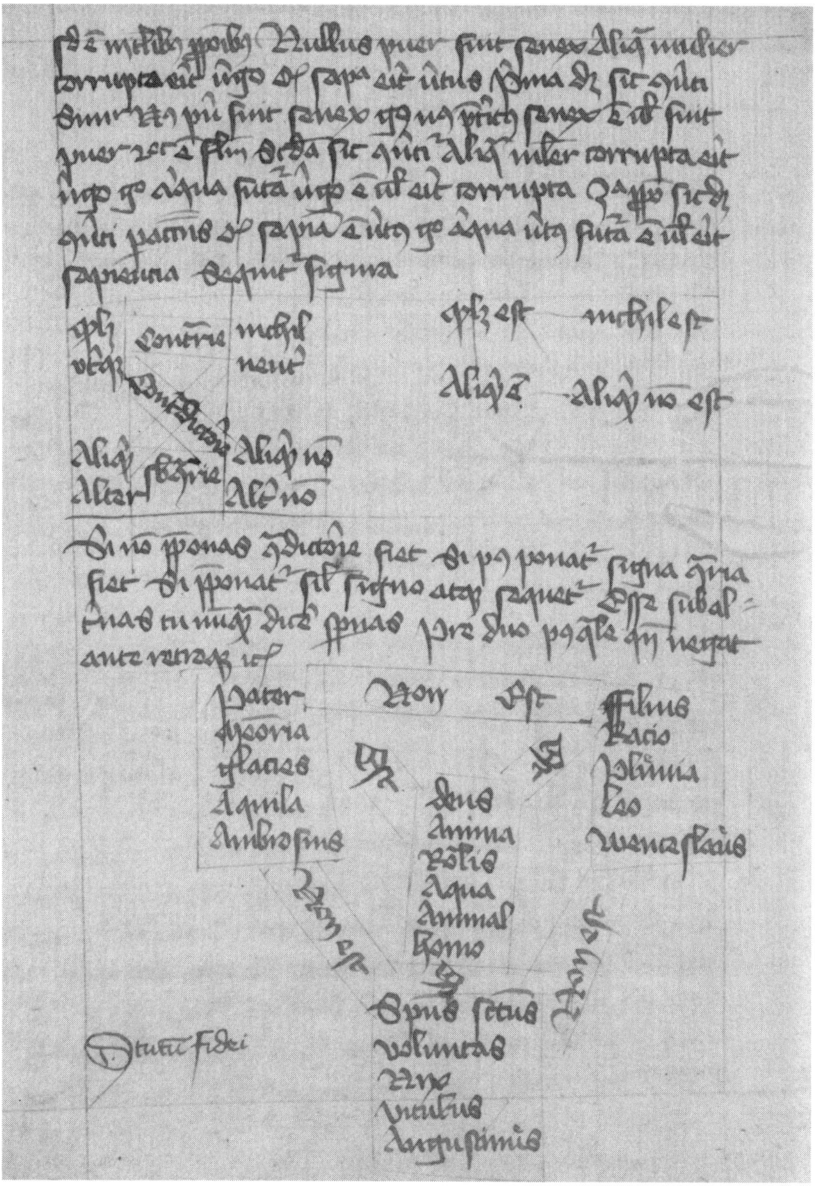

Figure 4-1. Jerome of Prague's *Shield of Faith*. Erfurt, Universitätsbibliothek, Dep. Erf. CA. 4° 253, fol. 12v. Courtesy of Universitätsbibliothek Erfurt.

theologically colored arguments.[100] Nevertheless, through this *quaestio*, Jerome joined a group of medieval Atomists which includes Wyclif.[101]

According to Vilém Herold, Jerome's last doctrinal text, the *Quaestio de mundo archetypo*, is the most extensive independent treatment of ideas in the Czech lands in the Hussite and pre-Hussite period. Jerome once again focused on the subject of ideas and their relation to the sensible world. As in the preceding cases, we find in this treatise numerous doctrinal allusions and correspondences with Wyclif. As Vilém Herold showed, Jerome developed Wyclif's ideas partly using arguments he had found in the texts of his Czech colleagues, which is evidenced by borrowings from the works of Štěpán of Páleč and Stanislav of Znojmo. Jerome also used some authorities that Wyclif did not employ, as for example Plato's *Timaeus*. In consequence, his treatise on the topic that was extraordinarily interesting for the Prague Wycliffites shows originality and only a partial reliance on Wyclif's doctrine.[102]

To conclude, we can confirm that Jerome's *quaestiones* show the significant influence of Wyclif's doctrines. This influence appears in all his *quaestiones*, and in relation to all of the main topics that we find in them: namely, the subject-matter of God and divine ideas; the question of the creation of the world in two steps; the *ens analogum* as the most common created entity, the prime matter and essence of all things including God; teachings about real universals; and realist logic. The primary treatises by Wyclif that influenced Jerome were *De universalibus*, *De ideis*, *De materia et forma*, and also *De logica* and *Logicae continuatio*. In addition, the *Trialogus* influenced Jerome's conception of prime matter and primarily from *De dominio Divino* Jerome adopted the central component of his teaching: the *ens analogum*. Although Jerome primarily adopted Wyclif's philosophical basics, he was also influenced by his theology of creation in two steps.

The conclusion that Jerome's doctrine, as present in his *quaestiones*, essentially conforms to Wyclif's does not mean, however, that Jerome's teaching is unoriginal or that he adopted everything that he found in Wyclif. It is necessary to emphasize that in Jerome's *quaestiones* we find many more sources and influences that are likewise important, which he arranged into a more or less harmonized whole. Of these sources, the most influential was Calcidius's translation of Plato's *Timaeus* with its commentary. In addition, we find in Jerome's texts responses, emphases, and motives that he could not have found in Wyclif. Jerome also avoided many of Wyclif's heterodox claims, such as Wyclif's emphasis on philosophical realism as a prerequisite for the orthodox faith. In this respect, we have to attend not only to which of Wyclif's treatises and ideas Jerome employed in his own texts, but also to what he did *not* adopt from Wyclif, which treatises he did *not* use, and what he intentionally omitted. From this point of view, it follows that Jerome's claim that his reception of Wyclif's thought was limited was not fabricated, and that he carefully chose from Wyclif's texts what he would use, and what he would *not* use, for his own.

NOTES

Work on this essay received financial support from the Czech Science Foundation (GA ČR) project "Cultural Codes and Their Transformations in the Hussite Period" (P405/12/G148), realized at the Institute of Philosophy of the Czech Academy of Sciences. I wish to thank Michael Van Dussen for his help with the English translation. Thanks also to the Jan Hus Educational Foundation and the Foundation of Josef, Marie, and Zdeňka Hlávka for supporting my research.

1. For the reception of Wyclif's texts in Bohemia, see František Šmahel, "Wyclif's Fortune in Hussite Bohemia," in *Die Prager Universität im Mittelalter / Charles University in the Middle Ages*, ed. F. Šmahel (Leiden, Netherlands: Brill, 2007), 467–489; Vilém Herold, *Pražská univerzita a Wyclif* (Prague: Univerzita Karlova, 1985); Anne Hudson, "From Oxford to Prague: The Writings of John Wyclif and his English Followers in Bohemia," in *Studies in the Transmission of Wyclif's Writings*, ed. Anne Hudson (Aldershot, England: Ashgate, 2008), 2:642–657; Włodzimierz Zega, *Filozofia Boga w Quaestiones Sententiarum Mikolaja Bicepsa* (Warsaw: IFiS PAN, 2002), 88–101; František Šmahel, *Život a dílo Jeronýma Pražského* (Prague: Argo, 2010), 179–183; Michael Van Dussen, *From England to Bohemia: Heresy and Communication in the Later Middle Ages* (Cambridge: Cambridge University Press, 2012), 63–85; František Šmahel, *Jan Hus: život a dílo* (Prague: Argo, 2013), 37–39. Cf. Anne Hudson, "The Survival of Wyclif's Works in England and Bohemia," in *Studies*, 16:29–41 and Anne Hudson, "From Oxford to Bohemia: Reflections on the Transmission of Wycliffite Texts," *Studia mediaevalia Bohemica* 2 (2010): 25–37. For more literature on the topic, see Zega, *Filozofia Boga*, 88–89n251.

2. Zega, *Filozofia Boga*, 88–101.

3. See Zega, *Filozofia Boga*, 99–100 and 160, lines 38–45; cf. ibid., 142–143 and Ota Pavlíček, "Two Philosophical Texts of Jerome of Prague and his Alleged Designation of Opponents of Real Universals as Diabolical Heretics," *The Bohemian Reformation and Religious Practice* 8 (2011): 52–76, particularly 75–76. For Biceps's text, cf. n. 10 infra.

4. Zega, *Filozofia Boga*, 56–57.

5. See Williel R. Thomson, *The Latin Writings of John Wyclyf* (Toronto: Pontifical Institute of Mediaeval Studies, 1983), 67–69. Stephen Penn dates three of Wyclif's texts in support of remanence (*De simonia, De eucharistia, De apostasia*) to 1380. See "Wyclif and the Sacraments," in *A Companion to John Wyclif*, ed. Ian Christopher Levy (Leiden, Netherlands: Brill, 2006), 250, 255–256.

6. See Zega, *Filozofia Boga*, 56. For Peter of Candia and his *Sentences* commentary, see Franz Ehrle, *Der Sentenzenkommentar Peters von Candia, des Pisaner Papstes Alexanders V* (Münster: Aschendorff, 1925).

7. For the whole argument concerning the date of the commentary's composition, see Zega, *Filozofia Boga*, 33–37, 59–60, 62–65, 71n188 (for the 1390s dating of the manuscript), and passim. Zega, 59, prints the colophon that is important for the *ante quem* date of the A version of Biceps's commentary: "Expliciunt questiones Sentenciarum quarti libri. Finitus in festo s. Francisci. Amen. Anno Domini millesimo trecentesimo octogesimo primo."

8. The text was printed in Zega, *Filozofia Boga*, 57. I am indebted to Professor Christopher D. Schabel for bringing my attention to this passage and in general to the possibility of 1384 as *terminus post quem* of the A version. For his solution of this topic, see Chris Schabel, Monica Brinzei, and Mihai Maga, "A Golden Age of Theology at Prague: Prague Sentences Commentaries, ca. 1375–1385, with a Redating of the Arrival of Wycliffism in Bohemia," *Acta Universitatis Carolinae—Historia Universitatis Carolinae Pragensis* 55 (2015), forthcoming.

9. For condemnations of Wyclif's doctrinal views during Wyclif's life, see Andrew E. Larsen, "John Wyclif, c. 1331–1384," in *A Companion to John Wyclif*, 38–42, 44–49, 50–58. The condemned articles were edited in *Fasciculi zizaniorum*, ed. W. W. Shirley (London, 1858), 110–111. Cf. Stephen Penn, "Wyclif and the Sacraments," 250–252.

10. Cf. Biceps's own words in Zega, *Filozofia Boga*, 160–162, lines 34–81: "In hac enim materia, praesertim in universitate ista, fere haec positio tot habet opponentes, quot non intelligentes. Ideo, quia tempus non patitur, cras me ad eandem materiam reducam secundum doctores quam plurimos et quantum potuero destruam positionem oppositam. In ista materia materiam errandi ministrant discipuli fratris Wilhelmi Occan, quos venerabilis Anselmus vocat dialecticae hereticos." Cf. the review on Zega's book by Efrem Jindráček, *Filosofický časopis* 58 (2010): 463.

11. The reference from Municipal Library of Nuremberg, MS Cent. I, 78, fol. 151v was published by František M. Bartoš, *Husitství a cizina* (Prague: Čin, 1931), 255. For the life and work of Mařík Rvačka, see Bohumil Kvapil, "Mistr Mařík Rvačka," in *K dějinám československým v období humanismu. Sborník prací věnovaných Janu Bedřichu Novákovi k šedesátým narozeninám 1872–1932*, ed. Bedřich Jenšovský and Bedřich Mendl (Prague: Československá archivní společnost, 1932), 192–199. Recently, Pavel Soukup, "Mařík Rvačka's Defense of Crusading Indulgences from 1412," *The Bohemian Reformation and Religious*

Practice 8 (2011): 77–97, points out that Mařík could have been born several years earlier than circa 1365, as suggested by Kvapil. For the system of colleges at Prague University, see Michal Svatoš, "The Carolinum and the College System," in *A History of Charles University*, vol. 1, *1348–1802*, ed. František Kavka et al. (Prague: Karolinum, 2001), 39–55.

12. František Svejkovský, ed., *Veršované skladby doby husitské* (Prague: Nakladatelství Československé akademie věd, 1963), 163; for description of the treatise, see ibid., 40–42. The relation between the reference in the Nuremberg MS and the *Veršované letopisy* testimony is unclear.

13. Josef Petráň, ed., *Památky univerzity Karlovy* (Prague: Karolinum, 1999), 11, 21–22.

14. Since Rvačka obtained his bachelor's and master's degrees *in artibus* in Prague in 1385 and 1387, it seems more likely that his journey took place sometime before he started his studies, perhaps in 1380–1381. See *Monumenta Historica Universitatis Carolo-Ferdinandae Pragensis* Tom. 1, Pars I (Prague, 1830), 230, 250; hereafter *MUPR*.

15. Jan Hus, "Contra Johannem Stokes," in *Polemica*, ed. Jaroslav Eršil, Corpus Christianorum, Continuatio Mediaevalis 238 (Turnhout, Belgium: Brepols, 2010), 48, lines 48–49: "egoque et membra nostre universitatis habemus et legimus illos libros <Iohannis Wyclif>, ab annis viginti et pluribus."

16. Šmahel, *Život a dílo Jeronýma Pražského*, 24.

17. See the index in the new edition of the catalogues, *Catalogi librorum vetustissimi universitatis pragensis*, ed. Zuzana Silagiová and František Šmahel, Corpus Christianorum, Continuatio Mediaevalis 271 (Turnhout, Belgium: Brepols, 2015), 244; cf. Jiří Kejř, "Kdo je Parisiensis ve spisech Husových," *Studie o rukopisech* 18 (1979): 26n13, and Jindráček's review in *Filosofický časopis* 58 (2010): 460n2.

18. M. Jan Hus, "Confirmate corda vestra," in *Universitní promluvy*, ed. Anežka Schmidtová (Prague: Státní pedogogické nakladatelství, 1958), 125–126.

19. See Kejř, "Kdo je Parisiensis," 12–26.

20. Cf., however, the introduction in Štěpán of Páleč, *Commentarius in I–IX capitula tractatus De universalibus Iohannis Wyclif Stephano de Palecz ascriptus*, ed. Ivan Müller (Prague: Filosofia, 2009), 9–30, and a pertinent review by František Šmahel in *Studia mediaevalia Bohemica* 2 (2010): 150.

21. Jan of Jenštejn, "Tractatus de consideracione," in *Studie a texty k náboženským dějinám českým* II/1, ed. Jan Sedlák (Olomouc: Nákl. Matice Cyrilometodějské, 1915), 105. Jenštejn refers to Wyclif in the context of Wyclif's theory of civil dominion. For more, see Van Dussen, *From England to Bohemia*, 68–69.

22. Cf. František Šmahel, "Circa universalia sunt dubitationes non pauce I–III. Studie a texty k pražskému sporu o universalia realia," in *Filosofický časopis* 18 (1970): 988–991. For the text, see Štěpán of Páleč, *Commentarius in I–IX capitula tractatus De universalibus*, 306.

23. See John Wyclif, *Tractatus de universalibus*, ed. Ivan J. Mueller (Oxford: Oxford University Press, 1985), xli, lxxxvi.

24. The treatise was mistakenly published as a work of Wyclif in *Iohannis Wyclif Miscellanea Philosophica II*, ed. Michael Henry Dziewicki (London: Trübner, 1905), 1–151.

25. On the glosses, see Jiří Daňhelka, "Das Zeugnis des Stockholmer Autographs von Hus," *Die Welt der Slawen* 27 (1982): 225–233, cf. František Šmahel, *Jan Hus*, 39–41, 269. On the emancipation endeavors, see Martin Nodl, *Dekret Kutnohorský* (Prague: Nakl. Lidové noviny, 2010), passim.

26. For his life and work, see Jaroslav Kadlec, *Leben und Schriften des Prager Magisters Adalbert Ranconis de Ericinio, Aus dem Nachlass von Rudolf Holinka und Jan Vilikovský* (Münster: Aschendorff, 1971).

27. For the life and work of Jerome of Prague, see especially Šmahel's introduction to *Magistri Hieronymi de Praga Quaestiones, Polemica, Epistulae*, ed. František Šmahel and Gabriel Silagi, Corpus Christianorum, Continuatio Mediaevalis 222 (Turnhout, Belgium: Brepols, 2010), xi–cxxviii, hereafter Šmahel-Silagi, and Šmahel, *Život a dílo Jeronýma Pražského*, passim.

28. See *MUPR* 1/I, 333, 338.

29. On this journey, cf. František Šmahel, "Drobné otázky a záhady v studentském životě mistra Jeronýma Pražského," *Český časopis historický* 106 (2008): 9–16.

30. See Herman von der Hardt, ed., *Magnum oecumenicum Constantiense concilium*, vol. IV (Frankfurt-Leipzig, 1699), cols. 635, 649, 651; hereafter Hardt IV. The alleged treatise *De hypocritis* noted in Hardt might actually be the treatise *De hyppoteticis*. In that case, the treatise in question is most probably the *tractatus tercius* of *Logicae continuatio*, published in Michael H. Dziewicki, ed., *Iohannis Wyclif Tractatus de Logica* II–III (London: Trübner, 1896–1899). It is unclear what *De morte* stands for.

31. See Šmahel-Silagi, xv–xxix, with a list of relevant literature.

32. See *Pražské synody a koncily předhusitské doby*, ed. Jaroslav V. Polc, Zdeňka Hledíková (Prague: Univerzita Karlova, 2002), 288. For the historical background, see František Šmahel, *Die Hussitische Revolution* (Hannover: Hahnsche Buchhandlung, 2002), 2:788–878.

33. Šmahel-Silagi, 214–215, lines 437–470. For Jerome's approach to Scripture, see Ota Pavlíček, "'Ipsa dicit, quod sic est, ergo verum.' Authority of Scripture, the Use and Sources of Biblical Citations in the Work of Jerome of Prague," *Bohemian Reformation and Religious Practice* 10 (2015): 70–89.

34. For Jerome's performance at the very end of the disputation, cf. the distorted and opposing testimonies from Vienna, *Processus iudiciarius contra Jeronimum de Praga habitus Viennae a. 1410–1412*, ed. Ladislau Klicman (Prague: Nákladem České akademie císaře Františka Josefa pro vědy, slovesnost a umění, 1898), 5, 8, 15, 17–19, 22, 24, 28, 31–32, and 34, which I mainly leave aside in the following passages for reasons of reliability. See, for example, "Johannes

Wikleph esset hereticus, et magister Jeronimus teneret *in magna parte* suas opiniones heresim sapientes" (22); and "Jeronimus et Huss tamquam principales essent Wikleviste, *presertim quoad opinionem universalium realium*" (25). On the honorary title *doctor evangelicus*, see Šmahel, "Wyclif's Fortune," 478. For the fullest account of the history of the Oxford letter, see Van Dussen, *From England to Bohemia*, 86–105.

35. See *Processus iudiciarius*, 26–27, 29–30, and 33. The expression "via veritatis" could imply that the discussions between the Prague masters were related to the subject of the *Wegestreit*. On this topic, see Maarten J. F. M. Hoenen, "*Via Antiqua* and *Via Moderna* in the Fifteenth Century: Doctrinal, Institutional, and Church Political Factors in the *Wegestreit*," in *The Medieval Heritage in Early Modern Metaphysics and Modal Theory, 1400–1700*, ed. Russell L. Friedman and Lauge Olaf Nielsen (Dordrecht, Netherlands: Kluwer, 2003), 9–36. Cf. Šmahel, "Wyclif's Fortune," 473, and Šmahel-Silagi, liv–lxiii. According to several sources, Wycliffite realism was one of the factors that led to the secession of the German masters from the University of Prague in 1409. See František Šmahel, "Universalia realia sunt heresis seminaria. Filosofie pražského extremního realismu ve světle doktrinálně institucionální kritiky," *Československý časopis historický* 16 (1968): 809.

36. *Processus iudiciarius*, 5 and 8 (articles 1 and 11).

37. Hardt IV, col. 751. Cf. František Šmahel, "Eine hussitische *Collecta de probationibus propositionum*," in *Die Prager Universität im Mittelalter*, 581–598.

38. Hardt IV, col. 654 and 750 (article 25).

39. See Šmahel-Silagi, 143, lines 74–6. Cf. Hardt IV, col. 646 and *Processus iudiciarius*, 9–10 (articles 15, 16, and 17).

40. For the articles against Jerome, see Hardt IV, cols. 634–691. For Jerome's replies, see Hard IV, cols. 634–646 and 751–762.

41. Hardt IV, col. 751. The collocation "magnus Philosophus" is a reference to Aristotle, not Wyclif.

42. Ibid., col. 635–636

43. Ibid., col. 637.

44. Ibid., col. 761.

45. Ibid., col. 761, cf. cols. 767–768.

46. For clarity's sake, I should point out that many implicit borrowings from Wyclif in Jerome's *quaestiones* remain unrecognized in the modern edition. I will not stress this fact in what follows; the reader can compare my findings with the index in Šmahel-Silagi, 303–305. For a detailed doctrinal analysis of Jerome's *quaestiones*, see especially Zénon Kaluza, *Études doctrinales sur le XIVe siècle* (Paris: Librarie Philosophique J. Vrin, 2013), particularly the following sections: "Le chancelier Gerson et Jérôme de Prague," 207–252; "Jérôme de Prague et le *Timée* de Platon," 253–300; "La question de Jérôme de Prague disputée à Heidelberg," 301–332; as well as Ota Pavlíček, *La dimension philosophique et théologique de la pensée de Jérôme de Prague* (PhD diss., Paris and Prague, 2014). Cf. also

Vilém Herold, *Pražská univerzita a Wyclif,* 204–219; Herold, "Wyclifs Polemik gegen Ockhams Auffasung der platonischen Ideen und ihr Nachklang in der tschechischen hussitischen Philosophie," in *From Ockham to Wyclif,* ed. A. Hudson, M. Wilks (Oxford: Blackwell, 1987), 185–215; Herold, "Wyclif und Hieronymus von Prag. Zum Versuch einer ‚praktischen' Umwandlung in der spätmittealterlichen Ideenlehre," in *Knowledge and the Sciences in Medieval Philosophy,* ed. Reijo Työrinoja, Anja Inkeri Lehtinen, and Dagfinn Føllesdal (Helsinki: Yliopistopaino, 1990), 3:212–223; Herold, "Der Streit zwischen Hieronymus von Prag und Johann Gerson. Eine spätmittelalterliche Diskussion mit tragischen Folgen," in *Société et Église: Textes et discussions dans les universités de l'Europe centrale au moyen âge tardif,* ed. Sophie Włodek (Turnhout, Belgium: Brepols, 1995), 77–89; Christine Blättler, *Delikt: Extremer Realismus* (Sankt Augustin: Academia-Verlag, 2002); Šmahel, *Život a dílo Jeronýma Pražského,* 239–337. For the doctrinal content of Jerome's *Recommendatio* which I keep aside in the next part of my essay, see Šmahel-Silagi, xxxviii–xxxix.

47. See the first part of Jerome's *quaestio,* Šmahel-Silagi, 5–7, lines 5–72; cf. the first chapter of Wyclif's *De ideis.* On Wyclif's theory of ideas, cf. Herold, *Pražská univerzita,* 67–138; Herold, "Wyclifs Polemik," passim; and Alessandro D. Conti, "Wyclif´s Logic and Metaphysics," in *A Companion to John Wyclif,* 86–89 and 96. I thank Vilém Herold for putting his and Ivan J. Mueller's edition of *De ideis* at my disposal.

48. See Šmahel-Silagi, 6, lines 36–37, and 7–8, lines 73–106. For the formal distinction in the *Quaestio de veritatibus generalibus,* see Kaluza, *Études doctrinales,* 321–325; cf. Jerome's explication in Vienna, *Processus iudiciarius,* 8–9 and 12. For the formal distinction in Wyclif, see, for example, *Tractatus de universalibus,* 91–92, lines 138–158, and 368, lines 369–372. Cf. Alessandro D. Conti, "Wyclif's logic and metaphysics," 72–78, and Kaluza, *Études doctrinales,* 321–325.

49. Šmahel-Silagi, 7–8, lines 73–98. For Wyclif, see, for example, John Wyclif, *De dominio Divino* I, ed. Reginald L. Poole (London: Trübner, 1890), 58–59, lines 21–19, and Wyclif, *Tractatus de universalibus,* 22, lines 102–223, and 200, lines 418–439.

50. Šmahel-Silagi, 7, lines 67–69.

51. Šmahel-Silagi, 8–11, lines 107–203. For a doctrinal interpretation, see Kaluza, *Études doctrinales,* 314–315 and 327–330. On this subject in Wyclif, see, for example, Michael H. Dziewicki, ed., *Iohannis Wyclif Tractatus de Logica* I (London: Trübner, 1893), 15, lines 12–22, and Wyclif, *Tractatus de universalibus,* 22, lines 102–112. Cf. Laurent Cesalli, *Le réalisme propositionnel* (Paris: Librairie philosophique J. Vrin, 2007), 309–390 and Conti, "Wyclif's logic and metaphysics," 78–89.

52. On Wyclif's theory of double creation, see Kaluza, *Études doctrinales,* 333–369.

53. See my exposition of Jerome's other *quaestiones* later in this essay and the

echoes from the Parisian disputations summarized by Kaluza, *Études doctrinales*, 207–252. Cf. Kaluza, *Études doctrinales*, 270–277.

54. Šmahel-Silagi, 15, lines 9–11; cf. Wyclif, *Tractatus de universalibus*, 363, line 255.

55. See, for example, the *rationes*, Šmahel-Silagi, 25, lines 310–333, and 26, lines 346–356, which are influenced by Wyclif, *De ideis*, chap. 1, in Stockholm, Kungliga Biblioteket, Codex Holmiensis, MS A.164, fols. 36v (the first *ratio*) and 35v (the second). I am using the medieval foliation of this manuscript throughout the essay. In *De ideis*, Jerome also read arguments from Pseudo-Dionysius the Areopagite. Since he used similar but not the same arguments for his own texts (27–30) and we know that his real source was the Parisian *Corpus Dionysiacum*, it seems likely that based on Wyclif's treatises, he searched in some cases for the full versions of texts that Wyclif referred to. He was excerpting from these texts a series of new arguments that he noted in his extensive notebook known as the *magnum volumen*. His efforts to find arguments and authorities in support of real universals were extraordinary. On Jerome's use of the *Corpus Dionysiacum*, see Kaluza, *Études doctrinales*, 241–252. For the *magnum volumen*, see Šmahel-Silagi, 69, lines 578–581. Herold, *Pražská univerzita*, 215–218, previously noted the influence of Wyclif's *De ideis* on this *quaestio*.

56. Wyclif also used Augustine and Eustratios of Nicea to confirm the legitimacy of his teaching on the plurality of ideas. See *Tractatus de universalibus*, 60–61, lines 186–206; cf. 62–63, lines 226–248. Jerome quotes Augustine very often. For citations from Eustratios, see Šmahel-Silagi, 18, lines 92–104, and 20–21, lines 170–182. On Eustratios's doctrine of ideas, see, for example, Kimon Giocarnis, "Eustratios of Nicaea's Defense of the Doctrine of Ideas," *Franciscan Studies* 24 (1964): 159–204.

57. Šmahel-Silagi, 16–17, lines 25–67.

58. Šmahel-Silagi, 17–31, lines 68–507.

59. Šmahel-Silagi, 30–31, lines 472–507.

60. In his extant *quaestiones*, Jerome mentioned Wyclif's name only twice. See Šmahel-Silagi, 143, line 74, and 164, line 53.

61. Šmahel-Silagi, 33–34, lines 585–599 (cf. Wyclif, *De dominio Divino*, 58–59, lines 21–19).

62. Šmahel-Silagi, 34, lines 600–602 (cf. Wyclif, *Tractatus de universalibus*, 15–16, lines 8–16); 34, lines 602–623 (cf. *Tractatus de universalibus*, 74, lines 88–97; 70, lines 13–16; 70, lines 17–19; 74, lines 88–97); 34–35, lines 624–642 (cf. *Tractatus de universalibus*, 16–17, lines 24–37); 35, lines 643–656 (cf. *Tractatus de universalibus*, 19–20, lines 66–73; 19, lines 55–65); 35–36, lines 657–676 (cf. *Tractatus de universalibus*, 18–19, lines 50–60; cf. 238–272); 37, lines 695–727 (cf. Wyclif, *De logica*, 5, lines 14–18, cf. 40, lines 36–41, and 41, lines 1–17; cf. also *Tractatus de universalibus*, 179–180, lines 721–729). I am completing here the list published by Kaluza, *Études doctrinales*, 272n2.

63. See, for example, Šmahel-Silagi, 43–44, lines 927–932 (cf. *Tractatus de universalibus*, 355, lines 68–72).

64. See, for example, Šmahel-Silagi, 45–46, lines 996–1010 (cf. *Tractatus de universalibus*, 353–354, lines 23–35); 46–47, lines 1023–1036 (cf. *Tractatus de universalibus*, 327, lines 638–640); 47–48, lines 1038–1078 (cf. *Tractatus de universalibus*, 144–149); 48–49, lines 1090–1099 (cf. *Tractatus de universalibus*, 19, lines 60–65, cf. 241–244, lines 97–155).

65. Šmahel-Silagi, 49, lines 1118–1127 (cf. *Tractatus de universalibus*, 211, lines 67–76), 50, lines 1128–1136 (cf. *Tractatus de universalibus*, 211–212, lines 77–93), 50, lines 1137–1147 (cf. *Tractatus de universalibus*, 212–213, lines 107–118).

66. See, for example, *Tractatus de universalibus*, 175, lines 623–626, and 357, lines 102–120.

67. Šmahel-Silagi, 38, lines 738–753.

68. Šmahel-Silagi, 44–49, lines 935–1099, particularly lines 1038–1078; for the arguments concerning Scripture, see 46, lines 999–1010, and 46–47, lines 1023–1037.

69. Kaluza, *Études doctrinales*, 285.

70. The borrowings from Wyclif in the *Quaestio de convertibilitate terminorum* include the following: Šmahel-Silagi, 76, lines 103–128 (cf. *De dominio Divino*, 13–14, lines 17–13); 76, lines 129–132 (cf. *De dominio Divino*, 14, lines 22–25); 76–77, lines 133–137 (cf. *De dominio Divino*, 12, lines 20–23); 77, lines 155–161 (cf. *De dominio Divino*, 38, lines 2–20; and 38–39, lines 31–3); 77–78, lines 162–176 (cf. *De dominio Divino*, 39, lines 4–19); 78, lines 176–180 (cf. *De dominio Divino*, 39, lines 26–33); 78, lines 180–184 (cf. *De dominio Divino*, 40, lines 7–11); 185–193 (cf. *De dominio Divino*, 21, lines 9–17); 78, lines 196–200 (cf. *De logica*, 11, lines 4–5); 81, lines 287–293 (cf. *De dominio Divino*, 11–12, lines 30–33); 81, lines 300–303 (cf. *De dominio Divino*, 44–45, lines 33–34); 82, lines 304–310 (cf. *De dominio Divino*, 45, lines 13–15, 19–23).

71. Cf. especially Šmahel-Silagi, 77, lines 155–161 and *De dominio Divino*, 38–39, lines 2–4.

72. On Wyclif's theory on divine dominion, see Stephen Lahey, *Philosophy and Politics in the Thought of John Wyclif* (Cambridge: Cambridge University Press, 2003), passim; for metaphysical and theological prerequisites see 68–107.

73. Šmahel-Silagi, 76–77, lines 103–137.

74. Ibid., 81, lines 283–294.

75. Ibid., 77, lines 138–161, cf. n. 71 supra.

76. Ibid., 77–78, lines 162–193.

77. Ibid., 78–80, lines 193–246.

78. Ibid., 81–82, lines 297–309.

79. On this theory, see especially chapter 13 of Wyclif's *Tractatus de universalibus*, 301–329, cf. Alessandro D. Conti, "Annihilatio e divina omnipotenza nel Tractatus de universalibus di John Wyclif," in *John Wyclif: logica, politica, teologia*, ed. Mariateresa Brocchieri and Stefano Simonetta (Florence: SISMEL, 2003), 71–85; and Kaluza, *Études doctrinales*, 333–363.

80. Šmahel-Silagi, 89, lines 144–157 (cf. Wyclif, *De dominio Divino*, 58–59, lines 21–19).

81. Cf. Kaluza, *Études doctrinales*, 289–293.

82. See Šmahel-Silagi, 92–95, lines 230–331 and Calcidius, "*In Platonis Timaeum*," in *Commentaire au Timée de Platon*, vol. 1, ed. Béatrice Bakhouche (Paris: J. Vrin, 2011), para. CCCIV, 532, lines 17–20.

83. See Kaluza, *Études doctrinales*, 255–256, 261–263, and 265. Cf. Pavlíček, *La dimension philosophique et théologique*, 311–315, 335–381, where I show that Jerome knew and used at least *Timaeus* 28a–29c, 30c–31c, 32c–33c, 39c, 41a–41b, and 49a. As for the commentary, I show in the same place that Jerome used mainly the parts devoted to creation out of necessity and to prime matter. In Jerome's *Quaestio de potentia materiae primae*, we find influences from the following paragraphs of Calcidius's exposition: 20, 21, 22, 123, 222, 269, 272, 273, 274, 276, 289, 303–304, 308, 319, 321, 326, 337, 354.

84. Kaluza, *Études doctrinales*, 286.

85. Šmahel-Silagi, 90–91, lines 158–221. On this, see Ota Pavlíček, "Otázka a kontext problematiky sufficientia praedicamentorum u Jeronýma Pražského a Robert Alyngton jako oxfordský zdroj jeho odpovědi," *AITHÉR: Časopis pro studium řecké a latinské filosofické tradice* 5/III (2011): 175–221.

86. Šmahel-Silagi, 103–137.

87. See mainly Šmahel-Silagi, 112, lines 46–63; 119, lines 69–77; 124, lines 196–218; 135–137, lines 1–47. On this theory in Wyclif, cf. Kaluza, *Études doctrinales*, 270–279, 293–295 and Conti, "Wyclif's logic and metaphysics," 103–107, both of whom mention important passages in Wyclif.

88. Šmahel-Silagi, 111, lines 15–35 and 116, lines 190–194.

89. See mainly Šmahel-Silagi, 119–123.

90. Šmahel-Silagi, 119, lines 69–81. Herold, *Pražská univerzita*, 89–90, previously called attention to this statement in Wyclif's treatise.

91. Cf. Šmahel-Silagi, 118, lines 40–53 (cf. *Tractatus de universalibus*, 304, lines 86–96).

92. Šmahel-Silagi, 117, lines 2–24.

93. See the edition in Šmahel-Silagi, 195–197. For the diagram, see also Figure 4-1.

94. See Šmahel-Silagi, 238–239, lines 91–111. For Jerome's *Shield of Faith* and the interconnection between realism and theology in Wyclif, see Ota Pavlíček, "*Scutum fidei christianae*: The Depiction and Explanation of the Shield of Faith in the Realistic Teaching of Jerome of Prague in the Context of His Interpretation of the Trinity," *The Bohemian Reformation and Religious Practice* 9 (2014): 72–97, which lists further literature in note 80. Jerome's testimony is also confirmed by the wording of an accusation presented by the German masters to the papal curia in 1407–1408. See František M. Bartoš, "V předvečer Kutnohorského dekretu," *Časopis národního musea* 102 (1928): 107–108. On the tradition of the *Shield of Faith*, cf. František Šmahel, "Das 'Scutum fidei christianae magistri Hieronymi Pragensis' in der Entwicklung der mittelalterlichen trinitarischen Diagramme," in *Die Bildwelt der Diagramme Joachims von Fiore. Zur Medialität*

religiös-politischer Programme im Mittelalter, ed. Alexander Patschovsky (Ostfildern, Germany: Thorbecke, 2003), 185–210.

95. I thank Dr. Mark Thakkar for informing me about this exemplar of Jerome's *Shield of Faith.*

96. The *Quaestio de potentia materiae primae* was published in Šmahel-Silagi, 141–159.

97. The *quaestio* contains at least the following influences and borrowings from Wyclif's treatises: Šmahel-Silagi, 141–142, lines 18–32 (cf. *Trialogus,* 87); 143, lines 74–81 (cf. *Trialogus,* 87); 143–144, lines 82–88 (cf. *Trialogus,* 86); 144, lines 88–101 (cf. John Wyclif, *De materia et forma,* ed. Michael Henry Dziewicki, in *Iohannis Wyclif Miscellanea Philosophica I,* London: Trübner, 1902, 163, lines 3–15); 144–145, lines 103–133 (cf. *De materia et forma,* 163–164, lines 13–23); 145, lines 134–148 (cf. *De materia et forma,* 185–186, lines 21–3); 146, lines 149–159 (cf. *De materia et forma,* 191, lines 26–35); 146, lines 165–177 (cf. *De materia et forma,* 192, lines 5–11, lines 25–31); 145–146, lines 177–187 (cf. *De materia et forma,* 212–215, lines 25–9); 147, lines 188–193 (cf. *De materia et forma,* 192–193, lines 31–1); 148, lines 212–216 (cf. *De materia et forma,* 193, lines 27–31); 149–150, lines 265–279 (cf. *Trialogus,* 87–88); 153–154, lines 395–416 (cf. *De materia et forma,* 199, lines 3–31); 157, lines 517–523 (cf. *Trialogus,* 89); and perhaps also 146, lines 170–172 (Cf. *De materia et forma,* 189–190, lines 23–2). For the influence of Wyclif's *De universalibus* on this *quaestio,* see n. 98 infra.

98. Šmahel-Silagi, 153, lines 370–376 (cf. *Tractatus de universalibus,* 301–304, lines 87–96).

99. The editors made significant discoveries as to the sources of this text. For emendations, some newly discovered sources, and interpretation, see Pavlíček, *La dimension philosophique et théologique,* 335–381. In this *quaestio,* I trace an influence of *Timaeus* 49a. As for the passages from Calcidius's commentary and from Wyclif, see nn. 83 and 97 supra.

100. See Šmahel-Silagi, 149, lines 257–270 (cf. *Trialogus,* 87).

101. See mainly the second part of the *Quaestio de potentia materiae primae,* Šmahel-Silagi, 153–159; cf. 114, line 105. For medieval Atomism, see Bernhard Pabst, *Atomtheorien des lateinischen Mittelalters* (Darmstadt: Wissenschaftliche Buchgesellschaft, 1994) and *Atomism in Late Medieval Philosophy and Theology,* ed. Christophe Grellard, Aurélien Robert (Leiden, Netherlands: Brill, 2009). For Wyclif's atomism, see Emily Michael, "John Wyclif's Atomism," in *Atomism in Late Medieval Philosophy and Theology,* 183–220.

102. The borrowings from Wyclif include at least the following: Šmahel-Silagi, 177–178, lines 448–503 (cf. *De ideis,* fol. 51v); 181–182, lines 584–635 (fols. 42v–43r); 183, lines 672–674 (fol. 35r); 183–185, lines 675–708 (fols. 45r–46r); 186, lines 762–766 (fol. 36r); 186–187, lines 767–775 (fol. 37v); 187, lines 776–789 (fol. 37r); 187, lines 790–804 (fol. 36r); 188, lines 807–828 (fol. 39v). Vilém Herold noted some of these influences or borrowings. On this and Herold's other conclusions, see Herold, *Pražská univerzita,* 97–98, 204–218.

CHAPTER FIVE

DETERMINISM BETWEEN OXFORD AND PRAGUE: THE LATE WYCLIF'S RETRACTIONS AND THEIR DEFENSE ASCRIBED TO PETER PAYNE

Luigi Campi

I n his *Essais de Théodicée* (1710), Gottfried Leibniz aimed to amend a number of doctrinal errors that had emerged in previous and contemporary theological debates, which he considered to be obstacles to the pursuit of his ecumenical ideal. One of these was extreme determinism, the belief that everything will come to pass by absolute necessity—a view that leaves no room for divine or human liberty. Mentioned four times in the *Essais* in this regard, John Wyclif is charged with having followed Abelard in maintaining the thesis "contrary to the doctrine of the saints and to reason" that "God cannot but do what he does": according to Leibniz, this is the root of the belief in a "mathematical necessity" imputed to Wyclif at the Council of Constance.[1]

When Leibniz was writing, Wyclif's determinism had long since become a commonplace. During his lifetime, however, Wyclif was never formally accused of philosophical and theological determinism. The first charge is found in the posthumous condemnation, promulgated by Archbishop Thomas Arundel in 1397, of eighteen propositions extracted from Wyclif's *Trialogus* by William Woodford, of which item 17 reads "Everything that will come to pass, will come to pass by absolute necessity [Omnia quae evenient, absolute necessario evenient]." In 1403 some German members of the Prague Theological Faculty added twenty-one conclusions to a list of twenty-four already condemned during the council at the London Blackfriars in 1382; item 27 of this new list reads "Everything comes to pass by necessity [Omnia de necessitate veniunt]." Charles University renewed the condemnation in 1412, and the theological note *haereticus* was added to item 27, now reading "Everything comes to pass by absolute necessity [Omnia de necessitate absoluta eveniunt]." As is well known, the forty-five articles collected in Prague were definitively condemned at Constance in 1415.[2]

As already mentioned, article 27 is taken from the *Trialogus*—a late writing of Wyclif's which is by no means illustrative, however, of the attitude toward necessity and contingency that he took while lecturing in the Oxford schools. I have recently devoted a paper to the attempt that Wyclif made in his earlier writings to keep his philosophy and theology safe from deterministic outcomes; its main arguments are summarized for the sake of discussion in the first part of this essay.[3] I then take into account the doctrinal points which Wyclif retracted from around 1375 to the compilation of the *Trialogus* and the *Opus evangelicum*, where his opinions on the necessity of created beings and events appear significantly altered. Finally, I deal with a startling defense of article 27 found in a text written in Prague after the Constance condemnations, and ascribed to Peter Payne—a profession of determinism so radical that it would hardly have been upheld by Wyclif even in his later years.

THE EARLY WYCLIF

"Even if it is true that Wyclif, early or late in his career, was a determinist, it is certainly not true that his determinism was derived from his realism," concludes Anthony Kenny in a 1987 article. Kenny was the first to take issue with the standard view on Wyclif's determinism, basing his argument almost exclusively on chapter 14 of the *De universalibus*, published by Ivan Müller two years before.[4] By enlarging the scope of the enquiry to all Wyclif's edited—and some unedited—works dating from 1368 to 1374, one may improve Kenny's argument on the grounds of textual witnesses that so far have been mostly overlooked.

A cornerstone of Wyclif's ontology is that the divine ideas—conceived as specific essences of individuals considered in their intelligible being—are the metaphysical constituents of God's essence, and are therefore absolutely necessary. That said, problems with determinism would arise if Wyclif did not draw any distinction between ideas as principles of divine cognition of creatures (*rationes*), and as models for their production (*exemplaria*). For, since God absolutely necessarily thinks of himself, he absolutely necessarily thinks of ideas; hence, were every idea a pattern for creation, God would absolutely necessarily create whatever he thinks of. To state this differently, given God, everything would come to pass by absolute necessity.[5]

Actually, Wyclif's early writings give evidence of his restless effort to avoid such a conclusion. In the *De intellectione dei*, Wyclif maintains that there are many things that have intelligible being, but which neither have nor can have temporal existence. Accordingly, in the *De dominio divino*, Wyclif states that there are more ideas in God's mind than created essences in the world.[6] In so saying, Wyclif is not referring to ideas of past or future beings which no longer exist or do not yet exist; as is made clear in works like the *De ente praedicamentali* or the *Determinatio* against Kenningham, he is rather referring to those logical possibilities which are never the case, and exist only in God's mind.[7] Ideas of such never-existing possibles, obviously, are not patterns for creation.

Again, in the *De intellectione dei* and in the *De potentia productiva dei ad extra*, Wyclif argues that God's absolute power covers more than God's ordained power does, and that the latter is contingent. For God has chosen to enact a certain set of things from among all the possible things he is able to create, but he could have chosen otherwise.[8] In this regard, Wyclif sometimes enriches his metaphysical taxonomy—customarily including the intelligible being that creatures have in God's mind, the essential being that creatures have in their created causes, and creatures' individual existence[9]— with a further ontological level, long neglected by scholarship: the intentional being. In some tracts, like the *De ente praedicamentali* and the *De scientia dei*, the intentional being is described as eternal and in God's mind, like the intelligible being, but contingent, as is the level on which God produces only what he chooses to bring into existence at the appropriate time.[10] That being so, one is entitled to consider the production of something in its *esse intentionale* as a result of the *ordinatio* of divine power. For among the many things that God thinks of, only those toward which he directs his *intentio* and *voluntas* fall within the subset of his ordained power, and come therefore into actual existence at the appropriate time. Hence, God neither is necessitated by his ideas to create this world, nor does he create everything he can think of; conversely, he creates *de potentia ordinata* in its temporal existence what he has chosen to create, namely what he has eternally produced in its contingent intentional being.

In this connection, the *De universalibus* and other contemporary tracts describe the contingency of God's choice as grounded in the liberty of contradiction, understood as the power of doing something or not, and not as the capability to do something and then to cease doing it. Once the choice is made—once the power is ordained, once something is produced in its intentional being—God can no longer change it.[11] All events therefore necessarily come to pass, as they follow from God's choice; still, this happens by suppositional necessity ("necessitate ex supposicione"), not by absolute necessity, as God could have chosen otherwise.[12]

Finally, Wyclif conceives of divine acts toward creatures as relations of reason. Interestingly, he dismisses the long-established notion of relation as a form inhering in only one extreme and simply referring to the other one as to its object. Instead he favors an unusual notion of relation as a form that inheres in two extremes at once. Relations of reason are also conceived by Wyclif as dyadic: such relations arise when one of the extremes is not a substance with a foundation (i.e., an absolute accident—for Wyclif, quality or quantity), when none of the extremes is a substance, or when the extremes are substances, but none has a foundation. Since God, according to Wyclif, is neither a substance, nor is he affected by accidents serving as foundations, creatures are involved only in relations of reason with him. Now, given their dyadic nature, all relations are caused by both the extremes—relations of reason included.[13] Hence, if God knows—or wills—that Peter exists, God's act is a relation of reason depending on both the extremes, and the same must be said of the converse relation at stake in Peter's existence being known by God. As noticed by Anthony Kenny, in sum, it is therefore both true for Wyclif to say that Peter exists because God knows him to exist, and that God knows Peter to exist because he exists: a temporal truth can cause an eternal truth.[14] Of course, this has significant theological implications: God thinks of all possible actions Peter might perform at time t, and these are absolutely necessary on the level of intelligible being; yet, it is insofar as Peter freely chooses to sin at time t that God eternally knows and wills this state of affairs in its intentional being. So Peter's sin at t is necessary by suppositional necessity; however, had Peter chosen otherwise, God would have eternally known and willed correspondingly.[15]

RETRACTIONS

From about 1375 onward, while developing his theological thought, Wyclif came to retract many of his earlier views.[16] A first move is made in the *De statu innocencie*, where Wyclif recants his past reliance on suppositional necessity, now regarded as a *superficialis sophisticatio*, a quibble which befits untrained students and/or nominalists. Wyclif shows an ambivalent attitude toward "academic-rationalist tools available to medieval scholasticism," to quote Kantik Ghosh, and this might be the case here with suppositional necessity: its rejection seems connected to his colleagues' abuses of it in oversimplifying treatments of difficult topics, like that of future contingents.[17]

Whatever his opinions on suppositional necessity at this stage, in the *De statu innocencie* Wyclif continues to maintain his former soteriological views,[18] requiring—as he remarks, a propos of ambivalence—that skills in grammar and logic must be fully grasped. Thus, he still claims that God does not will someone to sin, but permits sin to occur as it contributes to "beautify" the world: by punishing it, in fact, God has the occasion to restore the order broken by the sinner, and reestablish the legality of the world that Wyclif—following Augustine—considers at once as ontological, axiological, and aesthetical.[19] Again, Wyclif still relies on the mutual causality of God and creatures to claim that, though ordained from all eternity, God's punishments are partially caused by sinful actions freely performed in time by human agents.[20]

In the following years, Wyclif's retractions keep pace with the evolution of his views on the church as a congregation of all predestinate persons, and the more that time passes—one might suggest, the more inflamed ecclesiological controversies become—the more Wyclif's doctrine of salvation takes overtones of determinism. Granted, Wyclif never retracts his opinion that the elect are those whom God eternally wills to save as he knows that, before dying, they will be contrite for past sins and will accept his offer of grace. Nonetheless, Wyclif's soteriological discourse becomes not entirely consistent and somewhat confusing. Thus, while in the *De veritate sacre Scripture* he retraces his steps on suppositional necessity, and states that human actions are both eternally known by God and freely performed by human beings,[21] in the *De ecclesia* he argues that everything will come to pass by necessity—whether absolute or suppositional he leaves unsaid.[22]

Incidentally, in this latter work Wyclif maintains that baptism is ineffective in removing the original sin of those who are foreknown to damnation, as their nature is so defective that even sacramental grace cannot restore it. In this regard, Ian Levy has rightly stressed that the *De ecclesia* is more concerned with the outcomes of the process of salvation (ecclesiology) than with the process itself (soteriology). Nevertheless, that baptismal grace merely assists the foreknown in living in a state of temporal righteousness remains puzzling: their original sin is ineradicable because God eternally knows that they will not repent; but then again, how could they repent if their original sin is ineradicable?[23]

In his final work, the *Opus evangelicum*, Wyclif insists that rewards and punishments depend upon God's foreknowledge of human behavior. This does not entail that God wills someone to sin. For God eternally ordains and produces in its intentional being the *malum pene* for sinful actions, but he has no idea—no intelligible being—of the *malum culpe*, nor can he ordain it, as it is a defect of being under the sole responsibility of human choices. This seems consonant with Wyclif's earlier stances, though in the *Opus evangelicum* he never mentions human or divine liberty of contradiction, nor suppositional necessity. Parenthetically, in this work Wyclif reports that he is under suspicion of heresy by the ecclesiastical authorities, whom he considers to lack the intellectual means to understand both how the necessity of all events does not make human prayers and deliberations vain, and how such necessity is compatible with the human capability to merit anything before God.[24]

In his *Trialogus*, written shortly before his death, the lines of retraction are fully displayed. First Wyclif lowers the liberty of contradiction to the rank of a misleading scholastic technicality ("terminus magistralis erronee introductus"). In his academic tracts, Wyclif used to draw on liberty of contradiction to emphasize that God's choice of the world's order is no less free insofar as it is unchangeable, and that such an order is no less contingent insofar as follows by suppositional necessity from God's choice. In his *Trialogus*, instead, he states that God's liberty is consistent with absolute necessity, and that no alternatives are required for God to be free.[25]

Another retraction concerns never-existing possibles, with which Wyclif no longer intends to waste time ("nolo multum vagari circa intelligentiam sive potentiam producendi res, quae non sunt"). His former views were grounded on the distinction between absolute and ordained powers, with which Wyclif prefers no longer to deal to avoid jumping to unsubstantiated conclusions, as in the past ("saepe lapsus sum in altitudinem maris multa balbutiens quae non valui clare fundare"). So, dismissing any reference to the intentional being of creatures, Wyclif merely states that God can produce whatever he can think of, and that everything as such is in the utmost level of being, the intelligible being.[26]

In emphasizing human ignorance of God's choices, then, Wyclif declares himself to be no longer prone to flights of fancy as to what could have been otherwise ("ne evagemur superflue in incerto"), and resolves to restrict the term *possible* to connote only what sooner or later comes into being. Thus, in contrast with his past views ("quondam defendi constanter hujus contrarium"), Wyclif resolves to apply what has been called the *principle of plenitude* to everything God can enact, so that everything will come to pass by absolute necessity ("omnia quae eveniunt, necessario absolute eveniunt"), and God cannot produce or think anything but what he thinks or produces.[27]

At the end of a process of retraction mostly oriented to avoiding arguments—or their abuse—that he reckoned to be misleading sophistries, and with the paradoxical result of reaching hardly defendable conclusions from supposedly more cautious premises, Wyclif came to maintain, as noticed by Leibniz, something close to Abelard's opinion that God cannot do but what he does—a tenet whose condemnation at Sens in 1140 was a watershed in Western theological debate on determinism.

A DEFENSE OF ARTICLE 27 ASCRIBED TO PETER PAYNE

In early fifteenth-century Prague, a short tract in defense of Wyclif's views on the necessity of futures is addressed against a certain *ingeniosus magister* who has taken issue with article 27. The tract has been edited recently and is generally ascribed to Peter Payne,[28] "the most outspoken Wycliffite at Oxford" at that time, who possibly left England to escape prosecution for his association with Sir John Oldcastle and reached Prague only after Hus's departure for Constance on 11 October 1414.[29] In Prague he became a leading figure among the Hussites as an advocate of Wyclif's theological teachings, a proficient mediator in doctrinal controversies within the Hussite movement, and a representative of Bohemian ecclesiological and political expectations on several diplomatic missions. In a contemporary tract in defense of Wyclif's views on the veneration of images, Payne labels himself "a certain, rural, simple disciple of the aforesaid Doctor" ("quidam ruralis simplex discipulus dicti Doctoris"), namely Wyclif; as Bartoš noticed, the author of the defense of article 27 describes himself in the same exact words, and shows himself to be an enthusiastic follower of Wyclif's.[30]

According to William Cook, who has agreed with Bartoš in attributing the tract to Payne, it may date from late 1419 to early 1420. At this time, Wyclif's theological views were the object of harsh criticism by many masters of the University of Prague. One of them was Nicholas Stoyčzín, who saw in the forty-five articles the root of Hussite doctrinal controversies. In April 1420 Payne challenged him to a public debate on Wyclif's realism, confessing to be surprised by Stoyčzín's rejection of the forty-five articles, since Jan Hus—to whom Stoyčzín was closely related—had defended them.[31]

Payne's assertion is intriguing, since during his trial at Constance Hus denied to have ever defended thirty-two of the forty-five articles, item 27 included ("Art. 27. Omnia de necessitate absoluta eveniunt—*Non tenui nec teneo*").[32] Hus's dissent from determinism was sincere: in his commentary on the *Sentences*, begun in late 1407, Hus distinguishes between absolute and suppositional necessity and claims the contingency of future events; he also copies a long passage from Wyclif's *De scientia dei*, where Wyclif makes a distinction between God's absolutely necessary knowledge of the intelligible being and his contingent knowledge of creatures' actual existence.[33] As a matter of fact, then, none of the thirty articles imputed to Hus at Constance explicitly concerns determinism.[34] Hence, Hus's ecclesiology and soteriology, so influenced by Wyclif's, were not based on arguments from absolute necessity, and even Jerome of Prague—who was nonetheless charged at Constance with maintaining, oddly enough, that everything will come to pass by conditional necessity ("Omnia futura de necessitate conditionata evenient")—seems to have been cautious in avoiding deterministic outcomes while developing his metaphysical views in the wake of Wyclif.[35] In sum, the extent to which Wyclif's late determinism was actually being defended in fifteenth-century Bohemia is a matter that deserves further enquiry. One may wonder if the twenty-eight conclusions— including Wyclif's article 27 as item 20—read at the Council of Basel in 1433, and said to be taught in Bohemia, actually reflected current debates.[36]

What is certain is that Payne's defense of article 27 is an astonishing profession of determinism, going far beyond what Wyclif ever argued. Payne is aware that Wyclif reached his condemned conclusion not during the

course of his academic career, but in his holy old age ("in sua sancta senectute").[37] As pointed out by Christina von Nolcken and recently by Michael
Van Dussen, the perception of Wyclif's sanctity was common among
his followers, who correctly denied that he was ever condemned for heresy during his lifetime, and—against all evidence—even after his death.
This latter allegation, for instance, is found in a well-known letter, affixed
with the seal of the chancellor of the University of Oxford and attested at
Prague from the beginning of 1409 at the latest.[38] In spite of Thomas
Gascoigne's later suggestion that Payne was implicated in the affair involving the testimonial letter, his part in this story has never been conclu-
sively documented.[39]

Nonetheless, when referring in his defense of article 27 to Wyclif's holiness in old age, and when claiming—groundlessly—that Hus defended the
forty-five articles at Constance, Payne appears as committed in promoting
a narrative of Wyclif's total orthodoxy, which also reflects the conviction
that in his late days Wyclif came closer to the truth than he ever had before.[40] Accordingly, Payne does not rely on arguments found in Wyclif's
earlier writings, which were circulating in Bohemia at that time; rather, he
endorses his later retractions, making use of them with a radical intent and
without some of the nuances that Wyclif never completely abandoned.[41]

Thus Payne never makes an appeal to suppositional necessity, but openly
states that God produces this world and everything happening in it by absolute necessity, and that this world and every creature or state of affairs
consequently come to pass by absolute necessity. To stress this point, Payne
compares God to an impersonal cause like the sun, which inevitably produces its effects according to its nature; God produces this world by absolute necessity, and it is impossible for him either to create or have created
another world, since this one is his sole and best effect.[42] As a matter of fact,
Payne does not distinguish between God's absolute and ordained powers,
but considers them to be coterminous, maintaining that God cannot but
produce what he produces, and that God cannot produce what he does not
produce. In this way, Payne applies the principle of plenitude to everything
that falls under God's power, so that every genuine potentiality of being
cannot but be fulfilled, sooner or later.[43] Likewise, he draws no distinction
between divine ideas as principles of cognition and as patterns for creation,
for he argues that everything God provides with intelligible being comes
to pass in temporal existence by absolute necessity, and—significantly—he

maintains that the number of divine ideas is no greater than the number of creatures. In short, as Payne puts it, God is necessitated by his eternal ideas to create this world.[44]

Moreover, Payne rejects liberty of contradiction: God's liberty does not consist in his ability to eternally choose between alternatives, but to act in accordance with his thought without any other nature being able to prevent him, compel him, or interfere with him somehow. Necessitated to create by his ideas, God cannot will to produce any world other than the current one, as his will is unfailingly determined by his thought, and both are equally absolutely necessary from all eternity. No alternatives are open to the human will either, since its choices are absolutely necessary, given the necessary order of the world, and nonetheless considered as freely made. Payne's rejection of liberty of contradiction goes along with a refusal of any form of mutual causality between human choices and God's thought or will. According to Payne, to admit such a mutuality would be to admit the possibility for human beings to act otherwise than God has ordered— which is absurd, as it would imply a variation in divine thought or will in time. On this ground, Payne draws the conclusion that the stability of the world's order has to be anchored to absolute necessity, excluding any alternative of choice for God and human beings.[45]

Among his eighteen arguments for the absolute necessity of future events and his six long objections to his opponent's opinions, Payne includes many traditional soteriological themes that are also found in Wyclif. So, for example, he relieves God of being the author of sin, as sin is a lack of being, whereas God can only be the cause of being; or he states that God permits men to sin as he eternally knows them to sin, though not approving it, and that God eternally wills to punish men for those sins he eternally foresees.[46] Nevertheless, in spite of his claims to the contrary, Payne's systematic upholding of Wyclif's retractions and his radical interpretations of them make his soteriological arguments hardly tenable, if not wholly ineffective, leaving the impression of some unresolved internal tension within the text. This is particularly apparent if one considers Payne's attempt to embrace the well-known doctrine—also shared by Wyclif—that God is to be regarded as the primary cause of every created effect, human actions included, and that in performing the latter, human agents exert a form of secondary or instrumental causality. In the framework of his withholding of suppositional necessity and of mutual causality between God and created agents, however, Payne's appeal to instrumental causality in fact results in a distressing view according to which there is no real cause for human meritorious works other than God—human will serving as a mere *causa sine qua non*, which simply provides an occasion for divine intervention and has no significant moral role in the performing of such actions. Instead, human beings are reckoned to retain the whole responsibility for those sinful actions they commit, and cannot but commit as they happen by absolute necessity.[47] In sum, in the light of Payne's defense of article 27, his use of traditional soteriological themes does not seem to lead to other than pro forma statements: for how could a human being be worthy of reward for a meritorious action if such action occurs by absolute necessity? If God cannot but enact it? If there is no real human contribution to the performance of such an action other than a mere *sine qua non* causality? And how could a human being be worthy of punishment for its sinful action, if God eternally knows no alternatives for its choice to show contempt of God's law?

Whatever our assessment of Wyclif's retractions and however these reshaped the scope of his former soteriology, undoubtedly Payne's *Defensio* substantially alters the Oxford master's opinions. He replaces skepticism toward some scholastic tools with a complete refusal to employ them, and he reduces the subtleties of Wyclif's argument to a crude determinism. In doing so, ironically, Payne does not deviate so much from the distorted accounts of Wyclif's views given by tireless opponents like Thomas Netter.[48]

NOTES

1. See Gottfried W. Leibniz, *Essais de Théodicée*, in Leibniz, *Die Philosophischen Schriften*, ed. Karl I. Gerhardt (Berlin: Olms, 1875–1890), 6.1:67, 139; 6.2:171–172, 215–216.

2. Cf. David Wilkins, ed., *Concilia Magnae Britanniae et Hiberniae* (London: Gosling et al., 1737), 3:229–330; 345; Edward Brown, ed., *Fasciculus rerum expetendarum ac fugiendarum* (London: Chiswell, 1690), 1:190; William Woodford, *De causis condemnationis articulorum XVIII damnatorum Johannis Wyclif*, in Edward Brown, ed., *Fasciculus rerum expetendarum ac fugiendarum* (London: Chiswell, 1690), 1:250–257; František Palacký, ed. *Documenta Magistri Johannis Hus* (Prague: Tempsky, 1948), 329, 453; Giovanni D. Mansi, ed., *Sacrorum Conciliorum Nova et Amplissima Collectio* (Venice: Zatta, 1784), 27:632–634; Heinrich Finke and Johannes Hollnsteiner, eds., *Acta Concilii Constanciensis* (Münster: Verlag der Regensbergschen Buchhandlung, 1896–1928), 2:48;

Charles-Joseph Hefele, *Histoire Des Conciles D'après Les Documents Originaux*, trans. Henri Leclercq (Paris: Letouzey et Ané, 1907–1938), 7.1:313.

3. See Luigi Campi, "Was the Early Wyclif a Determinist? Concerning an Unnoticed Level in His Taxonomy of Being," *Vivarium* 52, no. 1 (2014): 102–146.

4. See Anthony Kenny, "Realism and Determinism in the Early Wyclif," in *From Ockham to Wyclif*, ed. Anne Hudson and Michael Wilks (Oxford: Blackwell, 1987), 165–178: 165. Cf. John Wyclif, *De universalibus*, ed. Ivan J. Müller (Oxford: Clarendon Press, 1985).

5. Cf. Alessandro D. Conti, "Wyclif's Logic and Metaphysics," in *A Companion to John Wyclif: Late Medieval Theologian*, ed. Ian C. Levy (Leiden, Netherlands: Brill, 2006), 67–125, esp. 86–89.

6. See John Wyclif, *De intelleccione dei*, in Wyclif, *De ente librorum duorum*, ed. Michael H. Dziewicki (London: Trübner and Co., 1909), 101: "Cum igitur multa sunt que non possunt <existere> . . . videtur quod multa habent esse que non habent esse existere"; John Wyclif, *De dominio divino*, ed. Reginald L. Poole (London: Trübner and Co., 1890), 59: "Tot vel plura sunt raciones in Deo adintra quot essencie sunt adextra."

7. Cf. John Wyclif, *De ente praedicamentali*, ed. Rudolf Beer (London: Trübner and Co., 1891), 2: "oportet supponere quod ens dicatur de omni signabili per complexum, et sic quoddam sit ens actuale vel existencie, quoddam ens potenciale, quod habet esse in causis secundis . . . et quoddam ens est, quod solum habet esse intelligibile in Deo, ut omne quod solum Deus potest producere et non actualiter existit." Wyclif, *Determinatio contra Kylingham Carmelitam*, in *Fasciculi Zizaniorum Magistri Johannis Wyclif cum Tritico*, ed. Walter W. Shirley, *Rolls Series* 5 (London: Longman, 1858), 463–464: "dico cum S. Thoma quod omnia praesentia, praeterita et futura Deus intuitive cognoscit. . . . Multa autem sunt quae non existunt, ut possibilia; omnia tamen praeterita et futura existunt in tempore suo. Ideo secundum regulam S. Thomae omnia talia, et non omnia possibilia, intuetur."

8. See Wyclif, *De intelleccione dei*, 101: "multa potest deus de sua potencia absoluta que non sunt in potencia eius ordinata, nec in potencia cause secunde, ut omnia possibilia existere que non existunt." Wyclif, *De potencia productiva dei ad extra*, Praha, Národní knihovna, MS IX.E.6, fol. 51r, lines 35–39: "Potencia absoluta est que terminatur ad possibilia in esse intelligibili vel absolute possibili; potencia autem ordinata est que terminatur ad possibilia secundum suum existere pro alico tempore. Et illa potencia ordinata vocatur contingens, set non accidentalis deo, cum non potest talem ordinanciam adquirere vel deperdere, set multas quas habet potest non habere et multas quas non habet potest habere."

9. Cf. Wyclif, *De universalibus*, 126–127. Cf. Conti, "Wyclif's Logic and Metaphysics," 89–95.

10. See Wyclif, *De ente praedicamentali*, 146: "Res creata secundum quadruplex suum esse habet quattuor gradus notabiles producendi. Primo enim producitur omne producibile a Deo ad intra secundum esse intelligibile, et

omnis talis produccio est absolute necessaria, consequens formaliter primum necesse esse. Secundo modo producitur res secundum esse intencionale, cum Deus intendit et wlt eternaliter rem illam non solum fore, sed existere actualiter suo tempore, et omnis talis produccio est contingens, sed eterna." Wyclif, *De scientia dei*, Praha, Národní knihovna, MS IX.E.6, fol. 23r, lines 27–33: "Ex istis dictis patent tria. Primum, quod multe res habent esse intelligibile que non habent esse existere.... Secundo, patet quod in eternitate non sunt fuisse et fore, set tantum esse, cum omne eternum sit proprie secundum totum presens. Et tercio, patet quamlibet creaturam habere esse eternum inmobile in eternitate non solum secundum esse intelligibile, ut talia que non existunt, set secundum esse intencionale dei ad producendum talia ad extra pro suo tempore."

11. Cf. Wyclif, *De universalibus*, 304: "Libertas contradictionis consistit in posse libere facere vel non facere, non autem in posse facere atque desistere."

12. Cf. ibid., 346–347: "Omnia futura necessario—necessitate ex suppositione—sunt futura, quae tamen contingentissime sunt futura." John Wyclif, *De volucione dei*, in Wyclif, *Summa de ente*, 176: "Deus libere necessitat seipsum per suam creaturam.... Et talis necessitas ex supposicione arguit graciam et libertatem in deo voluntarie se obligante. Nec est color ex tali necessitate concludere deum aut eius volucionem non esse liberam." Cf. John Wyclif, *De logica*, ed. Michael H. Dziewicki (London: Trübner and Co., 1893–1899), 3:181.

13. Cf. Wyclif, *De scientia dei*, fol. 17r, lines 6–9: "Omnis relacio requirens duo extrema dependet ab utroque eorum ut eius causa; sciencia dei quecunque ... est relacio racionis requirens tam deum quam scitum ad eius esse; igitur causatur ab utroque illorum." Wyclif, *De dominio divino*, 159: "Volicio divina et effectus temporalis se causant reciproce." On Wyclif's nonstandard theory, cf. Conti, "Wyclif's Logic and Metaphysics," 110–113.

14. See Kenny, "Realism and Determinism," 175. Cf. Campi, "Was the Early Wyclif," 108–111.

15. See Luigi Campi, "Mutual Causality in Wyclif's Political Thought. Some Logical Premises and Theological Results," in *Legitimation of Political Power in Medieval Thought. XIX Annual Colloquium of the International Society for the Study of Medieval Philosophy*, ed. Pedro Roche and Josep Puig Montada (Turnhout, Belgium: Brepols, forthcoming).

16. For further examples, see Michael Wilks, "The Early Oxford Wyclif: Papalist or Nominalist?," *Studies in Church History* 5 (1969): 69–98; repr. in Wilks, *Wyclif: Political Ideas and Practice*, ed. Anne Hudson (Oxford: Oxbow Books, 2000), 33–62.

17. See John Wyclif, *De statu innocencie*, in Wyclif, *Tractatus de mandatis divinis*, ed. Johann Loserth and Frederic D. Matthew (London: Trübner and Co., 1922), 518: "Propter difficultatem istius materie multi ... contrarie sunt locuti, ut hii propter istud specialiter negantes quod aliqua necessario sunt futura nisi ad istum sensum quem quondam tenui quod sunt futura necessitate ex supposicione,

hoc est, Deus vult quod erunt et necessario, si Deus vult quod erunt, ipsa erunt, et cum ista necessitate stat summa contingencia. Sed videtur mihi quod ista superficialis sophisticacio non ingreditur difficultatem materie." Cf. Kantik Ghosh, "Wycliffism and Lollardy," in *The Cambridge History of Christianity*, vol. 4, *Christianity in Western Europe 1000–1500*, ed. Miri Rubin and Walter Simons (Cambridge: Cambridge University Press, 2009), 439; Ghosh, "Logic and Lollardy," *Medium Aevum* 76, no. 2 (2007): 251–267.

18. Cf. Ian C. Levy, "Grace and Freedom in the Soteriology of John Wyclif," *Traditio* 60 (2005): 279–337.

19. Cf. Luigi Campi, "'But and alle thingus in mesure, and noumbre, and peis thou disposedist.' Some Notes on the Role of *Wisdom* 11, 21 in Wyclif's Writings," *Recherches de Théologie et Philosophie Médiévales* 80 (2013): 114, 134–135.

20. See Wyclif, *De statu innocencie*, 518: "Tercia autem via Lincolniensis, quam sepe tenui et adhuc teneo, presupponit arcium rudimenta, scilicet grammaticam et dialecticam, dicens quod peccatum . . . habet duplex esse, scilicet esse primum quod est deesse, et esse secundum quod est prodesse. . . . Et ita peccata sunt, ymmo sunt necessaria et felicia . . . et multum prosunt hominibus, pulcrificant mundum et iustissime sunt dampnanda." Ibid., 520: "Non sequitur Deum necessitare hominem ad peccandum; Deus tamen scit sed non ordinat quod quis peccet, et ita peccatum ordinat quod ipsum proficit aut punitur." Ibid., 514: "Hic videtur mihi quod omnis homo sive prescitus sive predestinatus debet sperare suam beatitudinem, cum Deus non possit dampnare hominem nisi suum demeritum sit in causa." Cf. Luigi Campi, "'Iusti sunt omnia': Note a margine del *De statu innocencie* di John Wyclif," *Dianoia* 12 (2007): 115–123.

21. See John Wyclif, *De veritate sacrae Scripturae*, ed. Rudolf Buddensieg (London: Trübner & Co., 1905–1907), 3:219: "perpetuo manet in omni creatura racionali possibilitas ad fruendum deo et contingencia ad utrumlibet ad merendum in deum intuendum. . . . Dampnati itaque habent ex lege dei unam morulam, in qua debent mereri, et non faciendo necesse est deum subtrahere se in racione obiecti excitantis ad meritum vel quietantis ad premium. Et quia in omnibus dampnatis tale tempus preteriit, ideo oportet eis inesse peccatum, a quo non possunt desistere, licet possint illud facillime non habere . . . Et sic necessario necessitate ex supposicione volunt perpetuo malum male."

22. See John Wyclif, *De ecclesia*, ed. Johann Loserth (London: Trübner and Co., 1886), 107: "Videtur quod omnia futura de necessitate evenient et quod nichil anichilari potest. Nam Deus qui non potest impediri ordinat cuncta esse perpetua. . . . Si enim pretericio rei non potest destrui, multo minus eius esse quod est previe requisitum. . . . Quando autem variavi ab ista sentencia, non cognovi ut modo quomodo res habet multiplex esse, sed omne esse posui existenciam individuam rei in suo genere."

23. Ibid., 467–468: "Nullus prescitus recipit rite baptismum quo deleatur simpliciter suum originale peccatum. . . . Nam omnis prescitus manet perpetuo

in defectu finalis perserverancie, quod est peccatum gravissimum et indelebile, et per consequens non tollitur simpliciter per baptismum. . . . Nam omnis prescitus habet perpetuum et originalem defectum, ille tamen ad tempus in malicia sua suspenditur per graciam secundum presentem iusticiam, ut graciam baptismalem et alias, et ideo dixi quod peccatum originale non deletur simpliciter." Cf. Levy, "Grace and Freedom," 331–332.

24. Cf. John Wyclif, *Opus evangelicum*, ed. Johann Loserth (London: Trübner and Co., 1895), 1:446: "malum pene habet ideam eternam in Deo sed non taliter malum culpe. . . . Pena peccati fuit ante mundi exordium ordinata. Causa enim peccati est a Deo volita, licet non sit a Deo volitum quod sic peccet." Ibid., 445: "Quidam concedunt quod malum pene habet esse ideale vel intencionale eternum in Deo; cum Deus eternaliter intendit quod peccatum ad mundi pulcritudinem et beatorum gaudium puniatur. Peccatum autem Deus non intelligit per ydeas, sed . . . per eternam carenciam idearum." Ibid., 267: "Nec sequitur si omnia que evenient de necessitate evenient, tunc non expedit sic orare, cum ex isto formaliter infert oppositum." Ibid., 101: "Sed quia pauci in hoc conveniunt quod omnia que evenient de necessitate evenient, immo superiores nostri dicerent quod hoc sit summe hereticum." Ibid., 2:196: "Ideo illi qui replicant contra hoc veritatem fidei 'omnia que evenient de necessitate evenient' in vanum laborant contrarii sibi ipsis."

25. John Wyclif, *Trialogus cum Supplemento Trialogi*, ed. Gotthard V. Lechler (Oxford: Clarendon Press, 1869), 71–72. "Quantum ad libertatem divinae potentiae, patet quod est summe libera, et tamen quidquid facit, necessario eveniet; sicut Deus pater summe libere producit filium, et tamen necessario absolute. Et quantum ad 'libertatem contradictionis', patet quod est terminus magistralis erronee introductus, ut illud quod Deus potest facere si voluerit, et non facere si noluerit, cum hoc sit contingens ad tempus, dicunt 'libere contradictorie' est productum."

26. Ibid., 69–70: "Vellem tamen addiscere in ista materia, quia nihil diffinio de Dei potentia, nec audeo profundare me in distinctione de absoluta Dei potentia et potentia ordinata. Scio tamen quod saepe lapsus sum in altitudine maris multa balbutiens quae non valui clare fundare. . . . Nec video nunc quare deus posset multa non existentia intelligere, quin per idem intelligat infinita, quae tu non potes intelligere, vel e contra utrobique deficere. . . . Ideo signata quacunque creatura, doceo quod ista potest esse sive intelligi, concedo quod Deus potest illam producere. Sed nolo multum vagari circa intelligentiam sive potentiam producendi res quae non sunt, concedens quod nihil est producibile nisi quod est, cum si hoc sit intelligibile, vel producibile, hoc est res quae potest intelligi vel produci. Et sic intellectus divinus ac ejus notita sunt paris ambitus, sic intellectus creatus et ejus notitia."

27. Cf. Arthur O. Lovejoy, *The Great Chain of Being: A Study of the History of an Idea* (New York: Harper and Row, 1960), 52: "no genuine potentiality of being can remain unfulfilled." Wyclif, *Trialogus*, 154–155: "Sed quo ad lapsum meum de

necessario, recolo me dixisse in libro primo, quod omnia quae eveniunt, necessario absolute eveniunt. Et sic Deus non potest quidquam producere vel intelligere nisi quod de facto intelligit et producit. Sed quia quondam defendi constanter hujus oppositum, nec claret mihi adhuc demonstratio quae hoc probat, ideo utor communiter hac cautela: proposito mihi tanquam possibili uno quod non est de facto, suppono hoc tanquam possibile, si Deus voluerit; sed quia non scio quod Deus determinavit oppositum, et scio quod multa sunt de facto, quorum dubia et sententias ignoramus, ideo ne evagemur superflue in incerto vellem quod tractaremus de veritate possibili quae est de facto, cum multas tales culpabiliter ignoramus."

28. See Peter Payne, *Defensio proposicionis venerabilis Doctoris Ewangelici de absoluta necessitate eventuum*, in Luigi Campi, "Una difesa del determinismo dell'ultimo Wyclif attribuita a Peter Payne," *Rivista di storia della filosofia 70*, no. 4 (2015): 829–871. The edition—based on the only two extant copies preserved in Prague, Národní knihovna, MS V.F.9, fols. 68v–75v, and Vienna, Österreichische Nationalbibliothek, MS 4937, fols. 28r–34v—is preceded by a historical and philological note.

29. František Šmahel, "Payne, Peter (d. 1455/6?)," in *Oxford Dictionary of National Biography* (Oxford: Oxford University Press, 2004), www.oxforddnb.com/view/article/21650. In addition to Šmahel's essential bibliography on Payne, see: William Cook, "John Wyclif and Hussite Theology, 1415-1436," *Church History 42*, no. 3 (1973): 335–349; Anne Hudson, *The Premature Reformation: Wycliffite Texts and Lollard History* (Oxford: Clarendon Press, 1988), 99–103; Hudson, "From Oxford to Prague: The Writings of John Wyclif and his English Followers in Bohemia," in Hudson, *Studies in the Transmission of Wyclif's Writings* (Aldershot: Ashgate, 2008), 2:642–657.

30. See František Bartoš, *Literární činnost M. Jana Rokycany, M. Jana Příbrama, M. Petra Payna* (Prague: Česká akademie věd a umění, 1928), 98. Cf. Jana Nechutová, "Traktát 'De ymaginibus', připisovaný Petru Paynovi," *Husitský Tábor 9* (1986–1987), 325–334: 326; Campi, "Una difesa del determinismo", 832n8.

31. See William Cook, "Peter Payne, Theologian and Diplomat of the Hussite Revolution" (PhD diss., Cornell University, 1971), 96–97, 106–108; Jan Sedlák, *Studie a texty k náboženským dějinám českým* (Olomouc, Czech Republic: Arcibiskupská knihtiskárna, 1915), 2:114–115; František Šmahel, "Magister und Studenten der Prager Medizinischen Fakultät bis zum Jahre 1419," in Šmahel, *Die Prager Universität im Mittelalter/The Charles University in the Middle Ages* (Leiden, Netherlands: Brill, 2007), 151. Cf. Campi, "Una difesa del determinismo", 833nn11–12.

32. Cf. *Responsiones Magistri Johannis Hus ad Articulos Johannis Wyclef*, in Jan Sedlák, ed., *M. Jan Hus* (Prague: Dědictví sv. Prokopa, 1915), 305*–310*: 308*.

33. See Jan Hus, *Super IV Sententiarum*, ed. Václav Flajšhans (Praha: Jaroslav Bursík, 1904), 69: "Notandum eciam est hic de necessitate, que duplex est, scilicet simplex necessitas dicta. . . . Alia necessitas est condicionata." Ibid., 161: "posita

presciencia Dei nec tollitur libertas arbitrii nec necessitate absolute omne futurum contingens eveniet." Ibid., 154: "Videtur Deum habere duplicem scienciam de qualibet creatura: unam, que est absolute necessaria, cum sit suum intelligere terminatum ad scitum secundum esse intelligibile; et aliam, que est contingens, terminata ad scitum secundum esse existere" (excerpted from Wyclif, *De scientia dei*, fol. 16r, lines 36–39).

34. Cf. Mansi, *Sacrorum Conciliorum*, 754–755.

35. Cf. Jerome of Prague, *Quaestiones, Polemica, Epistulae*, ed. František Šmahel and Gabriel Silagi (Turnhout, Belgium: Brepols, 2010), 144, 150, 182; Hermann von der Hardt, ed., *Monumenta Oecumenicum Constantiense Concilium* (Frankfurt, Leipzig, and Helmstadt: Gensch-Schnorr, 1698), 4: col. 646.

36. Cf. Hefele, *Histoire des Conciles*, 7.2:770–771. Cf. Campi, "Una difesa del determinismo", 833n10. On the gradual decline of interest in Wyclif's philosophy in favor of his ecclesiology at Prague since 1410, see František Šmahel, "'Doctor evangelicus super omnes evangelistas': Wyclif's Fortune in Hussite Bohemia," *Bulletin of the Institute of Historical Research* 43 (1970): 16–34.

37. Payne, *Defensio*, lines 3–5: "in sua sancta senectute fideliter asseruit quod omnia que evenient absolute necessario evenient."

38. See Christina von Nolcken, "Another Kind of Saint: A Lollard Perception of John Wyclif," in *From Ockham to Wyclif*, ed. Anne Hudson and Michael Wilks (Oxford: Blackwell, 1987), 429–443; Michael Van Dussen, *From England to Bohemia: Heresy and Communication in the Later Middle Ages* (Cambridge: Cambridge University Press, 2012), 86–111.

39. Cf. Thomas Gascoigne, *Loci e libro veritatum: Passages Selected from Gascoigne's Theological Dictionary Illustrating the Condition of the Church and State, 1403–1458*, ed. James E. Thorold Rogers (Oxford: Clarendon Press, 1881), 20.

40. At the Council of Basel, Payne jointly defended Wyclif and Hus, and stated that he had read "aliquos de libris" of Hus, without finding "aliquid erronei"; see František Palacký et al., eds., *Monumenta Conciliorum Generalium seculi decimi quinti* (Vienna: Typographia Aulae et Status, 1857), 270. Piccolomini met Payne in Basel, and described him as a "versipellis cavillator" and "solis elenchis in disputatione confidens", guilty of spreading the heresy of Wyclif— surprisingly considered as a pupil of Ockham's—in Bohemia; cf. Eneas Silvius Piccolomini, *Der Briefwechsel des Eneas Silvius Piccolomini*, ed. Rudolf Wolkan, in *Fontes Rerum Austriacarum* (Vienna: Hölder, 1912), 2:167, 179–180; Eneas Silvius Piccolomini, *Historia Bohemica*, ed. Joseph Hejnic and Hans Rothe (Cologne: Böhlau, 2005), 368–369.

41. It is worth noting that Payne never quotes any writing of Wyclif's in his defense of article 27; still, he takes excerpts from Wyclif's *De universalibus* and *Trialogus* without attributing them to Wyclif. See Campi, "Una difesa," 835–837, 860–866, esp. 862–863.

42. Payne, *Defensio*, lines 11–18: "deus absolute necessario producit istum mundum qui est aggregatum ex omnibus que evenient, ergo iste mundus et sic

omnia que evenient absolute necessario evenient. Antecedens arguitur sic: eo ipso quo deus producit mundum, producit istum mundum; ergo cum absolute necessario producit mundum, sequitur quod absolute necessario producit istum mundum. Maior huius racionis sic arguitur: eo ipso quo deus producit mundum, producit mundum optimum possibilem." Ibid., lines 361–364: "Sicud enim sol est ante diffusionem sui luminis in medio et tamen non potest non diffundere suum lumen in medio, sic intelligendum est de deo quod, licet sit ante produccionem effectuum suorum, non potest non producere eos." Ibid., lines 370–375: "Sicud melius est deum producere hunc mundum optimum possibilem quem producit quam foret si per inpossibile alium mundum qui non est iste mundus produceret, sic melius est deum producere creaturam quamcunque quam efficit in suo ordine quam foret si per inpossibile in alio mundi ordine creaturam produceret meliorem."

43. Payne, *Defensio*, lines 41–50: "deus non potest producere aliquid quod non producet, ergo a pari non potest non producere aliquid quod producet; et cum producet quidquid producet, sequitur quod absolute necessario producet quidquid producet. Antecedens sic: deus non habet potenciam ad producendum aliquid quod non producet; ergo et cetera. Antecedens sic: deus est actualissima res possibilis, ergo in eo non est aliqua potencia ad faciendum aliquid quod non est in actu, et per consequens non habet potenciam ad producendum aliquid quod non producet." Ibid., lines 236–240: "potencia productiva ad intra non potest esse in deo propter eius actualitatem nisi habeat omnem actum suum possibilem, ergo a pari cum potencia productiva ad extra sit in deo, sequitur quod ipsa non potest esse in eo propter eius actualitatem nisi habeat omnem actum suum possibilem."

44. Payne, *Defensio*, lines 35–40: "eo ipso quod deus est, mundus est; ergo cum mundus non potest esse nisi deus producat illum, sequitur quod absolute necessario deus producit mundum. Antecedens sic: eo ipso quod deus est, ydea mundi est; et si ydea mundi est, mundus est, cum eo ipso ydeatum per ydeam mundi est; ergo et cetera." Ibid., lines 123–131: "necessitatur deus a racionibus eternis precedentibus suam ordinacionem producere ea que producet . . . non subiacet potestati dei propter raciones eternas precedentes eius ordinacionem respectu futurorum eventuum producere alia quam producet, seu ordinare aliam ordinacionem quam ordinavit eternaliter." Ibid., lines 206–209: "deus perfecte facit quidquid facit . . . , ergo nulla creatura producitur a deo in esse intelligibili que non producitur ab eo in esse existere, et per consequens quecunque creatura intelligitur a deo producitur effectualiter a deo." Ibid., lines 161–165: "si non omnia que evenient absolute necessario evenient, tunc maior est numerus omnium producibilium quam producibilium que producentur. Quo dato, sequitur quod deus est productivus plurium producibilium quam producet, et per consequens deus potest plus benefacere quam benefacit."

45. Payne, *Defensio*, lines 176–183: "deus non potest velle producere mundum qui non est iste mundus . . . nulla voluntas quam deus habet eternaliter est

contingens ad utrumlibet; cum ergo deus non potest habere voluntatem nisi quam habet eternaliter, sequitur quod deus non potest habere voluntatem contingentem ad utrumlibet." Ibid., lines 192–200: "raciones eterne que faciunt deum velle producere istum mundum non possunt contingenter facere deum velle producere istum mundum . . . faccio illa, qua raciones ille faciunt deum velle producere istum mundum, est faccio eterna non dependens ab aliquo temporali, ergo est absolute necessaria." Ibid., lines 476–479: "non ideo deus dicitur summe liber quia sine limitacione alterius nature potest agere contingenter ad utrumlibet, set quia potest racionabiliter agere sine limitacione vel direccione sui per alteram naturam." Ibid., lines 480–484: "sicud non ex hoc quod deus absolute necessario vivit virtuose sequitur quod non libere vivit virtuose, sic non ex hoc quod Petrus absolute necessario agit datum opus sequitur quod non libere agit illud . . . nulla est libertas contradiccionis." Ibid., lines 101–110: "si non omnia que evenient absolute necessario evenirent, tunc Petrus posset non currere postquam deus ordinavit de eo quod curreret; cum ergo hoc sit falsum, sequitur quod antecedens ex quo sequitur sit falsum. . . . Petrus post istam ordinacionem non posset non currere nisi deus post illam ordinaret de eo quod non curret; cum ergo deus post illam ordinacionem non potest ordinare quod non currat, sequitur quod non subiacet potestati Petri post illam ordinacionem facere se non currere."

46. Payne, *Defensio*, lines 488–495: "arguit magister dictus sic: si, inquit, omnia que evenient et cetera, tunc omnia que evenient necessitantur evenire a deo, et per consequens, cum peccatum moris eveniet, sequitur quod necessitatur a deo evenire. Et ex consequenti, deus est auctor illius peccati. Hic dicitur negando quod peccatum moris eveniet proprie loquendo, et racio est quia tunc huiusmodi peccatum foret proprie effectus et non defectus, et per consequens haberet causam efficientem." Ibid., lines 505–507: "deus non approbat omnia necessitancia ad primum peccatum moris eo quod tunc approbaret voluntatem secundum racionem qua deficit ab observancia legis dei." Ibid., lines 527–535: "non est verum quod quia permittit deus hominem peccare, ideo peccat, set e contra est verum quod quia homo peccat, ideo deus permittit hominem peccare . . . est verum quod quia homo peccat ideo deus vult voluntate eterna punire ipsum pro peccato suo. Nec obest huic quin causa quare deus permittit hominem peccare est quia prescit eternaliter eum esse peccaturum, et prescit eternaliter eum esse peccaturum quia peccabit."

47. Payne, *Defensio*, lines 455–462: "non sequitur 'Petrus non potest facere datum actum quem deus vult ipsum facere, nisi deus velit ipsum facere istum actum; set non est in potestate Petri facere deum velle ipsum facere istum actum; ergo non est in potestate Petri facere datum actum'. Antecedens enim est verum, et consequens falsum. Hoc tamen sequitur ex dicto antecedente quod non est in potestate Petri facere originaliter, set secundarie seu instrumentaliter facere datum actum." Ibid., lines 513–520: "videtur quod sicud creatura racionalis benefaciens absolute necessario benefacit per hoc quod deus vult eam benefacere,

sic creatura racionalis malefaciens absolute necessario malefacit per hoc quod ipsa vult seipsam malefacere. . . . sicud in benefaciendo dei volicio causat originaliter benefaccionem creature racionalis benefacientis, sic in malefaciendo creature racionalis peccantis volicio causat originaliter malefaccionem ipsius creature malefacientis."

48. Cf. Thomas Netter of Walden, *Doctrinale Antiquitatum Fidei Catholicae Ecclesiae*, ed. Bonaventura Blanciotti (Venice: Bassani, 1747–1797), 1:117–131.

CHAPTER SIX

BEFORE AND AFTER WYCLIF: CONSENT TO ANOTHER'S SIN IN MEDIEVAL EUROPE

Fiona Somerset

I n this essay I will trace the history of an idea: that one person might be guilty of another person's sin because he or she has consented to it. I call this social consent: consent that goes beyond the interpersonal consent of a contract between people, in which mutual responsibilities and obligations are usually fairly explicitly spelled out, to a more nebulous web of relationships between people in larger groups (the realm, the city, the university, a monastery, a guild, even a household) in which some obligations and responsibilities may never have been explicitly articulated, let alone agreed. Indeed, the theory that one person might be guilty of another person's sin through consent lays bare a fairly basic difficulty in thinking through the relationship between persons and the groups to which they belong—one that continues to trouble us in the present day. While individuals may be held responsible for their actions, within larger groups wrongful actions may be the result of complex interactions between persons who do not agree at all on how to apportion responsibility.

Tracing the history of this idea requires us to investigate how ideas move, and what changes when they do. I first encountered social consent in lollard writings, then discovered that their distinctive formulation of it is drawn from Wyclif. In what follows I will suggest that Wyclif's extremist position on consent was fundamental to his thought, and to that of lollards and Hussites, in ways that have not yet been explored. Yet Wyclif's version of social consent was influenced by scholarly interchange in Europe at least as much as it influenced that interchange in turn in the fifteenth century. Wyclif drew heavily upon consent theory's development in canon law and its commentaries, an intellectual debt that has occasionally been remarked but never explored in depth.[1] But he did not merely adopt consent theory; he also adapted it to new purposes.

My interest began with lollard writings that present the social dimensions of consent as an important element of moral teaching. I take the example that follows from a late fourteenth-century commentary on the Decalogue that draws heavily on Wyclif's exposition of the Ten Commandments in his *Sermones*. There are twenty-seven known versions of this commentary, and they vary widely in scope and tone; many are not overtly polemical.[2] This particular version, extant only in Oxford, Bodleian Library MS Bodley 789, is one of the most outspoken:

> As clerkis seyn, upon sixe maneris is þis consent doon, and men schulden wel knowe it. He consentit to þe yuel þat wirchiþ wiþ þerto [participates]; he þat defendiþ and conseiliþ þerto [advises]; he þat bi whos auctorite is þe yuel don; or he þat wiþdrawiþ his helpe or scharp repreuynge [does not help to prevent it or sharply reprove the sinner], whanne he miȝte don it [he is able to do this] and schulde bi Goddis lawe. And among alle synnes bi whiche þe feend bigiliþ [beguiles] men, noon is moore sutil þan such consent. And þerfore þe prophetis of þe olde lawe tolden men hire periles [the danger they were in], til þei suffriden deeþ; and in þis cause þe apostilis of Crist weren martrid, and we schulde, ȝif we weren trewe men. But cowardise and defaute of [fol. 115v] loue of God makiþ us sterte abac [step back], as traytours don.[3]

As clerks say, there are six kinds of consent, and men should know them well. You consent to sin if you work with the person who commits a sin; or if you defend him, counsel him, authorize his action, fail to help stop him, or fail to speak out against him when you can and should do so according to God's law. For lollard writers, this set of injunctions gives concrete shape to one of their core ideals, central to their self-definition and their descriptions of what they and others should do. The minimal, yet sometimes most powerfully effective, means of opposing sin is to speak the truth rather than remaining silent. True men, as lollard writers like to call the group they belong to, are men who speak the truth (or aspire to do so, amid fear and doubt) even under threat of martyrdom.[4] For otherwise they would consent to the sin they see around them.

This commentary does not cite him, but this six-fold definition of consent comes from Wyclif: a mnemonic verse on the six types of consent listed in this Decalogue commentary, or references to one or another of these six types of consent, show up over and over in Wyclif's writings.[5]

Wyclif himself sometimes comments on how famous the verse is, and how very frequently he has repeated it in his writings. It is added in the lower margin of Wyclif's short polemical treatise *De novis ordinibus* in Prague National Library MS XI.E.3, an early fifteenth-century Bohemian manuscript containing writings by Wyclif, Hus, the Englishman Richard Wyche, and other Hussites:[6]

> Nota sex sunt species consensus:
> Consentit cooperans, defendens, consilium dans
> Ac auctorisans, non iuuans, non reprehendens.
> [Note that there are six kinds of consent:
> One consents by cooperating, defending, giving counsel
> And authorizing, not helping, nor reprehending.][7]

This annotation adumbrates the evidence for Wyclif's influence in Bohemia that I will survey later, demonstrating that consent theory was important to Hussites as well as lollards. But what it should also suggest is that it is only by paying close attention to the extant books and institutional settings through which this idea moves (indeed, by looking closely at where and how and in what forms this *verse* moves) that we can understand how it changes as it does so.

Where, then, did Wyclif get this verse, and these ideas? It turns out that he is drawing on canon law—a source that may explain why the topic was not pursued in depth by nineteenth-century Protestant historians.[8] In what may be his earliest and is certainly one of his lengthiest expositions of consent theory, in *De officio regis*, Wyclif cites the *Glossa ordinaria* by Bernard of Parma on the first book of the *Decretals*, 1.29.1. Consent is six-fold, Wyclif says, as saints and the laws of the church tell us: the gloss on "De officio delegate," "Quia quesitum est" cites many laws about such consent.[9] Indeed it does, in a gloss on the words "pari pena," and Wyclif, like many others, seems to have studied this gloss and its cited sources carefully. But in many manuscripts, and in the version printed in the 1582 edition of the *Corpus Iuris Canonici*, the *Glossa ordinaria* by Bernard of Parma is annotated in turn by a verse on consent—one that varies considerably, as it turns out, in both its content and its placement, across the transmission and reception of the *Decretals*.

The title surveys the duties and powers of papal judges delegate, who were prelates commissioned on an ad hoc basis to adjudicate appeals to the pope in their own locales.[10] "Quia quesitum est," its first chapter, quotes a letter by Alexander III written in response to an inquiry about how a judge should behave when he knows that justice is being impeded through bribes or threats that compel a complainant to keep silent:

> Sic tibi respondemus, quod sicut agentes et consentientes pari poena (scripturae testimonio) puniuntur, sic tam eos qui trahuntur in causam, quam principales eorum fautores (si eos manifeste cognoueris iustitiam impedire) districtione ecclesiastica poteris coercere.[11]

> [Thus we respond to you, that just as agents and consenters are punished with equivalent punishments ("pari poena") according to the testimony of Scripture, so you should use your ecclesiastical jurisdiction to coerce both those who are involved in a case, and their principal helpers (if you know that they have clearly impeded justice).]

If it is clear to the judge delegate that the helpers of the accused have impeded justice, then their actions are culpable and lie within his jurisdiction. The quoted portion of Alexander's letter seems unconcerned by the equivalence or parity in punishment he attests in citing Romans 1:32, "Qui talia agunt, digni sunt morte: et non solum qui ea faciunt, sed etiam qui consentiunt facientibus" / "they who do such things, are worthy of death; and not only those that do them, but those also that consent to the ones that do them."[12] In this excerpt, Alexander III is more anxious to establish his judge's jurisdiction over those who might help a defendant to escape justice. The same cannot be said of the glossators of the *Compilatio prima*, in which Bernard of Pavia had first included this quotation circa 1190, or of the *Decretals*. In explaining "pari poena" and its troubling implications, the commentators distinguish different types of consent in an effort to reconcile conflicting cases that had been presented in the *Decretum*.

Here is the version of what had become the standard gloss on "pari poena," printed in the 1582 edition of the *Decretals*, complete with an added verse on consent, labeled here as an "Additio" to the gloss. The *Glossa ordinaria* as printed here is largely consistent in its content, although often annotated in turn by more layers of glossing, across the extant copies of the *Decretals* where it appears.[13] The verse mnemonic is anything but consistent:

> Consensus spernit, suadet, iuuat, atque tuetur.
> Hic minus, hicque minus luit, hic aequaliter, hic plus:

Consentiens, operans, defendens, non reprehendens.
[Consent spurns, persuades, helps, and protects.
This less, and this less is culpable, this equally, this more.
Consenting, working, defending, not blaming.][14]

As is obvious, this is not Wyclif's verse, and these are not Wyclif's six types of consent, although they do bear some resemblance to them. Nor are they cited for the same purpose. Like Alexander III's letter, Wyclif's verse and his discussions of consent implicitly or explicitly assert parity in culpability for various kinds of action and consent. In contrast, the first two lines of this verse support the Gloss in its effort to reconcile conflicting treatments of consent in the *Decretum* through a fourfold distinction between negligence (*spernit* or elsewhere *spectat*), counsel (*suadet*), cooperation (*iuuat*), and authorization or defense (*tuetur*).[15] They provide a mnemonic summary: the second line pithily differentiates levels of blame, reinforcing the Gloss where it assigns lesser blame to negligence and counsel, equal blame to cooperation, and greater blame to authorization or defense. In some manuscripts, as for example Brno, Moravian Regional Library MS 1161, where *negligit* replaces *spernit*, the verbs in the first line and differential valuations in the second are numbered for easy cross-reference.[16] The third line of verse, however, in either this manuscript or the printed version, pulls in a different direction—and uses four of the same verbs, and in the same order, as Wyclif's verse. "Consentit operans, defendens" lacks Wyclif's "consilium dans, / Ac autorizans, non iuuans" but like his version finishes with "nec reprehendens."

My investigation of these verses and their development is ongoing, but the third line seems to be a later addition. Manuscripts of the *Compilatio prima* contain a version of the standard gloss passage but no verse; early manuscripts of the *Decretals* from Italy do likewise; verse mnemonics on consent first appear in later thirteenth-century Italian manuscripts but both their content and their placement within the *Decretals* vary; none, however, include the third line. In the Smithfield Decretals, produced like the Brno manuscript in the fourteenth century, the third line appears first, not last.[17] "Consentit operans defendens ut reprehendens. / Consensus negligit suadet iuuat atque tuetur. / Hic minus hicque minus luit equaliter hic plus."[18] The variance in this version seemingly includes two fairly obvious copying errors, *ut* for *nec* in the first line and an omitted *hic* before *equaliter* in the third; yet placing the third line first was presumably a deliberate decision, whenever it occurred.

Each of the three-line versions of the verse we have examined differs in wording and order, then, and only the line added later closely resembles the content of Wyclif's verse. Wyclif may have adapted a version of the three-line verse by dropping its two earlier lines, or adapted or adopted a verse that discards the differential valuations of consent found in the two-line verse. In either case, the contrast between the variance found in the canon law verse glosses and the remarkably consistent verse found in Wyclif's and Wycliffite manuscripts is striking. In these contexts, the verse is surprisingly stable, even as it moves between languages, centuries, and realms: *operans* may substitute for *cooperans* in the first line, and *nec* for *non* in the second, but the six types of consent remain consistent within Wycliffite and (as I will show shortly) Hussite writings, as do the reasons for their deployment.

Wyclif may have consulted a copy of the *Decretals* as he was first formulating his ideas about consent; but it is just as likely that he encountered a version of the verse that he may then have modified, as well as the key concepts that underlie it, in a heavily annotated and cross-referenced canon law commentary, compilation or text book.[19] The copy of Gratian's *Decretum* that we know Wyclif owned at one point, British Library MS Royal 10 E ii, is one sample of such a book, like the Smithfield *Decretals* first copied in the earlier part of the fourteenth century.[20] Into its margins has been copied the revised *Glossa ordinaria* on the *Decretum* by Bartholomew of Brescia, and it includes nearly all the *paleae*, that is, the added materials accreted to the *Decretum* as it was used in legal teaching in Bologna.[21] The opening pages contain an index that cross-references the *Decretum* with passages cited in the various successive collections of decretals; the margins and flyleaves are replete with notes on canon law, mnemonic verses, and additional materials including a purported papal letter, poems, and a miracle story. Clearly this book passed through several hands and acquired annotations and apparatus of various kinds as it did so. There are many canon law books like it: the clean copy of a single compilation that we find in the Smithfield *Decretals* is by no means the most common kind of book from which students and scholars learned, consulted, and quoted canon law. It is easy to imagine how a heavily used and multiply repurposed book like Royal 10 E ii was conducive to the fluid adaptation and repurposing of mnemonic verses, rather than their stabilization.

More to the point, however, the citation of versions of this mnemonic verse in glossed canon law books is one end product of a much longer process in which the theory of social consent was developed, in genres ranging from exegesis, penitential writings, and legal commentary to public letters, sermons, and political treatises. As John W. Baldwin, Brian Tierney, Philippe Buc, and Peter D. Clarke have shown, one key setting in which concepts of consent and representation were intensively developed and influentially deployed was late twelfth-century Paris, in the circle of Peter the Chanter.[22] His student Stephen Langton (and his probable student Lothario dei Segni, the future Innocent III) then brought these concepts to the papal curia, where they profoundly influenced new legislation on heresy and the papal interdict in the early thirteenth century, as well as the papal reforms of Lateran IV more broadly.[23] My story is not only about Europe after Wyclif, then, but about Wyclif after Europe. Wyclif in his theorizing about social consent consciously looks back to the early thirteenth century for models for the kind of reform he wants to promote.

While these ideas about consent and representation were widespread and much discussed in late twelfth- and early thirteenth-century Europe, Philippe Buc has claimed that they more or less went underground in the mid-thirteenth century as their revolutionary potential became evident, coming into their own again only with Wyclif and Hus as well as their opponents.[24] Ockham's extended treatment of consent through silence in his *Dialogus*, one of the political works he wrote after his break with Pope John XXII in 1328, might be presented as the exception that proves the rule.[25] But even if it was only opponents of the papacy who were deploying consent theory in poetry and prose that sought wider audiences, consent theory remained broadly current in canon law. It became a rule of law in the legal maxim "Qui tacet consentire videtur," presented as the forty-third of eighty-eight legal principles drawn from Roman law in the *Regulae Iuris* that conclude a new supplement to the *Decretals* compiled under Gregory IX.[26] Like Ockham, and indeed like many Wycliffite or (as we will see) Hussite commentators, this maxim focuses on the last of the six types of consent, *nec reprehendens*, interpreted here as keeping silence rather than speaking out. From one perspective, speaking out might be seen as the most minimal refusal of consent; from another, the most disruptive possible.

Even if the prominence (or absence) of ideas about social consent in public discourse between the mid-thirteenth and mid-fourteenth century remains under-researched, what is already clear is that Wyclif gave this theory of consent a particular kind of boost, heightening and sharpening some of its claims. He did so in a way that lollards and Hussites were intellectually prepared to receive, that they found nothing short of electrifying in its potential, and that they deployed to new ends in their own work. Certainly Wyclif himself presents the theory of social consent as having fallen into desuetude. Rather than a principle for determining responsibility and administering justice, it has become business as usual in a church whose affairs are everywhere tainted by the sale of spiritual services:

> Hodie namque sunt plures fautores partis diaboli ad defendendum Dei iniurias vel serviliter tacendum iusticiam quam sunt ex parte iusticie, in tantum quod ad tantum invaluit pars adversa quod aput multos non reputantur isti consensus esse peccata: sed sunt aput alios approbata, aput yppocritas colorata, et aput plurimos pretermissa. Ymmo peccatum symonie ad tantum invaluit quod comissione omissione vel consensu maiorem partem ecclesie maculavit. Et cum illud sit peccatum gravissimum non mirum si ecclesia sit adeo rethi diaboli intricatum.[27]

> [For today there are more supporters on the side of the devil intent on defending injuries to God or servilely keeping quiet about justice, than there are on the side of justice. So much so that the opposing part prevails, and among many these kinds of consent are not reputed to be sins. Instead, they are among some approved, among hypocrites colored, and among many passed over. Indeed, the sin of simony prevails to such a great extent that by commission, omission, or consent the greater part of the church has been stained. And since that is the gravest of sins, no wonder if the church is so much snarled in the devil's snare.]

As elsewhere in his references to consent, whether or not he articulates this point explicitly, Wyclif separates himself from the consent he deplores here by speaking out. The moral corruption and pastoral failure of the clergy are the reasons why his instruction on consent is needed. With some instruction, his readers will recognize their culpability, or the culpability of Wyclif's target—often both. Wyclif sometimes moves from a description of a general state of moral corruption to specific suggestions about how to combat it. But his main emphasis is on pointing fingers: at a person or group that needs to take responsibility for another group, at a group that needs to take responsibility for its own members, or at everyone for doing nothing. Unlike the lollard quotation I began with, his favorite pronoun is *they*, or *isti*, rather than *we*.

The discussion of consent in *De officio regis* may be one of Wyclif's earliest extended treatments of the various forms of consent to another's sin. This is the only work in which Wyclif lists five rather than six manners of consent: he folds *non reprehendens* into his discussion of authorizing and of defending—a strategy that makes sense in this case, for as he shows, any social superior who fails to blame a sin implicitly authorizes and defends it by virtue of his social role.[28] In contrast with the verse he so often quotes, here Wyclif treats the five kinds of consent he discusses more or less in reverse, as follows: authorizing, counseling, defending, cooperating, and not helping. This is also the only extant work in which he cites several precise canon law sources for each of his claims, even if in concluding he comments that he has done so many times before. While in this quotation he addresses simony, his broader target in *De officio regis* is the endowment of the clergy, a sin that corrupts them all. The king should take charge and seize their possessions, "quia aliter consentiret [because otherwise he would consent]" (87/17). It is the king's responsibility for bringing an end to clerical endowments that concerns Wyclif most, but the theoretical discussion of consent tends, here as elsewhere, to drag him off course.

As well as the idea that one person might consent to the sin of another, Wyclif is fascinated by the common medieval idea that an individual person might be said to consent to his or her own sin, in a moral psychology of the human faculties where the will consents to poor arguments offered it by the reason, or to urgings offered by the passions in response to the senses, imagination, or memory. The twelfth chapter of Augustine's commentary on the Sermon on the Mount is one of the most famous and earliest of these moral psychologies: Wyclif quotes and comments on it at great length in *De mandatis*, in his commentary on the ninth commandment, and also returns to it in his last work, the *Opus evangelicum*.[29] This account of individual human action is significant to Wyclif's theory of social consent because like many medieval writers on this topic, Wyclif bridges the gap between individual and group culpability through frequent analogy.[30] A convent of friars or a realm is *like* an individual body, for example, in that the head must take responsibility for its members, just as the intellect must for the whole person's wayward impulses. Thus, even though Wyclif has far more to say about culpability for consent between or among persons than he does about consent within the person, he does often revert to accounts of individual culpability in order to explain group culpability.

What is fascinating about analogies of this kind is how poorly they work. A person is not a social group writ small, nor is a realm a person writ large, nor can either of them adequately explain or justify an argument made about the other. Some medieval writers play up this difficulty in order to demonstrate just how difficult these ethical questions are, as Wyclif's contemporary Geoffrey Chaucer does in his Clerk's Tale.[31] Others seemingly want to override it, as Stephen Langton does in his letter to the English people, or indeed as Wyclif does in his Sunday gospel sermon on Luke 7:11 (printed in Sermones vol. 1 as Sermon 48).[32] While in De officio regis Wyclif seems to be working out ideas that are relatively new to him, in close conversation with their development in canon law commentary, Sermon 48 in contrast seems to provide a retrospective summary and further development of many of his previous claims.

Sermon 48 may indeed have been composed to provide just this sort of overview and development of Wyclif's previous claims about both individual and group culpability. The table in Appendix 1 (at the end of this essay) surveys Wyclif's references to social consent in his published works, subdivided into extended treatments, shorter treatments, and brief citations.[33] It includes works in Wyclif's monumental twelve-volume Summa Theologie; short polemical works, all but one aimed at the friars; the four volumes of collected sermons; De officio pastorali, a short work on the pastoral office extant in many Bohemian manuscripts, and the Trialogus, a late summa of Wyclif's ideas that attempts to address an audience beyond the schools— as indeed in a different way do the Sermons and the late polemical tracts.

Those who are familiar with Wyclif's writings will notice right away that his references to consent are clustered in the writings that he produced or revised most heavily in his final years, at Lutterworth, after he had left Oxford. Anne Hudson has argued that the writings that make up the Summa Theologie underwent extensive revision in this period, to the point where one cannot disentangle their intended order or mutual relationships.[34] She has also shown that the first three volumes of sermons in particular were probably composed or revised from notes in the wake of Wyclif's departure from Oxford.[35] The Trialogus dates to this period, as do the vitriolic short tracts against the friars. The De officio pastorali is cross-referenced in the *De officio regis* and refers to the friars as *pseudofratres* in Wyclif's characteristic late polemical idiom, so it was probably also revised in this period.[36] It may be the case, then, that most, if not all, of the references to social consent across this corpus were added after Wyclif's retreat to Lutterworth: many of them take the form of shorter or longer theoretical excurses, where they are not brief citations of a kind that would have been even easier to insert. In the products of Wyclif's wide-ranging revisions to his written oeuvre in these years, many of which may have aimed more fully to document his oral teaching and preaching now that he was no longer engaged in these activities, we can see that social consent theory was something of an obsession for Wyclif at the end of his life. He seems to have been well aware of this, and to have thought of it as something he was known for, and wanted to be known for.

More than anywhere else, the systematic explanation of the six kinds of consent in Wyclif's Sunday Gospel Sermon 48 seems to provide the consolidated and further extended account of social consent that Wyclif wanted to be remembered for. And by a happy accident of history—or perhaps through someone's careful planning—this in fact is the discussion of consent through which Wyclif's ideas on this topic were remembered. The whole of Wyclif's discussion of consent in Sermon 48 is included, lightly redacted or else in a previous recension, in the Wycliffite alphabetical encyclopedia known as the *Floretum*, compiled in England (probably in Oxford) but widely distributed in Bohemia as well as in England.[37] In Sermon 48, the six-fold discussion of consent is tacked on at the end, with a brief introduction that presents it as the third thing to be noted about sin, for among all the sins of the church it is more dangerous, more hidden, and less attended to. It may be, as with many components of the sermons, that this exposition started life as a separate tract, though it is not extant in that form.[38]

What is most striking about the systematic exposition in Sermon 48, though, is how far it reaches, especially in its treatment of the first three kinds of consent: this is not an introductory exposition designed to convince new readers, but an illustration of how far the consequences of these claims can be made to stretch. Stephen Lahey has shown us how Wyclif's metaphysics undergirds his political thought.[39] Here in this exposition we see metaphysics run riot, not so much explaining and justifying Wyclif's thought on consent as upping the ante to make his claims invincible—yet only, I think, for those who already accept the underlying theory. Wyclif reinforces each of his claims with a similitude of parts and wholes, an image to fix them in the mind. What he does not do, however, as we might expect in a practical moral guide, is to explain what each of these consenting actions might consist of, or how persons of various kinds might avoid them in particular situations.[40]

I will begin with Wyclif's expositions of the first three kinds of consent, through cooperating, defending, and giving counsel.

First, consent by cooperation: "omnis prescitus vel predestinatus operans viciose consentit omni peccato mundi . . . existens in crimine cooperatur cum alio criminoso ubicunque fuerit, quia omnes illi sunt unum corpus cooperans cum patre mendacii" (321/17–18, 28–31). The foreknown or *presciti*, in Wyclif's parlance, are those who will be damned. The predestined will be saved. Only God knows which is which, but his knowledge does not infringe upon human free will. Regardless of this future outcome, Wyclif insists here that anyone, whether foreknown or predestined, who commits any sin, consents to and participates in all sin in the world. There is such a huge hill of it, Wyclif says; every one of us is part of it. Anyone sinning cooperates with any other wherever he may be, for we are all one body cooperating with the father of lies.

Second, consent by defense: "Sicut enim multorum navem trahencium quilibet eorum trahit ipsam et quamlibet eius partem, sic multorum trahencium currum peccati in iugo peccati dyaboli quilibet eorum trahit ipsum et quamlibet eius partem. . . . tam mali quam boni faciunt participitative tam opera bona quam mala, cum tam boni quam mali sunt ambo una persona, que promovet opera suarum parcium" (322/7–11, 21–24). Everyone participates in both good works and bad, since we are all one person who promotes the work of its own parts. Just as when a group of people drags a boat, each one drags the boat and whatever part of it, so do the many dragging the chariot of sin in the yoke of the devil.

Third, consent by counsel: "cum quelibet creatura dicit se ipsam, patet quod posicio cuiuscunque operis mali dicit cuicunque malo per modum consilii quod est taliter operandum, ut medicus secundum Anselmum dicit efficacius hanc herbam esse salutiferam, dum avide ipsam edit quam diceret asserendo verbis ipsam esse pestiferam, et sic de contrario, quia minus verbis quam operibus est credendum" (322/26–33). Any evil act is itself, in a sense, a counsel to perform that evil, since every created thing bespeaks itself simply by existing and acting as it does, and actions speak louder than words. (Here Wyclif is relying on his realist understanding of propositional logic, according to which arrangements of words ["Peter is sitting"] and states of affairs in the world [that Peter is sitting] have the same kind of reality.[41]) Just as a doctor more effectively says that a particular herb is healthful by avidly eating it than by asserting in words alone that it is harmful, so our works are more to be believed than our words alone.

We might read the extremity of these claims as the product of Wyclif's prolonged frustration that his theoretical development of an imperative toward reform had fallen on so many deaf ears. Be that as it may, these sweeping claims build cumulatively to a larger point. Whenever we sin, we cooperate with all sinners and partake in all the sin in the world. All of us, regardless of our own personal virtue, partake of all the actions of other human beings in the world, both good and bad. We all influence others to imitate our own personal sins simply and most powerfully by committing them, even if we do not also recommend them in words. How then is there any hope of *not* participating in sin—of refusing social consent? Only in a world without sin, it seems, could any of us be without sin, and such a world is not possible.

How can this account promote any kind of reform, rather than simply despair? Let us contrast it, before going on to the final three conclusions, with the more case-based, rhetorically persuasive discussions of the six modes of consent in two of Wyclif's other works that were widely distributed and influential in both England and Bohemia. Here is Wyclif's *De simonia*, a work that Jan Hus translated, adapted, and expanded into his own treatise against simony. Wyclif's version refers to consent repeatedly throughout, but its most extended treatment of the topic is in chapter 8:

[O]mnis symoniace heresi consenciens symoniacus est censendus. Consentit enim homo sex modis et modis compositis resultantibus ex ipsis, sicut alias diffuse exposui ex sentenciis sanctorum et legum ecclesie; continentur autem in istis versibus:

Consentit operans, defendens, consilium dans
Ac auctorisans, non iuvans nec reprehendens.

Ille autem qui cooperatur cum symoniaco vel medians vel mercando est symoniacus ex consensu, sicut ille qui defendit symoniam scolastice vel contenciose, sicut tercio ille qui consulit ad pravitatem symoniacam et quarto potentatus qui auctorisat homines ut suos vel facta sua que debet cognoscere esse symoniaca. Sicut enim quilibet fidelis racionis capax debet cognoscere peccata mortalia ut evitet ipsa, sic quilibet racionis capax et specialiter secularis dominus debet cognoscere symoniam ... Quinto modo et sexto symonia comittitur, quando homo habens a deo oportunitatem et noticiam datam mutescit non reprehendens taliter viciosos. Et in isto casu sunt maior pars fratrum vel omnes et speculativi cuiuscunque status, etatis vel sexus fuerint, qui propter timorem servilem vel comodum temporale tacent in causa dei atque ecclesie.[42]

[(A)nyone who consents to simoniacal heresy must be regarded as a simoniac. For a person consents in six ways and in compound ways that result from these six, as I have explained in much detail elsewhere, relying on the opinions of saints and church law; furthermore, they are contained in these verses:

The person who acts, defends, gives counsel and authorizes,
the one who does not resist and does not reprehend, all give consent.

The person who cooperates with a simoniac either as an intermediary or by directly doing business with him is a simoniac by consent, just as the person is who defends simony in a scholastic or public dispute; thirdly, the one who gives counsel to simoniacal corruption, and fourthly, the powerful man who authorizes his own people or their actions which he should recognize as simoniacal. For just as any Christian with the use of reason should recognize mortal sins in order to avoid them, so anyone with the use of reason, particularly a secular lord, should recognize simony. . . . In a fifth and sixth way simony is committed when a person has the opportunity and knowledge given by God, but keeps quiet and does not reprehend such vicious people. And in this category are the major part of or all the friars, and thinking people of every state, age, or sex who are silent in God's and the church's cause because of servile fear or for their own material advantage.][43]

Here we see consent theory applied to a specific case, demonstrating specifically what actions might constitute consent to simony in daily life. Associated with each of the consent verbs familiar from Wyclif's verse are activities carefully differentiated and associated with particular social roles. Businessmen cooperate; scholars defend; ecclesiastical administrators give counsel; powerful men authorize. Any Christian with the use of reason should recognize simony; any thinking person who keeps quiet when they see it commits simony along with its perpetrators. Yet this anatomy of participation in sin is also a practical guide to reform, if the participants were to recognize and then refuse their participation.

The rather different emphases in *De novis ordinibus* may help us to see what impels the metaphysical impulses behind Sermon 48, for this work similarly strives to convince those who might think that they are not participants in sin that they are in fact implicated by their consent. *De novis ordinibus*, I noted earlier, has the consent verse copied into its lower margin in one Bohemian copy. At its beginning and end a polemical tract against the friars, it includes a long theoretical digression on consent to sin and soteriology in the middle, from which this quotation comes:

[P]redestinati in via communiter, licet insensibiliter, consenciunt criminibus aliorum, ut alii cooperando cum illis, alii defendendo et alii consulendo. Et sicut hoc fit communiter in sacerdotibus sive religiosis, sic quartus consensus, qui fit auctorizando, est communiter in dominis secularibus et prelatis. Quintus autem consensus et sextus sunt faciles et communes, ut quidam consenciunt differendo adiutorium quod debent intendere. Et sic consenciunt homines peccatis presentibus proximorum quantumcunque distantes fuerint, dum differunt spiritualiter adiuvare. Et sic iusto dei iudicio puniuntur tam presciti quam predestinati, qui videntur esse iusti et omnino immunes a crimine perpetrato, et tamen propter desidiam sui spiritualis adiutorii peccant cum principaliter peccantibus plus vel minus. Sexto vero et ultimo consenciunt qui differunt reprehendere sicut debent, sicut Eli consensit criminibus puerorum, et ita ex fide capimus, quod non est possibile quod aliqui temporaliter vel eternaliter pro aliorum criminibus puniantur nisi propocionaliter consenserunt[.][44]

[(T)he predestined in life all together, although without sensing it, consent to the crimes of others, some by cooperating with them, others by defending them, others by counselling them. And just as these come about commonly among priests or religious, so the fourth kind of consent, which happens through authorizing, is common among secular lords and prelates. The fifth kind of consent and the sixth are easy and common to all, as when some consent by deferring the help that they ought to offer. In this way men consent to the present sins of their neighbors, however far off, while they put off helping them spiritually. And thus by the just judgment of God are punished both the foreknown and the predestined who seem to be just and in every way innocent of the crime that has been perpetrated, and nonetheless because of their apathy in spiritual help, they sin with the principal sinners, more or less. Sixth and last, they consent who put off blaming as they should, as Eli consented to the crimes of [his] boys. Thus, from faith we understand that it is not possible that anyone should be temporally or eternally punished for the crimes of others unless they have consented in proportion to that punishment.]

Recall that the predestined (although only God knows who they are) are those who will attain salvation; the foreknown are those who will be damned. Yet even the predestined who seem in every way innocent are participants in the sin they fail to prevent through their apathy toward spiritual help. However, *De novis ordinibus* is seemingly much more sympathetic and reassuring than *De officio regis* or Sermon 48 about the sin of consent in which we all consequently find ourselves. While the predestined as well as the foreknown are punished for their consent to the sin of others, a sin nobody can entirely avoid, nonetheless the predestined are punished only temporally, as for example by plagues and their consequent decimation of the population (331). Only the foreknown are punished eternally for the sins of others; the predestined receive what Wyclif presents as an equivalent punishment, but it does not last forever.

Like *De simonia*, *De novis ordinibus* divides up the kinds of consent according to the three estates: priests and religious cooperate, defend, and counsel; lords and prelates authorize; common people and of course others too refuse help and fail to reprehend. These and other associations between kinds of consent and social position are common in Wyclif's writings, although they do not always associate the same kinds of consent with the same social groups. What is consistent across his writings, though, as in both these examples, is that he is characteristically most interested in commenting at length on the final three modes of consent (authorizing, withdrawing help, and not reprehending), rather than the first three (cooperating, defending and counselling). Let us now turn to consider what he does with these remaining three kinds in his extended discussion of consent in Sermon 48.

Wyclif continues, in Sermon 48, to develop his exposition through similitudes illustrating the distribution of parts within wholes, through analogies between corporate and individual action, and through assertions of universal corporate personhood—all of them seeming a bit elephantine in proportion to the discussion as a whole. In his discussion of the final three kinds of consent, however, it becomes clearer what this is all for: he aims to make untenable one particular kind of objection to his theory. He articulates this objection in his exposition of the fifth kind of consent, withdrawing help:

> Stulte locuntur quidam insciii quod non faciunt nec consenciunt talibus malis sed preservant se in persona sua nec admittunt subditorum regimina. (323/31–33)

> [Some ignorant people say foolishly that they do not commit, nor consent to, such evils, but look out for themselves, within their own persons; nor do they admit to their governing roles over their own subjects.]

Wyclif sets this argument up for a fall by the way he poses it, of course—he characterizes it as stupid, and makes it seem more so by assigning it to a group, each of whom speaks in the plural for his individual insistence on looking out for himself and refusing the responsibilities of community. He has chosen the right moment, too, for raising this objection: of all the kinds of consent, refusing help to those in peril most obviously infringes upon the demands of ordinary Christian charity, as Wyclif has in fact just pointed out.[45] Wyclif has also set this argument up as stupid in advance, by dismissing it while treating the fourth kind of consent, authorizing:

> [L]icet omni peccatori conveniat, principaliter tamen convenit perversis magnatibus et prelatis cum robore et defensione eorum fiunt multe iniurie. Nec capit excusacionem quod non faciunt illas in persona sua propria, cum principali consensu ipsas efficiant et consencientes ac agentes (ut patet ad Rom. I) sunt pariter puniendi. Quam ergo excusacionem habebit prepositus qui capit regimen de subiectis et vendicat retribucionem

de bonis que fecerint, et tamen de malis que in defectu sui regiminis perpetraverint non sperat participium? Talis indubie racionis adversarius blasphemat in Deum. Sic enim animus presciti dampnabitur ex peccato cuiuscunque sensibilis partis quod in defectu sui regiminis perpetraverit hic in via. (323/5–19)

[Although it pertains to every sinner, it is especially associated with perverse magnates and prelates, for many injuries come about with their defense and support. Nor can any defend himself that they do not do these things in their own proper person, for theirs was the principal consent that brought them about, and consenters and doers, as is clear in Romans 1, are to be punished equally. What excuse will he have then, a superior who exerts control over his subjects and seeks retribution for the good things they have done/made, and nonetheless does not expect to be a participant in the evils they have perpetrated because of his misrule? Such an adversary of reason no doubt blasphemes against God. In just the same way, the soul of a foreknown person will be damned by the sin perpetrated by of any of his sensible parts in this life because of his misrule.]

Rulers who think they are not responsible for the actions of their subjects, even while they have authorized or at the very least failed to properly govern them, are as foolish as foreknown individuals who will not take responsibility for the actions of their own bodies. Similarly, ignorant fools who refuse to acknowledge any mutual responsibilities between themselves and others are wrong to think they have no responsibility for governance even if they refuse to look beyond their individual human persons.

Here, then, Wyclif condenses the analogies between corporate and individual claims that are common in consent theory, and the specific practical conclusions that follow from them, in an especially useful way. He may even rescue his readers from despair at his previous evocations of the huge hill of sin, the yoked chariot, the bad counsel their own sins unwittingly perform, their failure to govern their own impulses or to help others as unstintingly as they should, through his concluding exposition of the sixth kind of consent, consent through remaining silent. However, he may also unravel the participatory relationships between parts and wholes that he has worked so hard to establish, where parts are distributed through wholes and shared among all rather than easily separated:

Sextum genus consensus est quando quicunque prelatus vel alius videns quod clamore vel reprehensione posset detegere vel destruere peccati maliciam et tacet vecorditer. Et licet prelatis et regibus peccatum istud ut priora conveniant, tamen nimis realiter convenit cuilibet peccatori. Quilibet enim debet se ipsum reprehendere secundum illam partem qua sic peccat, et per consequens consentit peccato, correccionem dissimulans. Et sic si fidelis servus Domini ex integro non consenciens dyabolo foveat partem suam, non multiplicarentur in ecclesia tot hereses, sed pars dyaboli habet maiores et plures pro parte sua contra Dominum procurantes. (324/3–14)

[The sixth kind of consent occurs when any prelate or other person sees they could deter or destroy sin through clamor and blame, but foolishly remains silent. Although this sin pertains especially to prelates and kings, nevertheless really it pertains to each sinner. For anybody ought to blame himself, in that part in which he sins in this way, and consequently consents to the sin, dissembling correction. And thus if the faithful servant of the Lord, not consenting to the devil as a whole, would sustain his own part, so many heresies would not be multiplied in the church. But the part belonging to the devil has greater and many agents for its part, against the Lord.]

Here, Wyclif seems instead to assert an easier partitive understanding where each of us, in something very like the individualistic account he has just rejected, is responsible only for his or her own part (of a larger whole) or parts (within himself). But what size are these parts, and what do they consist of? "Secundam illam partem," "partem suam," "pars dyaboli," and "pro parte sua": are these parts of a person? Parts the same size as a person who is part of a larger whole? The larger whole itself? Or a part of that whole? It is not clear. Wyclif may think he is being consistent here, but at the very least he has mightily confused the issue he seems to have been trying to elucidate.

What Wyclif presents here is a difficult lesson, even if in his sermons he claims, and perhaps attempts, to make it more accessible to a wider audience.[46] Perhaps it is not at all an accident that although the *Floretum* incorporates the whole of this exposition into its entry on consent, nevertheless the *Floretum* version does not include the more troubling analogies to individual consent and talk of parts and wholes that I have focused on here.

The *Rosarium*, a redacted, much shorter version of the *Floretum*, goes further: it centers its exposition around Wyclif's six kinds of consent, leaving only a tiny stub of the discussion of individual consent based on Wyclif's use of Augustine's commentary on the Sermon on the Mount in *De Mandatis* that had also appeared in the *Floretum*. But it grounds each of the six kinds of consent in a biblical quotation rather than in Wyclif's exposition, cutting out all of the material also found in Sermon 48. While these widely circulated versions of Wyclif's teaching on consent may have been easier for their intended audiences in England and Bohemia to accept, they still demonstrate the wider spread of the theory through Bohemia as well as England. They also suggest that in moving between audiences and genres, some of the more radical implications of Wyclif's particular spin on consent theory may have been especially prone to modification.

Here there is only room for a sketch of where and how Wyclif's theory of consent travelled in the late fourteenth and fifteenth centuries. Even a sketch is worth providing, if it may foster the collaboration between fields of study that the present volume aims to promote. I have written, and will write more, about how Wyclif's views on consent were received among English writers ranging from the compilers of the *Floretum* and *Rosarium* to the authors of *The Fyve Wyttes* and *Book to a Mother* to *Mum and the Sothsegger*.[47] Edwin Craun, too, has addressed the implications of consent theory through his work on Wyclif's and Wycliffite justifications of sharp speech, contrasting them with previous, less extreme theories of fraternal correction.[48] Hostile responses in England and beyond deserve attention too: one fertile ground for exploring them is the lists of condemned propositions drawn from Wyclif's and Hus's writings presented at the Council of Constance. These drew out the more radical implications of Wyclif's theory and its development by Hus—even as the debate over how to justify deposing the rival popes generated writings that drew deep upon the very same theories of political representation and culpability.

Perhaps most in need of further study, though, and least familiar to most scholars of medieval western Europe, is how Wyclif's consent theory was received in Bohemia. Czech scholars are certainly aware that Hussite writings frequently discuss consent, but as in English scholarship on Wyclif, the topic has not been a focus of interest. The development of consent theory in Bohemia was far from slavish. It is worth emphasizing again that social consent was not a new topic, and it was by no means unfamiliar to any European with academic training, especially if they had spent much time with moral theology, canon law, or political exegesis. I think we have some compelling evidence, though, that readers of Wyclif's writings in Bohemia found his particular take on consent theory highly engaging. Shaped by their own discussions and the particular political pressures they faced, Bohemians developed Wyclif's spin on consent into a central tenet of their own reform movement and its defense and justification.

That the Wycliffite *Floretum* and *Rosarium* were widely copied and distributed is one kind of evidence for Bohemian interest in Wyclif's take on consent; that the alphabetical indexes to Wyclif's works in Bohemian manuscripts often include an entry for consent is another.[49] More informative and revealing, however, is the plethora of marginalia about consent in the Bohemian copies of Wyclif's works. I have found forty-eight separate annotations about consent in manuscripts of Wyclif's writings. Of those, thirty-seven appear in twelve Bohemian manuscripts, while other Bohemian manuscripts have none.[50] Negative evidence in this form is difficult to interpret: a manuscript with clean margins may variously be a byproduct of design, ownership, or use, rather than simple disinterest. Positive evidence, on the other hand, gives us a great deal of information, especially since most of the annotations are far more closely engaged with the text than the simple numbering or labelling of points in the margin common everywhere in manuscript culture (and here too) or else the sort of post-Reformation political marginalia common in English manuscripts.[51] Most of these manuscripts can be more or less securely dated to between 1400 and 1420, and most of the annotations are either by the scribe, or in a similar rather than a later hand. Four manuscripts copy in the consent verse at the end of shorter works that make use of it. Others do not merely repeat or summarize the text, but engage with it, noticing for example that each person is obliged to help his neighbor; that a person acting sinfully consents to all the sin of the world; that there are two ways something is done, either in the strict sense of doing it oneself or through participation; that someone who stays silent betrays truth; that someone is punished for another's sin.[52] None revives the differential evaluation of guilt by consent that assigned lesser culpability than direct action to some kinds of consent, in the versions of the consent verse that we examined first. But some do weigh one or another kind of consent even heavier than direct action: defense of error is worse than error; counsel toward sin is graver than the sin itself; those who do not prevent sin, sin equally or more than those who commit it.[53] What these marginal comments demonstrate is deeply engaged interest among a group of people who were very probably in conversation with one another as well as with Wyclif's writings on consent.

Another compelling piece of evidence for the reception of Wyclif in Bohemia is, of course, Jan Hus's treatise on simony, which engages closely with Wyclif's *De simonia* but also extends and adapts it. In chapter 9 in particular, Hus gives a lengthy exposition of how persons should beware of participating in simony through their consent:

> From this discourse a spiritually discerning person may perceive that he who himself commits simony and defends others committing simony along with him is a heretic above heretics and a prince of heretics. Next to him are his underlings, who in turn defend him; and of such there are very many. For a better recognition of this type, let me cite an example: Suppose that a king owns a town which he himself had built; and when he had lost it, he won it back from his enemies at the risk of his own life. If then someone should, without the king's consent, turn over that city to another for money, he who bought it would be guilty equally with the intermediary who arranged the sale; likewise the scribes of both the seller and the buyer; also the messengers of both parties and the hostages; also the negotiators; equally guilty would be the person who did not oppose it when he could, and he who would defend one or both although he could reprove them; likewise he who would counsel one or both of them, or who would loan money for the transaction; he also who would submit voluntarily, along with the town crier who would not oppose it, and anyone else who would voluntarily aid in the surrender of the town against the king's will. Similarly in simony, as when a bishop desires to be and is installed in a simoniacal manner in a town. . . . Those who alienate the city from the king receive very severe punishment; but they care not about Christ's city when thieves and robbers scale it in order to plunder not only the goods but the souls as well![54]

Everyone who has consented to simony committed by another person sins, and is an accomplice. Such consent takes six forms: abetting, defense, counsel, approval, neglect of duty, and failure in correction. In this passage Hus develops at length an analogy with secular governance that lays out in detail (I might even say, far more compelling and useful detail about everyday life than any of Wyclif's attempts) all the roles and institutions of daily life that might place a person in the position of consenting to any such transaction.

Jan Jesenic, too, seems to have been keenly interested in Wyclif's take on consent, as we learn from his 1409 determination on the question of whether a judge, who decides in favor of a party he knows has presented false testimony, sins more gravely than the false witness.[55] Jesenic says that the judge does indeed sin more gravely, for he consents to the sin of lying and also sins himself by giving false judgment. Wyclif too had set himself against the ruling that a judge must not let his personal knowledge about the falsity of testimony influence his judgment, but much more briefly, in *De mandatis*.[56] What might not be apparent to anyone but a canon law specialist or a lawyer, however, is that in making this affirmative judgment, Jesenic, like Wyclif, is deploying consent theory in opposition to what had been perceived as an even more fundamental principle of legal ethics: that judges may not allow their personal knowledge of the veracity of witnesses to affect their decisions on evidence presented in court, for otherwise they would act as witnesses themselves, rather than as judges.[57] This is an issue of considerable importance, indeed, for papal judges delegate, whose duties and powers were the topic of the title in the Decretals where consent theory first becomes an intensive focus of commentary. Jesenic was the most talented legal thinker among the first generation of Hussites, and a key player in the establishment of their movement: he was at least as knowledgeable about canon law as Wyclif, probably more. Wyclif may have provided the spark here, but Jesenic develops the point in his own terms, in response to the power struggle between Czech and German scholars at the University of Prague.[58]

Finally, the Four Articles of Prague of 1420 include under the fourth article a discussion of consent, and citation of the key passage on "pari poena" from Romans 1:32. One version containing an expansive interpretation of the fourth article asserts:

Quod omnia peccata mortalia et specialiter publica alieque deordinaciones legi dei contrarie in quolibet statu rite et racionabiliter per eos, ad quos spectat, prohibeantur et destruantur. Que qui agunt, digni sunt morte, non solum qui ea faciunt, sed qui consenciunt facientibus.[59] (Rom. 1:32)

[That all mortal sins and especially public ones and other disorders contrary to the law of God, in whatever estate, rightly and reasonably should be prohibited and destroyed by those who look upon them. Those who engage in any such sins are worthy of death, and not only those doing them, but those who consent to those doing them.]

The Four Articles were a common statement of core belief between the various strands of Bohemian reform, and went through many recensions.[60] In 1433, a later version was the basis of the defense of their religious practice presented by the Bohemians at the Council of Basel.[61] Nicholas of Pelhřimov and Ulrich of Znojmo, assigned to speak second and third in defending the Four Articles, not only dispute the justice of Hus's condemnation at Constance; they also quote and discuss the *Sermo de pace* that Hus had not been permitted to deliver, in which Hus contrasted the false peace of conformity through consent to the sins of others with the true peace of war on sin.[62]

There is much more to be learned about the Bohemian reception of Wyclif's particular take on consent theory. But we can already see how much the results will have to tell us about Europe after Wyclif, as well as Wyclif after Europe. I want to conclude, though, by returning to two of John Van Engen's observations about institutional and religious change in fifteenth-century Europe that my research on consent seems to bear out. First, his observation about the importance of locales in the fifteenth century. Academics become less mobile, he suggests, in part because there are more universities. But perhaps at the same time texts, especially very short texts, become *more* mobile.[63] They move very fast from one locale where they have a set of local meanings, to another, where that context may be lost, and their significance and impact may develop in very different ways. Second, let me recall Van Engen's comment about fifteenth-century tensions between the community of the parish on the one hand, and on the other, forms of elective or imagined religious community within and between parishes and other forms of locale. I think that it is very clear in Wyclif's Sermon 48 in particular that one reason why consent theory rose to new prominence in the early fifteenth century is that it gave people a way to address, if not resolve, these tensions. Consent theory was a potent tool for them in thinking about wholes and parts of various sizes, the relationships between them, and the parts they might play in them.

APPENDIX 1: CONSENT IN WYCLIF'S PRINTED WORKS

Works marked ST are from Wyclif's *Summa theologica*; works marked PW are late polemical writings.

Lengthy systematic discussion of the kinds of consent:

De officio regis[64] (ST) WT 33
Sermones 1: 48 WT B2.I

Shorter discussions of consent that develop the theory significantly:

De officio pastorali[65] WT 53 B1
De simonia[66] (ST) WT 35
Sermones 1: 42 WT B2.I
De novis ordinibus (PW) WT F8
De oracione et ecclesie purgatione[67] (PW) WT A21
De septem donis spiritus sancti[68] (PW) WT A25

Citation of the six kinds or mention of one or another to develop another point:

Sermones 1: 11 WT B2.I, 3: 8 WT B2.III, 3: 55 WT B2.III, 4: 43 WT B2.IV
Speculum secularium dominorum[69] (PW) WT E5
De religionibus vanis monachorum[70] (PW) WT F20
De fundatione sectarum[71] (PW) WT F17
Purgatorium sectae Christi[72] (PW) WT F14
De perfectione statuum[73] (PW)
De ordinatione fratrum[74] (PW)
De civili dominio[75] (ST)
De mandatis[76] (ST)
De blasphemia[77] (ST) (several times)
De apostasia[78] (ST)
De ecclesia[79] (ST)
De officio regis[80] (ST)
Trialogus[81]

APPENDIX 2: MARGINALIA ABOUT CONSENT IN WYCLIF'S EXTANT OEUVRE

Shelf Mark	Title of Annotated Work	Transcription of Annotation or Buddensieg's Transcription (B)	Folio	Origin and Date	Printed Edition	Noted in edition	Online	WT #
Vienna, ONB MS 1337	De novis ordinibus	Consensus multiplex		Boh. ca. 1410	Pol. Wks. 1:323–336	330n43	no	422
Vienna, ONB MS 1337	De novis ordinibus	Punitur quis pro peccato alterius		Boh. ca. 1410	Pol. Wks. 1:323–336	330n58	no	422
Vienna, ONB MS 1337	De oracione et ecclesie purgacione	Consenciens non excusatur	70v	Boh. ca. 1410	Pol WksPol. Wks. 1:343–354	349n8	no	46
Vienna, ONB MS 3928	Sermones 4	Versus de consensu		Boh. ca. 1410	Sermones 4:355–360	359n17	no	277
Vienna, ONB MS 3929	De religionibus vanis monachorum	Deo gracias, Nota 6 species consensus: Consentit cooperans, defendens, consilium dans / Ac autorizans, non iuvans nec reprehendens	208v	Boh. ca. 1409	Pol. Wks. 2:435–440	440n48	no	434
Vienna, ONB MS 3930	De religionibus vanis monachorum	Discussed in text fol. 166c		Boh. 1412	Pol. Wks. 2:435–440		no	434
Vienna, ONB MS 3934	Sermones 1	De genera consensus. Declarat subtiliter sex genera consensus (and in another hand) Operans viciose consentit omni peccata mundi.		Boh. XV/1	Sermones 1:317–324	321n14	no	102

Vienna, ONB MS 3934	Sermones 1	Cooperans		Boh. XV/1	Sermones 1:317–324	321n18	no	102
Vienna, ONB MS 3934	Sermones 1	Quare dampnati sese odiunt		Boh. XV/1	Sermones 1:317–324	321n25	no	102
Vienna, ONB MS 3934	Sermones 1	Nota bene		Boh. XV/1	Sermones 1:317–324	321n28	no	102
Vienna, ONB MS 3934	Sermones 1	Defendens		Boh. XV/1	Sermones 1:317–324	321n32	no	102
Vienna, ONB MS 3934	Sermones 1	Nota		Boh. XV/1	Sermones 1:317–324	322n3	no	102
Vienna, ONB MS 3934	Sermones 1	Dupliciter intelligitur aliquid fieri vel proprie et per se vel participative		Boh. XV/1	Sermones 1:317–324	322n12	no	102
Vienna, ONB MS 3934	Sermones 1	Desperacio peccatorum		Boh. XV/1	Sermones 1:317–324	322n18	no	102
Vienna, ONB MS 3934	Sermones 1	Consilium ad peccandum		Boh. XV/1	Sermones 1:317–324	322n26	no	102
Vienna, ONB MS 3934	Sermones 1	De reali dicencia. Ans.		Boh. XV/1	Sermones 1:317–324	322n29	no	102
Vienna, ONB MS 3934	Sermones 1	Auctoritas		Boh. XV/1	Sermones 1:317–324	323n5	no	102
Vienna, ONB MS 3934	Sermones 1	Quilibet obligatur adiuvare proximum		Boh. XV/1	Sermones 1:317–324	323n27	no	102
Vienna, ONB MS 4515	De religionibus vanis monachorum	Nota VI species consensus: Consentit cooperans defendens consilium dans / Ac autorisans non rimans nec reprehendens	84v	Boh. ca. 1420	Pol. Wks. 2:435–440	440n48	no	434

(continued)

Shelf Mark	Title of Annotated Work	Transcription of Annotation or Buddensieg's Transcription (B)	Folio	Origin and Date	Printed Edition	Noted in edition	Online	WT #
Vienna, ONB MS 4527	De religionibus vanis monachorum	Discussed in text fol. 145v		Boh. 1410	Pol. Wks. 2:435–440		no	434
Vienna, ONB MS 4529	Sermones 1	Consensus sex genera		Boh. ca. 1420	Sermones 1:317–324	321n14	no	102
Prague, NK MS III.G.11	De novis ordinibus	Discussed in text fol. 58r near btm		Boh. XV/1	Pol. Wks. 1:323–336		yes	422
Prague, NK MS III.G.11	De novis ordinibus	Crimini consenciunt, qui adiutorium differunt	58v	Boh. XV/1	Pol. Wks. 1:323–336	330n47	yes	422
Prague, NK MS III.G.11	Speculum secularium dominorum	Domini consenciunt dotacioni sacerdotum	65v	Boh. XV/1	Op. Min. 74–91	82n9	yes	409
Prague, NK MS III.G.11	Speculum secularium dominorum	Dotacionem consencientes excidunt a caritate cleri	66r	Boh. XV/1	Op. Min. 74–91	83n10	yes	409
Prague, NK MS V.F.9	De novis ordinibus	Consensus	124r	Boh. 1408	Pol. Wks. 1:323–336		yes	422
Prague, NK MS V.F.9	De novis ordinibus	Reprehendere	124v	Boh. 1408	Pol. Wks. 1:323–336		yes	422

Manuscript	Work	Incipit	Folio	Date	Edition			Page
Prague, NK MS X.C.23	De religionibus vanis monachorum	Nota sex sunt species consensus: Consentit cooperans defendens consilium dans / Aut autorisans non iuuans nec reprehendens	195r	Boh. 1410	Pol. Wks. 2:435–440		yes	434
Prague, NK MS X.D.11	De officio regis	Tacens veritatis est proditor	154v	Boh. ca. 1410	De Off. Reg. 79			33
Prague, NK MS X.D.11	De officio regis	consensuum sunt modos 5	155v	Boh. ca. 1410	De Off. Reg. 83			33
Prague, NK MS X.D.11	De officio regis	Nota tres consensus regis	156r	Boh. ca. 1410	De Off. Reg. 83			33
Prague, NK MS X.D.11	De officio regis	consilii peccatum est gravius quam facte	157r	Boh. ca. 1410	De Off. Reg. 87			33
Prague, NK MS X.D.11	De officio regis	defensio erroris est peior errore	157r	Boh. ca. 1410	De Off. Reg. 87			33
Prague, NK MS X.D.11	De officio regis	nota intelligitur quod non impedientes peccatam peccant equaliter cum commitentibus aut grauius	157v	Boh. ca. 1410	De Off. Reg. 89			
Prague, NK MS XI.E.3	De novis ordinibus (redacted?)	Nota sex sunt species consensus: Consentit cooperans defendens consilium dans / Ac autorisans non iuuans non reprehendens	13v btm	Boh. 1416	Pol. Wks. 1:323–336	336n99	yes	422

(continued)

Shelf Mark	Title of Annotated Work	Transcription of Annotation or Buddensieg's Transcription (B)	Folio	Origin and Date	Printed Edition	Noted in edition	Online	WT #
Manchester, John Rylands Library English MS 86	Purgatorium sectae Christi	None, but mentioned in text fol. 52r		Eng. XV/1	Pol. Wks. 1:298–316	309	yes	428
Cambridge, TCC B.16.2	Sermones	Nota sex genera consensus. Versus.	177d	Eng. ca. 1400	Sermones 1:317–324	321n14	no	102
Cambridge, TCC B.16.2	Sermones	2	177d	Eng. ca. 1400	Sermones 1:317–324	321n32	no	102
Cambridge, TCC B.16.2	Sermones	Aliquid fieri potest accipitur dupliciter	177d	Eng. ca. 1400	Sermones 1:317–324	322n12	no	102
Cambridge, TCC B.16.2	Sermones	Tercium	177d	Eng. ca. 1400	Sermones 1:317–324	321n26	no	102
Cambridge, TCC B.16.2	Sermones	4	177d	Eng. ca. 1400	Sermones 1:317–324	323n5	no	102
Cambridge, TCC B.16.2	Sermones	Contra prelatos	177d	Eng. ca. 1400	Sermones 1:317–324	323n13	no	102
Cambridge, TCC B.16.2	Sermones	5	177d	Eng. ca. 1400	Sermones 1:317–324	321n27	no	102
Cambridge, TCC B.16.2	Sermones	6	177d	Eng. ca. 1400	Sermones 1:317–324	324n3	no	102

NOTES

1. For remarks see, for example, Herbert B. Workman, *John Wyclif: A Study of the English Medieval Church* (Oxford: Clarendon Press, 1926), 1:101–102, G. R. Evans, *John Wyclif: Myth and Reality* (Downers Grove, IL: Intervarsity, 2005), 129–134. The one more detailed study of Wyclif's engagement with law is William Farr, *John Wyclif as Legal Reformer* (Leiden, Netherlands: Brill, 1974).

2. The relationships between these versions have been thoroughly described in Judith Jefferson, ed., "An Edition of the Ten Commandments Commentary in BL Harley 2398, and the Related Version in Trinity College Dublin 245, York Minster XVI.L.12 and Harvard English 738: Together with Discussion of Related Commentaries," 2 vols. (PhD diss., University of Bristol, 1995).

3. From Bodley 789, fol. 115r–v. My transcription and glosses; for a fully modernized version see J. Patrick Hornbeck II, Stephen E. Lahey, and Fiona Somerset, eds. and trans., *Wycliffite Spirituality* (New York: Paulist Press, 2013), 17.

4. On the appellation "true men" and other lollard self-descriptions, see Anne Hudson, "A Lollard Sect Vocabulary?," in *So Meny People Longages and Tonges: Philological Essays in Scots and Mediaeval English Presented to Angus McIntosh*, ed. Michael Benskin and Michael L. Samuels (Edinburgh: n.p., 1981), 15–30, repr. in Anne Hudson, *Lollards and their Books* (London: Hambledon Press, 1985), 164–180; and Matti Peikola, *Congregation of the Elect: Patterns of Self-Fashioning in English Lollard Writings* (Turku, Finland: University of Turku, 2000).

5. For a list, though scarcely an exhaustive one, see Appendix 1 at the end of this essay.

6. Prague National Library MS XI.E.3, fol. 13v. The manuscript also contains miscellaneous documents associated with Charles University in Prague and with the Council of Constance. A full description and hyperlinks to digital images of the entire manuscript can be found at www.manuscriptorium.com/apps/main/mns_direct.php?docId=set20060315_118_43.

7. My translation; all translations are my own unless otherwise noted. In transcriptions, I silently expand abbreviations and impose modern punctuation, capitalization conventions, and word division, but do not normalize spelling.

8. Note that Buddensieg does meticulously transcribe and cross-reference marginalia about consent in his John Wyclif, *Polemical Works in Latin*, ed. Rudolf Buddensieg, 2 vols. (London: Trübner, 1883); and F. D. Matthew provides an entry on the six manners of consent in his topical index to *The English Works of Wyclif: Hitherto Unprinted* (London: Trübner, 1880).

9. John Wyclif, *Tractatus de officio regis*, ed. Charles Sayle and Alfred W. Pollard (London: Trübner, 1887), 68/2–7. The title Wyclif gives for 1.29.1 abbreviates the usual full title, "De officio et potestate iudicis delegati." I silently modify punctuation in quotations from the Wyclif Society volumes as needed to elucidate sense.

10. On papal judges delegate, see most recently James A. Brundage, *The Medieval Origins of the Legal Profession: Canonists, Civilians, and Courts* (Chicago: Chicago University Press, 2008), 135–137, 154, 381–388; Charles Duggan, "Papal Judges Delegate and the Making of the 'New Law' in the Twelfth Century," in *Cultures of Power: Lordship, Status, and Process in Twelfth-Century Europe*, ed. Thomas N. Bisson (Philadelphia: University of Pennsylvania Press, 1995), 172–199.

11. X 1.29.1, quoted from *Corpus iuris canonici* Liber Primus, col. 327, in the online facsimile in the UCLA Digital Library, 164; punctuation modified. See http://digital.library.ucla.edu/canonlaw/index.html. See also Peter D. Clarke, *The Interdict in the Thirteenth Century: A Question of Collective Guilt* (Oxford: Oxford University Press, 2007), 90.

12. I quote the Vulgate, and provide the Douay-Rheims Bible translation.

13. See Rudolf Weigand, "The Development of the *Glossa ordinaria* to Gratian's *Decretum*," in *The History of Medieval Canon Law in the Classical Period, 1140–1234: From Gratian to the Decretals of Pope Gregory IX*, ed. Wilfried Hartmann and Kenneth Pennington (Washington, DC: Catholic University of America Press, 2008), 55–97.

14. For this verse, see col. 327 at http://digital.library.ucla.edu/canonlaw/librarian?ITEMPAGE=CJC2_B01&NEXT.

15. On *spectat* see, for example, Vatican Library, MS Chigi E.VIII.237.

16. See fol. 60vb, lower margin. For a description and digital facsimile of Brno, Moravian Regional Library MS 1161, see www.manuscriptorium.com/apps/main/en/index.php?request=show_record_num&param=0&mode=&client=.

17. The most recent argument on the dating and provenance of the Smithfield Decretals concludes that they were copied in Toulouse, and their images finished in England: see Alixe Bovey, "A Pictorial *Ex Libris* in the Smithfield Decretals: John Batayle, Canon of St Bartholomew's, and his Illuminated Law Book," *English Manuscript Studies, 1100–1700* 10 (2002): 60–82.

18. London, British Library MS Royal 10 E iv, fol. 59ra. For a description and digital facsimile, see www.bl.uk/manuscripts/FullDisplay.aspx?ref=Royal_MS_10_e_iv.

19. On the literature of the canon law see the brief overview in R. H. Helmholz, *The Spirit of Classical Canon Law* (Athens: University of Georgia Press, 2010), 1–32. For a more extensive treatment see, Wilfried Hartmann and Kenneth Pennington, eds., *The History of Medieval Canon Law in the Classical Period, 1140–1234: From Gratian to the Decretals of Pope Gregory IX* (Washington, DC: Catholic University of America Press, 2008).

20. In what follows I draw upon the description of the manuscript published on the British Library website: to access it, search for the shelf mark at http://searcharchives.bl.uk/primo_library/libweb/action/search.do?vid=IAMS_VU2.

21. Scholars do not agree on the stages or some aspects of the process by which the *Decretum* was revised; they do agree that the text as we have it was

multiply revised and that many of the accretions were the byproduct of its use in teaching at Bologna. For introductory remarks, see Helmholz, *Spirit of Canon Law*, 1–32; for more detailed discussions, see, for example, Anders Winroth, *The Making of Gratian's Decretum* (Cambridge: Cambridge University Press, 2000) and Hartmann and Pennington, *History of Canon Law*.

22. Although it is not the central theme of his exposition, Baldwin exhaustively demonstrates the importance of consent in the social thought of Peter the Chanter and his circle as expressed in their exegetical and penitential writings: see John W. Baldwin, *Masters, Princes, and Merchants: The Social Views of Peter the Chanter and His Circle*, 2 vols. (Princeton, NJ: Princeton University Press, 1970). Brian Tierney places these thinkers in a wider scope in his marvelous *Religion, Law, and the Growth of Constitutional Thought, 1150–1650* (Cambridge: Cambridge University Press, 1983). Philippe Buc focuses on biblical exegesis, but considers as well how later writers developed ideas about correction of the prince by the people in other genres: see especially chap. 6 of *L'Ambiguïté du Livre: Prince, Pouvoir et Peuple dans les Commentaires de la Bible au Moyen Âge* (Paris: Beauchesne, 1994), 312–398. Peter D. Clarke's work on consent and collective guilt has greatly advanced my own owing to the breadth and depth of his archival knowledge and understanding of the workings of papal government: see especially Clarke, *Interdict*.

23. Baldwin, *Masters, Princes, and Merchants*, suggests that Innocent III had been influenced by Peter the Chanter and his circle (see esp. 1:342–343); Peter D. Clarke develops the suggestion in "Peter the Chanter, Innocent III and Theological Views on Collective Guilt and Punishment," *Journal of Ecclesiastical History* 52, no. 1 (2001): 1–20. As his argument reveals, however, what is truly startling is the number of learned thinkers who passed through or taught in Paris or Bologna and who deployed consent theory in a wide array of genres, beginning with its widespread use in legal and theological commentaries in the late twelfth century. The line of influence between Peter the Chanter and Innocent III need not have been direct.

24. Buc is speaking specifically about the correction of superiors by inferiors: see *L'Ambiguïté du Livre*, 395–398.

25. Takashi Shogimen too addresses thinking on fraternal correction, demonstrating that Ockham's position is strikingly innovative: "From Disobedience to Toleration: William of Ockham and the Medieval Discourse on Fraternal Correction," *Journal of Ecclesiastical History* 52 (2001): 599–622. For the online edition of Ockham's *Dialogus* by John Kilcullen, George Knysh, Volker Leppin, John Scott, and Jan Ballweg, see www.britac.ac.uk/pubs/dialogus /ockdial.html. On fraternal correction more broadly, see Edwin D. Craun, *Ethics and Power in Medieval English Reformist Writing* (Cambridge: Cambridge University Press, 2010); see also Daniel Wakelin, *Scribal Correction and Literary Craft: English Manuscripts 1375–1510* (Cambridge: Cambridge University Press, 2014), 19.

26. This was the *Liber Sextus* compiled under Boniface VIII and completed in 1298: see VI.5.12.43, and Clarke, *Interdict*, 38n82.

27. Wyclif, *De officio regis*, 89/6–16.

28. On tacit authorization and defense see Wyclif, *De officio regis*, 83/28–30, 88/20–28. Unusually too, Wyclif allows (perhaps because of the social prominence of these offenders) that for any of the types of consent, they may sometimes sin not equally, but more gravely, than those doing the deed: "in quolibet istorum quinque generum contingit consencientes peccare gravius quam ipsos principaliter delinquentes." 83/21–23.

29. Augustine, *De sermone Domini in monte*, book 1, chap. 12, in *Patrologia Latina*, ed. Jacques P. Migne, vol. 34, cols. 1246.34–1247.35. For Wyclif's treatment see John Wyclif, *Tractatus de mandatis Divinis*, ed. Johann Loserth and F. D. Matthew (London: Kegan Paul, 1922), esp. 447–454; John Wyclif, *Opus evangelicum*, ed. Johann Loserth (London: Trübner, 1895–96), 1:149–152.

30. Giles Constable succinctly surveys medieval corporate metaphors and previous studies of them, see "Medieval Latin Metaphors," *Viator* 38, no. 2 (2007): 7–8.

31. For the *Clerk's Tale* see Geoffrey Chaucer, *The Canterbury Tales*, ed. Jill Mann (London and New York: Penguin Classics, 2005). Particularly useful on its ethical difficulty are Linda Georgianna, "The *Clerk's Tale* and the Grammar of Assent," *Speculum* 70, no. 4 (1995): 793–821, and Michaela Paasche Grudin, "Chaucer's *Clerk's Tale* as Political Paradox," *Studies in the Age of Chaucer* 11 (1989): 63–92.

32. John Wyclif, *Sermones*, ed. Johann Loserth (London: Trübner, 1887–1890), 1:317–324. Parenthetical references to this sermon will be given in the text. For Langton's letter see *Acta Stephani Langton Cantuariensis Archiepiscopi A.D. 1207–1228*, ed. Kathleen Major (Oxford: Oxford University Press, 1950), 2–7; John W. Baldwin, "Master Stephen Langton, Future Archbishop of Canterbury: The Paris Schools and Magna Carta," *English Historical Review* 123, no. 503 (2008): 824–825; and Clarke, *Interdict*, 170–71.

33. This list is derived from biblical and topical indexes of these and other works and from editorial annotations, as well as from searches on digitized texts; there may well be yet more references to be discovered. Each work is followed by a WT number: these refer to the numbers assigned them in Williell R. Thomson, *The Latin Writings of John Wyclyf: An Annotated Catalog* (Toronto: Pontifical Institute of Mediaeval Studies, 1983). Works not provided with full bibliographical details in Appendix 1 are cited earlier in this essay.

34. Anne Hudson, "The Development of Wyclif's *Summa theologie*," in *John Wyclif: Logica, politica, teologia*, ed. Mariateresa Fumagalli Beonio Brocchieri and Stefano Simonetta (Florence: SISMEL—Edizioni del Galluzzo, 2003), 57–70, repr. in Anne Hudson, *Studies in the Transmission of Wyclif's Writings* (Aldershot, England: Ashgate, 2008), V.

35. Anne Hudson, "Wyclif's Latin Sermons: Questions of Form, Date and

Audience," *Archives d'Histoire Doctrinale et Littéraire du Moyen Âge* 68 (2001): 223–248, repr. with additional appendix from "Aspects of the 'Publication' of Wyclif's Latin Sermons," in *Late-Medieval Religious Texts and their Transmission: Essays in Honour of A. I. Doyle,* ed. A. J. Minnis (Woodbridge, England: Brewer, 1994), 124–126, and in Hudson, *Studies in the Transmission,* VI.

36. On cross-referencing see Anne Hudson, "Cross-Referencing in Wyclif's Latin Works," in *The Medieval Church: Universities, Heresy, and the Religious Life: Essays in Honour of Gordon Leff,* ed. Peter Biller and Barrie Dobson (Woodbridge, England: Boydell and Brewer, 1999), 193–215, repr. in Hudson, *Studies in the Transmission,* IV, esp. 207. On dating Wyclif's works, see also Thomson, *Latin Writings.*

37. On the *Floretum* and its redacted version the *Rosarium* and their dissemination in England and Bohemia see Anne Hudson, "A Lollard Compilation and the Dissemination of Wycliffite Thought," *Journal of Theological Studies* n.s. 23 (1972): 65–81 (repr. in Hudson, *Lollards and their Books,* 13–29); and "A Lollard Compilation in England and Bohemia," *Journal of Theological Studies* n.s. 25 (1974): 129–140 (repr. in Hudson, *Lollards and their Books,* 30–42). See also Christina von Nolcken, "Notes on Lollard Citation of John Wyclif's Writings," *Journal of Theological Studies* n.s. 39, no. 2 (1988): 411–437. There is no critical edition of either work. For the *Floretum* I have consulted and collated Brno, University Library MS Mk 35, and Prague, University Library MS VIII.B.5; for the *Rosarium,* Prague, University Library MS IV.G.19.

38. On components in Wyclif's sermons that circulated as separate tracts as well, or may originally have done so, see Hudson, "Wyclif's Latin Sermons," 13–15.

39. Stephen E. Lahey, *Philosophy and Politics in the Thought of John Wyclif* (Cambridge: Cambridge University Press, 2003).

40. Such analyses are found everywhere in Baldwin, *Masters, Princes, and Merchants.*

41. I thank Stephen Lahey for a helpful discussion of this point.

42. John Wyclif, *Tractatus de simonia,* ed. Herzberg-Fränkel and Michael H. Dziewicki (London: Trübner, 1898), 98/14–99/3.

43. I quote the published translation: John Wyclif, *On Simony,* trans. Terrence A. McVeigh (New York: Fordham University Press, 1992), 149/7–150/8.

44. *De novis ordinibus,* in *Polemical Works,* ed. Rudolf Buddensieg, 1:323–336, on 330/3–19.

45. Here is how Wyclif introduces the fifth kind of consent: "Quintum genus consensus consistit in negacione iuvaminis, dum subtrahens iuvamen teneatur ex mandato Dei ad subsidium apponere vires suas. Et sic quilibet committens vel omittens culpabiliter consentit omnibus malis mundi . . . Unicuique enim mandavit Deus de proximo ut mutuo se iuvarent [The fifth kind of consent consists in denying help, while the one withdrawing help is obligated by the commandment of God to apply his powers to aid. And anyone committing or

omitting in this way culpably consents to all the evils in the world. . . . For God commands each person with respect to his neighbour that they should help one another]" (323/27–35).

46. As Hudson notes, the preface to the first set of sermons extant in some manuscripts describes them as "sermones rudes ad populum," yet their content, as well as their language is not particularly suitable to uneducated laymen; it seems most likely that the primary audience was clerics in need of materials that might be suitably redacted for lay instruction. Hudson, "Wyclif's Latin Sermons," 5, 16–17.

47. Fiona Somerset, *Feeling Like Saints: Lollard Writings after Wyclif* (Ithaca, NY: Cornell University Press, 2014), esp. 36–39.

48. Craun, *Ethics and Power*, 101–119.

49. Twelve Bohemian copies of the *Floretum* and twenty-six of the *Rosarium* are extant. On topical and biblical indexes to Wyclif's works, as well as lists of his works and chapter-by-chapter summaries, see Anne Hudson, "*Accessus ad auctorem*: The Case of John Wyclif," *Viator* 30 (1999): 323–344, repr. in Hudson, *Studies in the Transmission*, VII.

50. A spreadsheet of these results appears in Appendix 2. In some cases, as noted, I rely upon editors who have noted marginal annotations.

51. For samples of this kind of annotation see the apparatus to the "Dialogue between a Clerk and a Knight" in Fiona Somerset, *Four Wycliffite Dialogues*, EETS o.s. 333 (Oxford: Oxford University Press, 2009), 54–67, and Helen L. Spencer, "The Fortunes of a Lollard Sermon-Cycle in the Later Fifteenth Century," *Mediaeval Studies* 48 (1986): 352–396.

52. "Quilibet obligatur adiuvare proximum"; "Operans viciose consentit omni peccata mundi"; "Dupliciter intelligitur aliquid fieri vel proprie et per se vel participative"; "tacens veritatis est proditor"; "punitur quis pro peccato alterius."

53. "defensio erroris est peior errore"; "consilii peccatum est gravius quam facte"; "non impedientes peccatam peccant equaliter cum commitentibus aut grauius."

54. Jan Hus, *On Simony*, in *Advocates of Reform, from Wyclif to Erasmus*, ed. and trans. Matthew Spinka (Philadelphia: Westminster Press, 1953), 196–278.

55. For an extended paraphrase of Jesenic's argument see Howard Kaminsky, *A History of the Hussite Revolution* (Berkeley: University of California Press, 1967), 63–66. As Kaminsky explains on 63n23, the question is edited and its legal implications discussed by Jiří Kejř, "Husitská kritika soudobé theorie soudních důkazů," in *Dvě studie o husitském právnictví* (Prague: ČSAV, 1954), 19–52, text on 53–65.

56. Wyclif, *De mandatis Divinis*, 342/27–343/20.

57. Brundage, *Medieval Origins*, 381–383, citing Knut W. Nörr, *Zur Stellung Des Richters im Gelehrten Prozess Der Frühzeit : Iudex secundum allegata non secundum conscientiam iudicat* (Munich: Beck, 1967). Kejř, "Husitská kritika," 21, also notes the contrast with classical canon law.

58. For Jesenic's later determination on a related question about corrupt judges, and his conclusion that the recent banishment of the German masters from the university was rightful, see Kaminsky, *Hussite Revolution*, 69–70.

59. This version of the Four Articles of Prague, from late July 1420, is printed in František M. Bartoš, *Manifesty města Prahy z doby husitské. Les manifestes de la ville de Prague de l'époque des guerres hussites* (Prague: Nákl. Obce hlavního města Prahy, 1932), 284. Kaminsky, *Hussite Revolution*, 373n32, compares it closely with an early July version used by the papal legate.

60. On the versions see Mathilde Uhlirz, *Die Genesis der vier Prager Artikel* (Vienna: Hölder, 1914), František M. Bartoš, *Do čtyř pražských artikulů : Z myšlenkových a ústavních zápasů let 1415–1420* (Prague: Nákladem Blaho-slavovy společnosti, 1925), Bartoš, *Manifesty*.

61. For the version presented at Basel, formulated in a manifesto of July 21, 1431, see *Monumenta conciliorum generalium seculi decimi quinti*, ed. František Palacký et al. (Vienna and Basel: Typis C.R. Officinae typographicae aulae et status, 1857–1935), 1:147. For comparison of the wording of the fourth article as formulated in 1420, in summer 1433, and as negotiated in November 1433, see Uhlirz, *Genesis*, 21n1. For detailed overviews of the debates between the Bohemians and their opponents at Basel see E. F. Jacob, "The Bohemians at the Council of Basel, 1433," in *Prague Essays*, ed. Robert W. Seton-Watson (Oxford: Clarendon Press, 1949), 81–123; Paul de Vooght, "La Confrontation des Thèses Hussites et Romaines au Concile de Bâle," *Recherches de Théologie Ancienne et Médiévale* 37 (1970): 97–137, 254–291. See also Gerald Christianson, "Church, Bible, and Reform in the Hussite Debates at the Council of Basel, 1433," in *Reassessing Reform: A Historical Investigation into Church Renewal*, ed. Christopher M. Bellitto and David Zachariah Flanagin (Washington, DC: Catholic University of America Press, 2012), 124–148.

62. For Nicholas's and Ulrich's speeches see František M. Bartoš, *Orationes: Quibus Nicolaus de Pelhřimov, Taboritarum Episcopus, et Ulricus de Znojmo, Orphanorum Sacerdos, Articulos de peccatis publicis puniendis et libertate verbi Dei in Concilio Basiliensi Anno 1433 ineunte defenderunt* (Tabor: Soc. Jihočeská Spol., 1935). Nicholas defends Hus, Jerome of Prague, and Wyclif on 24–25 and quotes Hus's sermon on 49; Ulrich defends Hus on 97 and 133–134, and blames the lack of true peace in the church on corrupt priests on 98.

63. See for example, Daniel Hobbins, "The Schoolman as Public Intellectual: Jean Gerson and the Late Medieval Tract," *American Historical Review* 108, no. 5 (2003): 1308–1337.

64. *Tractatus de Officio Regis*, ed. Charles Sayle and Alfred W. Pollard, Wyclif Society, (London: Trübner, 1887). As explained in the main text, WT numbers refer to the numbers assigned each work in Williel R. Thomson, *Latin Writings of John Wyclyf*.

65. *Tractatus de Officio Pastorali*, ed. G. V. Lechler, (Leipzig: A. Edelmannum, 1863).

66. *Tractatus de Simonia*, ed. Michael H. Dziewicki, and Sigmund Herzberg-Fränkel, Wyclif Society (London: Trübner, 1898).

67. *Polemical Works*, 1:337–54.

68. Ibid., 1:208–30.

69. *Opera minora*, ed. J. Loserth, Wyclif Society (London: Kegan Paul, 1913), 74–91.

70. *Polemical Works*, 2:435–40.

71. Ibid., 1:3–80.

72. Ibid., 1:293–316

73. Ibid., 2:443–82.

74. Ibid., 1:83–106.

75. John Wyclif, *De Civili Dominio*, 4 vols., ed. Johann Loserth, Wyclif Society (London: Trübner, 1885–1904).

76. John Wyclif, *Tractatus de Mandatis Divinis*, ed. Johann Loserth, Wyclif Society (London: Kegan Paul, 1922).

77. John Wyclif, *Tractatus de Blasphemia*, ed. M. H. Dziewicki, Wyclif Society (London: Trübner, 1893).

78. John Wyclif, *Tractatus de Apostasia*, ed. M. H. Dziewicki, Wyclif Society (London: Trübner, 1889).

79. John Wyclif, *Tractatus de Ecclesia*, ed. Johann Loserth, Wyclif Society (London: Trübner, 1886).

80. John Wyclif, *Tractatus de Officio Regis*, ed. Alfred W. Pollard, Wyclif Society (London: Trübner, 1887).

81. John Wyclif, *Trialogus*, ed. G. Lechler (Oxford: Clarendon Press, 1869).

CHAPTER SEVEN

INTERPRETING THE INTENTION OF CHRIST: ROMAN RESPONSES TO BOHEMIAN UTRAQUISM FROM CONSTANCE TO BASEL

Ian Christopher Levy

O n 15 June 1415, in the thirteenth session of the Council of Constance, the assembled fathers formally ratified the custom of offering communion to the laity solely under the species of the bread to the exclusion of the wine. The council fathers freely admitted that Christ had administered the Eucharist to his apostles under both species, and that it was received by the faithful under both species in the early church. Nevertheless, custom had developed such that only those confecting the sacrament would receive the chalice. The decree states: "And because this custom was introduced for good reasons by the church and holy fathers, and has been observed for a very long time, it should be held as a law which nobody may repudiate or alter at will without the church's permission. To say that the observance of this custom or law is sacrilegious or illicit must be regarded as erroneous. Those who stubbornly assert the opposite of the aforesaid are to be confined as heretics."[1]

Because Utraquism—lay reception of the Eucharist under the species of both bread and wine—possessed ancient and orthodox credentials, the practice itself could not be reckoned heretical. Heresy is a theological matter and the council was not primarily concerned with rendering a theological determination. The decree does assert that Christ's body and blood are present beneath both species—a point on which all sides agreed—but makes no further attempt to clarify questions of sacramental presence or efficacy. Consequently, the condemnation was not directed at those who would deny some foundational principle of Eucharistic doctrine (cf. the Wycliffite condemnations of 4 May 1415). Instead, what evoked the threat of prosecution was any assertion that the custom ratified by the council was itself sacrilegious. For to claim that chalice withdrawal is an impious custom that perforce cannot be lawfully sanctioned amounts to declaring the council's decision invalid and thus nonbinding. And that, in turn, is to call the authority of the council itself into question.

It was only about a year before the Constance decree that the Prague master Jakoubek of Stříbro had begun publicly advocating for lay chalice reception.[2] Focusing on Christ's words and actions at the Last Supper, Jakoubek insisted that the exact form of this event had direct, perduring, and universal application. When Christ offered the bread to his disciples he specifically told them to eat, just as the chalice was offered for the express purpose of drinking. The Lord instituted the sacrament in exactly this way for the greater good of the faithful, with the result that those who only receive bread are not drinking Christ's blood in a sacramental manner. Although Jakoubek did not question the doctrine of concomitance, whereby Christ's body and blood are wholly present under both species, he still insisted that this metaphysical fact does not erase the essential sacramental value of the chalice. No text made this clearer than Christ's admonition in the Gospel of John 6:53, "Unless you eat the flesh of the Son of Man and drink his blood, you have no life in you." Christ has promised his body as food only to those who came to the species of the bread, and his blood as drink solely to those who received the chalice. That the whole living Christ is present under the species of the bread does not mean that his blood is consequently present there in a sacramental manner. The chalice is not a superfluous addendum, therefore, but is necessary for receiving the full salvific benefit of the Eucharist.[3]

As important as these points of sacramental theology were to the Utraquists, the weight of their argument finally rested upon a historical foundation: Christ had personally instituted this Eucharistic practice and then, through the primitive church, had commanded (*praecepit*) what was to be done in future generations. It is because lay reception under both kinds constitutes a direct precept of Christ designed to unite the faithful with their Lord that it cannot be abrogated by subsequent custom.[4] It was this assertion that drew the chalice debate into larger questions of law, and thus authority, which had deep roots in the medieval tradition.

The language of precept (*praeceptio/praeceptum*) traditionally bore the sense of an injunction or command, a writ, or an imperial rescript.[5] The jurisprudential dimensions of the chalice debate must not be overlooked. The Constance decree had been precisely worded along the lines of canon law texts. In their discussions of rights and obligations, the medieval canonists not only examined duties relative to positive law but also those falling under the category of custom. The canonists pointedly acknowledged that longstanding and widely accepted custom (*consuetudo*) could be taken as law (*lex*). Custom might even attain force against a previous written law if that custom could be shown to be both reasonable (*rationabilis*) and as having gained force through the passage of time (*praescripta*). There were limits, however—limits which were directly applicable to the Utraquist debate: No custom, no matter how old, could stand if it derogated from either natural or divine law—the transgression of which induces sin, since both originate with God.[6]

The Constance decree seems to have been designed, therefore, to meet the aforementioned criteria outlined by canon law: this custom (*consuetudo*) has been introduced for good reasons (*rationabiliter introducta*), has been observed for a very long time (*diutissime observta*), and thus should be regarded as law (*pro lege*). The great question to be resolved, however, was whether the council had actually exceeded its authority by attempting to derogate from divine law. In its attempt to elevate custom to a principle of law was it overturning a direct precept of Jesus Christ?

So it was that the controversy over lay chalice reception that ensued brought to the fore once again, here at the outset of the fifteenth century, the perennial search for the locus of authority. Yet this is not the well-worn tale wherein the authority of Holy Scripture is set against that of Holy Mother Church. For in the main, the Roman anti-Utraquists either tacitly acknowledged the principal authority of Holy Scripture or made a point of professing it, so that they could move the debate beyond this noncontested ground. The fundamental issue was development of doctrine; not whether doctrine develops, however, but the means to determine legitimate development. The Utraquists were not primarily attempting to prove that the early church had communicated the laity under both species; everyone already knew that. Rather, they contended that lay chalice reception remained an integral part of the sacrament that could not be lawfully altered. It was this claim that forced the Romanists to provide warrant for chalice withdrawal based upon the analysis of a set of mutually recognized authoritative texts: Holy Scripture, the church fathers, and canon law. The stage was set for a battle over access to, and ultimately control over, a shared tradition.

When the tradition is shared, and the authoritative sources are embraced by both sides, the debate is soon narrowed to questions of methodological competence. Who possesses the hermeneutical skills requisite for the discovery, and subsequent application, of the intended meanings that rest within these sacred texts? Who, moreover, can rightfully claim to be guided by the Spirit which speaks throughout, and by means of, the tradition? In light of such questions it is not surprising to find that the Romanists consistently attempted, in one form or another, to delegitimize the Utraquists, casting them as unworthy participants in this exegetical quest. The Utraquists have not simply reached incorrect conclusions; they are incapable of grasping the truth. Having removed themselves from the society of the faithful, they can only misread key biblical and legal texts. In the case of Jakoubek of Stříbro the process of delegitimization was deeply personal. He could not be taken seriously as a proper master; lacking the appropriate academic degree, he based his authority on purported mystical visions. This is not to say that the Roman theologians employed such tactics to the exclusion of substantive arguments. Indeed, there was a strong case to be made against the Utraquists which takes into consideration not only important texts from the tradition, but also the very nature of tradition itself as organic and evolving. As we shall see, however, Roman attempts to fit central texts into this tradition, to demonstrate seamless conformity, could result in over-readings as texts were pressed to address a specific set of concerns that had only recently emerged. Indeed, it was the inherent ambiguity of so many authoritative texts relied upon by both sides that rendered the debate all but intractable.

ANDREW OF BROD

The Prague master Andrew of Brod was among the earliest and most persistent opponents of the Utraquists.[7] For Andrew, the chalice question was most clearly framed in terms of obedience, which is the glue that holds Christendom together. As salvation depends upon obeying God in all things, by extension we must obey the prelates that God has constituted, not only in good and licit matters but even in those that are deformed and evil, since disobedience is the root of all discord. Jakoubek and his fellow Utraquists were thereby cast as destroyers of Christian peace and thus agents of the devil. By administering the cup to the laity they revealed themselves as heretics and seducers who extinguish the charity of God in the hearts of the faithful and sow hatred in its place.[8]

Basic protocol was breached, moreover, as university masters, such as Jakoubek of Stříbro and Nicholas of Dresden, have taken the stuff of lecture hall disputation into the streets. A small cadre of renegade schoolmen has deceived the uncultured and the unlettered (*rudes et simplices*) into believing that under one species they receive only part of Christ. Offering the chalice to the laity was not merely a doctrinal error; it amounted to a destabilization of the social order. For Jakoubek was illicitly extending to the laity rules applicable to the confecting priest, thereby confusing the two estates. Yet these laymen, along with undereducated clerics, cannot be expected to grasp the subtle metaphysics at work in the Eucharist. Such simple people ought not to occupy themselves with questions of accidents without subjects. They should just believe devoutly and sincerely. Jakoubek was instead filling their heads with lofty ideas that they could scarcely understand and only creating scandal in the process.[9]

The lower clergy, it seems, were now taking it upon themselves to decide matters of sacramental practice. Andrew lamented that there were certain unlearned priests (*presbyteri vere ydiotae*) who in their "undisciplined zeal" (Romans 10:2) hold the rites and observances of the church in contempt. Believing that they are conforming themselves to the practices of the primitive church, these low-level clerics follow their own understanding rather than the sayings of the holy fathers. Andrew induced a series of texts from Augustine and Jerome to Bernard of Clairvaux, all to the effect that the general populace must be obedient to their ecclesiastical superiors in all matters that are not contrary to the sacred scriptures—which withdrawal of the chalice is not. Simple priests, therefore, have no such authority to confect the Eucharist outside the parameters of the divine office.[10]

Much to Andrew's dismay, questions regarding precept and custom were no longer confined to the magisterial class, but were filtering down to the populace. And so Andrew feared that some unsophisticated layman (*simplex laicus*) would speak up and demand the chalice on the grounds that many maintain that it is necessary for salvation, since it is grounded in a precept of Christ (*ex precepto Christi*).[11] Yet, according to Andrew, reception of the lay chalice is not actually a divine precept and therefore falls within the hierarchy's competence to regulate. More to the point, Andrew contended that ecclesiastical authority itself bears divine sanction. Despite Utraquist claims to the contrary, this custom is no mere human precept (*preceptum hominis*). It is the practice of God's beloved holy church, such that whatever she does has received his approval.[12] In other words, far from being contrary to divine law, chalice withdrawal has been sanctioned by it.

Andrew thereupon laid out his theory of doctrinal development: Although God is the supreme lawgiver who does not change, he has given laws to suit the needs of the times; first to man in the state of nature, then under the Mosaic law, and finally in the state of grace. All the while, though, there remains one immutable faith expressed through different sets of laws. God has, moreover, ceded to the church the right to change ceremonies and traditions over the ages.[13] Thus even as the Lord of the church remains constant, his bride is free to alter some traditions for good reason.[14] The church—which for Andrew meant the hierarchically constituted church—operates under the guidance of her Lord; nothing she does can ever be "merely human." Her decisions, therefore, amount to divine precepts.

PETER PULKA

Peter Pulka, a master at the University of Vienna, was asked to review the debate between Jakoubek and Andrew, and then present his conclusions to the theology faculty at the Council of Constance for their final deliberation.[15] In the document that he produced, Peter was determined to refute "that false preacher master Jacobellus," charged with leading astray certain simple people and unlearned priests. In an effort to discredit Jakoubek as a reliable theological disputant, Peter seized upon—and indeed misunderstood—Jakoubek's reference to a "revelation" (revelatio) that had led him to take up the cause of Utraquism. Although Jakoubek had been describing the understanding that he attained through careful study of biblical and patristic texts (cognitio ex lege et scriptis authenticis), Peter took this as a claim to some kind of private mystical awakening. Peter henceforth portrayed Jakoubek as a false prophet whose teaching has not been informed by a spirit of wisdom and understanding, nor of knowledge and piety; rather, his so-called revelation proceeded from a spirit of folly and blindness, ignorance and impiety.[16] The point being that Jakoubek cannot be trusted to read the legal and theological sources correctly, precisely because he operates outside of the received tradition.

Hence when Jakoubek appealed to the Decretum canon Comperimus—in which Pope Gelasius had insisted upon reception of both species—his interpretation of the text was not simply revealed as erroneous, but it has also unmasked his heretical pride. For this canon, according to Peter, clearly refers to the priest confecting the Eucharist; he alone is the one who must consume both species. Citing the Ordinary Gloss on the *Decretum*, as well as Thomas Aquinas's reference to this canon as pertaining solely to the priest, Peter derided Jakoubek for claiming to understand this text better than the glossator and the saint. Charges of prideful ignorance aside, however, these texts are actually much less precise than Peter acknowledged. We should be clear that Pope Gelasius was responding specifically to reports of priests abstaining from the chalice; he made no reference to the laity one way or the other. As for the gloss, it could lend support to either side: While it affirms that Christ is entirely consumed under either species, it goes on to state that neither form of reception is superfluous, since the species of bread refers to flesh and wine to soul, thereby signifying the totality of our participation in Christ who assumed the fullness of human nature. The gloss too is silent on the question of lay reception. Thomas came closest to supporting Peter's position, but he was principally concerned with securing the completeness, and thus the validity, of the sacrament rather than addressing lay reception as such.[17] Thus, even were one to concede that Jakoubek could not effectively make his case on the basis the *Comperimus*, neither could Peter definitively refute the Utraquist position on the strength of these texts. This is quite simply because the texts were not designed to resolve the present dispute. To demand that they provide answers for questions that they had never been asked is to press them to the breaking point.

For all that, however, Peter wanted to raise the stakes beyond the typical magisterial dispute over the correct interpretation of ancient texts. It would come down to ecclesiastical authority—specifically the hierarchical church's capacity to depart from old traditions and institute new ones. That, in turn, hinged upon determining which aspects of the received tradition remain fixed and which were subject to change. Peter conceded that Christ had not given the church the power to alter anything substantial in the sacrament of the Eucharist, but he did grant her the authority to determine various uses that are accidental, that is, nonessential to that immutable substance. When it comes to the rites surrounding the use of this sacrament, the church—inasmuch as she operates under the direct inspiration of the Holy Spirit—can make certain changes both to increase devotion and avoid irreverence. Christ, therefore, reserved to the apostles and their successors a certain degree of latitude in the handling of nonessential features that do not affect the sacrament's validity or effectiveness. As such, the church can establish or prohibit such accidental rites for reasonable causes (ex causis rationalibus). Peter's emphasis upon the principal role of the Holy Spirit must not be missed: Christ promised the apostles that he would send the Spirit, who would instruct them in the truth (John 16:12).[18] Withdrawal of the chalice from the laity is ultimately a divine precept, therefore, precisely because the bishops—in their unique role as successors of the apostles—have been led to implement this practice under the guidance of the Third Person of the Trinity.

NICHOLAS OF DINKELSBÜHL

Nicholas of Dinkelsbühl was a colleague of Peter Pulka at the University of Vienna and a member of the faith commission at Constance.[19] At the outset of his address Nicholas located two central errors in Jakoubek's "Conclusions" on lay communion: that communion under both species is necessary for salvation (de necessitate salutis) and a precept of Christ (de precepto Christi); and because it is a divine precept, the rite of communicating the laity under both species is not, and never was, subject to annulment by the pope or general council nor any custom of the universal church. Nicholas had immediately homed in on the fundamental question of determinative authority. Moreover, he too recognized the social ramifications of the Utraquist challenge and therefore sought to defend the legitimacy of this established practice lest simple and less learned folk (simplices ac minus docti) be led astray. As we have seen, the prospect of unsettling the lower orders of lay and clerical society was a persistent concern of the Roman anti-Utraquists. At all events, Nicholas set himself to demonstrate that these two Utraquist errors not only ran contrary to the holy doctors, saints, and the reasonable custom of the church; they directly contradicted the recent determination of the general council gathered at Constance.[20]

Nicholas readily granted that nothing that proceeds from the truth of Holy Scripture, divine law, or a precept of Christ can be undone through a custom of the church, a statute of the pope, or that of a general council. It is telling that Nicholas frankly acknowledged the proximity of both sides on this central matter; no reason to debate this point, he said, for here we all agree. Where the Utraquists go wrong, however, is in their contention that lay communion under both kinds proceeds from gospel truth and divine law. The rite of communicating the people under both species is something that the church is within her rights to change, according to Nicholas, for the very fact that it is not a precept of Christ.[21] And because it is not a divine precept, the rules governing authoritative custom can be applied. As it stands, lay communion under one kind is "a custom that has been approved for the longest time and by all throughout the kingdom of Bohemia." Echoing the canon law texts, Nicholas concluded that this practice has therefore obtained the force of law through longstanding public acceptance which cannot now be overturned by "some private person (*privata persona*) merely on his own whim and without sufficient evidence."[22] An outrider, not aligned with the faithful community, Jakoubek's demand for the chalice—absent the support of a direct divine precept—was thus reduced to one man's ravings.

Even as he made the case for authoritative custom, Nicholas never had any intention of subordinating the authority of Holy Scripture to that of the church. The task at hand was getting at the true sense of scripture— that meaning which the Holy Spirit has intended to convey.[23] And so too, when it comes to interpreting the authoritative texts of canon law, one must look beyond the strict grammatical construction of the words (*ad rigorem verborum*) to the intention that underlies them if one is to grasp the authentic meaning of the text. The key here, though, is that the Spirit's intended meaning remains dynamic; it unfolds in its fullness all the way into the present age. Thus whatever those decrees that seem to favor lay reception of the chalice might have meant in their own time, they were never presented as unalterable divine precepts.[24] Christ granted to the church— which always operates under the guidance of the Holy Spirit—the power to make certain changes for reasonable cause in matters that are extrinsic and accidental to the sacrament.[25] Development of practice, if not doctrine, is a process directed by the Spirit—the very Spirit who is also the author of Holy Scripture.

Applying this principle of normative interpretation, Nicholas was keen to expose the alleged subjectivity, and thus basic unreliability, of Utraquist exegesis. Again, therefore, in determining the correct reading one must not explicate texts based upon "the wishes of some private man (*secundum voluntatem cuiuscumque privati hominis*)," but instead according to "the authentic expositions of the saints and of the approved glosses (*secundum*

expositiones authenticas sanctorum et approbatarum glosarum)."[26] That is
to say, one is not free to explicate authoritative biblical and legal texts as
one chooses, but must follow the received commentary tradition found, for
instance, in the Ordinary Glosses on both the Bible and the *Decretum*.
What Nicholas neglected to mention, however, was that even those authoritative sources had never been uniformly interpreted throughout the later
Middle Ages and often proved to be sources of further debate.

With regard to the central Utraquist biblical text, John 6:53, Nicholas
would distinguish between two kinds of eating and drinking: sacramental
and spiritual. The former refers to the consumption of the true body under
the species of bread and true blood under the species of wine with the intention of consuming them as such. The latter, spiritual eating and drinking, is itself two-fold: There is spiritual consumption of the first reality (*res
prima*) of this sacrament, namely the true flesh and blood of Christ, done
devoutly in recognition of the body that was offered up in the passion. In
this way the believer is incorporated into Christ through an act of love. Yet
there is another form of spiritual eating that does not involve actual consumption of the species under which the true flesh and blood abide. This
second form refers to what medieval theologians traditionally referred to
as the ultimate reality (*res ultima*), that is, the mystical union with the body
of Christ through faith and charity which unites the members to their
head. And, according to Nicholas, this is the eating to which Jesus refers
in John 6:53. Nicholas backed up this reading with citations of the Gloss
on John 6:53 and 1 Corinthians 11:27. Spiritual eating, therefore, is a mystical consumption of Christ's flesh which signifies union with the body of
Christ.[27] Hence when priests confect in the sight of the people and consume
under both kinds, the people assist them in their devotion by eating and
drinking spiritually the body and blood in sincerity of faith, through their
pious meditations and by consuming with the mouth of their heart, and
thus being united to Christ through the affection of love.[28]

JEAN GERSON

The Parisian theologian Jean Gerson produced a concise tract on lay communion in 1417 which remained free from *ad hominem* attacks and focused
principally upon the means to achieve authoritative determinations.[29]
Gerson began the work with a meditation on scriptural authority and in-

terpretation, commending Holy Scripture as the rule of faith (*regula fidei*) which, when correctly understood, cannot be contravened by any human authority or custom. In fact, Gerson admitted—as had Nicholas of Dinkelsbühl—that on this front the council fathers and the "heretics" all agree. It was not the unimpeachable authority of scripture that was at issue, therefore, but its correct interpretation. Arriving at such an interpretation of scripture requires that the exegete adhere to a rigorous methodology. By laying out such a system, Gerson hoped to show, by way of contrast, that the Utraquist hermeneutical program was hopelessly flawed. Now the first thing that one must recognize, according to Gerson, is that all the parts of scripture are interconnected and should therefore be read comprehensively. Only then can one begin to understand the intention of its divine author, the Holy Spirit. The exegete needs to compare one passage with another to weigh up the totality; he cannot isolate certain passages to make his case—the very thing that Gerson accuses the Bohemians of doing when they (supposedly) fasten upon only those portions that seem to support lay reception of the chalice. On the other hand, biblical exegesis is not simply a matter of harnessing a set of linguistic skills, as valuable as these may be. There is a subjective, even if not an individualistic, component to the exegetical process. Exposition of Holy Scripture relies upon learned men who are not merely operating by the strength of their own wits, but under the inspiration of the Holy Spirit. Thus when comparing the various expositions of the doctors, we must pay close attention to those that appear to exhibit certain spiritual gifts. It is not enough to cite any given doctor of the church in support of one's case; one has to cite the right doctors. Beyond this, one must have respect for the interpretative authority of those expositions embodied in the glosses, the canons, and the decrees—all of which will assist us in making sense of the biblical text. Indeed, Holy Scripture receives its interpretation not only in the examination of the original words, but also as its meaning comes to light in later expositions. Where, then, does this layered interpretation reach its conclusion? Authentic reception and exposition, says Gerson, is finally resolved in the authority, reception, and approbation of the universal church, especially that of the primitive church (*praesertim primitivae*), which received this interpretative acuity directly from Christ by the revelation of the Holy Spirit.[30]

The problem for Gerson was that the Bohemians had specifically appealed to this same primitive church which they regarded as the uncorrupted guardian of Christ's original intentions. This fact was not lost on Gerson as he sought to move the discussion from the patristic texts themselves to the Spirit that informed them. Who, then, will determine the genuine patristic sense which, in turn, unlocks the original meaning of scripture? For Gerson (as we shall see) that will ultimately fall to modern doctors who are themselves operating under the infallible inspiration of the Holy Spirit.

With regard to the specific question of lay communion, Gerson focused on the Bohemian claim that reception of the chalice is "necessary for salvation" (de necessitate salutis). Not unlike the Vienna theologians, Gerson argued that one must distinguish between those aspects of the sacrament that are regulated by divine law (iure divino) and those that fall under human law (iure humano). The precise form of the words of consecration fall under the former since they are essential components of the sacrament. Yet other matters such as vestments, lights, prayers, and fasting are human precepts subject to variation. The church can, for good reason, change these precepts such that what was once sinful for a man would now be meritorious. Lay reception of the chalice, according to Gerson, is one example of a practice that had never been a necessary precept of divine law (de necessitate praecepti iuris divini), but had been left up to the church to decide. But how can we know which practices fall under which rubric; which belong to immutable divine law and which to variable custom? That decision remains with the church; she is the best interpreter of laws. It is not for presumptuous factions—here the Bohemians are likened to the fifth-century Donatists—to take it upon themselves to disturb and scandalize the church. Thus they are advised to be obedient and to work for the common good (bonum commune).[31]

In keeping with his broader discussion of the evaluation of sources, Gerson addressed the authoritative status of custom. When sacred authorities speak of communion under both species having the force of a precept with respect to the laity, such texts must be restricted to the specific time and custom of the church in which they were observed. Ecclesiastical custom which has its origin from a reasonable cause—whether throughout a nation, province, or diocese—has "the obligational force of law and precept (vim habet obligativam legis et praecepti)." Hence it is unlawful to contravene such customs where they are commonly observed. At no point, however, was lay communion under both kinds mandated altogether for the entire church. Custom may have indeed been taken for law (*consuetudo pro lege habetur*), yet such precepts were always restricted to a given locale; and when the custom came to an end, so then did the obligation. One must recognize, said Gerson, that genuine authority proceeds from cause; when the cause of its truth ceases, so too does the truth and its allegation cease. Here Gerson appealed to the rules governing time-dependent propositions. Consider the following: "Christ is going to become incarnate," which was once true because the cause of its truth was some future time that had not yet arrived. But with the advent of Christ, when what was once future is now present, the cause of that truth has been removed. That original statement is now false, therefore, since it is no longer true that "Christ is going to become incarnate."[32]

Gerson concluded by emphasizing that no authoritative text or doctor can effectively present an authentic conclusion in some matter of faith or doctrine concerning the salvation of souls except to the extent that his determination is in keeping with existing ecclesiastical doctrine or has been formally approved by the church. For all the doctors rightly submit their teachings to the church's judgment, even as the Apostle Paul—notwithstanding that he had received the gospel by revelation—sought authorization in Jerusalem where the primitive church principally resided (Galatians 2:1–2).[33] For Gerson, the conciliarist, the universal church gathered at Constance can render such infallible judgments under the guidance of the Holy Spirit—just like the church gathered in Jerusalem fourteen centuries earlier. Ultimately, Gerson put his trust in a general council which he regarded as a perfect representation of the hierarchy that had been instituted by God. It is the infallible council—under the aegis of the Holy Spirit who can neither deceive nor be deceived—that will render final determinations in matters of faith.[34]

JOHN OF RAGUSA

On 20 June 1432, the Bohemians were formally granted safe conduct to attend the Council of Basel and explain the Four Articles of Prague for which they claimed the support of "divine law, the apostolic practice of Christ, and that of the primitive Church."[35] The Dominican theologian John of Ragusa (Ivan Stojković of Dubrovnik) was chosen by the council to respond specifically to the article regarding communion under both species.[36]

Despite the fact that Jakoubek of Stříbro had died in 1429, and the leader of the Bohemian cause at Basel was now Jan Rokycana, the Dominican nonetheless took aim at Jakoubek as the first to break the universal custom of the church; he was the inventor of this novelty which has spread throughout the kingdom of Bohemia. John was reviving an earlier tactic of personally discrediting Jakoubek and, by extension, the entire movement that he had engendered. John found that Jakoubek was bereft of all the essential qualities of the reliable exegete. Where was his skill, his understanding of divine matters, his personal holiness, and profound learning? Where were the miracles that attest to his sanctity of life as the saints possess? Where was his magisterial or doctoral grade (Jakoubek was only a master of arts); and where the writings to lend sufficient credibility to his claims? Jakoubek was thus maligned as an unstable and unqualified interlocutor with no rightful claims to anyone's affections. This left John to muse that while there is nothing unusual about one man lapsing into such a reprobate understanding, it remains astonishing that so many otherwise faithful people might follow after him. Jakoubek's errors now fill the university of Prague and have spread throughout the whole kingdom of Bohemia, which had once abided by the teachings of the illustrious schoolmen.[37] Again we see that Utraquist arguments, and more fundamentally the men who advanced them, were not simply discounted as erroneous, but positively perverse.

John signaled the broader direction of his argument early on when he declared that among the articles of faith none is more important than the Creed's affirmation of the Holy Catholic Church which is governed by the Holy Spirit. Indeed, all the other articles are ultimately grounded upon this ecclesial foundation. By this, John did not intend to minimize the authority of Holy Scripture in the determination of doctrine. Rather, as with Gerson, the question was not one of scriptural authority but its authoritative interpretation. John promptly admitted that we must turn immediately Holy Scripture when doubt arises regarding other articles of faith. Yet because scripture does not proceed as the natural sciences do—from rational proofs that bind the intellect—there must be further recourse to authority. For although it is the weakest proof among the human sciences, authority remains a mainstay of divine science which is founded upon divine revelation. Even as John conceded that scripture is the principal authoritative source to which we turn in matters of doubt, when it comes to its subsequent interpretation we must then turn to the church, in keeping with Augustine's maxim: "I would not have believed the gospel had not the church compelled me." Well aware of all the difficulties that arise in scriptural interpretation, most notably the variety of opinions, there needs to be some single determinative standard, namely the Holy Catholic Church under the guidance of the Holy Spirit which cannot err in matters necessary for salvation.[38]

As John proceeded to expound upon the different senses of scripture he echoed almost verbatim the teachings of his former master Jean Gerson. Suffice it to say that John equated the literal sense with the meaning of the Divine Author; when rightly understood this divinely intended sense stands as the infallible and sufficient rule of faith. The greater point, however, is that for all of its inherent authority, the authentic reception and exposition of scripture will ultimately be determined by the reception and approbation of the universal church guided by the Holy Spirit.[39]

John maintained his consistent confidence in the Holy Spirit who will teach the church all truth (John 16:12) in matters necessary for salvation. The Utraquists had no quarrel with this principle, of course, but argued that it applied to the primitive church which had received the promise of the Spirit when she most truly imitated Christ in life and doctrine. Now that the church has fallen away from Christ, and has thus receded from the Spirit, she has fallen into all manner of errors and heresies. Once again, therefore, we seem to be at an impasse as the Bohemians held up the perfect model of the *ecclesia primitiva* by which to measure the corrupt state of the present church. Hence John would have to make the case for continuity: There are not two churches, but only one, which retains all that she had received during the apostolic epoch. Such confidence was grounded in Jesus Christ himself, who had promised his indefectibility to the church until the consummation of the age (Matthew 28:20). Christ never intended that his promise would apply only to the primitive church; he was speaking of the church as she endured forever. And what was promised to his apostles was thus guaranteed to their successors. Claims to such continuity hinge upon the veracity of Christ himself. For if the church could err at any time, and had erred in fact, then Christ's promise to remain with her to the end would have been false, as would his promise of the assistance of the Holy Spirit. Furthermore, if the church could err in matters necessary for salvation, there would be no security, since there would be no assurance that any dogma was true. It is the true church that has correctly grasped the meaning of Christ as intended by both his words and deeds recorded in the Gospels. Indeed, there would be no certitude of doctrine if the church were unable to discern Christ's intended meaning. Here John recalled the Waldensians: They followed the literal sense (*sensus litteralis*) but missed its meaning because they did not possess Christ's true meaning (*sensus Christi*). Only the church grasps the genuine signification of Christ's words and thereby secures the Catholic faith; she alone is directed by the Spirit and thus cannot err (*errare non potest*).[40]

Thus while the Bohemians protested that they wish only to understand the scriptures according to the expositions of the holy doctors, John recognized that such debates over the interpretation of these authoritative sources would be interminable. Recourse must finally be had, therefore, "to the judgment of the church which stands as an infallible and divine rule (*ad iudicium ecclesiae tamquam ad infallibilem et divinam regulam*)." Christ and the church have entered into a spiritual marriage wherein he has conferred his own infallibility upon his spouse from whom he can never be separated. And under the guidance of the Holy Spirit she will never err in matters necessary for salvation.[41]

The very fact that withdrawal of the chalice has been widely accepted over some time now, and has been formally approved and declared by a general council, proves that it cannot be contrary to the divine will nor opposed to the precept of Christ. While coming very close here, John never explicitly bestowed the mantle of infallibility upon the Basel council. Nevertheless, he remained so confident in the assembled church's inspired ratification of custom that (he says) even were the Utraquists to fend off all other arguments, a faithful Catholic could still rely completely upon the principle of the universal church's indefectibility, which by itself can defeat all the other arguments.[42] John's final unwillingness to invest the Council of Basel with the sort of infallible authority that Gerson located at Constance is telling and even unsettling. For in the end John made his appeal to the very same universal church of which the Bohemians likewise regarded themselves full members.

NICHOLAS OF CUSA

Nicholas of Cusa was officially incorporated into the Council of Basel on 29 February 1432, and on 11 February 1433 he was assigned to the team that would negotiate with the Bohemians.[43] It was in this capacity that Cusanus composed *On the Use of Communion* in the second half of 1433, after the Bohemians had left Basel.[44] Cusanus began his address in the sharpest terms: "You Bohemians, however, are cut off from the rest of the church's body, rupturing its peace and unity."[45] He dismissed the Bohemians' claim that they were committed first of all to obeying the precept of Christ (*praecepto Christi*) and thereafter the church, even to the point of disobeying the church when she commands otherwise. Herein lay, according to Cusanus, "the beginning of all presumption when individuals judge their own understanding of divine commands to be more conformed to the divine will than that of the universal Church."[46]

What follows is a full-throated, if not entirely cautious, exaltation of ecclesiastical authority, which can tend toward the sort of papalism notably absent from the oration of his Basel colleague, John of Ragusa. Of greater import, perhaps, is that whereas previous respondents had emphasized the continual guidance of the Holy Spirit, the thrust of Cusanus's argument turned on the fundamental identification of Christ with his body the church. Against Bohemian appeals to the practice of earlier generations, Cusanus argued for a process of adaptation overseen by Jesus Christ himself: "The Scriptures are both adapted to the times and understood in various ways . . . as Christ dispenses mysteries according to the changing of the times."[47] Cusanus rejected out of hand, therefore, the Bohemian argument that would censure the universal rite of the church based upon the writings of earlier saints and doctors. Rather than focusing on the interpretation of sacred texts, Cusanus emphasized the living authority of the presently assembled church. He observed that the Apostles themselves transmitted the faith not only through writings, but also by the oral expression of a short creed wherein they emphasized that the communion of the Holy Church is necessary for salvation. It is the church herself who will endure forever even were all the scriptures destroyed.[48]

Cusanus was thus keen to steer the question away from scriptural authority to the teaching authority of Christ manifested in his body, the church, which is enlivened by his Spirit and thus does only what Christ himself wishes. "And so the change of interpretation depends upon the will of Christ who now wills it so by his inspiration, just as once this very precept was practiced otherwise, according to the need of the time. And, therefore, this power to bind and loose is no less in the church than in

Christ." Far from deviating from "this very precept of Christ," as the Bohemians charge, the church is fulfilling it as he commanded. And here Cusanus went so far as to say: "There are no precepts of Christ (*praecepta Christi*) other than those accepted as such by the church."[49] For Cusanus, therefore, the actions and determinations of the hierarchically constituted church on earth amount to an extrapolation of Christ's unique sovereignty and perfect will.

Although a committed conciliarist at this time (see his *De concordantia catholica* [1433–1434]), Cusanus nevertheless proceeded to locate the heart of the church's authority in the Petrine office. Forestalling Bohemian appeals to the authority of the Catholic church at large, Cusanus argued that it is the See of Peter which is the guarantor of the truth of the church. The "refuge of infallibility" is to be found in union with the prince of the church who holds the power of universal spiritual rule. Here Cusanus designated the pope as sole legitimate successor of both Peter and Paul—the implication being that he embodies the fullness not only of jurisdictional, but also doctrinal, authority. This sort of language does have the ring of extreme papalism, and thus appears to be out of step with the young Cusanus's conciliarist sympathies. It may be, however, that such statements had a wider scope: Against those whom he considered schismatics, Cusanus wished to emphasize the unique authority of the divinely constituted hierarchical church that can never fail and is thus worthy of obedience.[50]

When Cusanus returned to the Utraquist matter in 1452, his commitment to the hierarchical church's authority had only grown stronger. His *Letter to the Bohemians on Church Unity* was written during his stint as papal legate to the lands of the Holy Roman Empire.[51] Even as the Bohemians pointed to passages that would seem to promote lay reception of the chalice, Cusanus charged that they had given themselves over to a crudely literalistic reading of scripture. Such a charge would hardly be remarkable except for the fact that, as Cusanus pursued his point, he succeeded in driving a wedge between scripture and the church, thereby creating a division that the other respondents had assiduously avoided. For Cusanus contended that the Catholic church cannot be bound to the letter (*ad literam*) of Holy Scripture, but must instead follow the spirit (*ad spiritum*). Indeed, it is the church alone who can draw out the spiritual sense of the biblical text such that it does not remain a mere dead letter. Because Christ had not wished to constrain (*astringere*) future generations, he left it to the church to interpret the text at different times in different ways: interpretation that conforms with good practice constitutes the life-giving spirit.[52]

Cusanus then proceeded to make a rather astonishing remark, the larger import of which repays more sustained analysis than we can grant it here. No doubt wearied with the Bohemian situation by this time, he wrote "The Scriptures follow the church which is prior to them and for the sake of which (*propter quam*) the Scriptures exist, and not the converse."[53] It seems that, for Cusanus, the sacred scriptures could be reckoned a collection of texts that have been assembled by, and are subject to, the church which subsequently authorized them. Cusanus has thereby set aside the classic medieval conception of Holy Scripture, extolled in countless magisterial inception sermons as the eternal font of Divine Wisdom according to which all human sciences are judged. Now the authority of Holy Scripture, precisely as a constructed text (*litera*), is determined to be derivative; it remains at the disposal of the church by which, and for which, it has been compiled.

CONCLUSION

That Nicholas of Cusa was willing to speak in such stark terms of scripture's subordination to the church may be indicative of the hermeneutical impasse that had been reached—or at least the perceived impasse in the minds of the higher clergy—by the second half of the fifteenth century. Although Cusanus was not appealing to some separate extra-scriptural deposit of divine revelation, he was nevertheless attempting to forestall the authority of written texts, the debate over which seemed irresolvable. That the respective authority of church and scripture were diverging on the eve of the Reformation is almost a cliché, but we found no such divorce among the other Roman respondents to Utraquism. For Jean Gerson and his one-time student John of Ragusa, the authority of the church under the guidance of the Holy Spirit was never intended to be set over against Holy Scripture as though its judge. Rather, the church stood alongside scripture as its infallible interpreter, guided by the same spirit by which scripture itself had been authored. Yet one is still left to ask where, concretely, this infallible interpretation could manifest itself. Precisely where would the self-authenticating tradition of the church reveal the true and unfolding intention of Christ? According to Gerson, it remained for the general council, "legitimately assembled in the Holy Spirit," to render that final and infallible decree on the lay chalice. John of Ragusa stopped just short of saying the same in answer to the Bohemians at Basel. In the event, however, the council of Basel soon disintegrated, which led a disillusioned Nicholas of Cusa to turn his eyes to the unique authority of the Petrine office. History tells us, however, that even Rome failed to show the way forward. Soon again Christendom would be clamoring for a council—*Veni Sancte Spiritus.*

NOTES

1. *Decrees of the Ecumenical Councils*, ed. Norman Tanner, 2 vols. (London: Sheed and Ward, 1990), 1:419; *Enchiridion Symbolorum*, ed. Henry Denzinger and Adolf Schönmetzer 36th ed. (Rome: Herder, 1976), 1198–1200; *Sacrorum conciliorum nova et amplissima collectio*, ed. J. D. Mansi, 54 vols. (Paris, 1901–1927), 28:157–159; *Rerum concilii oecumenici constantiensis*, ed. Hermann von der Hardt, 6 vols. (Frankfurt and Leipzig, 1697–1700), 4:333–334. Note that Hardt (and thus the Tanner volume which is based upon it) provides the heading: "*Condemnatio communionis sub utraque, a Iacobo de Misa nuper inter Bohemos resuscitata*," thereby naming Jakoubek of Stříbro specifically, although no one is actually mentioned by name in the text of the decree.

2. The most recent work is that of Dušan Coufal, *Polemika o kalich mezi teologií a politikou 1414-1431: Předpoklady basilejské disputace o prvním z pražských artikulů* (Prague: Kalich, 2012), which provides an extensive bibliography of primary and secondary sources. See also: Helen Krmíčková, "Utraquism in 1414," trans. Zdeněk V. David, in *The Bohemian Reformation and Religious Practice* 4 (2002): 99–105; Thomas Fudge, *Jan Hus: Religious Reform and Social Revolution in Bohemia* (London: Tauris, 2010), 154–163; Fudge, "Hussite Infant Communion," *Lutheran Quarterly* 10 (1996): 179–194; Howard Kaminsky, *A History of the Hussite Revolution* (Berkeley: University of California, 1967), 98–140; Kaminsky et al., eds., *Master Nicholas of Dresden: The Old Color and the New* (Philadelphia: American Philosophical Society, 1965), 5–28; Fudge, "Václav the Anonymous and Jan Příbram: Textual Laments on the Fate of Religion in Bohemia (1424–1429)," *Filosofický Časopis, supplementum* 3 (2011): 115–132; William Cook, "The Eucharist in Hussite Theology," *Archiv für Reformationgeschichte* 66 (1975): 23–35.

3. *Jacobellus contra Brodam* 1.11, in Hardt, *Rerum*, 3:456–457.

4. *Jacobellus contra Brodam* 2.28, in Hardt, *Rerum*, 3:578–581.

5. Lewis and Short, eds. *Latin Dictionary* (Oxford: Clarendon Press, 2002), 1412–1413; *Revised Medieval Latin Word-List from British and Irish Sources*, ed. R. E. Latham (London: Oxford Press, 2004), 364.

6. See *Consuetudo autem*, D. 1, c. 5; *Corpus Iuris Canonici*, ed. Emil Friedberg, 2

vols. (Leipzig: 1879; repr., Graz: 1960), 1:2; and the gloss in *Corpus juris canonici emendatum et notis illustratum*. Gregorii XIII. pont. max. iussu editum. Romae: In aedibus Populi Romani, 1582, 3 parts in 4 vols.; *Decretum Gratiani*, 1:3–4; Friedberg, *Corpus Iuris Canonici*, 1:15; *Corpus juris canonici emendatum et notis illustratum, 1:31–32;* Friedberg, *Corpus Iuris Canonici*, 2:41; *Corpus juris canonici emendatum et notis illustratum, 1:96–97.* See the discussion in James Brundage, *Medieval Canon Law* (London: Longman, 1995), 157–159.

7. See Jaroslav Kadlec, *Studien und Texte zum Leben und Wirken des Prager Magisters Andreas von Brod* (Münster: Aschendorff, 1982).

8. *Tractatus contra commmunionem calicis (De obedientia)*, in Kadlec, *Studien und Texte*, 236–238.

9. *Tractatus de sumptione venerabilis pretiosque corporis ac sanguinis domini nostri Iesu Christi*, in Kadlec, *Studien und Texte*, 186.

10. *Lectura de communione laicorum sub utraque specie*, in Kadlec, *Studien und Texte*, 225–235. See the canon *Si dominus*, C. 11 q. 3 c. 93, in Friedberg, *Corpus Iuris Canonici*, 1:669.

11. *Tractatus contra commmunionem calicis*, in Kadlec, *Studien und Texte*, 247–248.

12. *Tractatus de sumptione venerabilis pretiosque corporis ac sanguinis domini nostri Iesu Christi*, in Kadlec, *Studien und Texte*, 207.

13. Ibid, 212–213.

14. Ibid., 216.

15. For a study of his life and work in addition to the edited text, see Dieter Girgensohn, *Peter von Pulkau und die Wiedereinführung des Laienkelches: Leben und Wirken eines Wiener Theologen in der Zeit des großen Schismas* (Göttingen: Vandehoeck and Ruprecht, 1964). See also Walter Brandmüller, *Das Konzil von Konstanz: 1414–1418*, 2 vols. (Paderborn: Schöningh, 1991), 1:360–370.

16. *Confutatio Iacobi de Misa*, in *Peter von Pulkau und die Wiedereinführung des Laienkelches*, 217–219. On the misunderstanding of Jakoubek's use of the term *revelatio*, see Ferdinand Seibt, "Die *revelatio* des Jacobellus von Mies über die Kelchkommunion," *Deutsches Archiv für Erforschung des Mittelalters* 22 (1966): 618–624.

17. *Confutatio Iacobi de Misa*, 245. For *Comperimus*, D. 2. De cons. c. 11, see Friedberg, *Corpus Iuris Canonici*, 1:1318; and the Gloss in *Corpus juris canonici emendatum et notis illustratum*, 1:2511–2512. See also Thomas Aquinas, *Summa theologiae* 3, q. 80, a. 12.

18. *Confutatio Iacobi de Misa*, 222–229.

19. On Nicholas's life and work see Alois Madre, *Nikolaus von Dinkelsbühl: Ein Beitrag zur Theologischen Literaturgeschichte* (Münster: Aschendorff, 1965), esp. 22–29. Nicholas's *Tractatus contra errores Hussitorum* has been edited by Rudolf Damerau, *Nikolaus von Dinkelsbühl Texte zum Problem des Laienkelchs Nikolaus von Dinkelsbühl (1360–1433)* (Gliessen: Wilhelm Schmitz, 1969), 33–111. Note that this work was attributed to Maurice of Prague in Hardt, 3:826–883.

20. *Tractatus contra errores Hussitorum*, 33–34. See also *Conclusiones Jacobelli De necessaria communicacione plebis sub utraque specie*, ed. Hardt 3:820–821.

21. *Tractatus contra errores Hussitorum*, 103–107.

22. Ibid., 110.

23. Ibid., 34.

24. Ibid., 65–66.

25. Ibid., 35–38.

26. Ibid., 39.

27. Ibid., 40–43. See also *Biblia Sacra cum Glosa Ordinaria novisque additionibus*, 6 vols. (Venice, 1603), 5:1131–1132; 6:298. Both glosses have a decidedly ecclesiological emphasis, speaking of believers abiding in Christ and the unity of the church.

28. *Tractatus contra errores Hussitorum*, 57.

29. *De necessaria communione laicorum sub utraque specie*, in *Jean Gerson: Oevres Complètes*, ed. P. Glorieux, 10 vols. (Paris: Desclée, 1960–1973), 10:55–68. On Gerson's involvement in these matters, which remained peripheral to his central concerns, see Brian Patrick McGuire, *Jean Gerson and the Last Medieval Reformation* (University Park: Penn State Press, 2005), 240–283.

30. *De necessaria communione*, ed. Glorieux, 10:55–59.

31. Ibid., 10:59–61.

32. Ibid., 10:65. Cf. Aristotle, *De interpretatione* 9 (18a–19b).

33. *De necessaria communione*, ed. Glorieux, 10:67–68.

34. *De examinatione doctrinarum*, ed. Glorieux, 9:460. See also Francis Oakley, "Gerson as Concilarist," in *A Companion to Jean Gerson*, ed. Brian Patrick McGuire (Leiden, Netherlands: Brill, 2006), 179–204; and G. H. M. Posthumus Meyjes, *Jean Gerson: Apostle of Unity* (Leiden, Netherlands: Brill, 1999), 309–311.

35. *Decrees of the Ecumenical Councils*, ed. Tanner 1:460–461. For an overview of the Basel respondents to the Four Articles, see Paul de Vooght, "La confrontation des thèses hussites et romaines au concile de Bâle," *RTAM* 37 (1970): 97–137; 254–291; and on Ragusa specifically, 97–120.

36. *De communione sub utraque specie*, in *Sacrorum conciliorum . . . collectio*, ed., Mansi 29:699–868. On Ragusa's life and career see Aloysius Krchňák, *De vita et operibus Ioannis de Ragusio* (Rome: Lateranum, 1961), 1–49; and John Kraljic, "John of Ragusa (1390/95–1443)," in M. Watanabe, T. Izbicki, G. Christianson, eds., *Nicholas of Cusa: A Companion to His Life and Times* (Aldershot, England: Ashgate, 2011), 90–92.

37. *De communione sub utraque specie*, 761–762.

38. Ibid., 713–715. Santiago Madrigal believes that Ragusa's debate with Rocykana led him to articulate the specifically ecclesial dimensions of the Eucharist—the church as *corpus mysticum Christi*—which set the stage for his great work of systematic ecclesiology, the *Tractatus de Ecclesia*. See Madrigal, "Eucaristía e Iglesia en la 'Oratio de Communione sub utraque specie' de Juan de

Ragusa," *Revista Española de Teología* 53 (1993): 145–208; 285–340. See also J. Kubalik, "Jean de Raguse: Son Importance pour L'Ecclesiologie du XV Siècle," *Revue des Sciences Religieuses* 157 (1967): 150–167; and Karl Binder, "Der 'Tractatus de Ecclesia' Johanns von Ragusa und die Verhandlungen des Konzils von Basel mit den Husiten," *Angelicum* 28 (1951): 30–54.

39. *De communione sub utraque specie*, 715–728.

40. Ibid., 780–785.

41. Ibid., 786–790.

42. Ibid., 864–868.

43. Paul Sigmund, *Nicholas of Cusa and Medieval Political Thought* (Cambridge, MA: Harvard University Press, 1963), 30–36.

44. F. M. Bartoš, "Cusanus and the Hussite Bishop M. Lupáč," *Communio Viatorum* 5 (1962): 35–46.

45. *On the Use of Communion* (*De usu communionis ad Bohemos*), in *Nicholas of Cusa: Writings on Church and Reform*, ed. and trans. Thomas Izbicki (Cambridge, MA: Harvard University Press, 2008), 4–5.

46. Ibid., 16–17.

47. Ibid., 20–21.

48. Ibid., 22–27.

49. Ibid., 28–29.

50. Ibid., 32–37. See Thomas Prügl, "The Concept of Infallibility in Nicholas of Cusa," in *The Legacy of Learned Ignorance*, ed. Peter Casarella (Washington, DC: Catholic University of America Press, 2006), 151–177. See also Thomas Izbicki, "The Church," in *Introducing Nicholas of Cusa: A Guide to a Renaissance Man*, ed. C. Bellitto, T. Izbicki, G. Christianson (New York: Paulist Press, 2004), 113–140; and Izbicki, "An Ambivalent Papalism: Peter in the Sermons of Nicholas of Cusa," in *Perspectives on Early Modern and Modern Intellectual History: Essays in Honor of Nancy S. Streuver*, ed. J. Marino and M. Schlitt (Rochester, NY: University of Rochester Press, 2001), 49–65.

51. *Letter to the Bohemians on Church Unity* (*Contra Bohemos*) in Izbicki, *Nicholas of Cusa: Writings on Church and Reform*, 356–357.

52. Ibid., 412–415.

53. Ibid., 415.

CHAPTER EIGHT

THE WANING OF THE "WYCLIFFITES":
GIVING NAMES TO HUSSITE HERESY

Pavel Soukup

One of the main chapters in the history of "Europe after Wyclif" indubitably took place in Bohemia. It is a well-known fact that Wyclif's teachings met with a much bigger reception in Bohemia than in any other country on the continent.[1] It suffices to recall the oft-quoted observation that more copies of Wyclif's works survive in collections of Bohemian manuscripts in Prague and Vienna than in libraries on the British Isles.[2] The adoption of Wyclif's thinking by Master Jan Hus and his colleagues gave a decisive momentum to a preexisting Bohemian religious movement. This in turn gave rise to a distinctive theological system and ecclesiastical structure. The Hussites proved able to survive despite their condemnation by the church and repeated calls for their extermination. While the English Wycliffites were increasingly pushed toward a clandestine existence during the fifteenth century, the Hussites in Bohemia and Moravia successfully defended their public presence and even fought off several international crusades.[3] By that time, the political and doctrinal autonomy of the Hussites was beyond doubt.

Yet, the nomenclature used to describe them was not so distinctive. Whereas the prevailing majority of modern historians use the term *Hussite* to describe the Wyclif-inspired movement in Bohemia,[4] the fifteenth-century usage was much more blurred and ambiguous. The crusade against Bohemia that was proclaimed in 1420 officially aimed to exterminate "the Wycliffites and the Hussites."[5] Nevertheless, the pope, when proclaiming the crusade, is understood to have meant one, not two groups, and this group consisted of the followers of Jan Hus in Bohemia. The formulation of the bull and of those many other documents which continued to use the term *Wycliffite* for Bohemian heretics raise some questions for historians. Did contemporaries mean to imply that the Hussite movement was thoroughly affiliated with the Wycliffites? Or was it a mere linguistic persistence, when in fact Bohemia's links to Wyclif were becoming increasingly weaker with time? This essay suggests that terminological developments in the first third of the fifteenth century reflected changing discursive as well as political circumstances. It shows how linguistic usage reacted to both church politics between the councils of Constance and Basel and the theological treatment of heresy within the framework of the anti-Hussite polemical campaign.

In the introduction to his book *Hussitica: Zur Struktur einer Revolution*, first published in 1965, Ferdinand Seibt expressed his astonishment that virtually no research into the late-medieval use of the term *Hussite* existed. "One can hardly understand why none of the numerous Hussite scholars took pains to do this," he commented.[6] However astonishing this may have been, Seibt's own four pages on the origins of the term *Hussite* remain to my knowledge the sole treatment of this subject. Seibt had his only predecessor in Johann Loserth's book on Hus and Wyclif, published in 1884. Loserth, well known as the editor of multiple volumes within the Wyclif Society's series of the *Latin Works*, first collected evidence for what Hus and his followers were called. By showing that contemporaries spoke about the Wycliffites in Bohemia, Loserth wanted to confirm his key thesis, namely that there was nothing original in Hus but paraphrases of, or direct copying from, Wyclif.[7] Seibt rejected this approach and offered his own interpretation, which rested on the evidence gained from the two volumes of letters from the Hussite wars published by František Palacký as *Urkundliche Beiträge zur Geschichte des Hussitenkrieges*. According to Seibt, the term *Hussite* first appeared during Hus's trial at Constance, and from that moment on, it dominated in theological discourse as well as in the usage of the papal curia. Its German version, *die Hussen*, was coined by the Nuremberg chancery, whereas North German towns preferred the word *ketzer* (heretics), and the imperial chancery under Sigismund of Luxemburg insisted on the term *Wycliffites*. In the Latin usage of church authorities, the label *Hussites* remained in exclusive use until it was displaced by the neutral appellation *Bohemians*, which prevailed at the time of the Council of Basel in the early 1430s.[8]

New evidence that has become available since Seibt's book makes it possible to revise his conclusions. In an attempt to do so, I shall examine what terms were used for the heretics of Bohemia in the first third of the fifteenth century. First, I shall focus on the early evidence from the Prague prosecution of Wycliffism and the Constance condemnation of Wyclif, Hus, and their followers. Then I shall trace subsequent developments and tendencies in assigning different names to Bohemian dissenters. In order to identify the agents of these developments, I will combine papal documents from the pontificate of Martin V with evidence gained from a survey of theological polemics against the Hussites.

"Can it be that Wyclif was crucified for us, or that we were baptized in his name?," asked Andrew of Brod, doctor of theology in Prague, in his letter to Jan Hus in 1414. Andrew was complaining about the religious split in Bohemia. "Look, venerable master: charity tends to unity. What should we say to this, if there are such dissensions and schisms between us, that this one is called Johannite, that one Wycliffite and the others Mohammedans, and Christ is divided?" Andrew obviously preferred to be called a Christian and nothing else. After pointing out that he was neither baptized nor could he be saved in the name of Wyclif, he added: "I thank my God that his [i.e., Wyclif's] opinions never entered my heart."[9] Still, his resentment toward naming opposing religious groups changed nothing about the fact that it was a common practice in Bohemia. Andrew's phrase "ille Johannita, iste Wiklefista, ceterique Machometiste nunccupentur" gives three interesting examples. Whereas the expression *Johannita* remains difficult to interpret,[10] the other two terms are well attested in other sources as names used by both the opponents and the adherents of Jan Hus to denote their respective adversaries.[11]

In one of his writings, Jan Hus noted that he considered the term *Wycliffite* offensive. On another occasion, he proclaimed: "I accept everything that Wyclif had right, not because it is Wyclif's truth, but because it is Christ's truth." In Constance, Hus said that Wyclif was neither his father nor was he a Czech, and added: "If Wyclif disseminated any errors, the English should see to it".[12] By that time, however, the Wycliffite affiliation of Hus's teaching was already in the spotlight. A list of forty-five Wycliffite articles was condemned at Prague University in 1403. Five years later, the term *Wycliffite* first emerged in the extant sources. The diocesan synod of June 1408 condemned "some Wycliffites [*Wiklephiste*] who hold wrong belief about the sacrament of the body and blood of our Lord Jesus Christ."[13] This statute was aimed at Hus's teacher, master Stanislav of Znojmo. The next complaint from the same year aimed directly at Hus. The Prague clergy's denunciation of Hus's preaching asserted that the Kingdom of Bohemia was considered heretical by Rome "because of some erring people and Wycliffites [*propter erroneos et Wyclefistas*]."[14] Bohemia's heretical fame indeed spread abroad. In 1410, the Viennese ecclesiastical authorities prosecuted Hus's friend Jerome of Prague, accusing him of "Wiclefiana haeresis."[15] While this early evidence from outside Bohemia shows certain morphological instability, soon the form *Wiclefista* became common in written records.[16] At approximately the same time the Czech priest John Korvík complained to the archbishop of Prague that anyone who voiced any critique of clerical behavior was arrested and "immediately called a Wycliffite and heretic [*Wikleffista et hereticus appelatur*]."[17] In 1413, Jan Hus complained in the same way about his former colleagues who became his adversaries: "Páleč calls us Wycliffites [*Wiclefistas*], as if we are deviant in the entire Christian faith; and Stanislav calls us infidels, treacherous, insane and cursed clergy."[18]

To the Council of Constance, Jan Hus's relationship to Wycliffism was clear. On 6 July 1415, the Council condemned Hus to death as "a disciple not of Christ, but rather of the heresiarch John Wyclif." In 1416, Jerome of Prague was condemned as a follower of both Wyclif and Hus.[19] The council, however, avoided any collective terms and named only the persons, books, and doctrines of Wyclif and Hus. Only after Hus's death at the stake did the council began to use the collective label the *Wycliffites*. In the summer of 1415, one letter mentions "pravitatis Wicleficae vitium," and a week later "secta haeresum Wiclefistarum" appears.[20] In the fall of 1415, the term *Hussite* is used for the first time in private correspondence from Constance. While the adherence of the leading Bohemian nobleman Čeněk of Vartemberk to the "Wycliffites" (*cum Wiclefistis*) is asserted in this report, the convention of the Catholic nobility with the archbishop is said to have been aimed "against the Hussites [*contra Hussitas*]."[21] In 1416, the anonymous accusations against the king and queen of Bohemia, which also originated at Constance, reproached them for supporting "haeresis Husitarum et Wiclefistarum."[22] Two letters of the Council of Constance from 10 June 1416 employ the whole range of terminology used so far. They mention the "damned doctrine of John Wyclif, which was blindly followed by the late Jan Hus and Jerome"; they speak of the "doctrine of the Wycliffites" and finally of "that sect of the Wycliffites and Hussites [*Wiclefistarum atque Hussitarum*]."[23]

The question arises whether the emergence of the new term *Hussite* reflected a change in perception or in assessment of the Bohemian heresy. It is possible that the council gradually came to realize that the heterodox doctrines in Bohemia could not be entirely reduced to Wycliffism. For instance, the practice of communion under both kinds (now called Utraquism), which was condemned by the same council even before Jan Hus was burned at the stake, had little to do with Wyclif's doctrine.[24] In the years and decades to follow, the Hussites developed their beliefs and practices further, thus giving the outside world a sign that their doctrine was not necessarily identical with Wycliffism. In 1429 a public debate took place in Bohemia between two Hussite masters, John Příbram and Peter Payne, to decide if Wyclif's thoughts were true or erroneous.[25] Was this emancipation from Wyclif reflected upon by the Roman Church?

We have at our disposal a coherent set of data that makes it possible to address this question. The published documents of the papal archives reveal the vocabulary used at the Roman curia in the years following the Council of Constance. From the 2256 documents edited in the seventh volume of the *Monumenta Vaticana res gestas Bohemicas illustrantia* (hereafter *MVB*) which covers the pontificate of Martin V, 201 documents mention the Bohemian heresy or heretics.[26] Put into a chart (see Figure 8-1), these data suggest that the church modified its language during the 1420s. The horizontal axis displays the years of the pontificate of Martin V; the vertical axis displays individual terms used. These are arranged from less to more specific or technical terms. The two bottom lines represent expressions where personal names are used: the first gathers evidence for the expression "heresy (error, sect etc.) of Wyclif," the second analogically the heresy "of Wyclif and Hus." Toward the top, collective names are displayed, starting with "the Wycliffites" (*Wiclefiste* and other orthographic variants, morphing as far as *Euclifiste* [*MVB* 7:946]). What follows in the chart is the twin designator of "the Wycliffites and the Hussites" (as such or with a preceding *secta, error* or similar), with the reversed form ("the Hussites and the Wycliffites") displayed above the line. The next line shows the evidence for the exclusive label "the Hussites" (*Hussite* or, much less often, *Husiste* [e.g., *MVB* 7:823, 1114, 1715]) with no appended reference to Wycliffism. The upper line represents the term *Bohemian heretics* (*heretici in Bohemia* and similar), which—as we shall see—seems to be a sort of technical term.

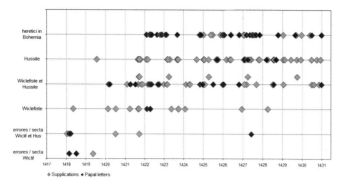

Figure 8-1. Bohemian heresy in supplications and papal letters.

In Figure 8-1, a diagonal tendency from bottom left to top right is apparent. It can be inferred that the older practice of referring to a heresy with the name of its originator was abandoned by the papal chancery as it appropriated the emerging collective names, with the term *Wycliffites* being gradually replaced by the term *Hussites*. However, before drawing conclusions concerning the agency of such development, a closer look at the nature of the sources is desirable. The evidence summarized in Figure 8-1 breaks down into two main types of document: papal letters proper, and other supplications submitted to the curia by clergy (or sometimes by lay persons) from the provinces located within the territory of the Bohemian Crown. In these supplications, clerics typically asked to be relieved from the duty of residence because their church was occupied by the Hussites, or to be able to hold multiple benefices, as one of them brings no revenue due to the heretics. If we distinguish between these two types, we see that the promoter of the change in vocabulary was not always the papal curia.

The label "secta Wyclif et Hus" was inherited from rhetoric that circulated at the time of Constance (when words like *errores*, *doctrina*, or *dogmata* were preferred to *secta*).[27] Martin V used such expressions on February 22, 1418, when he confirmed the Constance condemnations and introduced the inquisition against the Hussites (*MVB* 7:217–218). It is true that this usage was largely abandoned by the curia by 1419.[28] But the term *Wycliffites*, which gradually replaced the older expression, was not introduced by the curia but brought from the lands of the Bohemian Crown. We have seen that in Prague it was current from 1408 on. The papal chancery used it in September 1413 in an absolution of Prague Carmelites who had incurred excommunication for holding services under interdict (*MVB* 6:860). In the registers of Martin V, the word first appears in a supplication submitted by Stephen of Páleč in May 1418, and thus still in Constance (*MVB* 7:306). More supplications followed in 1420–1421, but it was only in 1422 that the papal administration itself employed the term *Wycliffites* (*MVB* 7:904 and 946). By early 1424, the term disappears even in supplications; it returns only in two documents from 1426–1428 (*MVB* 7:1688, 1939). Even before that, on 1 March 1420, the Pope used the twin expression "Wycliffites and Hussites" when he proclaimed the first crusade against Bohemia (*MVB* 7:565). This same expression was subsequently used in the context of anti-Hussite campaigns, above all on the occasion of appointing legates, giving them instructions, organizing the prosecution of heretics and fundraising.

The practice of referring to the Bohemian heretics with the single word *Hussites* was clearly brought to Rome from the province. An early piece of evidence dates to July 1419 (*MVB* 7:472). From 1421 on, documents in which this term was used were submitted to the curia in considerable numbers. The papacy, on the contrary, used it only exceptionally, such as when appointing Nicholas of Dinkelsbühl as a crusading preacher in 1427 (*MVB* 7:1715). Otherwise the evidence comes either from letters of grace granted in response to supplications,[29] or from special sources such as abjurations of heresy (*MVB* 7:1928, 1985). By contrast, the term *Bohemian heretics* was introduced by the papal curia in 1422–1423 in a number of letters, the first of which, from 13 February 1422, absolved from war crimes the participants in anti-Hussite crusades. A series of letters followed in April through May of the same year which aimed to amass resources in the Baltic for the war on Bohemian heretics (*MVB* 7:937, 949–950, 962–964). Subsequently, expressions like "heretici in regno Bohemie" were used as technical terms in all kinds of letters concerning the war against the heretics, be it crusading bulls or diplomatic correspondence with princes who were supposed to be waging such war. Perhaps a diplomatic tradition of crusading letters played a role here.[30]

Naturally, these general trends in terminology do not imply any absolutely uniform usage. In individual cases, we can even find contradictory evidence. For instance, in September 1421, the Carmelites exiled from the New Town of Prague asked for a concession to establish a house in a new place, to be relieved from chancery fees, and to be allowed to profit from indulgences (*MVB* 7:795, 797, 800). In the three supplications they submitted within nine days, they first spoke of "perfida secta Husitarum," then of "malediccionis alumni Hussite heretici," and finally of "malediccionis alumni Vicleviste heretici." When asking for a new benefice, the parish priest Matthias Kučka explained that his church was burned down by the "Hussites" and suggested he could take over another parish, the priest of which had joined the "Wycliffites." In reply to this, a letter was issued mentioning the "secta Husistarum et Wiclevistarum" (*MVB* 7:806–807). Most often, the papal chancery adopted the terms used by the petitioner when responding to a supplication.[31] This is how new terms leaked into curial usage. There is even evidence that the writers in the chancery were aware of the extraneous origin of some terms and kept a certain distance from such vocabulary. When first using the term *Wycliffite*, the curia under John XXIII noted that it was common people's language: "Wiclefiste vulgariter nuncupantur" (*MVB* 6:860). And as late as 1429, the chancery of Martin V spoke about the damages caused "per hereticos . . . Hussitas vulgariter nuncupatos" (*MVB* 7:2078). To summarize: Except for the expression *heretici in Bohemia*, all of the developments in antiheretical language (e.g., the replacement of multiword circumlocutions with one-word collective names, the employment of the neologism *Hussite*, etc.) were introduced as a reaction by the papacy to the usage preferred by the local clergy in Central Europe.

To discover a possible source for these developments, let us look at the language used in theological polemics against the Hussites. The preliminary data from a running inventory of anti-Hussite literature allow us to work with a total of some 230 treatises from the first four decades of the fifteenth century.[32] Not all treatises could have been taken into account for this study, as many of them are unpublished and their full texts remain inaccessible. Moreover, a number of works cannot be dated with sufficient precision, which makes them unsuitable for statistical processing. In some instances, it is impossible to determine if the term used in the title of the tract comes from the author of the text, or rather from a later scribe (or even a modern editor or cataloguer). In Figure 8-2, which summarizes the terminology used in polemical works, the evidence gained from headings is displayed separately in the top section of each column where applicable.[33] So far, data from 140 treatises have been collected. For statistical purposes,

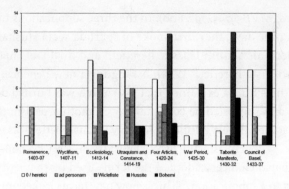

Figure 8-2. Bohemian heresy in polemical treatments.

I divide the period in question into eight time spans. The first covers the early Eucharistic polemics from 1406 to 1407, when the doctrine of remanence was the main controversial topic. In the next period, circa 1407 to 1411, other Wycliffite teachings were also debated. From 1412 to 1414, the concept of the church became the major topic in the debate. The practice of Utraquism, introduced in 1414, condemned by the Council of Constance in 1415, yet further discussed in 1417 and beyond, attracted most of the attention in the following period. In 1420, the proclamation of the Hussites' program in the form of the Four Articles of Prague opened a new chapter of the controversy. While the Hussite wars continued, the production of polemic slackened somewhat in the second half of the 1420s. Yet from 1430 to 1432, the debate was revived thanks to the Taborite manifesto, which circulated widely in Europe, and also thanks to the preparations for the Council of Basel. The disputation between the council representatives and the Hussites at Basel in 1433 and the subsequent negotiations including debates about the *Compactata* treaty of 1436 closed the first phase of the Hussite controversy.[34]

In many polemical works, no specific term for the opponent was needed. The argumentation was aimed against certain opinions that were at most described as heretical, or against a certain author who was identified by proper name or described with words like *adversarius* or *opponens*. At the early stage of the polemic, the Carthusian prior Stephen of Dolany's expressive treatises stood out for their rhetorical characterizations of opponents.[35] In one dialogic fiction, Stephen addressed Wyclif ("ausculta, Wikleff, et considera, erubesce et confundere") or Hus ("O Husska care"; "revertere,

Huska Magister"—*húska* is the diminutive of the Old Czech word *hus*, meaning "goose"). In another of his writings, Stephen called Wyclif a "superheretic."[36] The most frequent of the collective names were, unsurprisingly, Wycliffites, Hussites, and Bohemians. The term *Wycliffites* emerged around 1408, albeit in manuscript headings, which may have been added later to the texts.[37] In the same year, Master John of Rakovník warned Hus that through his advocacy of Wyclif he was losing not only his own words but also his name: "Iam propria cum iunctis perdidistis vocabula, a Wykleff suscepistis cognomen."[38] In 1411, a foreign author, Dietrich of Niem, spoke about Bohemian Wycliffites.[39] In the Prague debate of 1412–1414, the expression was already common usage, especially in the ecclesiological polemics of Stephen Páleč and Stephen of Dolany. The former explained in his *Antihus* why he called Hus and the likes of him Wycliffites: "You and your co-apostles have advocated and today advocate the pestiferous Wyclif . . . therefore you are deservedly called patrons of Wyclif and thus Wycliffites [patroni Wykleff et sic Wykleffiste appellamini]."[40]

At the same time (in 1413), Andrew of Brod—the same man who complained about assigning names, as was quoted above—used the term *Hussonitae*.[41] The form *Hussitae* had to wait for Stephen of Dolany to be used in polemical literature. In his 1414 *Dialogus volatilis*, Stephen spoke about the "Wycliffites and modern-day Hussites," presenting the Hussites as Wyclif's disciples. He also played with the signification of the name Hus and created the Latin term *aucarii*, which he used alongside the term *Wycliffites*.[42] In 1417, he used the word *Hussitae* in his polemical letters.[43] In the second half of the 1410s, the word *Wycliffites* began slowly to wane in preference for *Hussites*, although the former was still used by authors in both Bohemia and Constance. In 1420, the Hussite factions agreed on a common program of the so-called Four Articles and began to disseminate it, together with brief theological substantiation, in the form of manifestos within Bohemia and abroad. In the first reactions to the Four Articles, the term *Hussitae* prevailed, and it remained the most frequent name until the end of the period in question. Initially, it seems to have been preferred by authors outside of Bohemia, while Bohemian authors or those from neighboring lands still spoke about the "Wycliffites." In the latter part of the 1420s, the term *Wycliffites* largely disappeared from the debate. The Englishman Thomas Netter was one of only a few to apply it to Prague heretics. This was in accord with his polemical agenda: Netter insisted on the homogeneity of Wycliffite heresy, and its broad international impact confirmed how dangerous it was. At the time of the council of Basel, however, the term *Wycliffites* was almost completely out of use.

In contrast, the suspension of the hitherto thriving term *the Hussites* was sudden and had clearly political causes. It was deliberately abandoned by the representatives of the Council of Basel in order to facilitate communication with Bohemia. During the solemn disputation of the two parties at Basel, the labels "Hussites" and "heretics" were avoided and the somewhat neutral term *Bohemians* was used in their stead. Significantly, the only author of theological polemics in this period to employ the expression "haereticus Hussita" was the Camaldulensian John Jerome of Prague—himself a Bohemian, yet not a Hussite.[44] Theological opponents had been on occasion described as Bohemians since the later 1410s—in those times usually as "heretics from Bohemia." This can be understood as a term situating the particular heresy geographically, like when Gerson wrote about "haereses in Bohemia" and "apud Bohemos."[45] A little later, some authors may have used it to emphasize the fact that they visited the heretical country personally: Martin Talayero experienced the "perfidia hereticorum de Boemia" during the first crusade; Johannes of Frankfurt participated in the second crusade and refuted Hussite teachings with the exclamation "o stulte Boheme!"[46] In 1430, we see quite the opposite: authors from distant regions who grasped the pen against the Taborite manifesto perceived the general geographical designation ("Bohemians") as a sufficient identifier.[47] In 1432, during the theologians' preparations for the Basel disputation with the Hussites, political correctness brought the term *Bohemians* to the fore—in this case without the annexed "heretics." At the same time, however, some of the authors involved, prominently Heinrich Kalteisen, still stuck to the term *Hussites*. When this term was abandoned out of precaution, factual emphasis on the opposing person or idea replaced it, a practice that had almost disappeared after 1421.

In addition to the expressions just mentioned, other terms were occasionally used in polemical tracts. In the most hostile writings, we find a whole range of figurative names derived from medieval antiheretical imagery (such as disease, plague, weed, venom, beasts, foxes, fools). Besides these, some authors came up with quite original expressions. In the debate of 1412–1414, the polemicists developed the term *quidamista*, mocking the frequent unspecific references to opponents on either side as "quidam."[48] Stephen of Dolany's neologism "aucarii" has already been mentioned. Hus's name of course gave birth to a collective designator for heretics, but his was not alone: Johannes Hoffmann, writing a polemic against communion under both kinds in 1421, made a reference to the originator of Utraquism, Jacob (Jakoubek) of Stříbro, and called the Utraquists "Jacobitae." The same term appears in Johannes Nider's refutation of the Taborite manifesto; and as late as 1452, Nicholas of Cusa spoke about "iacobelliani."[49]

Some authors were even able to distinguish between the Hussite parties. The wide range of names Johannes Hoffmann used in his treatise included "Wiccleffistae," "Hussitae," "Jacobitae," and also "Pragenses." In 1430, he was able to name three Hussite factions: "alius Thaborita, alius Orphanus, alius Pragensis."[50] Thomas Netter, too, was able to name the Orphans and the Taborites in addition to Prague Wycliffites.[51] Martin Talayero noted the lack of concord between the Hussite groups already in 1421 when he said that "the Taborites hereticate the Praguers and vice versa."[52] Nider's expression "Iacobite inter Hussitas" also signals an awareness of factions within Hussitism. Heinrich Kalteisen showed similar knowledge of the Hussite question when he spoke about the "sects" in Bohemia in his *Avisamentum*.[53] Andrew of Regensburg managed to distinguish five Hussite factions in his Dialogue: "quidam vocantur Pragenses, quidam equestres, quidam Thaborite, quidam orphani, quidam populares."[54] The name *Pragenses* appears more often in the sources, yet it does not always necessarily refer to a Hussite party. In the 1415 *Estote sine offensione*, the expression "per quosdam Pragenses" indicates the geographical theater and is equivalent to phrases like "hodie in Praga quidam."[55] At the time of the first crusade, some authors of responses to the Hussite program spoke about "illos de Praga" simply because they received the articles in question from that particular city.[56]

Geoffrey of Montchoisi, abbot of Lérins in France, suggested that the Bohemian heretics should be called not only "Hussiste" but also "Julianiste" after the emperor Julian the Apostate. Geoffrey then used the apostrophe "Boeme, Julianista, Apostolice, Hussista, heretice."[57] Integration of Hussitism in the history of Christian heresies was a widespread strategy. The *Disputatio contra communionem plebis sub utraque specie* spoke about Bohemian followers of Nestorius and Pelagius.[58] The connection between Hussitism and earlier heresies was inferred by other authors as well. George of Bor, listing reasons for excommunication, included subscription to an existing, already condemned, heresy such as that of the "Arians, Nestorians, Manicheans, and Wycliffites," as well as fabricating a new heresy. He was not explicit about the question of whether Hussitism belonged to the latter category, or whether it was just a variant of the old error of Wyclif.[59] An anonymous author wrote a short treatise on heresies, preserved in a manuscript now in Wrocław. He included a chapter titled "De heresi Wiclevistarum et Hussitarum et de conparacione illius heresis ad alias." In it, he mentioned a number of historical sects comparable to the "heresis Bohemorum," yet insisted that "this pestiferous heresy took its origin from a certain Englishman, Wyclif."[60] Another manuscript now in New York's Morgan Library contains a copy of Augustine's *De haeresibus* (PL 42:21–50) supplemented with three additional chapters: on the Nestorians, the Eutychians and the Hussites. "Hussitę a quodam Bohemo Pragensis ciuitatis eiusdem prouincię presbitero nomen est, qui Iohannes Hijs dicebatur," we read. The anonymous Carthusian author gives brief information about the immolation of Hus and Jerome at Constance, as well as about the major "blasphemies" of the Hussites, and he recalls the destruction of the charterhouse near Prague.[61] The scribe, however, perceived the need to mention John Wyclif as the originator of the Hussite heresy at least in the table of contents.[62] The chronicler Andrew of Regensburg explained the origins of the Hussites as follows: "The Hussites [*Hussiste*] are named after a certain Bohemian Jan Hus. . . . This Jan Hus was an imitator of the pestilential and damned dogma of an Englishman who was called John Wyclif, which means 'wicked life' [*mala vita*]."[63]

Other authors showed a more differentiated approach. They insisted on the Hussites' Wycliffite affiliation at certain points where it appeared appropriate. The time when the terms *Hussites* and *Wycliffites* were used as equivalents (such as in Andrew Escobar's "Hussisse seu Viclevisse in Bohemia"[64]) had passed. Even if some authors argued against the Utraquism of the "Wycliffites," they were aware that the lay chalice was not an idea of Wyclif's, but an independent intellectual development of his Bohemian adherents. This is especially true of the authors who refuted the Taborite manifesto of 1430. They mostly called their adversaries simply "Hussites," not bothering themselves with distinguishing the Taborite faction. They knew about the Wycliffite origin of certain ideas. The Dominican Johannes

Nider, for example, reminded his readers that Hus was a disciple of the heresiarch Wyclif ("Wickliff heresiarcha et Husso suus discipulus"). Nevertheless, he spoke about the "Wycliffites" specifically in connection with transubstantiation.[65] Nicholas of Jawór spoke about the "school of Wyclif" when it came to the polemic against the mendicants: "in the school of that greatest heretic, the Englishman Wyclif, who was exhumed after his death and incinerated because of his heresy, they [i.e., the Hussites] learned that all religious orders were illicit."[66] Similarly, the Viennese theologians who refuted the manifesto called Wyclif a "patron" of the Hussites because he inspired their call for the dissolution of religious orders.[67] Indeed, it seems that by this time, authors who specialized in anti-Hussite polemics arrived at a more balanced view of the Bohemian heresy. They classified certain tenets as Wycliffite, such as the Eucharistic doctrine of remanence or the opposition to the mendicant orders, but at the same time they acknowledged the doctrinal discreteness of Hussitism by refraining from calling the Bohemian heretics "Wycliffites," but giving them a unique, independent name.

This survey of names given to the Bohemian heretics in the first third of the fifteenth century has rendered a dynamic picture of a relatively wide range of expressions in use. The evidence used here stems from both institutional and individual usage. Documents issued by the Council of Constance and the papal chancery are joined by a number of other sources: supplications sent to Rome, but also theological treatises. These scholarly polemical texts originated in various local contexts and cannot be seen as official statements of the Roman church. Avoiding thus the "inquisitorial" perspective of one single kind of evidence, this study aims to show how the interplay between institutional and individual linguistic choices generated a number of designators for Central European dissenters. In contrast to the variety of names applied from the outside, members of the hereticated party did not go much beyond calling themselves "the faithful" or similar. Ferdinand Seibt was right when he pointed out that the Bohemian heretics did not use a technical term that would embrace them all.[68] Would it be appropriate to say that it was the language employed by the Roman Church that made Hussitism exist? In a certain sense it would. Terminology used by the clergy involved in fighting the Hussite heresy implied exclusion and coherence—exclusion from the universal church that the Hussites never intended, and a coherence to the Hussite movement that never existed.[69] On the other hand, we need not push the constructivist argument too far. All the internal divisions and quarrels notwithstanding, the Hussites were able to show unity when needed. They defended themselves in joint military ventures against the crusaders, and they negotiated collectively on a high theological level with the Council of Basel. Therefore, it was natural that they were being given one specific collective name, even though they did not come up with one themselves.

With their common program of the Four Articles, the Hussites were even able to shape the debate with Catholic theologians. Thus, their opponents had a good reason to search for an umbrella term for all Hussite factions. Nevertheless, the church struggled somewhat to find a fitting technical name for the heretics in Bohemia. The inference that Jan Hus and his followers were mere disciples of Wyclif gave rise to the term *Wiclefistae*; both the concept and (a little later) the term were adopted by the Council of Constance. Only gradually the word "Wycliffite" was displaced by the term *Hussite*. When using both terms coupled together, the authorities did not necessarily show their uncertainty about the subject, but possibly instead a juridical caution which recommended condemning the widest range of errors possible. A certain terminological persistence also played a role, especially when the papal curia insisted on the expression "heretics of Bohemia" specifically in a crusading context.

The assumption of earlier scholarship that the church coined and almost exclusively used the term *Hussitae* proves to be wrong. The move toward the word *Hussite* was a gradual one, and was driven by local usage, as the supplications submitted to Rome show. Where was the source and driver of this linguistic development? The evidence presented here suggests that it may be found in the anti-Hussite polemics. Very early on, the terms *Hussonitae* as well as *Hussitae* emerged in polemical writings. The publication of the Four Articles in 1420 aroused a wave of polemical reactions, most of which used the term *Hussites*. This was one to two years before the same term began to dominate the supplications to Rome, which in turn influenced the official usage of the church. Shortly before the Council of Basel, the neutral term *Bohemians* appeared more often in the polemics against the Taborite manifesto as well as in the preconciliar discussion. When the Basel fathers ended the period of crusades and started negotiation, they used precisely this term (*Bohemi*) in their communication with the Hussites. The assiduous polemical activity delivered more and more information about Hussitism and thus provoked shifts and alterations in naming the Hussite heresy. We can assume that it was an achievement of inventive and diligent Hussite propaganda. By disseminating their beliefs, the Hussites eventually achieved the extrication from the term *Wycliffites* and earned their own independent label. Ironically, when this label was at the peak of its use, it was dismissed again. In 1432, the council's envoys to Bohemia wrote in a letter to Basel: "It seems expedient that the Bohemians are not called 'Hussites' in conciliar letters for they feel much ashamed by this. They should be called 'Bohemi' in order not to tease them."[70] While the introduction of the term *Hussitae* was a side effect of Hussite propaganda, the Hussites themselves were not happy about it.

APPENDIX: SOURCES FOR FIGURE 8-2

A. Remanence, 1403–1407

No name: Stanislav of Znojmo, Tractatus de corpore Cristi, in Sedlák, *Miscellanea*, 288–297.

Ad personam: John Štěkna, Sermo contra Vikleff contra remanenciam panis: "Ex hoc infero, quod Joh. Wikleff fuerit hereticus," in Sedlák, *Miscellanea*, 300–301; Johannes von Frankfurt, Propositio contra Hieronymum de Praga, in František Šmahel and Gabriel Silagi, ed., *Magistri Hieronymi de Praga Quaestiones, polemica, epistulae*, Corpus christianorum. Continuatio mediaevalis 222 (Turnhout: Brepols, 2010), 263; John Sharpe, Declaratorium super tractatum Stanislay de eukaristia: "tractatus a quodam sacre theologie professore magistro Stanislao nuper editus," in Ursula Winter, *Die Manuscripta Magdeburgica der Staatsbibliothek zu Berlin— Preußischer Kulturbesitz* (Wiesbaden: Harrassowitz, 2001), 1:149; Andrew of Brod, Epistula ad Sbinconem archiepiscopum: "libri varii, ymmo pestilentes illius quondam Wycleff Anglici," in Jaroslav Kadlec, *Studien und Texte zum Leben und Wirken des Prager Magisters Andreas von Brod* (Münster: Aschendorff, 1982), 127–128.

B. Wyclifism, 1407–1411

No name: Disputacio contra duplicem posicionem magistri Hieronymi de Praga, in Šmahel and Silagi, *Hieronymi de Praga Quaestiones*, 265–271.

Ad personam: John Stokes, Materialia ad disputationem contra Johannem Hus (heading), in Friedrich Leitschuh and Hans Fischer, *Katalog der Handschriften der Königlichen Bibliothek zu Bamberg* (Bamberg: Buchner; Wiesbaden: Harrasowitz, 1887–1966), 718; Maurice Rvačka, Opposita Hussoni: "magister reverende," in Eršil, *Magistri Iohannis Hus Polemica*, 66; Stanislav of Znojmo, Induite novum hominem: "contra Hussonem" (heading), in Pavel Spunar, *Repertorium auctorum Bohemorum provectum idearum post universitatem Pragensem conditam illustrans*, 2 vols. (Warszawa et al.: Wydawnictwo PAN, 1985–1995), vol. 1, no. 812, 298; Stanislav of Znojmo, Tractatus de Anticristo: "contra Jacobellum' (heading), in Spunar, *Repertorium*, vol. 1, no. 786, 289; Stephen of Dolany, Medulla tritici seu Antiwiclef: "audi ergo Wicleph," in Pez, *Thesaurus*, 4.2, col. 166.

Wycliffites: Tractatus de dignitate sacerdotum: "contra Hus et alios Wiclephistas" (heading), in Spunar, *Repertorium*, vol. 2, no. 400, 200; Jacques de Nouvion, Disputacio cum Hussitis: "contra Wiclefistas" (heading), in Sedlák, *Jacobi de Noviano Disputatio*, 1; Dietrich of Niem, Contra dampnatos Wiclivitas Prage: "isti Wiclivite," in Erler, "Dietrichs von Niem Schrift," 186.

C. Ecclesiology, 1412–1414

No name: Maurice Rvačka, Articuli contra impedientes, in Pavel Soukup, "Mařík Rvačka's Defense of Crusading Indulgences from 1412," in Zdeněk V. David and David R. Holeton, eds., *The Bohemian Reformation and Religious Practice* (Prague: Filosofia, 2011), 8:77–97; Stanislav of Znojmo, Sermo contra quinque articulos Wiclef, in Sedlák, *Miscellanea*, 324–334; Stanislav of Znojmo, Tractatus contra XLV articulos Joannis Wiclef: "adversarii," in Hardt, *Magnum oecumenicum Constantiense concilium*, vol. 3, col. 272; Stanislav of Znojmo, Tractatus De Romana ecclesia, in Sedlák, *Miscellanea*, 312–322; Stanislav of Znojmo, Alma et venerabilis: "sentencie Wyklef et aliorum hereticorum," in Loserth, "Beiträge 4," 366; Stanislav of Znojmo, Epistola Catherinae de Crawar: "de libris Wikleff," in Loserth, *Hus und Wiclif*, 295; Stephen of Páleč, De aequivocatione nominis ecclesia, in Sedlák, *Miscellanea*, 356–363; Stephen of Páleč, Sermo contra duos articulos Wickleff, in Sedlák, *Miscellanea*, 336–353; Stephen of Páleč, Tractatus gloriosus, in Loserth, "Beiträge 4," 335.

Ad personam: George of Bor, Consilium contra Hus: "M. J. Hus cum suis complicibus," in Palacký, *Documenta*, 502; Stephen of Dolany, Antihuss:

"responsurus eidem Magistro Huss," "ultores et deffensores Wikleff," in Pez, *Thesaurus*, 4.2, cols. 366 and 386.

Wycliffites: Defensio prelatorum contra Hus: "Ad confutandam viclefistarum maliciam," in Jaroslav Weber [=Kadlec], Josef Tříška and Pavel Spunar, *Soupis rukopisů v Třeboni a Českém Krumlově* (Prague: ČSAV, 1958), 119; Tractatus de indulgenciis: "nonnulli Wyklefiste," in Brno, Moravská zemská knihovna, MS. Mk 100, fol. 181r; Tractatus de potestate remittendi peccata contra Wiclephistas (heading), in Spunar, *Repertorium*, vol. 2, no. 401, 200; George of Bor, Replicacio contra Hus: "in heresim iam dampnatam ut Arrii, Nestorii, Manichei, Wiklefistc," in Sedlák, *Miscellanea*, 234; Stephcn of Páleč, Antihus: "Audiant ergo Wikleffiste," "moderni heretici Wyklefiste," in Sedlák, *Miscellanea*, 451 and 142; Stephen of Páleč, Replicatio contra quidamistas: "sed diceret Quidamista vel Wiclephista," in Loserth, "Beiträge 4," 347; Stephen of Páleč, Tractatus de ecclesia: "vulgares Wiklefiste," "Hus cum suis Wiklefistis," in Jan Sedlák, *M. Jan Hus* (Prague: Dědictví sv. Prokopa, 1915), 244* and 231*; Stephen of Dolany, Dialogus volatilis: "nec detraho aucariis et Wiklefistis," "quidam Wiklefiticae sortis magister," in Pez, *Thesaurus*, 4.2, cols. 456 and 453.

Hussites: Andrew of Brod, Contra obiecciones Hussonitarum: Loserth, "Beiträge 4," 342; Stephen of Dolany, Dialogus volatilis: "in Wiklefitis et modernis Hussitis," "proverbium Hussitarum tuorum," in Pez, *Thesaurus*, 4.2, cols. 435 and 496.

D. Utraquism and Constance, 1414–1419

No name: Contra communionem sub utraque: Prague, Národní knihovna České republiky, MS. I F 18, fol. 195r–200r; Estote sine offensione: "in Praga nonnulli," "quidam heretici," in Hardt, *Magnum oecumenicum Constantiense concilium*, vol. 3, cols. 658 and 709; Havlík, Asserunt quidam, in Krmíčková, *Studie a texty*, 137–147; Maurice Rvačka, Tractatus contra Hussitas de sumpcione venerabilis sacramenti: "de istis assertoribus," in Hardt, *Magnum oecumenicum Constantiense concilium* 3, col. 802; Andrew of Brod, Contra communionem calicis: "multi," "moderni adversarii," "moderni novi corruptores fidei," in Kadlec, *Studien und Texte*, 238 and 245–246; Andrew of Brod, Lectura de communione laicorum sub utraque specie: "nostri temporis sacerdotes," in Kadlec, *Studien und Texte*, 233; Paul of Dolany, Litterae de ecclesia, in Johann Loserth, "Simon von Tischnow. Ein Beitrag zur Geschichte des böhmischen Wiclifismus," *Mittheilungen des*

Vereines für Geschichte der Deutschen in Böhmen 26 (1888): 235–237; Pierre d'Ailly(?), Conclusiones de communione plebis sub utraque specie: "praesumtores," in Hardt, *Magnum oecumenicum Constantiense concilium*, vol. 3, col. 589.

Ad personam: Brevis censura XLV articulorum Wiclef (heading), in Giovanni Domenico Mansi, ed., *Sacrorum conciliorum nova et amplissima collectio*, 53 vols. (Florence and Venice: Zatta, 1759–1927), vol. 28 (1785), cols. 57–83; De articulis Iacobelli (heading), in Spunar, *Repertorium*, vol. 2, no. 419, 207; Eloquenti viro: "frater mi dilecte cum caeteris in hoc facto tibi adhaerentibus," in Hardt, *Magnum oecumenicum Constantiense concilium*, vol. 3, col. 346; Nikolaus of Dinkelsbühl, Tractatus contra errores Hussitarum: "compilator libelli," in Rudolf Damerau, ed., *Texte zum Problem des Laienkelchs* (Giessen: Schmitz, 1969), 33; Andrew of Brod, Tractatus de sumpcione venerabilis et sacrosancti sacramenti: "adversarius," in Kadlec, *Studien und Texte*, 168.

Wycliffites: Questio de manducacione sub utraque specie contra Wyclefistas (heading), in Spunar, *Repertorium*, vol. 2, no. 429, 209; Johlín of Vodňany, Collacio de damnacione Iohannis Wyclef: "multi Wiclefiste," in Říčan, "Johlín z Vodňan," 141; Andrew of Brod, Tractatus de sacramento eukaristie contra Wyclefistas: "responsum ad obiecta et cavillaciones Wiclefistarum," in Kadlec, *Studien und Texte*, 273; Peter of Pulkau, Confutatio Iacobi de Misa: "Iacobelli et aliorum, presertim Wyklefitarum," in Girgensohn, *Peter von Pulkau*, 250; Rupertus de Bundancia, Prophete mortui sunt: "Wikklefiste," in Sedlák, *Miscellanea*, 245; Stephen of Páleč, Tractatus breves pro domino Paulo, plebano in Planan: "Contra Wycleffistas" (heading), in Sedlák, *Miscellanea*, 519.

Hussites: Paul of Dolany, Tractatus contra Hussitas: "secta Hussitarum," in Loserth, "Simon von Tischnow," 242; Stephen of Dolany, Epistola ad Hussitas: "quidam de synagoga Hussitarum," "in partem Wicleff et Hussitarum deditus," "secte illius Hussitarum," in Pez, *Thesaurus*, vol. 4.2, cols. 505, 516, and 520.

Bohemians: Disputatio contra communionem plebis sub utraque specie: "Nestorius et Pelagius et sequaces eorum Bohemi," in Hardt, *Magnum oecumenicum Constantiense concilium* 3, col. 412; Jean Gerson, De necessaria communione: "haereses in Bohemia," "apud Bohemos," in Jean Gerson, *Œuvres*, 10:62.

E. Four Articles, 1420–1424

No name: Fernando of Lugo, Responsio ad quatuor articulos, in František Palacký, ed., *Urkundliche Beiträge zur Geschichte des Hussitenkrieges*, 2 vols. (Prague: Tempsky, 1873), 1:33–37; Andrew of Brod, Planctus super civitatem Pragensem, in Jaroslav Kadlec, "Planctus super civitatem Pragensem a jeho autor," *Studie o rukopisech* 25 (1986): 50–72; Stanisław of Skarbimierz, De visione spirituali determinacio, in Zofia Włodek, "Stanislas de Skalbimierz, un court traité contre les hussites sur la vision spirituelle. Introduction et texte," in Paul J. J. M. Bakker, Emmanuel Faye and Christophe Grellard, ed., *Chemins de la pensée médiévale. Études offertes à Zénon Kaluza* (Turnhout: Brepols, 2002), 499–512; Simon of Tišnov, Epistola publica contra quattuor articulos Bohemorum, in Konstantin Höfler, ed., *Geschichtschreiber der husitischen Bewegung in Böhmen*, 3 vols., Fontes rerum Austriacarum I/2, 6, 7 (Vienna: K. k. Hof- und Staatsdruckerei, 1856–66), 3:167–169n1; Johann Loserth, "Urkunden und Traktate betreffend die Verbreitung des Wiclifismus in Böhmen," *Mittheilungen des Vereines für Geschichte der Deutschen in Böhmen* 25 (1887): 338; Loserth, "Simon von Tischnow," 243; Martin Talayero, Oracio ad Polonie regem: "Taborienses hereticant Pragenses," in Kadlec, "Magister Martin Talayero," 305; Pier Paolo Vergerio(?), Responsiones facte ad quatuor articulos: "illi de Praga," in Soukup, "Zur Verbreitung," 246–248; Responsiones ad quattuor articulos datos domino duci Austrie per illos de Praga, in Coufal, *Polemika*, 141.

Ad personam: Maurice Rvačka, Index errorum in tractatu Floretus theologicus: "sub auctoritate Vicleff," "doctrinam Wicleff," in Jerzy Wolny, "Maurycy Rwaczka i Floretus theologicus w rękopisach Biblioteki Jagiellońskiej i innych księgozbiorów," Biuletyn Biblioteki Jagiellońskiej 27 (1977): 12 and 14; Stanisław of Skarbimierz, Ad ostendendum: "sectatores Hus," in Zofia Włodek and Ryszard Tatarzyński, ed., *Scripta manent. Textus ad theologiam spectantes in Universitate Cracoviensi saeculo XV conscripti* (Kraków: Wydawnictwo Naukowe Papieskiej Akademii Teologicznej, 2000), 135; Stanisław of Skarbimierz, Determinatio Ad enervandum errores: "ex falsis Wycklif et Ioannis Hus damnatorum dogmatibus," "sectatores istorum," in Włodek, *Scripta manent*, 105 and 121.

Ad personam and Hussites: Stanisław of Skarbimierz, Determinacio contra sub utraque specie communicantes: "sectatores Iohannis Hus et

Iohannis Wycklif," "cum Glossis nostris Hussitarum" (in a quote), in Włodek, *Scripta manent*, 146 and 150.

Wycliffites: Andrew of Brod, Tractatus de origine Hussitarum: "Wiclefite," "Wiclefiste," "presbyterorum et scolarium wiclefficorum," "Wiclefica secta," in Jaroslav Kadlec, ed., *Traktát Mistra Ondřeje z Brodu o původu husitů* (Tábor: Muzeum husitského revolučního hnutí, 1980), 12, 16, 11, 29; Stephen of Páleč, Omnes et singuli catholici: "Tractatus Wiklefistarum" (heading), in Spunar, *Repertorium*, vol. 1, no. 923, 332.

Wycliffites and Hussites: Johannes Hoffmann, Debemus invicem diligere: "Wiccleffistae," "Hussitae," "Pragenses," "Jacobitae," in Machilek, *Ludolf von Sagan*, 188; Simon of Tišnov, Contra hereses Wiclefistarum et Hussitarum (heading), in Spunar, *Repertorium*, vol. 1, no. 960, 344; Stephen of Páleč, Tractatus contra quattuor articulos hussitarum (heading), in Spunar, *Repertorium*, vol. 1, no. 923, 331–333; Andrew of Escobar, Contra Taborienses necnon Pragenses: "Hussisse seu Viclevisse in Bohemia," in Bartoš, "Španělský biskup," 68.

Wycliffites, Hussites, Bohemians: Ludolf of Sagan, Tractatus de longoevo schismate: "Wyclefiste et Husite," "Wyclefiste et Bohemi," in Johann Loserth, "Beiträge zur Geschichte der husitischen Bewegung 3. Der Tractatus de longevo schismate des Abtes Ludolf von Sagan," *Archiv für österreichische Geschichte* 60 (1880): 522–523.

Hussites: Contra communionem sub utraque: "contra errorem tractatuli cuiusdam Hussitarum," in Spunar, *Repertorium*, vol. 2, no. 424, 208; Questiones contra Wiklefistas et Hussitas: "sacerdotibus hussitarum," in Soukup, "Zur Verbreitung," 252; De erroribus hereticorum hussitarum (heading), in F. M. Bartoš, "Veliké dílo protihusitské polemiky," *Jihočeský sborník historický* 13 (1940): 19; Andrew of Kokorzyn, Contra articulum communionis eukaristie sub utraque specie: "Secundus articulus Hussitarum," in Mieczysław Markowski, "Poglądy filozoficzne Andrzeja z Kokorzyna," *Studia mediewistyczne* 6 (1964): 76; Francis of Brzeg, Utrum sacramentum eukaristie sit dandum laycali populo sub utraque specie: "errorem Hussitarum," in Maria Kowalczyk BJ, "Franciszek z Brzegu," *Acta mediaevalia* 12 (1999), 137; Francis of Retz, Contra articulum de peccatis publicis: "quod Hussite pro parte sua allegant," in Olomouc, Vědecká knihovna, MS. M II 55, fol. 82rb; Konrad of Soest, Tractatus contra hussitas: "heretici hussite," in München, Bayerische Staatsbibliothek, MS. clm 5411, fol. 102v; Peter of Pulkau et al., Tractatus contra quattuor articulos Hussitarum (heading), in Girgensohn, *Peter von Pulkau*, 175; Simon of Tišnov, Tractatus de communione sub utraque . . . adversus Hussitas (heading), in Spunar, *Repertorium*, vol. 1, no. 961, 344.

Bohemians: Johannes of Frankfurt, Contra hussitas: "Bohemi," in Johannes von Frankfurt, *Zwölf Werke*, 111; Martin Talayero, Contra quatuor articulos Hussitarum: "perfidia hereticorum de Boemia," in Kadlec, "Magister Martin Talayero," 283.

F. War Period, 1425–1430

No name: Nicholas of Jawór, Quaestio de hereticis, in Adolph Franz, Der Magister Nikolaus Magni de Jawor. Ein Beitrag zur Literatur- und Gelehrtengeschichte des 14. und 15. Jahrhunderts (Freiburg im Breisgau: Herder, 1898), 217–223.

Wycliffites and Hussites: Thomas Netter, Doctrinale: "sectatores illius haeresis ibi appellantur Hussitae," "Pragensium Wiclevistarum quidam," in Van Dussen, *From England*, 116.

Hussites: Andrew of Regensburg, Dialogus de haeresi Bohemica: "Hussiste," in Andreas von Regensburg, *Sämtliche Werke*, 660; Tractatus contra quattuor articulos armatae haeresis Hussitarum (heading), in Spunar, *Repertorium*, vol. 2, no. 403, 200–201; Conrad Bitschin, Epistola ecclesiae deplanctoria: "hereticorum Hussitarumque congeriem," in Theodor Hirsch, Max Töppen and Ernst Strehlke, ed., *Scriptores rerum Prussicarum*, 5 vols. (Leipzig: Hirzel, 1861–1874), vol. 3 (1866), 513; George of Zella, Sermo contra Hussitas et Biclefistas: "abscisi heretici et perversi Bohemorum Hussitae," in Georg Buchwald, "Die Leipziger Universitätspredigt in den ersten Jahrzehnten des Bestehens der Universität," *Zeitschift für Kirchengeschichte* 36 (1915): 88; Heymeric van de Velde, Dialogus ad Martinum papam: "cum Husistis," in Heymericus de Campo, *Opera selecta*, vol. 1, ed. Ruedi Imbach and Pascal Ladner (Freiburg/Schweiz: Universitätsverlag, 2001), 78; Oswald Reinlein, Tractatus exhortatorius: "Hussite," in Anežka Vidmanová, "Stoupenci a protivníci Mistra Jana Husi," Husitský Tábor 4 (1981): 50.

G. Taborite Manifesto, 1430–1432

No name: Litera seu epistola ad universos Christi fideles: "ad partes regni Bohemiae, in quibus proh dolor haeresis tenebrae ab aliquibus citra temporibus jacent," in Palacký and Birk, *Monumenta conciliorum*, 1:172.

Ad personam: Johannes Hoffmann, Epistola infideli Procopio, in Neumann, "Francouzská hussitica I," 103–108.

Wycliffites and Hussites: Disputatio Cracoviensis: "Vyclifistae et Hussitae," in Włodek, *Scripta manent*, 185; Johannes Nider, Contra heresim hussitarum: "heretici Hussite," "Hussite et Wiklifiste," "Iacobite inter Hussitas," in Basel, Universitätsbibliothek, MS. E I 9, fols. 386rb and 408vb.

Hussites: Curandum summopere: "Hussitarum hereticorum ignorancia," in Prokeš, "Táborské manifesty," 27; Heinrich Kalteisen, Contra errores Hussitarum: "Hussitis," in Prügl, *Die Ekklesiologie*, 62; Heinrich Kalteisen, Contra sedecim articulos sive errores Hussitarum (heading), in Prügl, *Die Ekklesiologie*, 56; Heinrich Kalteisen, De possessione cleri: "hussitarum articulus," in Prügl, *Die Ekklesiologie*, 56; Heinrich Kalteisen, Responsio ad quaestionem de communione populi sub utraque specie: "pro articulo Hussitarum," in Prügl, *Die Ekklesiologie*, 57; Hendrik van Gorkum, Contra articulos Hussitarum: "hussyte occisores innocentum," "o ceci huyssite," in *Tractatus consultatorii venerandi magistri Henrici de Gorychum* (Köln: Quentel, 1503), fols. 65ra and 77vb; Matthias Döring and Johannes Bremer, Videte, ne quis vos seducat: "in hiis dampnatis et perfidis hussitis," in Jiří Petrášek, "Die Erfurter Reaktion auf das Taboritenmanifest aus dem Jahr 1430," *Studia mediaevalia Bohemica* 4 (2012): 223; Nicholas of Jawór, Scriptum contra epistolam perfidiae Hussitarum: "Non est ergo credendum Hussistis hereticis obstinatis," in Berlin, Staatsbibliothek Preußischer Kulturbesitz, Ms. theol. lat. fol. 672, fol. 25or; Stephan Bodeker, De oracione dominica: "perfidi Hussite," in Annette Wigger, "Weil die "Simplices" zu schützen sind. Die Stellungnahme des brandenburgischen Bischofs Stephan Bodeker (1383–1459) gegenüber die Hussiten," *Wichmann-Jahrbuch des Diözesangeschichtsvereins Berlin* NF 7 (2002–2003): 58; Valesius Hispanus, Confutatio errorum Hussitarum: "Hussitas pertinacissimos eclesiæ hostes evomuit," in Prague, Knihovna Národního muzea, MS. VIII E 67, fol. 1v.

Hussites, Bohemians: Geoffrey of Montchoisi: Libellus contra errores seu libellum famosum Bohemorum: "isti Boemi . . . non tantum Hussiste, sed pocius Julianiste merentur appellari," in Neumann, "Francouzská hussitica II," 79; Matthias Döring, De temporalitate clericorum: "Bohemi," "Hussite," in Petra Weigel, *Ordensreform und Konziliarismus. Der Franziskanerprovinzial Matthias Döring (1427–1461)* (Frankfurt am Main: Peter Lang, 2005), 315–316.

Bohemians: Contra epistolam Taboritarum: "Boemi," in Prokeš, "Táborské manifesty," 32; Gilles Charlier, Posicio super secundo articulo Bohemorum: "error oppositus Bohemorum" (heading), in F. M. Bartoš, "Husitika a bohemika několika knihoven německých a švýcarských," *Věstník Královské české společnosti nauk* (1931), no. 5, 41; Heinrich Toke, De ecclesia militanti catholica: "propter adventum et materiam Bohemorum Hussitarum" (heading), in Werner Krämer, *Konsens und Rezeption. Verfassungsprinzipien der Kirche im Basler Konziliarismus* (Münster: Aschendorff, 1980), 77; John Jerome of Prague, Contra quattuor articulos Bohemorum: "contra Bohemos haereticos," "Bohemi et Moravi sunt haeretici," in Mittarelli and Costadoni, *Annales Camaldulenses*, 9:755 and 800.

H. Council of Basel, 1433–1437

No name: Contra quattuor articulos Pragenses, in Berlin, Staatsbibliothek Preußischer Kulturbesitz, Ms. Ham. 198, fols. 161r–178v; Heymeric van de Velde, An maior gratia conferatur communicanti sub utraque specie, in Koblenz, Landeshauptarchiv, Best. 701, Nr. 220, fols. 113r–117v; John of Ragusa, Septem regule: "adversarii," in Mansi, *Sacrorum conciliorum nova et amplissima collectio,* vol. 29 (1788), cols. 864–868; John Palomar, De communione parvulorum, in Prague, Národní knihovna České republiky, MS. XIX C 17, fols. 172r–177r; John Palomar, De compactatis, in Prague, Národní knihovna České republiky, MS. XIX C 17, fols. 61r–142r; John Palomar, De temporalitate ecclesie: "adversus veritatis hostes," in Mansi, *Sacrorum conciliorum nova et amplissima collectio,* vol. 30 (1792), col. 476; John Palomar, Responsio Interrogasti me, in Prague, Národní knihovna České republiky, MS. XIX C 17, fols. 177v–179r; Juan de Torquemada, De aqua benedicta: "in mentibus hereticorum," in Johannes de Turrecremata, *Tractatus de aqua benedicta* (Rome: Bartholomeus Guldinbeck de Sultz, 1475), 16.

Ad personam: Gilles Charlier, Responsio ad replicas: "dicendum est opponenti," in Mansi, *Sacrorum conciliorum nova et amplissima collectio,* vol. 30, col. 421; Heymeric van de Velde, Epistola contra Iohannem de Rokycana, in Pascal Ladner, "Heymericus de Campo an Johannes Rokycana. Zur Laienkelchdiskussion am Basler Konzil," in *Variorum munera florum. Latinität als prägende Kraft mittelalterlicher Kultur. Festschrift für Hans F. Haefele,* ed. Adolf Reinle, Ludwig Schmugge and Peter Stotz (Sigmaringen: Thorbecke, 1985), 304–308; John Palomar, Responsio ad replicas: "magister

Petrus," in Mansi, *Sacrorum conciliorum nova et amplissima collectio*, vol. 29, cols. 1153–1154.

Hussites: John Jerome of Prague, Sermo modernus de corpore Christi: "haereticus Hussita," in Mittarelli and Costadoni, *Annales Camaldulenses*, 9:746.

Bohemians: Ad exercitacionem ingenii: "circa articulos 4or propositos per Bohemos," in Bartoš, "Husitika a bohemika," 17; Circa materiam primi articuli Bohemorum, in Bartoš, "Husitika a bohemika," 48; Dialogus militis cum monacho: "Boemi," in Třeboň, Státní oblastní archiv, MS. A 16, fol. 263v; Gilles Charlier, Oratio de punitione peccatorum publicorum: "nuncii Bohemorum oratores," in Mansi, *Sacrorum conciliorum nova et amplissima collectio*, vol. 29, col. 869; Heinrich Kalteisen, Avisamentum super concessionem calicis: "Bohemis," in Prügl, *Die Ekklesiologie*, 84; Heinrich Kalteisen, Oratio de libera predicacione: "inclyti Bohemie regni oratores," in Mansi, *Sacrorum conciliorum nova et amplissima collectio*, vol. 29, col. 971; Heinrich Kalteisen, Responsio ad replicas: "incliti regni Bohemie oratores," in Mansi, *Sacrorum conciliorum nova et amplissima collectio*, vol. 29, col. 1045; Heymeric van de Velde, Disputatio de potestate ecclesiastica: "radix controversie Bohemorum," in J. Marx, *Verzeichnis der Handschriften-Sammlung des Hospitals zu Cues bei Bernkastel a./Mosel* (Trier: Hospital zu Cues, 1905), 106; John of Ragusa, Oratio de communione sub utraque specie: "oratores inclyti regni Bohemie," in Mansi, *Sacrorum conciliorum nova et amplissima collectio*, vol. 29, col. 699; John Palomar, Oratio de civili dominio clericorum: "ambasiatores inclyti regni Bohemie," in Mansi, *Sacrorum conciliorum nova et amplissima collectio*, vol. 29, col. 1106; Juan de Torquemada, De sacramento eucharistie: "de primo articulo Bohemorum," in Jaroslav Prokeš, *Husitika vatikánské knihovny v Římě* (Prague: Orbis, 1928), 16; Nicholas of Cusa, De usu communionis: "vos vero Bohemi," in Nicolaus Cusa, *Accurata recognitio trium voluminum operum*, 3 vols. (Paris: Officina Ascensiana, 1514), vol. 3, Septem epistolae, fol. 5r.

NOTES

This study was supported by a grant from the Czech Science Foundation (GA ČR) "Cultural Codes and Their Transformations in the Hussite Period" (P405/12/G148), realized at the Institute of Philosophy of the Czech Academy of Sciences.

1. On Wyclif's influence in Bohemia, see František Šmahel, "Wyclif's Fortune

in Hussite Bohemia," in Šmahel, *Die Prager Universität im Mittelalter* (Leiden: Brill, 2007), 457–489; David R. Holeton, "Wyclif's Bohemian Fate. A Reflection on the Contextualization of Wyclif in Bohemia," *Communio viatorum* 32 (1989): 209–222. On communication of texts and ideas between the two countries, see Michael Van Dussen, *From England to Bohemia. Heresy and Communication in the Later Middle Ages* (Cambridge: Cambridge University Press, 2012).

2. On this subject, see the numerous publications by Anne Hudson, especially those collected in Anne Hudson, *Studies in the Transmission of Wyclif's Writings* (Aldershot: Ashgate, 2008); more recently see her "From Oxford to Bohemia: reflections on the transmission of Wycliffite texts," *Studia Mediaevalia Bohemica* 2 (2010): 25–37.

3. The best comprehensive survey of Hussite history available in a language other than Czech is František Šmahel, *Die Hussitische Revolution*, 3 vols. (Hannover: Hahn, 2002). See also Howard Kaminsky, *A History of the Hussite Revolution* (Berkeley: University of California Press, 1967); František Šmahel, *La révolution hussite, une anomalie historique* (Paris: Presses Universitaires de France, 1985); Thomas A. Fudge, *Magnificent Ride. The First Reformation in Hussite Bohemia* (Aldershot: Ashgate, 1998).

4. On the issues of modern terminology, see Phillip Haberkern, "What's in a Name, or What's at Stake When We Talk about 'Hussites'?," *History Compass* 9 (2011): 791–801, with further references.

5. Jaroslav Eršil, ed., *Monumenta Vaticana res gestas Bohemicas illustrantia*, vol. 7.1–2 (Prague: Academia, 1996–1998), no. 565, 247. Hereafter cited as *MVB* 7.

6. Ferdinand Seibt, *Hussitica. Zur Struktur einer Revolution* (Cologne and Graz: Böhlau, 1965), 10.

7. Johann Loserth, *Hus und Wiclif. Zur Genesis der husitischen Lehre* (Prague and Leipzig: Tempsky, 1884), 87–91; cf. Loserth, *Wiclif and Hus*, trans. J. Evans (London: Hodder and Stoughton, 1884) 82–87. On Johann Loserth's biography and approach, see Pavel Soukup, "Johann Loserth (1846–1936). Ein 'Gelehrter von Weltruf' in Czernowitz und Graz," in *Österreichische Historiker 1900–1945. Lebensläufe und Karrieren in Österreich, Deutschland und der Tschechoslowakei in wissenschaftsgeschichtlichen Porträts*, ed. Karel Hruza (Vienna, Cologne, and Weimar: Böhlau, 2008), 39–71.

8. Seibt, *Hussitica*, 10–14.

9. Václav Novotný, ed., *M. Jana Husi Korespondence a dokumenty* (Prague: Komise pro vydávání pramenů náboženského hnutí českého, 1920), no. 73, 186–187.

10. Loserth, *Hus und Wiclif*, 88n1, concluded this expression was "identical with Hussite" (apparently he considered it derived from Hus's first name). In Czech and German, however, the word is used for the Knights Hospitallers. While the order indeed played a role in the Prague religious controversy of 1412, the name "Johannitae" seems to date to a later period.

11. See also Pavel Soukup, "'Pars Machometica' in Early Hussite Polemics: The Use and Background of an Invective," in *Religious Controversy in Europe, 1378–1536: Textual Transmission and Networks of Readership*, ed. Michael Van Dussen and Pavel Soukup (Turnhout: Brepols, 2013), 251–287.

12. Jaroslav Eršil, ed., *Magistri Iohannis Hus Polemica*, Corpus Christianorum. Continuatio Mediaevalis 238 (Turnhout: Brepols, 2010), 299–300; František Palacký, ed., *Documenta Mag. Joannis Hus vitam, doctrinam, causam illustrantia* (Prague: Tempsky, 1869), 184; Václav Novotný, ed., *Fontes rerum Bohemicarum*, vol. 8 (Prague: Nadání Františka Palackého, 1932), 76.

13. Jaroslav V. Polc and Zdeňka Hledíková, *Pražské synody a koncily předhusitské doby* (Prague: Karolinum, 2002), no. LXIII/2, 285.

14. Novotný, *Korespondence*, no. 166, 343.

15. Palacký, *Documenta*, 419; cf. "Wiclefianis per sedem apostolicam damnatis erroribus implicatus," ibid., 417.

16. In 1413, for example, the University of Vienna used the words "Wycleffiste" or "Wycleffistica secta": Novotný, *Korespondence*, nos. 168 and 171, 350–358.

17. Ibid., no. 167, 347.

18. Ibid., no. 63, 170. Páleč indeed spoke of "sententiae Wiclefistarum" in 1413: Palacký, *Documenta*, 508.

19. Giuseppe Alberigo and Josef Wohlmuth, ed., *Conciliorum oecumenicorum decreta. Dekrete der ökumenischen Konzilien*, 3 vols. (Paderborn: Schöningh, 1998–2002), 2:426–434.

20. Palacký, *Documenta*, 572 and 578.

21. Ibid., 601–602.

22. Ibid., 639–640.

23. Jaroslav Eršil, ed., *Acta summorum pontificum res gestas Bohemicas aevi praehussitici et hussitici illustrantia*, 2 vols. (Prague: Academia, 1980), nos. 1097–1098, 625–629, hereafter cited as *MVB 6*. Simultaneously with the emergence of the term *Hussites*, the expression "Wycliffites" continued to be used at Constance. See Novotný, *Fontes 8*, 47; Palacký, *Documenta*, 541, 648, 654 (evidence from 1415 and 1416).

24. Dieter Girgensohn, *Peter von Pulkau und die Wiedereinführung des Laienkelches. Leben und Wirken eines Wiener Theologen in der Zeit des großen Schismas* (Göttingen: Vandenhoeck and Ruprecht, 1964), 120–164; Helena Krmíčková, *Studie a texty k počátkům kalicha v Čechách* (Brno: Masarykova univerzita, 1997); Dušan Coufal, *Polemika o kalich mezi teologií a politikou 1414–1431. Předpoklady basilejské disputace o prvním z pražských artikulů* (Prague: Kalich, 2012), 20–41.

25. František Šmahel, "Magister Peter Payne: Curriculum vitae eines englischen Nonkonformisten," in Albert de Lange and Kathrin Utz Tremp, ed., *Friedrich Reiser und die "waldensisch-hussitische Internationale"* (Heidelberg, Ubstadt-Weiher, Basel: Verlag Regionalkultur, 2006), 250–251; Šmahel, "Wyclif's Fortune," 486–487.

26. See *MVB* 7. In the following text, references in parentheses are to document numbers in this edition.

27. See *MVB* 6, nos. 1073, 1093, 1095, 1096, 1097. Jan Hus's name was added to that of John Wyclif in Constance after the former's condemnation. Previously, the Pisan popes typically aimed at the "errores/libros Johannis Wicleff" (*MVB* 6, nos. 419, 754, 761, 946, 968). The "heresy of Wyclif" (with no mention of Hus) is invoked in the nomination of Giovanni Dominici as papal legate in July 1418 and in a supplication from May 1419 (where, however, the Bohemian followers of Wyclif are subsumed in the expression "Johannis Wikleff suorumque sequencium heresis") and then disappear: *MVB* 7, nos. 325 and 431.

28. The evidence from after this date is a supplication from July 1420 and another two from September 1421 (*MVB* 7, nos. 644 and 809–810). The curia itself used the expression "haereses et errores Johannis Wiklef et Johannis Hus," outdated as it was by that time, in June 1427 when giving the bishop of Bamberg the right to absolve heretics (*MVB* 7, no. 1817). This can be explained with the specific contents of this letter, which could have easily been reminiscent of the introduction of the anti-Wycliffite / anti-Hussite inquisition in Constance.

29. *MVB* 7, no. 823, responding to 806; 1053, responding to 1028; 2229, responding to 2227. In case of *MVB* 7, nos. 1808 and 2078, the respective supplications are not extant but can be supposed.

30. As far as crusading against heretics is concerned, the situation in the Albigensian war is revealing and analogical to that in the Hussite wars. Although the term *Albigensians* existed even before the crusaders reached the region, Innocent III and Honorius III continued to use the older and quite vague expression "the heretics of Provence" in crusade-related documents: Daniel Power, "Who Went on the Albigensian Crusade?", *English Historical Review* 128 (2013): 1070–1075 (with references to the sources and a brief summary of the previous scholarship). The crusading letters against the Muslims from the twelfth and thirteenth centuries used specific ethnic or geographic names such as "Turci, Egypti, Persae," usually accompanied by a range of hostile expressions: see Ursula Schwerin, *Die Aufrufe der Päpste zur Befreiung des Heiligen Landes von den Anfängen bis zum Ausgang Innozenz IV. Ein Beitrag zur Geschichte der kurialen Kreuzzugspropaganda und der päpstlichen Epistolographie* (Berlin: Ebering, 1937), 53–57.

31. To mention one exception: when the town of Jihlava asked for permission to turn the synagogue into a chapel in 1427, they mentioned the devastation of churches through the Hussites; the response avoided this specific term and spoke just about heretics; see *MVB* 7, nos. 1710–1711.

32. I use data from a repertory of anti-Hussite treatises which I am compiling in the form of an online database. See Pavel Soukup, ed., *Repertorium operum antihussiticorum*, www.antihus.eu.

33. I disregard the heading when the text is available and contains terms different from the title.

34. The evidence underlying Figure 8-2 is summarized in the appendix. In cases where one treatise employs two or three relevant terms, it is counted as half or a third for each applicable category (e.g., if a treatise uses "Hussite" in one place and "Wycliffite" in another, it is counted as half a point in the column "Wiclefiste" and half a point in the column "Hussite").

35. See Jana Nechutová, "K literární morfologii husitské polemiky. Štěpán z Dolan, Diagolus volatilis," *Sborník prací filosofické fakulty brněnské univerzity* E 29 (1984): 209–218; Jana Nechutová, "Prology protihusitských traktátů Štěpána z Dolan," in *Nový Mars Moravicus aneb Sborník příspěvků, jež věnovali Prof. Dr. Josefu Válkovi jeho žáci a přátelé k sedmdesátinám*, ed. Bronislav Chocholáč, Libor Jan and Tomáš Knoz (Brno: Matice moravská, 1999), 119–126.

36. Bernhard Pez, ed., *Thesaurus anecdotorum novissimus*, 6 vols. (Augsburg and Graz: Veith, 1721–1729), vol. 4.2 (1723), 357, 371, 381, and 437.

37. Jan Sedlák, ed., *Jacobi de Noviano, Mgri Parisiensis, Disputatio cum Hussitis* (Brno: Papežská knihtiskárna benediktinů rajhradských, 1914), 1.

38. Novotný, *Korespondence*, no. 14, 45.

39. Georg Erler, "Dietrichs von Niem Schrift Contra dampnatos Wiclivitas Pragae," *Zeitschrift für vaterländische Geschichte und Altertumskunde* 43 (1885): 186.

40. Jan Sedlák, *Miscellanea husitica Ioannis Sedlák*, ed. Jaroslav V. Polc and Stanislav Přibyl (Praha: Katolická teologická fakluta Univerzity Karlovy, 1996), 492.

41. Johann Loserth, "Beiträge zur Geschichte der husitischen Bewegung 4. Die Streitschriften und Unionsverhandlungen zwischen den Katholiken und Husiten in den Jahren 1412 und 1413," *Archiv für österreichische Geschichte* 75 (1889): 342.

42. "[S]icut et haec dies in Wiklefitis et modernis Hussitis comprobat," in Pez, *Thesaurus*, vol. 4.2, col. 435; "viri Wiklefiticae sortis et Hussitae ejusdem discipuli," ibid., col. 446; "nec detraho aucariis et Wiklefistis," ibid., col. 456.

43. E.g., "in partem Wicleff et Hussitarum deditus," ibid., col. 516; "secte illius Hussitarum," ibid., col. 520.

44. Giovanni Benedetto Mittarelli and Anselmo Costadoni, ed., *Annales Camaldulenses Ordinis sancti Benedicti*, 9 vols. (Venice: Pasquali, 1755–1773), 9:746 (June 1433).

45. Jean Gerson, *Œuvres complètes*, ed. Palémon Glorieux, 10 vols. (Paris, Tournai, Rome, and New York: Desclée, 1960–1973), 10:62.

46. Jaroslav Kadlec, "Magister Martin Talayero aus Tortosa im Kampf gegen die Hussiten," *Annuarium historiae conciliorum* 12 (1980): 283; Johannes von Frankfurt, *Zwölf Werke des Heidelberger Theologen und Inquisitors*, ed. Dorothea Walz et al. (Heidelberg: Winter, 2000), 111.

47. This was the case with Geoffrey of Montchoisi or the anonymous Cambridge theologian: Augustin Neumann, "Francouzská hussitica II," *Studie a texty k náboženským dějinám českým* 4, nos. 3–4 (1925): 62; Jaroslav Prokeš, "Táborské

manifesty z r. 1430 a 1431. Příspěvek k politice Prokopa Velikého," *Časopis Matice moravské* 52 (1928): 32.

48. "[S]ed diceret Quidamista vel Wiclephista," Loserth, "Beiträge 4," 347; see also Václav Novotný, *M. Jan Hus. Život a učení I. Život a dílo*, 2 vols. (Prague: Leichter, 1919–1921), 2:289.

49. See Coufal, *Polemika*, 21 (with references).

50. Franz Machilek, *Ludolf von Sagan und seine Stellung in der Auseinandersetzung um Konziliarismus und Hussitismus* (München: Lerche, 1967), 188; Neumann, "Francouzská hussitica I," 103–108.

51. Thomas Netter, *Doctrinale antiquitatum fidei catholice ecclesie*, ed. Bonaventura Blanciotti, 3 vols. (Venice: Bassanesi, 1757–1759), 3: col. 250.

52. Kadlec, "Magister Martin Talayero," 305, cf. 299.

53. Thomas Prügl, *Die Ekklesiologie Heinrich Kalteisens OP in der Auseinandersetzung mit dem Basler Konziliarismus* (Paderborn, Munich, Vienna, and Zürich: Schöningh, 1995), 84.

54. Andreas von Regensburg, *Sämtliche Werke*, ed. Georg Leidinger (Munich: Rieger, 1903), 691.

55. Hermann von der Hardt, ed., *Magnum oecumenicum Constantiense concilium*, 6 vols. (Frankfurt and Leipzig: Genschius, 1697–1700), 3: cols. 706–707 (1698).

56. This is the case with two "Responsiones" to the Four Articles. See Pavel Soukup, "Zur Verbreitung theologischer Streitschriften im 15. Jahrhundert. Eine antihussitische Sammelhandschrift aus der Erfurter Kartause," *Studia mediaevalia Bohemica* 1 (2009): 246, and Coufal, *Polemika*, 141. On the other hand, from a remote perspective the name of the city of Prague could represent the entire Hussite movement, as it is, for instance, in French and Burgundian chronicles and other texts. See Jaroslav Svátek, "Pohled zvnějšku: husité a cizina," in *Husitské století*, ed. Pavlína Cermanová, Robert Novotný and Pavel Soukup (Prague: Nakladatelství Lidové noviny, 2014), 395.

57. Neumann, "Francouzská hussitica II," 79.

58. Hardt, *Magnum oecumenicum Constantiense concilium* 3: col. 412.

59. Sedlák, *Miscellanea*, 234.

60. "Ortum autem habuit hec pestifera heresis a quodam Wicleff Anglico." Wrocław, Biblioteka uniwersytecka, MS. Mil. II 25 (6078), fols. 235r–243v, quotes fols. 235v–236r. Most of the information provided on the Husssite and Wycliffite heresy is a simple reproduction of the respective articles condemned in Constance.

61. New York, The Morgan Library, MS.738, fols. 264v–265r.

62. "Principalis tamen fuerat Iohannes Oclyf Anglicus," ibid., fol. 249v.

63. Andreas von Regensburg, *Sämtliche Werke*, 660. For reasons obscure to me, Johlín of Vodňany translated Wyclif's name as "liar" ("Vicleff bohemice mendax"): Rudolf Říčan, "Johlín z Vodňan, křižovník kláštera zderazského," *Věstník královské české spolenosti nauk* (1929), no. 2, 139.

64. F. M. Bartoš, "Španělský biskup proti Táboru a Praze," *Jihočeský sborník historický* 11 (1938): 68.

65. Basel, Universitätsbibliothek, MS. E I 9, fols. 414va and 408vb.

66. Berlin, Staatsbibliothek Preußischer Kulturbesitz, Ms. theol. lat. fol. 672, fol. 254r: "in scola illius maximi heretici Wykleff Anglici, propter heresim post mortem eius diu exhumati et conbusti, didicerunt ordines religionum omnium esse illicitos."

67. Vienna, Österreichische Nationalbibliothek, Cod. 4268, fol. 65v.

68. Seibt, *Hussitica*, 14.

69. Analogically, the emergence of Protestantism as a discrete confession was also induced by opposition. See Dorothea Wendebourg, "Die Einheit der Reformation als historisches Problem," in *Reformationstheorien. Ein kirchenhistorischer Disput über Einheit und Vielfalt der Reformation*, ed. Berndt Hamm, Bernd Moeller and Dorothea Wendebourg (Göttingen: Vandenhoeck and Ruprecht, 1995), 34.

70. František Palacký and Ernst Birk, ed., *Monumenta conciliorum generalium seculi decimi quinti. Concilium Basileense. Scriptorum* t. I (Vienna: K. k. Hof- und Staatsdruckerei, 1857), 187.

CHAPTER NINE

ORTHODOXY AND THE GAME OF KNOWLEDGE:
DEGUILEVILLE IN FIFTEENTH-CENTURY
ENGLAND

Mishtooni Bose

Among the discursive modes of late-medieval English religious writing, "exploratory intellection" of the conceptual density and originality so abundantly exhibited in the writings of Julian of Norwich is a rare phenomenon.[1] But despite this challenge from the primary sources, better justice could still be done to the full range of cognitive and experiential modes of which English writers in this period appear to have been aware.[2] This essay is accordingly concerned with varieties of intellectual experience—thinking, knowing, the generation of insight, argument and judgment, and even the explicit enjoyment of such mental activities—that persisted in literature produced in England in the aftermath of the Wycliffite controversies. English intellectual life during this period can seem many things to the modern scholar: diffuse, diverse, intriguing, and difficult to bring into focus.[3] But one of the most obvious ways in which Europe made its presence felt in English religious and intellectual culture after Wyclif was through the medium of translation. Even if the sometimes controversial histories of their sources may not always have been known to English translators or readers, translations provided routes whereby a rich archive of intellectually engaged texts, comparable in density and ambition to Julian's writings, might be given expression in English.[4]

A group of texts that exemplify this process, the English translations of Guillaume de Deguileville's *Pèlerinage de l'âme* (1355; hereafter *PA*) and of both recensions of his *Pèlerinage de la vie humaine* (hereafter *PVH1* [1331] and *PVH2* [1350s]), appeared during a period of "curiously intimate as well as adversarial contact" between England and France.[5] *The Pilgrimage of the Sowle* (hereafter *Sowle*), an anonymous prose translation of *PA*, was made in 1413.[6] *The Pilgrimage of the Lyfe of the Manhode* (hereafter *Manhode*), an anonymous prose translation of *PVH1*, was in circulation by the mid-fifteenth century,[7] and a verse translation of *PVH2*, commonly attributed to John Lydgate, appeared in 1426.[8] William Calin's observation that "Guillaume's posterity proved to be richer in England than on the Continent" suggests the persistence of shrewd, focused, literary and spiritual connoisseurship among some groups of late medieval English readers.[9] Versions of Deguileville in English have already received attention from literary scholars interested in the way in which the *Roman de la Rose* and its literary progeny affected conceptions of authorship, authority, and allegory, and from others interested in his influence on particular English authors, from Geoffrey Chaucer and William Langland to John Lydgate and Thomas Hoccleve.[10] The straightforward comparison and contrast of these translations with Deguileville's originals is another productive and far from exhausted line of inquiry. Much closer to the concerns of the present volume, however, Rosemarie Potz McGerr has pointed out how much of the subject matter of *Sowle* may well have proved particularly congenial in an anti-Wycliffite climate.[11] Clearly, therefore, one way of contributing to the discussion that this volume is attempting to foster might be to speculate about the kind of impact these texts may have had purely as vessels of orthodox content. But that, in my view, would be to miss what is most valuable about them. During a period of heightened awareness about the risks of religious controversy, these translations provided opportunities, however discrete and localized, for fresh sources of intellectual nourishment. They released into new interpretative communities intellectually uninhibited narratives rich in theological argumentation, nourished by Cistercian learning that drew on the exegetical and argumentative creativity of Augustine and on the scholastic efflorescence of the twelfth and thirteenth centuries.[12] I have chosen, therefore, to consider those narrative qualities that may have enabled these translations to preserve a place for imaginative speculation within the capacious realm of orthodox discourse in the wake of the Wycliffite controversies.

Critics from Rosemond Tuve to Sarah Kay have borne witness to the complexity of Deguileville's original allegories, in which the mode of narration repeatedly challenges readers to experience different levels of engagement: intuitive and emotional, yet also ratiocinative and intellectual.[13] It is, in my view, a provocative experience for any scholar of the Wycliffite controversies and their intellectual legacies to encounter those same qualities, reproduced faithfully in these translations, in an English setting, and thereby rendered susceptible of comparison with other vernacular voices from the early fifteenth century, whether avowedly orthodox or self-consciously heterodox. They continuously invite their readers to ruminate, to far less obvious ends than those of religious pedagogy, on a range of advanced theological topics that were potentially or actually controversial, including the mystery of transubstantiation, the relations between the persons of the Trinity and the nature of the soul. Here, therefore, I concentrate on suggesting several of the ways in which they offer a distinctive and self-consciously speculative experience to their English readers, one characterized by repeated patterns of arousal and containment that in turn invite different kinds of engagement—intuitive, emotional, and intellectual—with the narrative. I focus on the two prose translations, *Sowle* and *Manhode*, not only because they are less well known than the verse translation (to date, *Sowle* lacks a complete modern edition) but also because keeping the focus on prose enables cogent comparison and contrast, later in the essay, between the handling of theological topics, and the Eucharist in particular, in these texts and the treatment of similar materials in prose works by Nicholas Love and an anonymous Wycliffite preacher. After undertaking a sequence of close readings of the prose translations, therefore, I put all of these disparate texts in conversation with one another, in order to suggest what the translations might have had to offer in terms of enriching the polyvocality and multimodality of vernacular religious discourse and experience in England during this period.

PLAY AND PROCESS

The *verba translatoris* that appear in several manuscripts of *Sowle* provide the raw elements of a critical language that does justice to the ways in which the structural workings of Deguileville's imagination were both preserved and, at times, subtly reshaped in the English translation. The translator justifies his mode of procedure on the grounds that he found some aspects of *PA*—"diffuse and . . . ouerderk. Wherfore I haue in dyuers places added and withdrawe litel, what as me semed needful: no thing changing of the processe, ne substaunce of the matiere, but as might be most lusti to the reder or herer of the matiere,"[14] Of particular significance here is the distinction between "processe" and "substaunce," a distinction that reflects

Deguileville's own self-consciousness about the relationship between rhetorical *dispositio* and the ruminative engagement that his allegories are designed to provoke. It is particularly rewarding in this context to recover the semantic richness that the term *process* enjoyed in Middle English. The senses listed under *MED* (3) are of particular importance here, denoting different types of narrative discourse: sense (c) denotes "an expository or descriptive discourse"; sense (d), "an argumentative discourse, an argument; a plea, an appeal, or exhortation; a statement in a debate"; sense (e), "a speech of praise, blame, or well-wishing"; and sense (f), "a play, pageant, or performance."[15] All of these are more than apt descriptions of the various kinds of narrative rhetoric, from epideixis and complaint to dialogue and disputation, that can be found throughout *Sowle* and *Manhode*.

The *Sowle* translator intends "processe" to indicate "argument" or "arrangement": the means by which content, or *substaunce*, has been presented to the reader, as for example in debate, dialogue, complaint or description. But it is also rewarding to test the critical consequences of allowing a deeper layer of signification, one enriched by the combination of some of these medieval and modern senses, to suffuse what is, in relation to these translations, nothing less than a keyword. For in these texts, "process" occurs not simply through stylistic choices regarding *ordo*, or sequence, the various surface structures of rhetorical arrangement, but also through the various means by which the reader *experiences substaunce*, or content. In order to refine our understanding of this amplified sense of "process" more fully, it is necessary to consider briefly the *OED* entry, which includes, under sense (1c), the term's use in philosophical discourse to indicate "the course of becoming as opposed to static being." This also connects with *OED* (1b): "the fact of going on or being carried on, as an action or series of actions."[16] The near-synonymy between the phrases "in process" and "in progress," a fact also acknowledged under (1b), cements the connection between modern English "process" and the concepts of movement, forward motion, or becoming—which are all essentially incomplete states.

In this section, I will argue that in relation to the narrative textures of *Manhode* and *Sowle*, the term *process*, in an enriched sense that combines both its medieval senses of "discourse" or "argument" and its modern philosophical sense of "becoming," succinctly focuses not only a text's uses of stylistic variation, but more precisely the discursive means whereby it attempts to stimulate intellectual and emotional experiences in its readers,

requiring that they engage in the continuous processing of fluid and meta-
morphosing images. A good example of writerly vitality soliciting readerly
engagement in this way occurs at the beginning of *Manhode*, in which a
conventional image is turned into "a wol gret wunder" that renders the
pilgrim-dreamer "gre[t]liche [greatly] abashed."[17] He sees how, as a result
of their having been nourished by St. Augustine and other "grete maistres
and doctours," "many folke bicomen briddes [birds] and after flyen euene
[straight] upright . . . [they] gadered hem [for themselves] feþeres [feathers]
and maden hem grete wynges and sithen bigunnen to flee and for to clymbe
hye into þe citee."[18] Avril Henry notes that this is "an image of religious instruction"; but here such instruction undergoes wholesale defamiliariza-
tion because of the manner in which it is presented. An opportunity, at the
very least, has been provided for the transformation of objective knowledge
into subjective experience. The dreamer witnesses the metamorphoses
without the intellectual comfort of prior explanation; and the experiential
imperatives of the narrative foreground collaboration, by the "folke," in
the physical *process of becoming* birds. It is the strangeness of the physical
metamorphosis, rather than its doctrinal significance alone, that is important here. It is left to the informed reader to complete the process, and
thereby to finish its "work," by translating this experience back into the
image identified by Henry; but this phase of the process remains unscripted
by the text.

A comparable example is provided by the climax of *Sowle*, when the
pilgrim-soul, through whose experiential adventures the narrative is focal-
ized, reports a transformation in his understanding. Marveling at the scale
of God's house, which cannot be "comprehended by thought of mannes wit
for it is infynyte" (V.ii.221), he reports that he was granted deeper understanding of something that he had previously read: "thane was I entalented
[stimulated] to knowe of seynt poule of whom I hadde radde in his own
scripture that he was rauished to the thridde heuene, and there he sawgh
sightes wher of he wolde not speke" (V.ii.222).[19] The distinction between the
bare fact of what he had read while embodied, and what he is now *entalented to knowe* as a journeying soul is typical of a narrative in which the
narrator's cognitive development is kept continuously in the foreground.
As this example also shows, such development is achieved by *revision*: by
reconsidering from different perspectives, and at different levels, what had
previously been digested by the mind in another way. The reader has long

been prepared for this development by exchanges such as that between the pilgrim-soul and Doctrine in which she informs him that "knowyng" must be achieved through "labor" and "exercise" (IV.xxx.185). Such labor is characterized by a process of searching into which the soul is provoked by perception: as part of a discourse concerning the differences between human and angelic kinds of knowledge, Doctrine describes "the clere polished myrrour of the diuinite" into which angels had originally gazed and seen "the verrey resemblaunce of alle creatures, and of all that shulde betide to the laste ende" (IV.xxx.184). In every creature, she goes on to explain, there is a beam from this bright mirror that gives to the creature a beauty not of itself. The soul, which is "fourmed lyk an aungel with abilite of knowing, kyndely [naturally] desireth to know and putte this abilite into verrey worchyng; he seketh by discourses of resoun the skiles [rationales] and the causes of the wonderful beauty of thise foreside creatures," and in this way it learns that "no thyng cometh of nought, that is to say, with oute bygynner" (IV.xxx.185). Philosophers once discovered this, she explains, "with oute mannes techyng, only by shewyng of resoun," and it was this ability that St. Paul was acknowledging in his Epistle to the Romans, "amonges who as at that tyme was the sotilte [*subtlety*] of philosophie," when he asserted that invisible properties of God are seen "by thise visible thynges that ben made faire and agreeable to oure bodily wittes" (IV.xxx.185–186).[20] A great deal more could be said purely about the speculative content of this passage. But for our immediate purposes, it is more important to notice how this sequence signals to its readers the kind of engagement that the text is soliciting. Perception, it argues, is understood to provoke desire, which in turn engenders discourse. This could equally be a reflexive observation about the narrative texture of *Sowle* itself, and about the notably "*busy* entendement" (IV.xxv.174 [my emphasis]) required from the reader, not only at this point in the narrative, but throughout *Manhode* and *Sowle*. *Play* and *process* are vital discursive means whereby these texts attempt to *entalenten*, that is, to stimulate such a response.

Processes of inquiry and investigation are repeatedly modelled throughout *Manhode*, as for example by a "vicarie," or parish vicar, who asks why he has horns, and thereby learns about his true identity—or perhaps acquires it incrementally, by a process of silent metamorphosis that mirrors the stages by which a mind gradually grasps a concept.[21] First, he is taught by Resoun that his name is Pontifex: that is, a mediator between God and man. Resoun's firm assertion that "þis is þi lessoun" seems to crown the vicarie's learning process with a definite answer, but this is only a short-lived moment of stasis.[22] Not long afterward, the vicarie's identity shifts further: as Avril Henry points out, he is first "like a representative of Aaron or Moses"; subsequently "he is told he 'would be' *goode Moyses* if he used his authority against evil." Later, "he *is* Moses, Type of Christ."[23] Has he been this all along, with his true nature veiled from him, or the reader, or both? Or does his nature actually change as the narrative progresses, completing or perfecting itself before the reader's eyes? Even the reader who comes to this passage familiar with the iconographic tradition of the horned Moses may be left in a state of uncertainty about what he or she has actually experienced here. And the calculated arousal of a spectrum of possible mental states—objective knowledge (for example, about the "horned Moses" tradition) turned into experience (the metamorphosis from "vicarie" to "Moyses"), provoking interpretative questions that in turn lead to rumination on what the "answers" themselves really signified all along—is as characteristic of both *Manhode* and *Sowle* as it is of their sources.

A different kind of discursive engagement is set in motion by the confrontation in *Manhode* between Nature and Grace Dieu concerning the mystery of the Eucharist. The miracle of transubstantiation is abhorrent to Nature because she hates "al mutacioun [transformation] þat is doon in haste."[24] Nevertheless, even though Nature is gradually brought to understand that arguing with Grace is futile, she wishes to press her case, and Grace allows this, "for I holde al þat euere ye mown [must] seyn and arguen today [more] game."[25] I will consider further implications of the translations' explorations of the Eucharist later, but for now it is sufficient to notice what is suggested here about the intrinsic productivity of "game." Grace may use "game" simply to indicate that Nature's objections are trivial to her, and easily refuted. But there is a separate dividend for the reader who might experience this kind of "game" in an altogether less trivial way: that is, as an intellectual exercise in which the mind is obliged to ruminate on, and evaluate, both Nature's objections and Grace's responses. The translation, therefore, faithfully renders something characteristic of the original texts: a sequence of significant narrative pauses that arrest the "pilgrim's progress," so that ideas and arguments might become subject to serious play in which both the reader and the allegorical figures may participate.[26]

Such a technique is deployed at greater length, and depth, in the "apple tree" sequence from *Sowle*, IV. In the first chapter, the soul experiences that "helle went a fer [far] fro me and . . . I also wente a fer fro it contynuely" (IV.i.141). It encounters a wondrous enigma ("a thing wher of I mervailed"): "a multitude of pilgrims pleynge with an appil by twen [between] two grete trees of whiche oon was faire and grene . . . & that other was drye" (141). The significance of what the pilgrim-soul is seeing is psychological as well as theological, his angelic guide emphasizing the emotional necessity of this play. There is no pilgrim so wise or so holy, she declares, "that somtyme he ne shal fynden heuynes [heaviness] and sorwe [sorrow] at his herte, wherfore hym nedeth som solace & disporte wher with to appesen [bring peace to] his herte" (141). The reader whose mind is well stocked with religious doctrine will be unsurprised at the simple doctrinal content perceptible beneath the allegorical layer in what follows: the pilgrims are playing with the apple that "for cause of Adam & hys lynage was honged upon this drye tree . . . and fro on [*one*] tree to a nother thus was he translated & born" (142). But at this particular moment in the narrative, Christ's function is purely emotional and consolatory. Moreover, the significance of this particular apple can be grasped intuitively long before the intellect is satisfied by the full explanation of its *raison d'être*. The apple that Christ has become is tossed about between the pilgrims to comfort them "as ofte tymes as they ben annoyed" (142). This play, then, is a figuration of the relationship with Christ to which all Christians, both within the narrative and beyond it, must return in a process of continuous reengagement, as well as a figuration in which the constant threat of abjection is both acknowledged and contained: "This fruyt is the appil with tho which men musten pleyen hem [play] for to avoydon [relieve] her heuynesse" (IV.ii.145). Thus, playing with the apple in *Sowle*, like the game between Grace and Nature in *Manhode*, is utterly serious without being remotely solemn. The exigencies of play and game enfranchise narrative modes through which doctrine can be made to serve a number of possible human needs, such as the intellectual stimulus achieved through disputation, or the containment of powerful emotions provided through consolation.

Having considered some of the functions of playful narrative space in these texts, we can return to the apple tree/incarnation sequence in *Sowle* in order to discover the significance of "process" to the English translations. Another opening-up of narrative space for discursive exploration occurs when Virginity asks Justice to make a dry and a green tree debate the matter of restitution for Adam's sin (IV.v.148). The ingenuity of the debate that results is derived from the fact that the reader knows its outcome—that Christ will become "mene and mediatour by twene sinful men and [God]" (IV.xviii.157)—but not the particular argumentative route by which that outcome will be reached in this particular text. And this, in turn, opens up a further forum for debate between the persons of the Trinity, which is concluded by the agreement that Christ will become the sacrificed apple. Throughout the latter debate, balance is carefully maintained between emotion and logic, complaint and disputation: just as IV.vi was taken up with the prose complaint of the dry tree for Adam's transgression, so IV.xxi contains the lengthy poetic lamentation of the green tree for the loss of its precious apple. In IV.xxii, the dry tree offers the green tree tender consolation in a register removed from the skilful language of debate: "[F]or in this wide worlde is ther no Iuel [jewel] so faire ne so precious wher with for to pleyen and take desport" (IV.xxii.169). Psalm 33:9 ("O taste and see that the Lord is sweet"), an unquoted but powerful intertextual presence, generates the dry tree's narrative: "The swot [moisture] and the sauour ther of shal glade euery wyght that wel is disposed. And that [for one who] often tasteth of the swetnes ther of and goodly can kepen it . . . it shal make hym to forȝete al maner greaunce [grievance], and it shal destroy and utterly awoydon it [render it void]" (IV.xxii.169–170). It is for this reason, the angel finally explains, that the pilgrims "maken hem so besy with this appil" (IV.xxiii.170). And it is for the same reason that the green tree "endeth this processe," as the rubric in New York, Public Library, MS Spencer 19 (fol. 82v) has it, by resolving to "pley and desporte, that I may forȝete al myn heuynesse" (IV.xxiii.170). This "process" thus ends where it began, with the playing pilgrims, returning the pilgrim-soul, and the reader, to the onward journey of pilgrimage. But their journeys to this point have been anything but linear.

This lack of linearity, signaled in the chronology-defying tableau that contains both the dry and green trees and pilgrims who could only have benefited many years later from Christ's sacrifice, prioritizes not the slow working-out of salvation history, but the ways in which knowledge of that history and its theological implications might be configured synchronically, rather than diachronically, in a reader's mind, as for instance by associative and imagistic shortcuts that enable the idea of "Christ-as-apple" both to be grasped immediately at an intuitive level and to require further rational explanation. The periodic use of synchronic tableaux is, therefore, simply one of several related ways in which a scholastic imagination, committed to the fostering of a distinctly dianoetic experience in the reader, is at work in these texts. Argument and dialogue in both translations also further the means whereby the reader is continuously involved in questioning and self-questioning. Sarah Kay has argued that Deguileville's principal theme in the *Pèlerinage de la vie humaine* had been "the imperative that one should know oneself."[27] The interactive techniques carried over into the translations—conversations, dialogues, and even imagistic sequences in which curiosity is both aroused and "assoiled"—ceaselessly provoke the reader toward self-understanding even as they emphasize the inevitable incompleteness, the continuous becoming, of such understanding *in via*, in this life. The interactive, and consequently dramatic, potential of *Sowle* seems to have been amply recognized by the London Carthusian readers whose discriminating use of the text, and particular focus on its "series of conversations" and dialogues, has recently been explored by Jessica Brantley.[28] Julian of Norwich was, it seems, far from being the only late-medieval English writer for whom the work of the text was "nott yett performyd."[29]

THE EUCHARIST IN THE ENGLISH
THEOLOGICAL IMAGINATION

In this section, I enlarge the perspective on dianoetic experience established in the previous section by placing these translations in conversation with other vernacular voices from this period. The intellectually capacious and emotionally nondefensive qualities of the translations may be more sharply appreciated when they are read alongside texts generated more immediately by the exigencies of theological controversy. But it is equally important to acknowledge that these very different kinds of writing could nevertheless achieve similar kinds and levels of dianoetic vitality.

Shannon Gayk has recently drawn attention to the fact that literary form, and the implications of stylistic variety, were as important to Wycliffite writers as to their contemporaries.[30] Among such writers, an early fifteenth-century anonymous Wycliffite preacher is among the most intellectually and stylistically resourceful.[31] The preacher's works provide an opportunity for comparison with the Deguileville translations in that both are engaged

in developing the vernacular for the expression and exploration of theological ideas, images, and arguments. In order to appraise this preacher's
scholastic imagination, I concentrate here on his *Tractatus de oblacione
iugis sacrificii* (also known as the "Titus tract" and henceforth referred to
as such for convenience). Like those of the Deguileville translations, many
of this writer's propositions can be readily grasped in outline; but what
gives this tract its exceptionally challenging density, and thereby its most
immediate point of comparison with the allegories, is its author's commitment to the pragmatic elaboration of those propositions: in short, to *processe* as the translator of *Sowle* might also have understood that term.

One of the preacher's contentions is that the institutional church has impeded the dissemination of Christ's teachings in the scriptures. This is
argued through an extremely elaborate allegorical narrative. Taking as
his text for this phase of the argument Job's complaint in Job 19:17 ("Mi
wiif haþ agrisid [abhorred] my breþe [breath]"), he develops his argument
by postulating an antagonism between Christ's spouse, the church, and
Christ's breath, which is "his lawe þat comeþ out of his mouthe." Moreover,
this mouth should also be understood as his "manheed," through which he
pronounced his law; and in a final development of the same image, this
"manheed" should be understood not only as his mouth, but also as "alle
trewe prestis and prophetis" of the old and new laws, and other "trewe feiþ-
ful men."[32] The preacher maintains that both while he was alive and after
his ascension, Christ "putt þis breþe of þe gospel vppon þe peple wiche
schuld be his spouse."[33] The preacher then elaborates this image, and argument, further into a narrative that requires quotation in full in order that
the richness of its allegorical potential may be adequately appreciated:

Naþeles, sum tyme þis breþe was blowe ful besili vpon Cristis spouse,
and it was ful swete and ful saueri to hir into þe tyme þat sche wax so
frike [eager] and lusti þour [through] grete plente [abundance] of
prouendur [nourishment] þat prekid [stimulated] hir; and namely in þat
partie of þis spouse þat is called þe clerge, þat schuld haue be most sibbe
[amicable] and chast [chaste], þis spouse specially in þis parte began to
loþe [loathe] þe breþe of hir uerri [true] spouse Crist. And þan, riȝt [just]
as vnclene and a schrewid [scolding] calat [harlot] þat is weri of hir trewe
wedded housbond first turneþ hir from her housbonde and loþiþ his
breþe, and aftur makiþ open playnt [public complaint] upon his breþe

seching [seeking] a deuors [divorce], and at þe last [in the end] mariiþ
hir [gets married] [t]o housbonde wiþ a newe breþ, so stondiþ it of þe
clergy þat schuld be streitli [strictly] weddid to Iesu Crist.[34]

The preacher's understanding of what a reader's mind requires in order to
immerse itself in the persuasiveness of an argument was evidently much
more sophisticated than his conventionally Wycliffite rhetoric, replete with
its inevitable hostility toward "glosers" (unreliable interpreters) and a con-
comitant, dogged commitment to what he calls "Cristis logic," might at first
suggest.[35] The imperatives of Christ's logic do not, for this writer, prevent
metaphorical elaboration, which often takes the reader sufficiently deeply
into the inner world of the image that it constitutes a mini-allegory at some
distance from the main thrust of the polemic. One possible effect for the
reader may be compared with the experience of wandering through a well-
stocked garden in a direction that is anything but linear; or of tracing each
ramification of an argument that is as branched and spreading as an abundant tree. It is a short distance from this phase of the writer's argument to
a full-blown complaint against spiritual adultery on the part of the clergy.
The exceptional commitment of this preacher to developing the allegory
from the argument, and *vice versa*, obliges the reader not simply to decode
such imagery, separating the notional chaff from the wheat, but rather to
approach the polemic more patiently and experientially, hearing, understanding and pondering its literal and allegorical levels simultaneously.
Indeed, to use an image that the preacher might have found congenial,
elaborate vehicle and simple tenor are allowed to coexist in this text like
the parabolic wheat and tares, growing together until the harvest time of
interpretation.

Later in the tract, there is an even closer convergence between the imagistic mentality at work here and that exhibited in the Deguileville translations when the preacher addresses the mystery of the Eucharist, his
theology obliging him to describe what he understands by the "mystik bodi
of Crist." He imagines this as having been "multepliid of þe whete [wheat]
corne þat Crist spekiþ of": "þe wiche fel into þe erthe and was dede, and so
multiplied into meche [much] frute oonyd [united] in Iesu Crist, rote [root]
and heed [head] þerof. And it is betokened into þe sacrid oost [sacred host]
þat is many whete cornys onyd togedre bi craft of man, and uereli is þe bodi
of Crist bi uertu and wirching of his worde; and so it is boþe figurre and

truthe."³⁶ Translating St. Augustine, an authority who nourishes this writer's sensibility as surely as he had that of Deguileville, the preacher turns to a Pentecost sermon for the image of many grains making up the sacred bread. These grains are ordinary Christians, for, according to the preacher's translation of Augustine, "[w]han ȝe we[re] exorciȝed, ȝe were in a maner igrounde [ground up in a way]. Whan ȝe were christened, ȝe were sprengid [mixed, i.e. with water]; and so in a maner made into past [paste], and afturword ibake [baked] and isaddid [made resolute] bi hote loue [devotion]."³⁷ He elaborates on this further by turning this image into one linking penance, baptism, and devotion ("hote loue"). The preacher seeks to show that Augustine might be quoted in support of a Eucharistic theology that seeks to preserve the substance of the bread and wine after consecration: for the sacred host "is Cristis mystik bodi figurali and uerreli [*truly*], þe wiche þe peple is þe same bodi reali and uerreli." Objecting to the orthodox doctrine that transubstantiation was to be understood as the annihilation of the physical properties of the sacraments, the writer maintains that "a sacrament is propurli a uisible forme or kynde of an vnuisible grace, and in antecristis sacrament is no uisible forme or kinde."³⁸

As we will see, the preacher's openness to the argumentative viability of the image of many fragments making up a whole, and to a patristic discourse in which the faithful for a moment become that which they ingest in the Mass, is on a continuum with some of the narrative processes in the Deguileville translations. However, in order to situate the translations in relation to another avowedly orthodox treatment of the Eucharist during this period, it is instructive to turn briefly to Nicholas Love's *De sacramento* (Treatise on the Sacrament), which was disseminated with his better-known translation, *The Mirror of the Blessed Life of Jesus Christ*, in many manuscripts.³⁹ In a text to which belief in miracles ("merueiles") is fundamental, Love argues that in order to grasp the miracle of transubstantiation, it is necessary that we "leuyn [abandon] oure kyndely [natural] reson" (226/6–7) in stark contrast to the "heritykes" who "falsly trowene [believe] & obstinately seyne þat it is brede in his kynde [in its nature] as it was before þe consecration, so þat þe substance of brede is not turnede in to þe substance of goddes body, bot duelleþ [remains] stille brede as it was before" (225/26–30). For Love, "ymaginacion of reson" cannot account for the "merueiles [miracles] of þis worthi sacrament" (227/27–28). He repeatedly castigates "manye grete clerkes, þe which leuen [rely] so miche vpon hir owne kyndely reson, & þe principales of philosophy, þat is mannus wisdame grondete [grounded] onely in kyndely reson of man" (235/13–16). For Love, this mentality is exemplified by Aristotle, who "techeþ as kyndely reson acordeþ [confirms] þat þe accidents of brede or wyne," such as color and taste, "mowe not be bot [must only be] in [þe] substance of brede or wyne after hir kynde [in accordance with their nature]." This contradicts the "doctrine of holy chirch" that teaches that after consecration, "accidents" such as color and taste "bene þere [there] with out hir kyndely [natural] subiecte" (236/30–37). Nevertheless, distaste for logical argument concerning the mystery does not preclude an imagistic explanation of the miracle whereby Christ's body is fully in each separate fragment of the host, as well as in the whole. He does this by drawing an analogy with the way in which "þe ymage of a mannus [man's] grete face, & of a grete body is seene in a litel Mirrour, & if it be broken & departede [shattered]. ʒit in euery parte it semeþ alle þe hole ymage, & not in partye after þe partes of þe glasse so broken" (227/18–21).

Returning to the Deguileville translations, we can see that several aspects of the transubstantiation sequence in *Manhode*—the routing of Aristotle (functioning there as Nature's emissary) and the image of the shattered mirror—make contact with some of the elements of Love's argument in the *Treatise*. *Manhode* is doctrinally uncontroversial: as Grace assures the pilgrim, "Flesh and blood it is in sooth, but bred and wyn it is figured. And sooth it is þat sumtime it was bred and wyn, but . . . into flesh and into blood it was remeeved [removed] bi Moyses."[40] And on hearing the words of consecration, the pilgrim must believe that "it is no more neiþer wyne ne bred, but it is þe flesh þat was spred on the cros for þee and hanged, and þat it is þe blood with which þilke [the same] cros was bidewed [moistened] and spreynt [sprinkled]."[41] However, the differences between these two avowedly orthodox treatments of this complex topic are as striking as their incidental similarities. In order to demonstrate this, rather than reprising the whole of the transubstantiation sequence in *Manhode*, I will focus on two of its most distinctive aspects, before briefly discussing the representation of the Eucharist in *Sowle*. The first aspect to note about the *Manhode* version is the fact that the argument between Nature and Grace, briefly discussed earlier in the context of "game," takes place at the same time that Moses, the priest, is dining (that is, celebrating the Eucharist).[42] The simultaneity of these two events brings about a rhetorical effect similar to that of a cinematic split screen, as the Mass is celebrated in the background even as a lengthy and vehement debate about its metaphysical underpinnings is staged. The narrative's doctrinal content is, again, uncontroversial: Grace will inevitably triumph in this debate. And a more conservative way of arranging the allegory might have been to grant Grace victory over Nature's "rude understondinge" before Moses's meal had commenced.[43] But this particular *dispositio* keeps the meal in the background throughout; rather than entirely displacing the debate, the mystery coexists with it, in a manner possibly suggestive of the way in which the intellectuality appropriate to scholastic disputation and the multimodal experience—including the imaginative, the sensory and the emotional—involved in the celebration of the Mass somehow had to coexist in the minds, souls, and lives of medieval theologians.

The discussion of the Eucharist in *Manhode* moves into a different phase with the argument between Aristotle and Sapience, and this brings me to the second of the aspects to be discussed here. The second significant aspect of this allegory is its discursive density: it demonstrates to an extremely elaborate degree a feature discussed above, namely the opening up of narrative space for discourse and exploration. The heart of this process is the discussion of "measure," which focuses on the paradox that the Eucharist obliges God, an immeasurable and infinite entity, to be contained in something finite. It is Sapience's task to ensure that each fragment of the Eucharistic host is as big as the whole loaf from which it comes.[44] The "process" with which Sapience confounds Aristotle revolves around the fact that God is great and yet needs to fill a little human heart. And the remarkable aspect of this phase of their disputation is the imagistic and conceptual density with which Sapience dilates her subject matter. Memory, she argues, contains vast things, but is enclosed in a tiny space, just as Aristotle can contain in his mind the images of populous places that he has visited.[45] The pupil of the eye is tiny, she points out, when compared with the size of the people whose faces it can see. And she too uses the image of the shattered mirror that contains a perfect image in each of its fragments. This image recurs in *Sowle* when the figure of Doctrine argues that each soul is made in God's image and thus can contain him, just as a shattered mirror can contain "the same figure hool" (IV.xxviii.176). And it is this aspect of the translation that makes contact, however briefly, with that of the Wycliffite preacher beguiled by Augustine's image of Christians as the grains of wheat that make up the whole of the Eucharistic host. Continuity between these kinds of imagination subsists, despite their contrasting attitudes toward the authority of the institutional church.

The representation of the Eucharist in *Sowle* is far less elaborate than its disputatious treatment in *Manhode*, but it is notable that this brief sequence, in which St. Peter invites Adam and Eve to see whether the "mete" that he has brought them "be better than the appil which ȝe eeten and wheyther [*which*] is more delicious, the olde fruyt or the newe," is a dramatic tableau in which the redemption of mankind is represented through synchronic compression (V.xx.252). It differs only slightly in content, therefore, from the tableau of the playing pilgrims discussed earlier, and it completes the argument that the first tableau initiated. It skilfully sidesteps the inflamed metaphysical terminology used in theological controversy by looking outward, to Christian history and the consolations of typology, the apple tasting staged by St. Peter providing another example of the profound playfulness that we have encountered elsewhere in these translations. This completes my appraisal of the various experiential and discursive perspectives on the Eucharistic mystery that the Deguileville translations unleash in English. But what emerges most forcefully from the final phase of this discussion, which builds in turn on the earlier analyses of play and process, is the spectacle of philosophical arguments being deployed with such relish, discrimination, and lack of inhibition in these translations, even in contexts in which Nature and Reason are so readily and inevitably confounded. This playful orthodoxy contrasts dramatically with Love's suspicion of "kyndely reson." as voiced with anxiety, or possibly irritation, at several points in the *Treatise*, determined as its rhetorical options are by the narrower exigencies of controversy. Even the Wycliffite preacher's tract provides more in the way of allegorical openings and nonlinear ruminations.

In concentrating so firmly on these translations in themselves, rather than comparing and contrasting them with their originals, I have sought to invite further reflection on their possible impact at a particularly complex moment in English religious and literary history. That impact cannot be known absolutely, but even the very selective material that I have presented here precludes the drawing of overly firm conclusions about the discursive and imaginative adventurousness of English texts and readers in the aftermath of the Wycliffite controversies. It might once have been thought an indictment of late-medieval English intellectual life that even as Degui-leville's allegories were being translated, *Piers Plowman* was gradually becoming, in James Simpson's words, "effectively unreachable."[46] After all, when differentiating *Piers Plowman* from other allegories of its time, David Aers once counselled: "[L]et us not impatiently turn the kind of process Langland seems to be creating, into that of the exegetes, homilists and normal medieval allegorical poets."[47] Aers positioned Deguileville as a representative of the "normal," an embodiment of the mediocrity transcended by Langland's poetic intuition. But as these translations remind us, Langland clearly learned a great deal about "process" from his French predecessor. The English versions remain as hospitable as their sources to enterprising fusions between theological matter and imaginative experience, engaging their readers in a simultaneously poetic and ratiocinative process closely analogous to the "jeu du savoir," the "game of knowledge," to which, it has been argued, some late fourteenth-century French translators of Aristotle had invited their readers.[48] They bring to their respective interpretative communities an armature derived partly from having originated in a different place and time; exhibit a challenging insistence on viewing the interior life as an experiential adventure in which objective knowledge is ceaselessly subjected to the unpredictable forces of process, play and game; and refresh the resources of allegory as a genre that suggests, invites and solicits, but cannot absolutely predict or control its readers' interpretative and experiential ruminations. Where original texts rather than translations are concerned, *Piers Plowman* might be regarded as the work that displays the most highly developed understanding of how a poetic "jeu du savoir" might be played in English, but in light of the narrative ingenuity preserved in these translations, let alone that of their sources, it might be time to reconsider the claim that it was also Langland who invented "experience as a literary category."[49] The material considered here suggests a different conclusion.

NOTES

1. As noted by Nicholas Watson, whose phrase this is, in "'Multi vocati pauci vero electi': affective spirituality revisited," a lecture delivered at the Faculty of English, University of Oxford, on 27 February 2013. See Nicholas Watson, "The Composition of Julian of Norwich's *Revelation of Love*," *Speculum* 68 (1993): 637–683.

2. An outstanding recent example of what can be achieved in this respect with apparently well-known texts is the revisionist essay by Valerie Allen, "Belief and Knowledge in Love's *Mirror*," in *Devotional Culture in Late Medieval England and Europe. Diverse Imaginations of Christ's Life*, eds. Stephen Kelly and Ryan Perry, Medieval Church Studies 31 (Turnhout, Belgium: Brepols, 2014), 553–572.

3. I address some of the consequences of this lack of focus in "Intellectual Life in Fifteenth-Century England," *New Medieval Literatures* 12 (2010): 333–370.

4. See Kathryn Kerby-Fulton, *Books Under Suspicion. Censorship and Tolerance of Revelatory Writing in Late Medieval England* (Notre Dame, IN: University of Notre Dame Press, 2006).

5. Susan Crane, "Anglo-Norman Cultures in England," in *The Cambridge History of Medieval English Literature*, ed. David Wallace (Cambridge: Cambridge University Press, 1999), 52. See also Jocelyn Wogan Brown et al., *Language and Culture in Medieval Britain. The French of England, c.1100–c.1500* (Woodbridge, England: York Medieval Press, 2009); Ardis Butterfield, *The Familiar Enemy. Chaucer, Language and Nation in the Hundred Years War* (Oxford: Oxford University Press, 2009); William Calin, *The French Tradition and the Literature of Medieval England* (Toronto: University of Toronto Press, 1994).

6. Rosemarie Potz McGerr, introduction to *The Pilgrimage of the Soul*, vol. 1: *A Critical Edition of the Middle English Dream Vision*, ed. Rosemarie Potz McGerr (New York: Garland, 1990), xxx. The cited edition covers only the first book of the English text. The full text of New York, New York Public Library, MS Spencer 19 is reproduced in *The Pilgrimage of the Soul*, ed. M. Dorothea Barry (PhD diss., University of Toronto, 1931), and all quotations from *Sowle* within this essay, except where otherwise noted, refer to a facsimile of Barry's edition parenthetically by section, chapter and page numbers.

7. *The Pilgrimage of the Lyfe of the Manhode*, ed. Avril Henry, 2 vols., EETS OS 288 and 292 (London: Oxford University Press, 1985–1988). All quotations from *Manhode* in this essay refer to this edition by volume, page, and line number.

8. *The Pilgrimage of the Life of Man*, ed. F. J. Furnivall and Katharine B. Locock, 3 vols. EETS OS 78, 83, and 92 (London: Kegan Paul, Trench, Trübner and Co., 1899–1904).

9. *The French Tradition*, 185. On such English readers, see Jessica Brantley, *Reading in the Wilderness. Private Devotion and Public Performance in Late Medieval England* (Chicago: University of Chicago Press, 2007), 240–259; Michael G. Sargent, "Censorship or Cultural Change? Reformation and Renaissance in the Spirituality of Late Medieval England," in *After Arundel. Religious Writing in Fifteenth-Century England*, eds. Vincent Gillespie and Kantik Ghosh. Medieval Church Studies 21 (Turnhout, Belgium: Brepols, 2011), 55–72; and Nicholas Love, *"The Mirror of the Blessed Life of Jesus Christ": A Full Critical Edition*, ed. Michael G. Sargent (Exeter, England: University of Exeter Press, 2005), 54–96.

10. The Pèlerinage *Allegories of Guillaume de Deguileville: Tradition, Authority*

and Influence, ed. Marco Nievergelt and Stephanie A.Viereck Gibbs Kamath (Cambridge, England: D. S. Brewer, 2013); Stephanie A. Viereck Gibbs Kamath, *Authorship and First-Person Allegory in Late Medieval France and England* (Cambridge, England: D. S. Brewer, 2012); Marco Nievergelt, "Paradigm, Intertext or Residual Allegory: Guillaume de Deguileville and the *Gawain*-Poet," *Medium Aevum* 80 (2011): 18–40; Josephine Elizabeth Houghton, "The Works of Guillaume de Deguileville in Late Medieval England: Transmission, Reception and Context with Special Reference to *Piers Plowman*" (PhD diss., University of Birmingham, 2006); Emily Steiner, *Documentary Culture and the Making of Medieval English Literature* (Cambridge: Cambridge University Press, 2003); Jennifer E. Bryan, "Hoccleve, the Virgin, and the Politics of Complaint," *PMLA* 117, no. 5 (2002): 1172–1187.

11. Rosemarie Potz McGerr, introduction to *The Pilgrimage of the Soul*, xlii.

12. On the complex religious, intellectual and literary cultures of England during this period, see Gillespie and Ghosh.

13. Rosemond Tuve, *Allegorical Imagery. Some Mediaeval Books and Their Posterity* (Princeton, NJ: Princeton University Press, 1966), 145–218; Helen Phillips, "Chaucer and Deguileville: The *ABC* in Context," *Medium Aevum* 62 (1993): 1–19; Sarah Kay, *The Place of Thought. The Complexity of One in Late Medieval French Didactic Poetry* (Philadelphia: University of Pennsylvania Press, 2007), 70–94.

14. The facsimile of the Barry edition, which reproduces New York, Public Library, MS Spencer 19, fols. 133r–v (265) is faint at this point, but the *verba translatoris* are also printed (and hence quoted here) from London, British Library, MS. Egerton 615 (fol. 106r) in the very selective edition of *The Booke of the Pylgremage of the Sowle*, ed. Katherine Isabella Cust (London: Basil Montagu Pickering, 1859), 82.

15. *MED*, "proces" (n.).

16. *OED*, "proces" (n.).

17. *Manhode*, 1:2/51.

18. Ibid., 1:2/57–58, 61–63.

19. II Corinthians 12:2–4.

20. Romans 1:20.

21. *Manhode*, 1:9/339ff.

22. Ibid., 1:10/381.

23. Ibid., 2:374–375, referring to lines 278, 430 and 434 respectively (my emphasis).

24. Ibid., 1:21/854–855.

25. Ibid., 1:24/997–998.

26. Sarah Kay explores Deguileville's sensitivities to the possibilities of spatial and temporal configurations in *The Place of Thought*, 70–94.

27. Kay, 71.

28. Brantley, 240–259.

29. Long Text, chap. 86, in Julian of Norwich, *A Book of Showings*, ed. Edmund College, OSA, and James Walsh, SJ, 2 vols. (Toronto: Pontifical Institute of Mediaeval Studies), 2:731.

30. "Lollard Writings, Literary Criticism, and the Meaningfulness of Form," in *Wycliffite Controversies*, ed. Mishtooni Bose and J. Patrick Hornbeck II, Medieval Church Studies 23 (Turnhout, Belgium: Brepols, 2011), 135–152.

31. *The Works of a Lollard Preacher. The Sermon* Omnis Plantacio, *The Tract* Fundamentum aliud nemo potest ponere, *and The Tract* de oblacione iugis sacrificii, ed. by Anne Hudson, EETS OS 317 (Oxford: Early English Text Society, 2001). Hereafter referenced as *WLP* with page and line numbers.

32. *WLP*, 179/862–869.

33. *WLP*, 179/877–880.

34. *WLP*, 180/899–909.

35. *WLP*, 169/467, and 172/588.

36. *WLP*, 195/1509–1514.

37. *WLP*, 195/1494–1496. On the source, see Hudson's note, 320.

38. *WLP*, 196/1524–1525, 1545–1547.

39. Nicholas Love, *The Mirror of the Blessed Life of Jesus Christ*, ed. Michael G. Sargent, 63–64, 67. As Potz Gerr points out, six manuscripts containing *Sowle* belonged to "people who either had Carthusian connections themselves or owned other books associated with the Carthusians" (*Pilgrimage of the Soul*, xliv).

40. *Manhode*, 1:36/1492–1495.

41. Ibid., 1:37/1519–1522.

42. Ibid., 1:19–26.

43. Ibid., 1:26/1043.

44. Kay's discussion of this sequence in the original text is pertinent here (*The Place of Thought*, 76–81).

45. *Manhode*, 1:42/1727–1740.

46. *Reform and Cultural Revolution. The Oxford English Literary History* (Oxford: Oxford University Press, 2002), 2:333.

47. David Aers, *"Piers Plowman" and Christian Allegory* (London: Edward Arnold, 1975), 88.

48. Caroline Boucher, "De la *subtilité* en français: vulgarisation et savoir dans les traductions d'*auctoritates* des XIIIe–XIVe siècles," *The Medieval Translator VIII*, ed. Rosalynn Voaden, René Tixier, Teresa Sanchez Roura, and Jenny Rebecca Rytting (Turnhout, Belgium: Brepols, 2003), 99.

49. Anne Middleton, "Narration and the Invention of Experience: Episodic Form in *Piers Plowman*," in *The Wisdom of Poetry: Essays in Early English Literature in Honor of Morton W. Bloomfield*, ed. Larry D. Benson and Siegfried Wenzel (Kalamazoo, MI: Medieval Institute Publications, 1982), 110.

CHAPTER TEN

PREPARING FOR EASTER: SERMONS ON THE EUCHARIST IN *ENGLISH WYCLIFFITE SERMONS*

Jennifer Illig

T he Fourth Lateran Council in 1215 decreed that "all the faithful of either sex, after they have reached the age of discernment, should individually confess all their sins in a faithful manner to their own priest at least once a year, and let them take care to do what they can to perform the penance imposed on them. Let them reverently receive the sacrament of the Eucharist at least at Easter."[1] Although some people in the late Middle Ages received the Eucharist more often, for most, receiving the sacrament became an annual event that took place only at Easter.[2] According to the late John Bossy, across medieval Europe, the Easter communion naturally brought together all members of the community. The Eucharistic celebration was commonly followed by a parish feast that would emphasize the ties of unity within the community.[3] As a result, sermons for Easter Sunday were designed to prepare people to have the proper disposition for the reception of communion.[4]

During the remainder of the year, sermons and devotional manuals from England and the Continent emphasized the importance of having a proper interior disposition in order to spiritually receive the Eucharist when a person attended Sunday mass. For instance, in *The Goodman of Paris* (*Le Ménagier de Paris*), a late fourteenth-century explanation of the sacraments and teachings of the church, the writer, a wealthy Paris burgher, wrote for his young wife: "when men and women be at church to hear divine service, their hearts should not be at home or in their fields, nor in any other things of this world; and they should not think of temporal things, but of God, in purity, singleness and sincerity, and should pray devoutly to Him."[5] While such manuals as well as sermons often describe the Eucharist in terms of the doctrine of transubstantiation, it seems that the primary focus of these writings is not to present theological treatises on the nature of the Eucharist, but to prepare members of their audience for the spiritual reception of communion most of the year and actual reception at Easter.[6]

Although emphasis on correct attention and participation in the sacramental life of the church, and particularly the Eucharist, is commonplace in the late Middle Ages, it is not something that is often commented upon in relation to Wycliffite texts. Wycliffite Christians are better known for their varieties of Eucharistic theologies, as laid out, for instance, by J. Patrick Hornbeck II, than for a pastoral Eucharistic theology focused on the reception of communion. In fact, much scholarship has pointed away from an emphasis on reception. Margaret Aston suggested in her essay "Lollard Women Priests?" that Lollards (to use her term) most often held meetings centered around preaching rather than the celebration and reception of the Eucharist.[7] More recently, Fiona Somerset, while pointing out that lollard writings do not necessarily deny the efficacy of the sacraments or suggest that people should not participate in them, has suggested that "lollard writings emphasize 'gostili' or spiritual reception [of the Eucharist] through knowing about Christ's life, believing he is God and man, and keeping the commandments."[8] It seems important to note that for most of the liturgical year, such spiritual reception was precisely what mainstream texts were calling for as well.[9] Following the pattern of the mainstream church, at least one group of Wycliffite writings seems to be particularly interested in providing instruction concerning both the spiritual and actual reception of communion: the *English Wycliffite Sermons* (*EWS*).

In this essay, I will first present some brief comments on reading *EWS* in their liturgical order, exploring the way in which the liturgical year influences the sermons' teaching about pastoral subjects. I have elsewhere shown the influence of the liturgical cycle on diverse pastoral topics such as Christ, Mary, and prayer to be significant.[10] For the sake of space here, I will focus on the Eucharist. I will begin my discussion of the Eucharist in *EWS* by establishing the contours of the Eucharistic theology found there. I will then show that during the Lenten season and at Easter, the writers of *EWS* discuss what the Eucharist is and how to have the proper disposition to receive it. By offering these teachings at this time of the year, the writers of *EWS* prepare the members of their audience for their Easter communion. This work of preparation situates *EWS* closer to mainstream church practice on the Eucharist than the varieties of Eucharistic theologies found in *EWS* would seem to suggest.

READING *EWS* LITURGICALLY

As is well known, the 294 sermons of *EWS* take their lections from the Sarum Missal. Although the sermons in *EWS* are clearly associated with specific liturgical days and events, scholars have most often used them as a source for Wycliffite understandings of specific doctrines rather than analyzed them as liturgical texts. There are at least two reasons for this. The first is the organization of many *EWS* manuscripts, which present the sermons as five separate sets: the Sunday gospels (set 1), the common of the saints used for saints' feast days when no specific sermon had been provided (set 2), the proper of the saints used on specific feast days (set 3), the weekday gospels (set 4), and the Sunday epistles (set 5).[11] The second reason has to do with the general approach taken by many scholars of Wycliffism and lollardy. Somerset notes that "selective readings of lollard writings often attend only to their most polemical passages, or what is most heretical in the terms set by bishops seeking out deviant belief and practice, or what is most similar to later protestant views."[12] By picking out sermons based on polemical issues, the wider context of the sermon cycle and the wider possible use of the sermons within the liturgical year are invariably ignored.

To resituate the sermons within their late medieval liturgical context, the sermons should be read, not thematically or according to their five sets, but according to their place in the liturgical year. Because *EWS* is based on a model year rather than an actual one, I arranged the sermons in the order of a year in which they might be used. By 1404/05, the year I chose, all of the sermons contained in *EWS* would have been composed, but the most severe restrictions on vernacular biblical translation and on Wyclifffism more broadly, namely those implemented by Archbishop Thomas Arundel's 1408/09 *Constitutions*, would not have been put into place. This method of reading the sermons uncovered a number of interesting things. For instance, themes presented on a Sunday are sometimes continued on the following weekdays. During the second week of Lent, for instance, almost all of the sermons discuss meekness or its opposite, pride.[13] In addition, Mary is mentioned throughout the liturgical year—at least once a month.[14] Such occurrences are easier to recognize when the sermons are arranged in liturgical order.

The most interesting findings from reading the sermons liturgically, however, have to do with the Eucharist. In *EWS*, there are twenty-one sermons that discuss the Eucharist.[15] Eighteen of these can be assigned to particular dates.[16] Nine of these occur in the period from Septuagesima to Easter. This means that half of the sermons that refer to the Eucharist in the course of the liturgical year occur disproportionally in the two-month period during the Lenten season up to Easter.[17] That there is a high concentration of sermons on the Eucharist during the Lenten season should come as no surprise. Given that most lay people would receive the Eucharist at Easter, Lent would be an appropriate time to make sure that believers were familiar with teaching on the Eucharist.

EUCHARISTIC THEOLOGY

The Eucharistic theology found among the sermons of *EWS* is largely dependent upon John Wyclif's teachings about the Eucharist. As is well known, Wyclif's Eucharistic theology developed over the course of his lifetime in reaction to the teachings of the mainstream church on the doctrine of transubstantiation.[18] The term *transubstantiation* was first officially used at the Fourth Lateran Council in 1215. At that time, it had only been in use in theological circles for about seventy years and was still subject to multiple interpretations. As both Gary Macy and Ian Christopher Levy point out, the council did not define what *transubstantiation* meant. Rather, it introduced it into the church's official vocabulary for discussions about the Eucharist and, specifically, used it to defend the notion of the real presence of Christ in the Eucharist.[19] In the years that followed, transubstantiation continued to have multiple definitions. However, by the middle of the thirteenth century, the definition formulated by Thomas Aquinas became dominant. Aquinas says that the substance of the bread and wine is changed into the substance of the body and blood of Christ.[20]

Wyclif did not deny the presence of Christ in the Eucharist. What he did deny is Aquinas's definition, which he dismisses as allowing for an "accident without a subject."[21] Despite very clearly dismissing Aquinas's definition of transubstantiation, Wyclif, according to Stephen E. Lahey, did not do much to develop an alternate theory of Christ's presence in the Eucharist beyond asserting that Christ is indeed present.[22] Wyclif's assertions are based on his belief that Christ in Scripture teaches that he is present in the Eucharist. Scripture must be read properly in order for Christians to hold correct beliefs. In the case of the Eucharist, Christ's presence is guaranteed by the scriptural words, *"Hoc est corpus meum."* There must be, according to Wyclif, a continual identification of the bread as bread with Christ's body because Christ, who Wyclif asserts cannot lie, says so.[23] If the substance of that bread were to be destroyed in the course of the statement, then Christ would be made a liar.

In many ways, the teaching on the Eucharist in *EWS* is influenced by Wyclif. With Wyclif, the writers of *EWS* reject the scholastic understanding and language of transubstantiation. In sermon 166 for feria three in the fourth week of Lent, the writer comments on John 7:16 that Christ sometimes speaks by his humanity and sometimes speaks by his divinity.[24] The writer then connects this to the Eucharist by insisting, "And wolde God þes heretikis in mater of þe sacrid oost conseyueden þis speche, and vndirstooden wel Ambrose þat þis oost is not bred aftir þat it is sacrid, for it is not aftir principaly bred but þe body of Crist by uertu of his wordis, and þanne shulden þey shame of þer feyned accidentis."[25] In support of the doctrine of transubstantiation, orthodox theologians often cited Ambrose's assertion that the host was not bread but God's body. According to the writer of sermon 166, these theologians have misunderstood Ambrose, who says that the host was not primarily bread, but the body of Christ by virtue of the words Christ spoke.[26] If they truly understood Ambrose, the writer concludes, they would be ashamed of their invented accidents. In this way, the writer makes very clear that the language of accidents, when associated with the Eucharist, is simply untenable.

In sermon E47, for the seventeenth Sunday after Trinity, the writer, glossing Ephesians 4:5–6,[27] condemns diversity in teachings about the Eucharist: "And heere trowen cristen men þat dyuersete of bileues þat ben in þe sacrid host makiþ dyuersete in þe chirche, and þis mot nedis make aftir dyuersete at þe day of doom, and make sum men be take to heuene and sum men to go to helle."[28] Multiple understandings of the Eucharist mean that some people are going to go to heaven and some people are going to go to hell because, as the writer goes on to explain, Paul teaches that there is only one faith. The particular problem that the writer identifies is not knowing what the host is. The writer explains that Christ says, and the saints that come after him affirm, that the consecrated host is Christ's body in the form of bread. This is what Christians believe: Christ's body and bread can coexist. What they should not hold is that it is either an accident without a subject or nothing at all. Those are the beliefs, the writer insists, that heretics hold.[29] The writer of sermon E47 explains that the source of heretical beliefs about the Eucharist is a false reading of scripture. In formulating heretical teachings about the Eucharist, the writer says that those other people are not following what Christ says. Rather, they deny what scripture actually says and present it in a way that supports their heretical teaching.[30]

This relationship between a proper understanding of scripture and the proper understanding of the Eucharist is emphasized by Wyclif and is seen in other *EWS* sermons.[31] Sermon 176 for Saturday of the fifth week of Lent takes as its lection John 6:54–72. Following the lection, the author emphasizes that there are two kinds of eating and two kinds of food, spiritual and bodily. The problem that the author identifies with the way that John 6 is commonly interpreted is that the words of the Gospel are often applied to the Eucharist. The writer points out that in the timeline of the biblical narrative, Jesus's discourse in John 6 took place well before the institution of the Eucharist at the last supper. As a result, Christ could not have been talking about the Eucharist when he was giving this particular speech.[32] However, the writer goes on to suggest that if the words are properly understood, many, though not all, can be applied to the Eucharist.[33]

In discussing the Eucharist, the writer of sermon 176 employs a distinction between bodily and spiritual presence. The writer explains that Christ had flesh here on earth, and that flesh can be identified with God's body, which is now in heaven. Because Christ's flesh and blood are in heaven, people can only partake of them through spiritual eating. The bread of the Eucharist is truly bread and is eaten bodily by those who receive it. At the same time, it is God's body "in figure" and God in nature.[34] This can seem confusingly contradictory: How can the sacred host be figuratively God's body and naturally God's body at the same time? The answer would seem to lie in Wyclif's notion of the sacramental sign.

In his discussion of Wyclif's Eucharistic theology in *De Eucharistia*, David Aers explains that orthodox discourse on the Eucharist had developed a binary: "*either* Christ's Galilean body is present in the sacrament *or* Christ's body is not present. *Either* the presence of Christ's body is of the real, literal, carnal kind apparently illustrated by Eucharistic miracles . . . ; *or* there is no real presence, merely tropes for an absent Christ."[35] Wyclif rejected this binary because he believed that it was the product of a misunderstanding of sacramental signs and the way that those signs function for humanity. Instead, Wyclif develops a different model of understanding sacramental signs that, disregarding this binary, presents Christ as both present and absent. As Aers explains, Wyclif "affirmed that the body of Christ is *both* present 'allegorically or sacramentally' *and* present transformationally, 'really but sacramentally' in the consecrated sign."[36] At the same time, Christ's physical body—the "Galilean body"—is absent.[37] The writer of sermon 176 likewise denies that Christ's physical body is present while he maintains that God's body is present.[38] It is figurative, but not merely memorial in the way that some later lollard texts are, such as *Wycklyffes Wycket*.[39]

After describing what the Eucharist is, the sermon writer discusses the reception of the sacred host:

> And, but ȝif þis be etun gostly in eting of þe sacrid oost, ellis men taken not wrþily þe sacrament more þan a beeste. And for þis gostly eting many of þe wordis heere ben referrid gostly to eting of þe sacrid oost. But þis oost is etun bodily and gostly of summe men. But Crist body in his kynde is not etun bodily . . . . But euere wite we þat þis oost is uery bred in his kynde, and in figure Goddis body by uertu of Cristis wordis. But þus it is not of Cristis fleyss and his blood in his kynde.[40]

People must receive the sacrament spiritually. If they do not, they are no better than animals. Some men—presumably those who accept the doctrine of transubstantiation—say that the host is eaten both bodily and spiritually. Christ's physical, fleshly body is not eaten—that would be cannibalism. God's body, though, is present in the host in a way not precisely defined. The sermon writer admits that he does not really provide a full explanation and quotes John 6:65: "'*But þer ben summe of ȝou þat trowen not* to þes wordus,' *for Iesu wiste fro þe bigynnyng which men weren not trowynge, and who was to traye hym.*"[41] The writer then points out that Christ sometimes spoke "mystely."[42] Hence, the precise way in which Christ is present is not defined, and the writer does not seem interested in pursuing a precise definition because that would push him beyond the limits of what scripture says.

While Stephen Pink has argued that for the writers of *EWS*, hearing the word of God replaces receiving the sacrament, it seems important to note that the host itself remains an object of discussion and never do the sermon writers say that a person should not receive it.[43] In fact, the Eucharist is repeatedly referred to with some reverence as the "sacrament of the auter"[44] or "þe sacred hoost."[45] The only negative language that the writers use about the Eucharist is to deny the doctrine of transubstantiation.[46] Rejecting the doctrine does not necessarily mean rejecting the practice. It could just mean assigning a different significance to it. In sermon 176, it seems that eating the host spiritually is a necessary addition to mere physical eating. As shown in the previously quoted passage, to eat only physically leaves a person no better than a beast. The sermon writer, though, does not seem to be saying not to receive the host at all, but rather adds further meaning to that reception.

From the sermons discussed, it should be clear that despite—or perhaps because of—the influence of Wyclif on the writers of *EWS*, the sermons do not articulate a uniform or particularly precise teaching on the Eucharist. However, they do maintain that Christ is present in some way and that misunderstandings of the Eucharist, rooted in a false reading of scripture, are heretical. Importantly, reception of the Eucharist is not excluded by the writers of the sermons.

PREPARING FOR EASTER

Although the sermons of *EWS* reject the contemporary formulations of Eucharistic theology, they maintain the importance of the Eucharist in the life of the Christian. During Lent, when the majority of the sermons on the Eucharist appear in *EWS*, the writers present catechesis and directives on the spiritual reception of the Eucharist. For instance, sermon E17 for the second Sunday of Lent teaches that people should "erre not in þis sacrud oost but graunte þat it is two þingis, boþe bred and Godus body, but principally Godus body."[47] The sermon writer offers a direct teaching about what he believes the Eucharist is: both bread and God's body, but principally God's body.[48] Sermon 44 for Passion Sunday offers a similar reading, referencing both Ambrose and Augustine: "And on þis maner semeþ Ambrose to graunte þat þe sacred breed is not aftur breed but Godis body, for hit is not aftur principally breed, but Godis body in maner as Austyn seiþ."[49]

Sermon 162 for feria five in the third week of Lent, like sermon 176, discussed earlier, describes the way to receive the Eucharist: "it shal be chewed in mouþ of soule, fortretid godely by skylis, and siþ it shal be hid in mynde, as mete is hid in mannus stomac and þere moue men to worche werkis of loue, as God biddiþ."[50] After a brief discussion of what typically happens to bread when it is eaten, the writer comments, citing Augustine, that when a person spiritually receives the Eucharist, the recipient is turned into Christ as a result of what he eats.[51] The writer continues that the Eucharist is the foundation of all virtues, and therefore, a person should maintain faith in it and by it, be moved to follow God's law.[52]

The writers of the two sermons for Easter Day, sermons E22 and 46, prepare the members of their audience for the Easter communion by using language that calls to mind the coming communion and by emphasizing the virtues. In this, they are very much like contemporary sermon writers. In his Easter sermon, John Mirk emphasizes the importance of purifying the soul by confessing sin and practicing virtue. Immediately before Mirk presents the exemplum that he includes in the sermon, he instructs: "good men and woymen, I charch you heyly in Godys byhalue þat non of you to-day com to Godys bord, but he be in full charyte to all Godis pepull; and also þat ʒe be clene schryuen and yn full wyll to leue your synne."[53] In this way, he connects the reception of communion, for which people would "com to Godys bord," with the life of virtue and the confession of sin.

In a dominical sermon collection from the late-fifteenth century, the writer of one of the Easter sermons claims that his purpose is to discuss "þe very disposicion þat every cristen sowle scholde have in resceyving of þis blessyd sacrament, it is neþer *in dente* ne *in ventre*, but pryncipally *in mente*. It is neþer 'In þe tethe ne in the wombe' ne in bodyly apparens owtewarde; but specyally grownde þe in stedfaste feythe of mans soule."[54] For this writer, as for the writers of *EWS*, reception of communion involves not just the ability to receive the Eucharist physically; it also means being prepared spiritually for reception. The writer of this Easter sermon, like the writers of *EWS*, then explains that the proper preparation involves instantiating the virtues in one's life. Using the language of a feast, he says that the table "must be sett vpon þe grownde of owre feythe and hope" and is covered with a cloth of charity.[55] These virtues, practiced in this life, prepare a Christian to worthily receive the Eucharist while he or she is alive and to enter heaven upon death.[56] The remainder of this essay will show that although the writers of the Easter sermons in *EWS* present variant Eucharistic theologies, they, like their contemporaries, call people to worthily receive the Eucharist at Easter.

Sermon E22 is cited by the sermons' editors, Anne Hudson and Pamela Gradon, and by Hornbeck as a sermon that presents a Eucharistic theology that is "purely memorial" or a "commemoration of Christ's passion."[57] The sermon describes that those who eat the sacred host "ete Crist goostly, þat is to haue muynde of hym."[58] According to Hornbeck, this phrase "seems to move beyond the notion of Christ's localized presence, however spiritual. For this preacher, to receive the host is to call to mind Christ and his passion, not to receive Christ as present in the Eucharistic elements."[59] As will be shown, this seems to be overstating the case.

In sermon E22, the writers' discussion of the Eucharist begins by quoting the third part of 1 Corinthians 5:7 and then continues with commentary:

> Þe þridde word þat Poul seiþ ȝyueþ cause of þes two byfore and seiþ *for certeyn þat owre pasc Crist is* now *sacrifised.* For, riȝt as fadris maden þerf breed for to ete þer pasc lomb, so men eton þe sacred oost to ete Crist goostly, þat is to haue muynde of hym, how kyndely he suffrede for man. And such a fruytous muynde of Crist is gostly mete to þe soule, and goostly etyng of Cristus body þat þe gospel of Iohn spekuþ of.[60]

The first thing to note is the interjected "now" in the biblical passage. In adding this "now" to the text of the scripture, the writer gives the paschal sacrifice of Jesus a present immediacy. The scriptural text on its own is in the passive present—"*Crist is sacrifised.*" By adding the "now," the writer firmly establishes the activity of Christ's sacrifice in the present of the community to whom he is speaking. The sacrifice of Christ—"how kyndely he suffrede for man"—is what communicants should have in mind as they eat the consecrated host. Having these ideas in their minds will be the proper spiritual food for the soul. With this appropriate mental disposition, the person will be able to spiritually eat of Christ's body in the way that "Iohn spekuþ of." It seems possible that this spiritual eating that John speaks of is that found in sermon 176, discussed earlier.

The problem with reading E22 as a merely memorial Eucharistic theology is that the writer seems to be uninterested, like most of the other writers of *EWS*, in theoretical discussions about Christ's presence in the Eucharist.[61] He admits that his notions of spiritual eating are colored by John's gospel, but there is nothing more beyond the reference. Elsewhere in *EWS*, such as in sermon 176, the description of spiritual eating does not necessarily exclude belief in the presence of Christ in the Eucharistic elements or even exclude reception of communion. Notably, sermon 176 was written for the Saturday of the fifth week of Lent and would have been used just a week before sermon E22.[62]

The way that sermon E22 is most like contemporary Easter sermons is in the writer's emphasis that Easter is the time when people should "clene forsake synne."[63] The writer points out that sin comes in many forms and that the best way to get rid of sin is to treat sins like weeds and pluck them out from their roots. It is only then that a person will begin to have a disposition that will not draw that person to sin again.[64] This is the disposition that is necessary for the Christian to receive the Eucharist.

The gospel sermon for Easter Day, sermon 46, also takes up a discussion of the Eucharist. Toward the end of the sermon, after the writer has completed his commentary on the scriptural passage, he notes that the person using the sermon for preaching might want to continue to speak about the gospel, but that it is common for the preacher to discuss "þe sacrament of þe auter, and how men schal disposon hem now to take þis sacrament."[65] As in sermon E22, the "now" in this passage emphasizes the immediacy of the writer's purpose: to prepare people to receive their Easter communion. The writer then compares those coming to church on Easter Sunday to the women who went to the tomb early in the morning. Likewise, the Christian believers should come to church early on Easter Sunday to receive the sacrament. They must leave behind their sins so as to be ready to properly receive the Eucharist.[66] The writer then tells the members of his audience that to properly receive the Eucharist, they should clothe themselves with the three virtues of faith, hope, and charity. As discussed earlier, this emphasis on the virtues is common in contemporary sermons.

Using the framework of the three virtues, the writer of sermon 46 is able to explain what the Eucharist is, the disposition that the person should have in approaching reception of the Eucharist, and the purpose of receiving the Eucharist. The first of the virtues, faith, is necessary to understand the nature of the sacramental elements the communicant receives. By the virtue of faith, the communicant knows that the Eucharist he or she receives is God's body because of Christ's words, although it remains naturally bread; the presence of God is a sacramental presence.[67] The writer denies, as other sermon writers do, the Thomistic definition of transubstantiation and insists that God's body need not be localized in a single place because the Trinity is present in all places. However, the sermon writer concludes with the rather ambiguous statement: "But owre byleue is set upon þis poynt: what is þis sacrede host, and not what þing is þere."[68] It would seem that the writer of the sermon is eschewing an interest in the mechanics of the Eucharistic presence to focus instead on what the sacred host is: God's body.

The second virtue that the communicant should possess is the virtue of hope for his or her life in this world and, more particularly, for the grace of God to come in heaven. The writer explains, "to þis entent men taken now þis sacrament, so þat by takyng herof þer muynde be fresched in hem to þenkon of kyndenesse of Crist, to maken hem clene in sowle."[69] By approaching the sacrament with hope of heaven, the communicants' minds are refreshed and they are able to think of Christ's kindness and have their souls cleansed in preparation for heaven.

The third virtue necessary to approach the sacrament worthily is the virtue of charity. Without charity, the writer suggests that a person will grow in sin.[70] On the other hand, possessing this virtue truly moves the person into the eschatological feast: "And ȝif we han þis cloþing, takyng þis mete in figure, hit schal bryngon vs to heuene þere to ete Godis body goostly wiþowten eende; and þat is mennys blisse."[71] If a person has the virtue of charity and receives the Eucharist as a sacrament of God's body, as suggested earlier in the sermon, the recipient will be brought into the heavenly banquet where he or she will spiritually eat God's body forever and be in perpetual bliss.

Over the course of the Lenten season and at Easter, the writers of *EWS* repeatedly turn to teaching about the Eucharist. While their theology is not uniform, it occurs at a point in the liturgical year when reception of communion would be common. This suggests that the writers of *EWS* saw at least part of their work as a preparation for Easter when "men schulden come to þe chirche to take þis hooly sacrament."[72]

CONCLUSION

The writers of *EWS*, like their contemporaries, are engaged in a process of formation in Christian life and faith. In this aim, the sermons of *EWS* reflect the mainstream church and the culture of that church. Just as the Eucharist was important in the life of any Christian, it remains important in the life of a Wycliffite Christian. What we have learned from the study of the few Wycliffite sermons presented here is that throughout the season of Lent and at Easter, the sermon writers prepare their audience for the reception of the Eucharist at Easter by offering catechetical teachings about what the Eucharist is and what the proper disposition is in approaching the Eucharist. It is important, after all, to know what is being received and how to receive it. At the same time, that person need not and should not understand the Eucharist in terms of transubstantiation.

The differences in Eucharistic theology between the Wycliffites and the mainstream church are significant. To focus solely on the differences, though, can miss the very purpose of the sermon cycle: to create a program of education and formation in Christianity by providing sermons on the Sunday lections from the Sarum Missal. I am not suggesting that we ignore the differences among *EWS* and contemporary sermon collections or even attempt to reconcile those differences. What I am saying is that those differences need not be the first or only thing that we focus on when we read these sermons. Rather, we should look at the ways in which the sermons of *EWS* are like the sermons of contemporary writers. In those instances of likeness, we might well discover that the sermons of *EWS* are less specifically "Wycliffite" and are, in fact, closer to the life and practice of the mainstream church then we thought.

NOTES

1. Norman P. Tanner, ed., *Decrees of the Ecumenical Councils*, vol. 1, *Nicaea I to Lateran V* (Washington, DC: Georgetown University Press, 1990), 245. "Omnis utriusque sexus fidelis, postquam ad annos discrestionis pervenerit, omnia sua solus peccata confiteatur fideliter, altem semel in anno proprio sacerdoti, et iniunctam sibi poenitentiam studeat pro viribus adimplere, suscipiens reverenter ad minus in pascha eucharistiae sacramentum."

2. Eamon Duffy, *The Stripping of the Altars: Traditional Religion in England 1400–1580* (New Haven, CT: Yale University Press, 1992), 93–94; Duffy points out that there were occasionally people who would receive more often. Margery Kempe received weekly and Lady Margaret Beaufort received monthly, but they were the exception rather than the rule (93).

3. John Bossy, "The Mass as a Social Institution, 1200–1700," *Past and Present* 100 (1983): 53–54.

4. Duffy, *Stripping of the Altars*, 94.

5. Eileen Power, trans., *The Goodman of Paris (Le Ménagier de Paris): A*

Treatise on Moral and Domestic Economy by a Citizen of Paris c. 1393 (Woodbridge, England: Boydell, 2006), 39. See also Miri Rubin, *Corpus Christi: The Eucharist in Late Medieval Culture* (Cambridge: Cambridge University Press, 1991).

6. For a sermon that presents the teachings of Lateran IV and clearly describes the Eucharist in terms of transubstantiation without using the word, see Stephen Morrison, ed., *A Late Fifteenth-Century Dominical Sermon Cycle* (Oxford: Oxford University Press, 2012), 183–185.

7. "It seems most unlikely that there were ever many Lollards—either men or women—who resorted to administering the Eucharist. We should certainly expect to learn more about it (in the way of formulated questions, if not answers) if they had, and the frequency with which they denied transubstantiation, coupled with their own belief in the sacramental value of the Word, makes it likely that such ceremony as they had centered upon preaching." Margaret Aston, "Lollard Women Priests?," in *Lollards and Reformers: Images and Literacy in Late Medieval Religion*, by Margaret Aston (London: Hambledon, 1984), 66.

8. Fiona Somerset, *Feeling Like Saints: Lollard Writings after Wyclif* (Ithaca, NY: Cornell University Press, 2014), 281.

9. See Rubin, *Corpus Christi*, 63, 83–98; Powers, *Goodman of Paris*, 40; Morrison, *Late Fifteenth-Century*, 177. It is possible that the descriptions of what constituted "spiritual eating" vary in lollard and mainstream texts, but that is the work of a different paper.

10. Jennifer Illig, "Through a Lens of Likeness: Reading *English Wycliffite Sermons* in Light of Contemporary Sermon Texts" (PhD diss., Fordham University, 2014).

11. This is also the organization of the sermons in Anne Hudson and Pamela Gradon, eds., *English Wycliffite Sermons*, 5 vols. (Oxford: Clarendon Press, 1983–1997). The sermons will be cited in the footnotes in the form: *EWS* sermon number/line number. Hudson and Gradon's extensive notes will be cited as: Hudson and Gradon, volume number:page number.

12. Somerset, *Feeling Like Saints*, 4.

13. The sermons that discuss meekness are: *EWS* E17, 41, 155, 156, 158. The sermons from that week that discuss pride or other vices are: *EWS* 153, 154, and 157.

14. The sermons that mention Mary, along with their dates in 1404/5, are: *EWS* 127 (19 December 1404: Feria 6 in week 3 of Advent), E4 (21 December 1404: Fourth Sunday of Advent), 89 (24 December 1404: Christmas Eve), 90 (25 December 1404: Christmas Day), 94 (28 December 1404: Sixth Day after Christmas), E7 (11 January 1405: Sunday within the octave of Epiphany), 32 (18 January 1405: First Sunday after the Octave of the Epiphany), 99 (2 February 1405: Candlemas), 42 (22 March 1405: Third Sunday of Lent), 102 (25 March 1405: Annunciation), 179 (17 April 1405: Good Friday), 180 (18 April 1405: Vigil of Easter), 189 (6 May 1405: Feria 4 in week 3 after Easter), 49 (10 May 1405: Third

Sunday after Easter), 107 (30 June 1405: Octave of St. John the Baptist), 110 (10 July 1405: Seven Brothers), 112 (14 August 1405: Vigil of the Assumption), 12 (6 September 1405: Twelfth Sunday after Trinity), 116 (8 September 1405: Nativity of the Virgin Mary), and 19 (25 October 1405: Nineteenth Sunday after Trinity).

15. In the order they would appear in the liturgical year, the sermons that discuss the Eucharist are: *EWS* 125, 30, E13, E17, 158, 162, 166, 44, 176, E22, 46, 197, 206, E35, 111, 8, 59, E47, 67, 75, 85.

16. *EWS* 125 (10 December 1404: Feria 4 in week 2 of Advent), 30 (11 January 1405: Sunday within the octave of the Epiphany), E13 (15 February 1405: Septuagesima), E17 (17 March 1405: Second Sunday of Lent), 158 (21 March 1405: Sabbath in week 2 of Lent), 162 (26 March 1405: Feria 5 in week 3 of Lent), 166 (31 March 1405: Feria 3 in week 4 of Lent), 44 (5 April 1405: Passion Sunday), 176 (11 April 1405: Sabbath in week 5 of Lent), E22 (19 April 1405: Easter Sunday), 46 (19 April 1405: Easter Sunday), 197 (28 May 1405: Ascension Day), 206 (18 June 1405: Feast of Corpus Christi), E35 (19 July 1405: Fifth Sunday after Trinity), 111 (25 July 1405: St. James), 8 (9 August 1405: Eighth Sunday after Trinity), 59 (10 August 1405: St. Laurentius), E47 (11 October 1405: Seventeenth Sunday after Trinity). The others are in the common of the saints: *EWS* 67 (Common of many martyrs with lection Luke 21: 14–19), 75 (Common of many martyrs with the lection Mark 13:1–13), and 85 (Common of a virgin not a martyr with lection Matthew 25:1–13).

17. In 1405, Septuagesima, beginning the penitential season nine weeks before Easter, would have occurred on February 15. Easter Sunday was on April 19. The sermons that reference the Eucharist in this period are E13, E17, 158, 162, 166, 44, 176, E22, and 46.

18. See Ian Christopher Levy, *John Wyclif: Scriptural Logic, Real Presence, and the Parameters of Orthodoxy* (Milwaukee, WI: Marquette University Press, 2003).

19. See Levy, *John Wyclif*, 172–173; Levy, "The Narrowing of Eucharistic Orthodoxy: Wycliffites and Their Opponents," *Lexington Theological Quarterly* 41 (2006): 131–147; Gary Macy, "The Dogma of Transubstantiation in the Middle Ages," *Journal of Ecclesiastical History* 45 (1994): 11–41.

20. *Summa Theologica* 3.75.1–8. For a history of this development, see Levy, *John Wyclif*, 172–201; Macy, "The Dogma of Transubstantiation"; Edward J. Kilmartin, *The Eucharist in the West: History and Theology*, ed. by Robert J. Daly (Collegeville, MN: Liturgical Press, 1998), 143–156.

21. As quoted in Stephen E. Lahey, *John Wyclif* (Oxford: Oxford University Press, 2009), 103.

22. Lahey, *John Wyclif*, 103.

23. Levy, *John Wyclif*, 246–247, see John Wyclif, *Trialogus, cum Supplemento Trialogi*, ed. G. V. Lechler (Oxford: Oxford University Press, 1869), IV.2.250. A full translation is available: John Wyclif, *Trialogus*, trans. Stephen E. Lahey (Cambridge: Cambridge University Press, 2013).

24. "Jesus answered them, and said: My doctrine is not mine, but his that sent

me." All biblical quotes are from the Douay-Rheims Bible translation available at www.drbo.org/index.htm.

25. *EWS* 166/11–16. See also 44/40–43 and 111/56–60 which use Ambrose to discuss the Eucharist.

26. See J. Patrick Hornbeck II, *What Is a Lollard? Dissent and Belief in Late Medieval England* (Oxford: Oxford University Press, 2010), 77–78 for a discussion of Ambrose on transubstantiation.

27. "One Lord, one faith, one baptism. One God and Father of all, who is above all, and through all, and in us all."

28. *EWS* E47/68–72.

29. *EWS* E47/76–79: "As Crist seiþ, and seyntis aftir, þat þe hoost, whan it is sacrid, is uerrili Cristis owene body in forme of breed, as cristen men bileuen, and neyþer accident wiþoute sugett, ne no[uȝ]t as heretikis seien."

30. *EWS* E47/79–82: "And errour in witt of holy writ haþ brouȝt in þis heresye: þei seyen þat holi writt is fals, and ȝeuen it witt aftir hemsilf; and þus þis witnesse moeueþ hem not þat Crist seiþ þus in hooli writt."

31. On Wyclif, see Levy, *John Wyclif*, 15.

32. *EWS* 176/59–64: "And heere ben many men marrid of þe sacrament of þe auter, and referren alle þes wordis to þis holy sacrament. But neþeles men witen wel þat þes wordis weren spokun of Crist longe bifore þat þis sacrament was maad of Crist or ony man. For þe sacrament was maad first upon Shier-Þursday, and longe bifore þat tyme weren þes wordis spokun of Crist." A similar assertion is also found in *EWS* 162/38–39 which is also a sermon on John 6.

33. *EWS* 176/64–66: "many of þes wordis may be wel vndurstonden of þis sacrid oost, who þat knowiþ hem soundely."

34. *EWS* 176/66–72: "And so we shulen vndirstonde first þat sum þing is Goddis body, and nouȝt ellis in his kynde, as þe fleyss þat Crist bar heere, and is nou in heuene glorified, as seyntis shulun be. And of þis fl[e]yss and þis blood in his kynde spekiþ þe gospel, and of þe gostly eting þat men moten ete þis. Þe bred of þe sacrid oost is uery bred in his kynde, and is etun bodily, but it is Goddis body in figure, and so it is þe same body þat is Goddis body in his kynde."

35. David Aers, *Sanctifying Signs: Making Christian Tradition in Late Medieval England* (Notre Dame, IN: University of Notre Dame Press, 2004), 61.

36. Aers, *Sanctifying Signs*, 61.

37. Ibid., 61.

38. The denial of Christ's physical presence is made even clearer in lines 82–83: "But þus it is not of Cristis fleyss and his blood in his kynde."

39. *Wycklyffes Wycket* (Oxford: Oxford University Press, 1828). It is important to distinguish Wycliffite Eucharistic theology from that of the sixteenth-century reformers. Those later reformers had a broad range of Eucharistic theologies. Although early historians of the English Reformation often wanted to identify reformation theologies with Wyclif, it is broadly unfair to do because he and the later reformers are operating out of different intellectual frameworks. For some

of the variety of Eucharistic theologies among the reformers, see Martin Luther, *The Pagan Servitude of the Church*, in *Martin Luther: Selections from his Writings*, ed. John Dillenberger (New York: Doubleday, 1962), 249–359; John Calvin, *Institutes of Christian Religion*, ed. John T. McNeill, trans. Ford Lewis Battles (Philadelphia: Westminister, 1960), 2:4/17–18; "The Marburg Colloquy," in *Great Debates of the Reformation*, ed. D. J. Ziegler (New York: Random House, 1969), 71–107.

40. *EWS* 176/73–83.

41. *EWS* 176/86–88. The italics appear in Hudson and Gradon's text and represent the biblical text which would have been underlined in the manuscripts.

42. *EWS* 176/89.

43. Stephen Pink, "Holy Scripture and the Meaning of the Eucharist in Late Medieval England, c. 1370–1430" (D.Phil. thesis, University of Oxford, 2011).

44. See, for instance, *EWS* 46/61; 176/59.

45. See, for instance, *EWS* 8/28; 46/77–78; E13/64; 166/12; 67/121; E47/69.

46. See *EWS* 162/49; 46/73–74; 67/164–165; 111/59–60; 59/20; E47/78; 85/108. See also Anne Hudson, ed., *Selections from English Wycliffite Writings* (Cambridge: Cambridge University Press, 1978), 21A/65–66. At least part of what the writers of *EWS* were doing was working toward finding a language to talk about the Eucharist, a topic that would more commonly be discussed in the Latin of the university rather than the vernacular.

47. *EWS* E17/71–73.

48. *EWS* 166, discussed earlier, presents a similar teaching on the Eucharistic elements. Such language is also found in *De oblacione iugis sacrificii*. See Anne Hudson, ed., *The Works of a Lollard Preacher*, Early English Text Society, o.s. 317 (Oxford: Oxford University Press, 2001), 200/1715–205/1901

49. *EWS* 44/41–43. It should be noted that it is possible that "aftur" here could also take on the sense of definition 8 for "after" in the Middle English Dictionary: "in conformity with, according to."

50. *EWS* 162/55–58.

51. *EWS* 162/61–65: "But þis bred þat is Crist, etyn gostly of man, may not wende þes þre weyes, for he may not be þus partid ne turnyd into anoþer kynde ne drawen þus into mannus body, but he turnyþ man into hym, as man turnyþ mete into his body."

52. *EWS* 162/65–67: "siþ þis beste bred is grounde of alle uertues of man, hou faste shulde a man holde clere bileue of þis bred."

53. John Mirk, *Festial: A Collection of Homilies*, ed. Theodor Erbe (London: Paul, Trench, Trübner, 1905), 131. This passage is also found in Morrison, *Late Fifteenth-Century*, 184.

54. Morrison, *Late Fifteenth-Century*, 177.

55. Ibid.

56. Ibid.

57. Hudson and Gradon, 4:51; Hornbeck, *What Is a Lollard?*, 78.

58. *EWS* E22/38–39.

59. Hornbeck, *What Is a Lollard?*, 78.

60. *EWS* E22/35–42.

61. Somerset has, likewise, noted, "it is a pervasive and widespread characteristic of lollard writing about the Eucharist to refuse to explain what happens to the bread and wine at consecration." Somerset, *Feeling Like Saints*, 280.

62. In 1405, sermon 176 would have been used on April 11 and Easter Sunday was on April 19.

63. *EWS* E22/1.

64. *EWS* E22/14–26.

65. *EWS* 46/61–62.

66. *EWS* 46/62–66: "And hit is seid comunly þat, as þese hooly wymmen hadden left þer formere synne and take þeir fresch deuocion, so men schulden come to þe chirche to take þis hooly sacrament, and þus come wiþ þese wymmen wiþ ly3t of þe sonne."

67. *EWS* 46/68–70: "Byleue is furst nedful, and algatis of þis breed, how hit is Godis body by uertew of Cristis wordis. And so hit is kyndely breed, as Powle seiþ, but hit is sacramentally verrey Godis body."

68. *EWS* 46/77–78.

69. *EWS* 46/81–83.

70. *EWS* 46/91: "And þus, as Austyn declaruþ, fowre poyntes þat fallen to makyng of breed techon us þis charite, and algatis to haue hit now, for ellys we gregien owre synne in etyng of þis breed."

71. *EWS* 46/91–94.

72. *EWS* 46/64–65.

CHAPTER ELEVEN

"IF YT BE A NACION": VERNACULAR SCRIPTURE AND ENGLISH NATIONHOOD IN COLUMBIA UNIVERSITY LIBRARY, PLIMPTON MS 259

Louisa Z. Foroughi

In the last quarter of the fifteenth century, Robert Gottes, a yeoman farmer from rural Norfolk, arranged for two tracts advocating open dissemination of English scripture to be copied into his small, parchment-bound notebook, now Columbia University Library, Plimpton MS 259.[1] The first of these tracts, "What Charyte Ys," is familiar to scholars from Mary Dove's edition of Cambridge University Library, MS Ii.6.26, and from two lollard-interpolated versions of the *Pore Caitif*.[2] The second tract, entitled "Crystys Wordys," appears for the first time in this essay. Its author argues that English scripture must be made widely available because England cannot be a nation unless its lay inhabitants have access to scripture in their mother tongue. This tract, together with other texts that emerged out of the contentious late fourteenth-century debates over vernacular Bible translation, reveals that these disputes sparked intense interest in the parameters of English nationhood among both lollard and orthodox believers.[3] Could a nation be a nation without a vernacular Bible? The author of "Crystys Wordys" implicitly argues that because a nation is by definition a reading community founded on scripture, England "ys none nacion" without widespread access to an English Bible.

The relationship between heresy and "nationalism" is contested.[4] Since the nineteenth century, John Wyclif and Jan Hus have played starring roles in English and Czech nationalist narratives, now the subject of much critique. But there is ample evidence that fifteenth-century Hussite authors were themselves interested in the meaning of nationhood and saw their reform work as bettering the Czech *natio*, meaning not only the Bohemian group at the university in Prague but also the greater Czech-speaking public.[5] Hus and later reformers used the vernacular to unite and mobilize this diverse audience; thus for these reformers, preserving the Czech vernacular became a key part of preserving the Czech nation.[6] Likewise, "Crystys Wordys" suggests that English reformers, both lollard and orthodox, found in the Bible debates a venue for exploring what it meant to be a nation.

This essay encounters "Crystys Wordys" at two moments in time: first, at the end of the fourteenth century, when debates about English nationhood and biblical translation gained new urgency in the face of Wyclif's challenges to the English church; and second, at the end of the fifteenth century, when Robert Gottes selected it for inclusion in his miscellany. The appearance of "Crystys Wordys" at this late date and in this lay context indicates that the relationship between English scripture and English nationhood was still of interest to some readers, though these later readers were very different from the original participants in the translation debates. At the end of the fourteenth century, academics and prelates argued openly at Oxford about the legitimacy of the English Bible.[7] By the end of the fifteenth century, after Archbishop Thomas Arundel's 1409 *Constitutions* had banned unauthorized Bible translations produced after the time of Wyclif, these discussions had retreated from the universities into the countryside where they passed informally among neighbors, as illustrated by the appearance of "What Charyte Ys" and "Crystys Wordys" in Gottes's notebook.[8] As in fourteenth-century Oxford, support for the English Bible in the fifteenth century was not a uniquely lollard position, but the contents of Plimpton MS 259 suggest that Robert Gottes may indeed have been sympathetic to lollardy's spiritual teachings, particularly the importance of direct engagement with scripture.[9] His notebook is an invaluable witness, then, both to a previously unattested text and to the development of lay interest in accessing the English Bible in late medieval England.

THE NATION AND THE BIBLE

The only known copy of "Crystys Wordys" appears in Robert Gottes's late fifteenth-century miscellany, but the tract had likely been circulating for nearly a century before it reached him. The debates at Oxford over Bible translation to which the tract responds were most fervent from circa 1390, when Henry Knighton noted with disdain the popularity of the Wycliffite Bible, through 1414, when heresy prosecutions and support for Archbishop Arundel's 1409 prohibitions increased following Oldcastle's Revolt.[10] Three formal determinations on the subject survive, all from circa 1401: two against Bible translation written by the friars Thomas Palmer and William Butler, and one in favor by the secular cleric Richard Ullerston.[11] In addition to these three texts, an anonymous compiler working sometime between 1410 and 1425 collected twelve tracts advocating English scripture in CUL MS Ii. 6. 26.[12] "What Charyte Ys," the first of the two tracts in Plimpton MS 259 that advocate for English scripture, appears in the Cambridge compilation and in two early fifteenth-century lollard manuscripts of the *Pore Caitif*.[13]

Internal evidence suggests that "Crystys Wordys" most likely emerged from the same context as "What Charyte Ys," and indeed the two tracts were likely travelling together by the end of the fifteenth century, perhaps in booklet form.[14] The text of "Crystys Wordys" indicates that the debates over English scripture were already underway when the tract was written, and that positions for and against—"lay pepyll" versus "menn of holy chyrch"—had been established. Nevertheless, when the tract was written "dyuers opynyons" on the subject could still be voiced openly: the question had not yet been resolved.[15] Thus "Crystys Wordys" was most likely written after circa 1390, when debates over translation began in earnest, and before circa 1414, when Arundel's "opynyon" found broader support. In the interim, participants in the debate found themselves grappling not only with the threat of heresy, but with larger issues about the status of the English language and the English nation.

The author of "Crystys Wordys" begins by expressing his or her wonderment at clerical opposition to vernacular scripture: "Whereas dyuers opynyons be hold that lay pepyll schold knowe nodyr vnderstond holy scripture, I merveyle gretly þerof that the menn of holy chyrch schold sey soo, or els perauenture they reputyth Englysch pepyll for none nacion." For this medieval author, English nationhood is assumed, though his or her conception of nationhood is contingent on the dissemination of vernacular scripture. How much more would he or she "merveyle," then, that medieval English nationhood is indeed contested among modern scholars of nationalism?[16] The debate hinges on the wide varieties of meanings attached to "nation," both medieval and modern. According to Benedict Anderson, one of the most influential scholars of the origins of national identity, nationalism first developed in the eighteenth century, with the rise of print media and the concurrent decline of dynastic reigns and the universal Catholic church. Without the guiding influence of the church, the general public sought another community to which they could belong: the national community, imagined on a monumental scale through the language of popular publications.[17]

Anderson's periodization of national development precludes the possibility of medieval nationhood, but his definition of "nation" as "an imagined political community" usefully highlights the constructed, rhetorical nature of national identity.[18] Anderson's emphasis, moreover, on the importance of the vernacular resonates with late medieval developments, particularly Bible translation, as "Crystys Wordys" suggests and as Adrian Hastings argues in his controversial book, *The Construction of Nationhood*. Hastings asserts that medieval England fulfills Anderson's definition of "nation," and that stirrings of English national identity are visible from the eighth century onward, starting with Bede.[19] Although Hastings's work has not passed without critique, it has stimulated interest in medieval conceptions of "Englishness." Recent studies highlight the variety in expressions of medieval English identity and the importance of vernacular language for medieval conceptions of the nation.[20]

Whether or not medieval England fulfills modern requirements for nationhood, texts like "Crystys Wordys" make it clear that medieval English people were themselves interested in what it meant to be a nation. But the definition of "nation" was as indeterminate in the Middle Ages as it is among modern scholars.[21] In ancient Rome, the personified *Natio* was the goddess of childbirth, and in classical contexts the word is best translated as "race" or "people."[22] *Natio* retained this sense in the Vulgate, though it appears only infrequently in comparison to its synonyms *gens* and *populus*.[23] Most medieval commentators drew on Isidore of Seville's *Etymologies*, in which the seventh-century archbishop identifies *natio* as a synonym of *gens*, that is, "a number of people sharing a common origin," and portrays language as the origin of nations at the Tower of Babel: "nations [*gentes*] arose from languages, and not languages from nations."[24]

Over the course of the Middle Ages, the term acquired a broader range of meanings, not only "ethno-cultural" but also "geopolitical."[25] In 1140 Bernard, the Bishop of St. David's, referred to the Welsh *natio* as distinguished by "language, laws, habits, modes of judgment and customs."[26] At the Council of Constance in 1415, England's representative Thomas Polton expanded upon the definitions offered by Bernard and Isidore when he outlined the range of meanings associated with *natio*:

Whether a nation be understood as a race, relationship, and habit of unity, separate from others, or as a difference of language, which by divine and human law is the greatest and most authentic mark of a nation and the essence of it . . . or whether it be understood . . . as an equality of territory . . . in all these respects the renowned nation of England or Britain is one of the four or five nations that compose the papal obedience.[27]

Polton's argument illuminates the different parameters of English nationhood, especially as imagined vis-à-vis other nations: geographic boundaries, ethnic descent, but especially linguistic difference.[28]

Language, "the greatest and most authentic mark of a nation," was thus a privileged element of the medieval sense of *natio*.[29] This direct link between a nation's identity and its unique vernacular language forms the basis for the argument in "Crystys Wordys" that nationhood depends on the availability of vernacular scripture. But the tract was also informed by a contemporary sense that national stability was in jeopardy, a fear exploited by advocates for the English Bible as they prepared to defend their position at the end of the fourteenth century.[30] This was indeed a period of substantial unrest. Abroad, England was only just emerging from wars in Scotland and France.[31] At home, the social order was in flux after successive waves of plague, political authorities were reeling after the 1381 Peasants' Revolt, and the church was struggling to respond to increasingly bold demands from the supporters of John Wyclif for social and ecclesiastical reform. These supporters, with Wyclif's approval and perhaps even his assistance, completed a full Bible translation in the 1380s.[32] It was immediately popular with both lollard and orthodox readers and remained so through the fifteenth century, even after the text was banned by Arundel's 1409 *Constitutions*. The many surviving fifteenth-century copies, and indeed the continued circulation of tracts like "What Charyte Ys" and "Crystys Wordys," demonstrate the continued demand for the English Bible and the selective application of Arundel's legislation.[33]

Vernacular preaching came under scrutiny at the Blackfriars Council in 1382; the English Bible was next.[34] But although opponents of scriptural translation were motivated by antilollard sentiment, not all of its supporters were influenced by lollard teachings. Some were undeniably followers of Wyclif, but others were entirely orthodox and saw vernacular scripture as a tool to combat heresy.[35] Thus it is crucial to attend closely to nuances of belief when approaching texts advocating English scripture: support for the English Bible is not a sufficient criterion to diagnose lollard sympathies. Such caution is equally necessary when approaching fifteenth-century sources, as will be evident in this essay's subsequent analysis of the spirituality of the Gottes family.

In its language and themes "Crystys Wordys" closely resembles the larger body of texts advocating English scripture. The argument its author advances—that English scripture is a necessary component of English nationhood—does not appear elsewhere, but assertions in favor of scriptural translation predicated on English national identity do exist, as explored by Jill C. Havens in her article on lollard "nationalism."[36] Moreover, the sense of the "nation" as a textual community that the author develops in "Crystys Wordys" underlies other contemporary discussions of English nationhood, though it only fully emerges in this tract. As the following analysis will reveal, the "nation" in "Crystys Wordys" is both a linguistically distinct people—a *gens* in the biblical sense advanced by Isidore—and an abstract entity unto itself, as in Polton's fifteenth-century description. According to the author of "Crystys Words," each nation is distinct from but comparable to other nations, and every nation must have appeared at Pentecost, as in Acts 2:5: "and there were dwelling at Jerusalem, Jews, devout men, out of every nation under heaven."[37] Finally, every nation must have a Bible in its own vernacular because the "nation" is imagined as an inclusive reading community of laymen and clerics seeking to know and understand holy writ.

The entire tract reads:

Whereas dyuers opynyons be hold that lay pepyll schold knowe nodyr vnderstond holy scripture, I merveyle gretly þerof that the menn of holy chyrch schold sey soo, or els perauenture they reputyth Englysch pepyll for none nacion. & If yt be a nacion me thynkyth they do wrong for this cause: for Cryst Rebukyd the Saduces & seyd they erryd by cause they knew no scripture, neythyr the virtu of godd, the wich is in the gospell [Mark 12:24; Matthew 22:29]. Seynte Paule seyth: Non erubesco euangelium quia virtus dei est [Romans 1:16]. All ye may rede on wytsonday yn the dedys of the postelys, þe ii chapter, how ther come to Ierusalem of all maner nacions of the world to hyre Cryst prech his word [Acts 2:1–13]. And he takyht yt to euery nacion seuerally in ther moder tonge. Wher-

fore, me thynkketh he gaue yt to Englysch men as well as to oder nacions, or els yt must be seyd ther ys none such nacion. Allso yt ys wrytyn
ad hebreos tercio Cap° iii yt is seyd by the holy gost: Today yf ye haue
herd his voyse ye wyll nat hard your hertes yn bytternys lyke the day of
temptacion [Hebrews 3:8].[38]

The first three lines introduce the author's thesis. By preventing the laity from learning scripture, clerics are denying English people a key feature of nationhood, the nation as a Christian reading community. Here,
then, a "nacion" is both an entity unto itself—"If *yt* be a nacion"—and a
group of people: "perauenture they reputyth *Englysch pepyll* for none nacion." As we have seen, medieval definitions of *natio* exhibit this same fluidity of meaning. The term can refer to a *gens* of common descent and
language, as in Isidore's *Etymologiae*; to a community bound together by
laws and customs, as in Bernard's 1140 definition; or to a socially, politically, and culturally distinct collective that encompasses all these senses,
as in Polton's 1415 defense at Constance.

The text continues: "& If yt be a nacion me thynkyth they do wrong for
this cause: for Cryst Rebukyd the Saduces & seyd they erryd by cause they
knew no scripture, neythyr the virtu of godd, the wich is in the gospell
[Mark 12:24; Matthew 22:29]." This reference to the Sadducees is unusual:
when the Sadducees or Pharisees enter into lollard discussions of Bible
translation, the invocation is generally used to accuse clerics of ignorance,
corruption, and hypocrisy.[39] In the *Holi Prophete David*, for example, the
author writes of churchmen who neglect their duties: "Sich proude clerkis
and blyndid in peyne of here synnes shulden taken hede what Crist seiþ, in
Mt. xxiii° ch., to þe blynde saduceis, where Matheu writiþ þus: 'Ʒe erren, ʒe
kunne not þe scripturis neiþir þe vertu of God.'" These clerks are "grete
foolis" and "prisoneris to þe deuyl."[40] But in the passage from "Crystys
Wordys," it is not entirely clear who is following the Sadducees' bad example: is it the "menn of holy chyrch" who limit vernacular scripture? Or
is it the "Englysch pepyll" who, deprived of holy writ, remain ignorant of
"the virtu of godd"? The equation of holy writ with God's power is particularly characteristic of lollard texts, as is the anticlerical bent of "Crystys
Wordys."[41] But the polemic in this tract is comparatively tame. Though
invoking the Sadducees certainly had negative connotations, the author's
subsequent argument builds on holy writ's power and not on clerical error.

"Crystys Wordys" is thus less an excoriation of clerical misdeeds than a corrective based on scripture.

The author turns next from the Sadducees to Pentecost and the main substance of his or her argument: "All ye may rede on wytsonday yn the dedys of the postelys, þe ii chapter, how ther come to Ierusalem of all maner nacions of the world to hyre Cryst prech his word [Acts 2:1–13]. And he takyht yt to euery nacion seuerally in ther moder tonge. Wherfore, me thynkketh he gaue yt to Englysch men as well as to oder nacions, or els yt must be seyd ther ys none such nacion." Whitsunday appears in two other tracts advocating for English scripture, *First Seith Bois*, a vernacular translation and adaptation of Ullerston's determination on the English Bible, and the first tract in CUL, MS Ii.6.26.[42] In both these texts, the appearance of the Holy Spirit at Pentecost demonstrates that it is licit for the gospel to appear in the vernacular, in the present as in Jerusalem. In *First Seith Bois*, the Spirit "ʒaf to many diuerse nacions knowing of his lawe be on tunge, in tokene þat he wolde alle men knewe his lawe."[43] In Cambridge Tract I, the Spirit's intentions are likewise pragmatic: because "þe most parte of þe world know[eþ] neyþer Ebrew, Grew ne Latyn . . . on Witsonday, wanne þe Holy Gost liʒtted on Cristi[s] disciplis, he . . . tauʒte hem . . . alle maner langages."[44]

In the passage from "Crystys Wordys," the author also establishes nationhood by comparison with "oder nacions." In contrast to Adrian Hasting's argument that England's national identity was "precocious" and that it established a prototype for other nations to follow, "Crystys Wordys" asserts that England is a nation only if it is equivalent to "oder nacions."[45] The author of "Crystys Wordys" does not name the nations he or she has in mind, but lists of nations where vernacular Bibles already existed or languages into which the Bible had been translated appear in four other texts advocating vernacular scripture.[46] Every one of these lists includes France, while the Low Countries, Germany, Spain, and Italy appear twice. Armenians, Britons, Bohemians, and Wendels (Slavic peoples) are each listed once.[47] These catalogues of comparable nations and peoples suggest that the contemporary sense of nation relied in part on a process of comparison.[48] Here, nations are distinguished by their respective vernaculars, and all are distinguished from England by their unchallenged possession of vernacular Bibles.

In the reference to Whitsunday in "Crystys Wordys," there is a still larger—and more conceptually complex—claim about the origins of nationhood. In this author's literal reading of Acts 2:5, nations only exist if they appeared at Pentecost.[49] This biblical precedent both validates a nation's vernacular as a suitable medium for scripture and establishes its very nationhood. If England is to be one of the nations of the world, the English people must understand scripture in English, as other nations do in their respective languages. If it does not, then "yt must be seyd ther ys none such nacion." There is no clear parallel to this argument in other tracts advocating the translation of scripture. These texts sometimes deploy threats of instability due to a lack of scriptural and moral education, as in Cambridge Tract I, which warns that England "schal be moued and chaungid from oure nacion to anoþer nacion, but we amende us."[50] But threats of rebellion or conquest do not invalidate English nationhood: they simply reveal the precariousness of a nation founded and maintained in the absence of widespread knowledge of God's law.

In playfully casting doubt on England's qualifications for nationhood, the author takes the vocabulary of Acts 2:1–13 to its logical extreme. If all the nations of the world were at Pentecost and could understand the Holy Spirit in their own language, and if the English vernacular is an unsuitable vehicle for Biblical translation, then it follows that it was excluded from this communal experience and cannot be numbered among the true nations. It is a nation without a mother tongue, without direct validation of its nationhood by the Holy Spirit. It is, then, by biblical precedent, no nation at all. But concluding his or her argument at this point shows that the author of "Crystys Wordys" is confident about English national identity as he or she understands it: even "the menn of holy chyrch" would not argue that English is "none nacion." And yet England's lack of nationhood is a logical but unintended consequence of their prohibitions. These prohibitions cannot stand when faced with such dire implications for the English nation. Vernacular scripture must be widely disseminated and efforts must be made to educate all "English pepyll" so that they may understand it.

This, then, is the last and most important qualification for nationhood in "Crystys Wordys": a nation is—or should be—a scripturally engaged textual community. The author construes national identity as necessarily grounded in vernacular engagement with scripture, and depicts England as a textual community based on direct engagement with the Gospels.[51] This reading community should be inclusive rather than exclusive, extending to both clerics and laymen, and indeed encompassing all "Englysch pepyll." This inclusivity is broadly characteristic of lollard formulations of the Christian community, but here there is none of the language of sectarian exclusion—the true church of the saved, as separate from the false church on earth—often found in lollard texts.[52] Instead, the reading community of the "nacion" is limited only by a desire and ability to "knowe [and] vnderstond holy scripture."

In most respects, the sense of English nationhood advanced in "Crystys Wordys" is entirely consistent with contemporary depictions. Here, as in other medieval definitions, England is both a *gens* and an abstract collective. In tracts that list nations where translated Bibles were already in circulation, England likewise appears as a distinct nation comparable to other nations. Pentecost is invoked elsewhere in texts advocating for the English Bible as a precedent for vernacular scripture. Finally, the driving goal of all the advocates for the English Bible was ultimately the cultivation of a national reading community, insofar as they all argue in favor of widespread and unimpeded study of scripture. What is distinct in "Crystys Wordys" is that England cannot be a nation *unless* it satisfies these requirements, "or els yt must be seyd ther ys none such nacion." English nationhood is, in fact, not assumed at all—it depends on scriptural engagement. "Crystys Wordys," then, encourages us to revisit the question of medieval English nationhood and its development. Isidore, Bernard, and Polton do not define *natio* as a reading community, but Benedict Anderson does. It may be that the development of a national reading community, as imagined both in modern scholarship on nationalism and in "Crystys Wordys," did not have to wait for the advent of print. Certainly, revisiting the texts of the Bible debates has the potential to expand our understanding of the term as it appears in late medieval sources.

This essay has thus far focused on the English nation as it appears in the fourteenth-century Bible debates, through the lens of "Crystys Wordys." But the manuscript containing the only known copy of this tract is a fifteenth-century miscellany. The next step, then, is to explore the tract's later manuscript context. Interest in "Englishness" had not decreased over the course of the fifteenth century; indeed, it intensified as a result of England's military campaigns, the ongoing centralization of government administration, and the overall rise of the English vernacular.[53] This trend was likely most pronounced among yeomen and husbandmen, who were starting to participate as never before in local administration and in foreign and domestic wars.[54] Plimpton MS 259 at once sheds new light on the theme of nationhood in the Oxford Bible debates and provides an example of the spread of interest in the English Bible within these newly prominent social groups.[55]

ROBERT GOTTES AND HIS BOOK

Plimpton MS 259 is a small softbound book of sixty-one folios. It is an untidy manuscript, with excised and blank pages, and as many as twenty different fifteenth- and sixteenth-century scribal hands. In it, the Gottes family recorded or had recorded a variety of short texts in Latin and Middle English, including two florilegia of Latin moral adages, quotations from scripture, a variety of religious tracts, and records of land and livestock transactions.[56] The identification of the compilers comes from these accounts, which pertain to members of successive generations of the Gottes family: Robert, Richard, and Nicholas, all of Little Ryburgh, Norfolk. Robert Gottes was earliest of these compilers.[57]

Manorial records and the Gotteses' accounts show that Robert's social and economic activities were typical of contemporary yeomen. But the survival of Plimpton MS 259 makes the Gottes family unusual: until the end of the sixteenth century, few manuscripts associated with yeomen survive. The Gotteses were likely more literate than most of their neighbors, but this does not mean that the texts in the manuscript were for the Gotteses' sole use.[58] They may well have read aloud to friends or taught them to read using the collections of adages, which were a feature of basic Latin instruction in grammar schools.[59] Certainly, the number of hands in the miscellany means that many different people were involved in its production from the late fifteenth century until it fell out of use in the sixteenth century.

Given the many different actors involved in the manuscript's compilation, it is not surprising that the spirituality evinced by its religious texts can be interpreted in a number of different ways. Both "What Charyte Ys" and "Crystys Wordys" include concepts and language that suggest that their authors may have been influenced by lollard spiritual ideals, but

neither is overtly heretical and both could equally appeal to devoutly orthodox readers. The same holds true of the other religious texts in Plimpton MS 259. In the analysis of the manuscript that follows, themes that
resonate with lollard ideas are noted as such, but none of these resonances
are sufficient to demonstrate the existence of self-conscious lollardy in
Little Ryburgh in the late fifteenth century. These ideas may instead bear
witness to the wide-ranging influence of lollard beliefs and practices on
orthodox religion.

Plimpton MS 259 contains six religious texts in hands dating from the
late fifteenth century, when the first Robert Gottes owned the book and
likely began its compilation: a series of scriptural quotations in Latin from
the readings for Lent (fols. 23v–25v); another list of Latin quotations, some
scriptural, entitled "Textus of Autorite" (fol. 27v); a short treatise on right
living entitled "Thes be the ix things þat pleasith god most spechially"
(fol. 29v); "What Charyte Ys" (fol. 30v); "Crystys Wordys" (fol. 31r); and a
final excerpt from the Latin Vulgate, Matthew 22:34–40, where the evan-
gelist describes Christ's confrontation with the Pharisees (fol. 31v).[60]

The first set of scriptural quotations focuses on themes central to lollard
spirituality, as recently characterized by Fiona Somerset. On fol. 23v,
Matthew 18:15–22 provides justification for correcting one's brother when
he or she errs, as in the emphasis on neighborly correction within lollard
communities identified by Somerset and Edwin Craun.[61] A list of the Ten
Commandments from Exodus 20:12–19—a key passage for both lollard
and orthodox moral instruction—appears on fol. 24r; and the shorter extracts on 24v–25v all condemn judging men unjustly.[62] In light of the
lollard commitment to pacifism—a belief grounded in charity as God's
law—the selection of Daniel 13:52–53 may have been particularly pointed:
"the innocent and the just thou shalt not kill."[63] The extracts included
under the heading "Textus of Autorite" on fol. 27v are less thematically
cohesive, but the final scriptural quotation on fol. 32v, Matthew 22:34–
40, focuses on a favorite lollard theme in its injunction to love: "Thou shalt
love the Lord thy God. . . . This is the greatest and the first commandment.
And the second is like to this: Thou shalt love thy neighbor as thyself. On
these two commandments dependeth the whole law and the prophets."[64]

"Thes be the ix things þat pleasith god most spechially" is a numbered
list of pious acts, each contrasted with another religious deed less pleasing
to God (fol. 29v).[65] The acts that God prefers are based on affective devo-

tion: "wepe I tere for þi synnys while þu lyuyst or for crystys love; þat pleast more cryst þan a C tymys so mich after þi deth." The lesser acts are performed postmortem, require monetary expenditure, or involve physical suffering: "sey no words of babbytyng ne of salanndyre for godds loue; for þat pleast more Jhesus þan þu wentist barefetid bledyng." This prohibition on gossip accords with Somerset's observation that well-regulated speech was particularly important in lollard spirituality. She found that the preservation of peace within the community was paramount in the active form of love featured in lollard texts, and this same understanding of charity appears here: beside the seventh injunction, "excuse þi neyghbor & torne all thing in to þe best," the scribe has written "Charite."[66]

The version of "What Charyte Ys" in Plimpton MS 259 is almost identical to Mary Dove's edition of the Cambridge text.[67] The author begins by asserting that charity, God, and holy writ are one and the same and that if we may not speak openly about any one of them, then we may not discuss the others either.[68] He or she extends this argument to the point of absurdity: because "holy wrytt spekeþ of all the werkes þat euer god made", if we cannot speak of holy writ then we cannot speak of anything at all, not "of hevyn, neyþer of erth, ne of hell, ne of no creature þat euer god made." Indeed, Christ "tawght yt hym selfe to all menne gode & yuell," because knowledge of scripture and Christ's law is crucial for salvation: "For we know nat gode frome Ivell but by wisdom of holy wrytt [Romans 7:7]. And þerfore Cryst cursith in his lawe all pepyll þat bow awey herre erys fro yt & blessith all pepill þat hyre yt & kepe yt justly." The author concludes that those who hearken to scripture are good executors of Christ's will, in both the sense of desire and the sense of testament, while those who ignore it are cursed.

According to Mary Dove, "there is nothing specifically Wycliffite" in "What Charyte Ys."[69] But in her analysis of the tract as it appears in the *Pore Caitif*, Nicole Rice notes that the author uses sect vocabulary to develop a sense of an "in-group": the "heuynly pepill" who keep Christ's law are contrasted with "pepyll þat bow awey herre erys."[70] This sense of a privileged community is emphasized by the use of plural pronouns: the *we* both includes and excludes.[71] Moreover, as Somerset notes, lollard authors often equate Christ's law with holy writ and interpret charity or love as "þe principall parte of holy wrytt."[72] As in "The ix things þat pleasith god," lollard understanding of "charyte" includes a focus on activity, on using scripture to relate to other members of the Christian community. "Char-yte" is active, it is based in holy writ, and it is found within a limited com-munity of believers.[73] In "What Charyte Ys," it is also linked with a speech act, with the capacity to proclaim scripture. Here, all speech refers back to God's creation, holy writ, and charity.[74] Speaking and hearing holy writ fulfills the testament of Christ and the requirements of love: to limit preaching on scripture, then, is to break the commandments. Given that this tract contains no overtly heterodox material, it is entirely possible that its arguments could have appealed to and circulated among devoutly or-thodox believers, but its author may have been familiar with lollard spiri-tual teachings.

Finally, while the opinions in favor of Bible translation expressed in "What Charyte Ys" and "Crystys Wordys" were part of an ongoing debate at the end of the fourteenth century, arguing for English scripture was a subversive act after Arundel's *Constitutions* passed into legislation in 1409. According to Margaret Aston, vernacular literature, whatever its content, acquired an edge of danger in this period.[75] Nicholas Watson famously at-tributed the derivative and hyperpious nature of fifteenth-century ver-nacular theology to the self-censorship occasioned by Arundel's laws.[76] Nevertheless, lollard spirituality became a part of the fabric of fifteenth-century piety. The generation of Oxford-trained ecclesiastics who led the English church in the decades after Arundel's prohibitions were heavily in-fluenced by Wyclif's arguments for reform and attempted to respond con-structively.[77] Some even supported producing an approved translation of the English Bible—Mary Dove suggests that Arundel himself may have in-tended to produce one.[78] But by the end of the fifteenth century, advocates for the English Bible had to tread a fine line or risk Reginald Pecock's fate.[79]

The question of lollardy's urban or rural afterlife is open for debate, but the material in Plimpton MS 259 suggests that some lollard ideas may have been circulating in rural Norfolk in the late fifteenth century.[80] It may be significant that while most of the heresy trials in East Anglia centered on towns grouped around the Suffolk border, two men from South Creake, a town only eight miles to the north where Robert Gottes later rented land, were prosecuted for heresy in 1429.[81] The Gotteses do fit the demographic profile of heresy suspects in fifteenth-century East Anglia developed by Maureen Jurkowski. These suspects tended to be locally prominent farm-ers in rural areas who worked to expand their landholdings and were active in local administration.[82] Also like the Gotteses, they were often literate and displayed a marked reverence for scripture.[83] Indeed, Gail McMurray Gibson has suggested that Norfolk was a county particularly amenable to religious dissenters, and that East Anglian religious culture was heavily influenced by lollard spiritual ideals.[84]

The 1537 will written by Robert Gottes's son Richard, however, offers a different picture of the family's piety.[85] Here, Richard exhibits a strong devotion to Mary and his local parish. He leaves money for building a new steeple in the parish church, and makes two additional bequests to supply lights before the Host and an image of Mary. Richard also leaves money to guilds, friaries, and the Cathedral in Norwich. The last of his religious bequests is the most extravagant: a yearly stipend for a priest "to sing for my sowle and for my frendes sowles witin the church of Ribrugh forsaid by the space of foure holl yeres."[86] Venerating images, supporting friars, endowing chantries—these are practices that are neither consistent with current assessments of lollard spirituality, nor with the texts in Plimpton MS 259.[87] Richard's bequests are all the more remarkable given the religious climate of the late 1530s, when Henry VIII began to implement protestant legislation at the parish level.[88] Wills respond only slowly to changes in church administration and practice, but it is striking that Richard chose to make these bequests even given the mounting pressure against images and religious institutions.

There are a few possibilities for reconciling the inconsistencies within the spirituality exhibited by members of the Gottes family. First, it may be that Richard and his father subscribed to different systems of belief and practice. The affective religious texts in Plimpton MS 259 from the mid-sixteenth century suggest, however, some continuity of belief within the family.[89] Second, it is conceivable that neither Plimpton MS 259 nor Richard's will accurately represent the Gotteses' religious affiliations. Wills are formulaic, and using them to interpret piety is controversial.[90] Likewise, miscellanies sometimes appear to be random collections of texts that the compilers happened upon.[91] It is possible that Plimpton MS 259 was assembled in this haphazard way, given the diversity of the manuscript's contents, but the loose grouping of thematically coherent religious texts implies that they were selected more carefully.

The most likely scenario is that the Gottes family participated in the wide range of practices and beliefs available in the fifteenth century, without clearly differentiating between lollard and orthodox spirituality.[92] As has been so often observed in recent scholarship, these two traditions were highly permeable and exhibit strong mutual influence. Both may have appealed to unusually pious believers for their stringency, their emphasis on community, and their promise of salvation. "Crystys Wordys" and Richard Gottes's will, then, lie at different points within a spectrum of contemporary beliefs and practices, but they were not incompatible. It may even be that vernacular scripture was a point of particular concord between them: as Ian Johnson notes, one mid-fifteenth-century scribe included a copy of Ullerston's defense of the English Bible immediately after Nicholas Love's anti-lollard *Mirror of the Blessed Life of Christ* in New York, Pierpont Morgan Library MS M.648.[93] Even as he or she endorsed antiheresy legislation with a marginal "Amen" written after Arundel's *memorandum* authorizing the *Mirror*, this scribe patently supported dissemination of English scripture. Like the Morgan manuscript, then, the inclusion of "What Charyte Ys" and "Crystys Wordys" in Plimpton MS 259 encourages us to explore the fluidity and inclusivity of English religious cultures after Wyclif. They suggest that both lollard and devoutly orthodox readers were interested in accessing English scripture directly, and that fourteenth-century arguments in favor of the English Bible were in circulation even as late as the end of the fifteenth century. Certainly, Plimpton MS 259 and its local context are ripe for further study.

NOTES

1. Hereafter Plimpton MS 259. My thanks to the editors of this volume and to the attendees of the Europe After Wyclif conference for their thoughtful comments. In particular, I would like to thank Maryanne Kowaleski, J. Patrick Hornbeck II, Richard Gyug, Susanne Hafner, and Salvatore Cipriano for their guidance and encouragement at different stages in this project. My thanks also to Maureen Jurkowski for her comments on this essay, to Anne Hudson for her insights on these tracts, and to Consuelo Dutschke at Columbia University Library for her archival assistance. Finally, my thanks to Ian Gottes for his generosity with his time and resources.

2. Mary Dove, ed., *The Earliest Advocates of the English Bible: The Texts of the Medieval Debate* (Exeter, England: University of Exeter Press, 2010), xlii and 117; Mary Teresa Brady, "*The Pore Caitif*, Edited from MS Harley 2336 with Introduction and Notes" (PhD diss., Fordham University, 1954), xix and xxv; Nicole Rice, "Reformist Devotional Reading: The *Pore Caitif* in British Library, MS Harley

2322," in *The Medieval Mystical Tradition in England: Papers Read at Charney Manor, July 2011*, ed. E. A. Jones (Cambridge, England: D. S. Brewer, 2013), 185–186.

3. For editions of many of these works, including "What Charyte Ys" but not "Crystys Wordys," see Dove, *Advocates*; see also Anne Hudson, "The Debate on Bible Translation, Oxford 1401," in *Lollards and Their Books* (London: Hambledon Press, 1985), 68–84; Nicholas Watson, "Censorship and Cultural Change in Late-Medieval England: Vernacular Theology, the Oxford Translation Debate, and Arundel's Constitutions of 1409," *Speculum* 70, no. 4 (1995): 822–864. Anne Hudson and Jill Havens have discussed lollardy and English "nationalism" in the English Bible debates: Hudson, "Lollardy: The English Heresy?" in *Lollards and Their Books*, 141–163; Jill Havens, "'As Englishe is comoun langage to oure puple': The Lollards and Their Imagined 'English' Community," in *Imagining a Medieval English Nation*, ed. Kathy Lavezzo (Minneapolis: University of Minnesota Press, 2004), 96–128. For Wyclif's own sense of the English church, see E. C. Tatnall, "John Wyclif and *Ecclesia Anglicana*," *Journal of Ecclesiastical History* 20 (1969): 19–43.

4. Hudson, "Lollardy," 143; Havens, "Englishe," 96–98. My thanks to the anonymous reviewer for directing me to literature on the Hussite idea of nationhood: see Pavlína Rychterová, "The Vernacular Theology of Jan Hus" and František Šmahel, "The National Idea, Secular Power and Social Issues in the Political Theology of Jan Hus," in *A Companion to Jan Hus*, ed. František Šmahel and Ota Pavlíček (Leiden, Netherlands: Brill, 2014), 170–213 and 214–253; and František Šmahel, "The Idea of the 'Nation' in Hussite Bohemia," *Historica* 16 (1969): 143–247.

5. Rychterová, "Vernacular," 174, 191; Šmahel, "Idea," 216–226.

6. Rychterová, "Vernacular," 172–173, 186–191.

7. Hudson, "Debate," 74–84; Kantik Ghosh, *The Wycliffite Heresy: Authority and the Interpretation of Texts* (Cambridge: Cambridge University Press, 2002), 61–111; Watson, "Censorship," 840–846; Hudson, "Debate," 74–84; Mary Dove, *The First English Bible* (Cambridge: Cambridge University Press, 2007), 6–36.

8. For lollardy within rural communities, see Maureen Jurkowski, "Lollardy and Social Status in East Anglia," *Speculum* 82 (2007): 120–152.

9. I follow Fiona Somerset's use of lollard in her recent book, *Feeling Like Saints*. Somerset understands *lollardy* as a reformed way of life, developed and sustained by communities of readers inspired by but not necessarily adhering to Wyclif's thought. The lowercase "l" and predominantly adjectival usage are intended to acknowledge that "lollard" is a series of characteristics and primarily a matter not of self-identification but of similitude. Fiona Somerset, *Feeling Like Saints: Lollard Writings After Wyclif* (Ithaca, NY: Cornell University Press, 2014), 15–20. On this point and for an overview of terminological trends, see J. Patrick Hornbeck II, *What Is a Lollard?* (Oxford: Oxford University Press, 2010), 3–18.

10. Dove, *Bible*, 6–8; Watson, "Censorship," 830.

11. Hudson, "Debate," 78.

12. Dove, "Introduction," in *Advocates*, xxxiii–xxxiv.

13. Ibid., 117; Rice, "Reading," 185.

14. In Plimpton MS 259, the two thematically linked tracts appear on facing folios in the same hand and with the same *mise-en-page*.

15. Plimpton MS 259, fol. 31r.

16. For modernist theories of nationalism, see Umut Özkırımlı, *Theories of Nationalism: A Critical Introduction* (New York: St. Martin's Press, 2000), 85–166. For a historiographic introduction to medieval English nationhood, see Andrea Ruddick, *English Identity and Political Culture in the Fourteenth Century* (Cambridge: Cambridge University Press, 2013), 1–13.

17. *Nationalism* is a modern concept and the term is generally avoided in studies of historical nationhood. *Nation*, however, is not a modern concept; see Ruddick, *English*, 3. See also Benedict Anderson, *Imagined Communities: Reflections on the Origin and Spread of Nationalism* (1983; repr., London: Verso, 2006), 9–26, 37–46. For critiques, see Özkırımlı, *Theories*, 152–156.

18. Anderson, *Imagined Communities*, 6. Historians have identified the origins of English nationhood in ever-earlier epochs. Anthony Smith and Liah Greenfeld argue that the English nation emerged in the early sixteenth century, in the bureaucratic Tudor state: Anthony Smith, "National Identities: Modern and Medieval?," in *Concepts of National Identity in the Middle Ages*, ed. Simon Forde, Lesley Johnson and Alan V. Murray (Leeds: Leeds Studies in English, 1995), 35; Liah Greenfeld, *Nationalism: Five Roads to Modernity* (Cambridge, MA: Harvard University Press, 1992) 29–31. Thorlac Turville-Petre identifies national consciousness in the early fourteenth century in *Language, Literature, and National Identity, 1290–1340* (Oxford: Clarendon Press, 1996), 22. For a modernist critique, see Krishan Kumar, *The Making of English National Identity* (Cambridge: Cambridge University Press, 2003) 39–55.

19. Hastings, *Construction*, 22–25, 36.

20. Turville-Petre, *Language*, 15–22; Ruddick, *English*, 156–167; Kathy Lavezzo, "Introduction," in *Imagining a Medieval English Nation*, ed. Kathy Lavezzo (Minneapolis: University of Minnesota Press, 2004), xix.

21. Lavezzo, "Introduction," xvi; David Green, "National Identities and the Hundred Years War," in *Fourteenth Century England VI*, ed. Chris Given-Wilson (Woodbridge, England: Boydell Press, 2010), 118–119.

22. Charlton Lewis and Charles Short, *A Latin Dictionary* (Oxford: Clarendon Press, 1879), s.v. *natio*.

23. Hastings, *Construction*, 17; Greenfeld, *Nationalism*, 52. *Natio* appears six times in the New Testament: Luke 21:24; Acts 10:45, 2:5, and 22:21; Philippians 2:15; and Revelation 5:9.

24. Stephen A. Barney, W. J. Lewis, J. A. Beach, and Oliver Berghof, ed. and trans., *The Etymologies of Isidore of Seville* (Cambridge: Cambridge University Press, 2006), 192; see also Ruddick, *English*, 120.

25. Ruddick, *English*, 120.

26. R. R. Davies, "The Peoples of Britain and Ireland 1100–1400 I: Identities," *Transactions of the Royal Historical Society,* 6th series, 4 (1994): 10; cited in Hastings, *Construction,* 17.

27. J. H. Mundy and K. M. Woody, ed., *The Council of Constance,* trans. L. R. Loomis (New York: Columbia University Press, 1961), 344; cited in Green, "National Identities," 118. For the context and an analysis of Polton's arguments, see J.-P. Genet, "English Nationalism: Thomas Polton at the Council of Constance," *Nottingham Medieval Studies* 28 (1984): 60–78. It was in Polton's best interest to endorse a broad definition: at universities and ecumenical councils, *nationes* were groupings of students or delegates from the same geographic area. At Constance in 1415, France challenged England's status as a *natio* distinct from the Germanic lands, and Polton was called on to defend England's legitimacy as its own congregation. Ruddick, *English,* 119; Hastings, *Construction,* 17.

28. These are the same criteria used in fourteenth-century depictions of England; see Turville-Petre, *Language,* 14.

29. Mundy and Wood, *Council of Constance,* 344. The Middle English sense of nacion/nation followed the Latin root; see Ruddick, *English,* 118–119, and Hastings, *Construction,* 17.

30. Havens, "Englishe," 97.

31. For an introduction to the role of the Hundred Years War in stimulating national sentiment, see Green, "National Identities," 115–129.

32. Dove, *Bible,* 68–82.

33. Ibid., 46–67. My thanks to Maureen Jurkowski for sharing her forthcoming paper on this topic, "The Selective Censorship of the Wycliffite Bible," in *The Wycliffite Bible: Origin, History and Interpretation,* ed. Elizabeth Solopova (Leiden, Netherlands: Brill, forthcoming in 2016). For the overwhelming popularity of the Wycliffite Bible, see Kathleen Kennedy, *The Courtly and Commercial Art of the Wycliffite Bible* (Turnhout, Belgium: Brepols, 2014), 1–16.

34. For the Blackfriars Council, see Andrew Cole, *Literature and Heresy in the Age of Chaucer* (Cambridge: Cambridge University Press, 2008), 3–22.

35. Fiona Somerset, "Professionalizing Translation at the Turn of the Fifteenth Century: Ullerston's *Determinacio,* Arundel's *Constitutiones,*" in *The Vulgar Tongue: Medieval and Postmedieval Vernacularity,* ed. Fiona Somerset and Nicholas Watson (University Park: Pennsylvania State University, 2003), 145–157; Dove, *Advocates,* xlix–l.

36. Havens casts the Oxford debates, which included both orthodox and lollard participants, as "the Lollard translation debate," and interprets "nationalism" in the debates as lollard. Havens, "Englishe," 97.

37. Acts 2:5, Douay-Rheims 1899 American Version.

38. Plimpton MS 259, fol. 31r. Louisa Foroughi, "'This was found in an olde written booke:' An Edition of Fols. 1–32 of Columbia University Library Plimpton MS 259, A Late Medieval Miscellany" (MA thesis, Medieval Studies, Fordham University, 2013), 67. My thanks to Anne Hudson for noting the rough

similarity between the biblical quotations here and corresponding passages in the Wycliffite Bible.

39. Clerics are disparaged as Pharisees in two Cambridge tracts: Dove, *Advocates*, 105 (Cambridge Tract II), 118 and 120 (both Cambridge Tract VII).

40. Dove, *Advocates*, 153.

41. Somerset, *Saints*, 63–67.

42. Dove, "Introduction," in *Advocates*, xxxv–xxxvi and 92 (CTI), xlix–liv and 144 (FSB).

43. Ibid., 144.

44. Ibid., 92.

45. Hastings, *Construction*, 35–65; Greenfeld, *Nationalism*, 29–31. For a refutation, see Kumar, *Making*, 39–55.

46. Havens, "Englishe," 103. She lists the prologue to the Wycliffite Bible (Dove, *Advocates*, 84), *First Seith Bois* (Dove, *Advocates,* 145), and Cambridge Tract VII (Dove, *Advocates*, 119). Similar statements also appear twice in Cambridge Tract I (Dove, *Advocates*, 89, 97).

47. Dove, *Bible*, 34–35.

48. See Kumar, *Making*, 60–62; and John Armstrong's theories of exclusion in Özkırımlı, *Theories*, 170–174.

49. Acts 2:5, Douay-Rheims 1899 American Version. Arguments for Bible translation rooted in human history are more common in texts advocating for the English Bible: see Havens, "Englishe," 102–103.

50. Dove, *Advocates*, 101. See also Havens, "Englishe," 107–108.

51. My interpretation is influenced by Brian Stock's famous chapter on heretical "textual communities" in his *Implications of Literacy* (Princeton, NJ: Princeton University Press, 1983), 88–91.

52. Somerset, *Saints*, 72–73; Van Nolcken, "Lay Literacy," 181.

53. Hastings, *Construction*, 47–51; Ruddick, *English*, 308–319.

54. Ruddick, *English*, 309; Mildred Campbell, *The English Yeoman* (London: Merlin Press, 1942), 3–4, 7–20.

55. My doctoral dissertation investigates the rise of the yeomanry in fifteenth-century England. Campbell's 1942 *The English Yeoman* is the key work. For a contemporary yeoman, see Christopher Dyer, *A Country Merchant, 1495–1520* (Oxford: Oxford University Press, 2012).

56. For a contents list, see Foroughi, "Booke," 3–6 and 19–20.

57. The transaction records include Roberts from multiple generations. The first known reference to a Robert Gottes appears in a 1475 charter from Great Ryburgh: British Library, Wodehouse Papers, Additional MS 39221, fol. 10r; Acker, "The Crafte," 78n7. This Robert died in 1494: British Library, Additional MS 39228, fol. 17r.

58. British Library, Additional MS 39221, fol. 96r: on a 1572 valuation of corn, two witnesses sign their own names—including Nicholas Gottes—while six use symbols.

59. Nicholas Orme, *English School Exercises, 1420–1530* (Turnhout, Belgium: Brepols, 2013), 1–42.

60. These tracts are part of a loose grouping of religious material in hands dating from the late fifteenth and the mid-sixteenth century.

61. Somerset, *Saints*, 36–41. On correction within lollard communities, see also Edwin Craun, "Discarding Traditional Pastoral Ethics: Wycliffism and Slander," in *Wycliffite Controversies*, ed. Mishtooni Bose and J. Patrick Hornbeck II (Turnhout, Belgium: Brepols, 2011), 227–242.

62. Somerset, *Saints*, 64–65.

63. Daniel 13:53, Douay-Rheims 1899 American Version. For lollard pacifism, see Ben Lowe, "Teaching in the 'Schole of Christ': Law, Learning, and Love in Early Lollard Pacifism," *Catholic Historical Review* 90, no. 3 (2004): 405–438.

64. Matt. 22:37–40, Douay-Rheims 1899 American Version.

65. I have not found this text attested elsewhere.

66. Somerset, *Saints*, 25–45.

67. Dove, ed., *Advocates*, 117; Foroughi, "Booke," 66–67. The version of "What Charyte Ys" in the Cambridge compilation is slightly longer than the version in Plimpton MS 259: it includes a list of the gospels and a curse upon those who fail to honor holy writ. These last few lines are also omitted in one of the *Pore Caitif* versions, British Library MS Harley 2336. Rice, "Reading," 185–186. A Latin testament of Christ appears in a mid-sixteenth century hand immediately before "What Charyte Ys" on Plimpton 259, fol. 30r, probably as a compliment to this passage; for Charters of Christ and lollardy, see Emily Steiner, *Documentary Culture and the Making of Medieval English Literature* (Cambridge: Cambridge University Press, 2003), 193–228.

68. The focus on speech suggests this tract is responding to limitations on preaching promulgated by the 1382 Blackfriars Council or the preaching licenses mandated by Arundel. Rice, "Reading," 185n41.

69. I take *Wycliffite* here as synonymous with *lollard*, as Dove uses "Wycliffite" and "Lollard" interchangeably.

70. Rice, "Reading," 186. In her manuscript, the phrase is "heuenly men," closer to lollards' self-identification as "trewe men."

71. Ibid., 182; Havens, "Englishe," 109.

72. Somerset, *Saints*, 63–67.

73. Ibid., 65–66. For a similar passage see the Prologue to the Wycliffite Bible in Dove, *Advocates*, 65.

74. My thanks to J. Patrick Hornbeck II for noting the resemblance here to Wyclif's theology of "universals by community," according to which all individual created things derive from and refer back to universal ideas in God's mind. See Stephen E. Lahey, *John Wyclif* (Oxford: Oxford University Press, 2009).

75. Aston, "Lollardy," 208–209.

76. Watson, "Censorship," 823–825.

77. Vincent Gillespie, "Chichele's Church: Vernacular Theology in England After Thomas Arundel," in *After Arundel: Religious Writing in Fifteenth-Century England*, ed. Vincent Gillespie and Kantik Ghosh (Turnhout, Belgium: Brepols, 2011), 19–20.

78. Dove, ed., *Advocates*, xx.

79. Stephen E. Lahey, "Reginald Pecock on the Authority of Reason, Scripture and Tradition," *Journal of Ecclesiastical History* 56, no. 2 (2005): 235–238.

80. See Jurkowski, "Lollardy," 120–152 and Derek Plumb, "The Social and Economic Spread of Rural Lollardy: A Reappraisal," in *Voluntary Religion*, ed. W. J. Sheils and Diana Wood (Oxford: Blackwell, 1986), 111–129.

81. Jurkowski, "Lollardy," 124, 129; for the South Creake suspects, see Norman Tanner, ed., *Heresy Trials in the Diocese of Norwich, 1428–31* (London: Offices of the Royal Historical Society, 1977), 89–92; and Jurkowski, "Lollardy," 121–124, 129.

82. Jurkowski, "Lollardy," 131–143.

83. Ibid., 123. For lollards and literacy, see Margaret Aston, "Lollardy and Literacy," in *Lollards and Reformers: Images and Literacy in Late Medieval England* (London: Hambledon Press, 1984), 196–206; and Jurkowski, "Lollardy," 123.

84. Gail McMurray Gibson, *The Theater of Devotion: East Anglian Drama and Society in the Late Middle Ages* (Chicago: University of Chicago Press, 1989), 30–31.

85. Norwich, Norfolk Record Office, Norwich Consistory Court Will Register, Mingaye 53, Richard Gottes (d. 1537). For piety in wills, see Robert Lutton, *Lollard and Orthodox Religion in Pre-Reformation England: Reconstructing Piety* (Woodbridge, England: Boydell Press, 2006), 11–19.

86. For chantry endowment during this period, see Lutton, *Lollardy*, 55–60.

87. Aston, "Lollards and Images," in *Lollards and Reformers: Images and Literacy in Late Medieval England* (London: Hambledon Press, 1984), 143–189; Somerset, *Saints*, 139–165; Lutton, *Lollardy*, 83–84. Richard certainly used the manuscript—fol. 11v contains a list of debts owed to him.

88. Official positions toward images and monastic houses were inconsistent but increasingly hostile, especially from 1536 to 1538; Christopher Haigh, *English Reformations: Religion, Politics, and Society under the Tudors* (Oxford: Clarendon Press, 1993), 132–133.

89. Robert Lutton's study of Tenterden, Kent, also found that spiritual beliefs attested in wills tend to remain the same within family groups. Lutton, *Lollardy*, 20.

90. Ibid., 19–26, 39–40.

91. Ibid., 11–19.

92. For a cogent discussion of lollardy's influence on fifteenth-century religious cultures and the "dissident orthodoxy" that developed out of reactions against Arundel's prohibitions, see Karen Winstead, *John Capgrave's Fifteenth Century* (Philadelphia: University of Pennsylvania Press, 2007), 51–87.

93. Ian Johnson, "Vernacular Theology/Theological Vernacular: A Game of Two Halves," in *After Arundel: Religious Writing in Fifteenth-Century England*, ed. Vincent Gillespie and Kantik Ghosh (Turnhout, Belgium: Brepols, 2011), 86–87. Likewise, Kathleen Kennedy suggests that the Wycliffite Bible was a point of particular "hospitality" among readers of different confessions: Kennedy, *Art*, 35–43.

CHAPTER TWELVE

RE-FORMING THE LIFE OF CHRIST

Mary Raschko

According to surviving manuscripts, Wycliffites represented the life of Christ in three primary forms: close translation of the Vulgate,[1] close translation interpolated with exegetical commentary, and harmonization of the four gospels into a single narrative. Notably, only one of these three affirms the conventional portrayal of Wycliffites as proto-Protestants who valued the whole text of the Bible in a plain form unadulterated by glossing. The other two lives of Christ, the *Glossed Gospels* and the gospel harmony *Oon of Foure*, convey only select biblical books and re-form those texts, adding to, and rearranging scripture in an effort to clarify its meaning.

Attempting to reconcile these gospel translations with a proto-Protestant paradigm, Anne Hudson has consistently minimized the active interpretive work involved in creating the *Glossed Gospels* and has refrained from including *Oon of Foure* in the corpus of Wycliffite biblical translation.[2] Essentially, she concludes that Wycliffites would clarify the basic text of scripture with reference to "the central Western orthodox tradition" but they would not distort that text through rearrangement.[3] Challenging common assumptions of post-Reformation historiography, in this essay I will demonstrate that Wycliffites presented scripture in a variety of ways and will explore how those different forms functioned together. With regard to the gospels specifically, I will argue that Wycliffite translators employed commentary and harmony as complementary forms that together convey the mystery of divine incarnation, portraying Christ as both the transcendent Word and the ultimate exemplar of right living.

My argument stems both from manuscript evidence and from a medieval European view of scripture that emphasized unity in multiplicity. As I will show, gospel harmonies enjoyed considerable popularity across medieval Europe, and in the preface to Jean Gerson's *Monotessaron* (ca. 1420) we find an apt explanation of their theological function. Describing harmony as a counterpoint to the perceived fragmentation that comes from expounding a text via subdivision and commentary, Gerson asserts that "all multiplicity can be reduced to one or a few things. And what can one take as that one or few, better than the Gospel?"[4] Gerson's principle of unity in multiplicity, likely borrowed from Bonaventure, finds expression in gospel harmonies like the *Monotesseron* and *Oon of Foure* that reconcile all distinct parts of the gospels into a coherent narrative.[5] Such harmonies, Gerson argues, demonstrate the integral unity of the life of Christ to which all other truths ultimately adhere. From this perspective, the gospel harmony *Oon of Foure* is not outlier text at odds with Wycliffite approaches to scripture but rather a logical counterpoint to the *Glossed Gospels*, grounding the generative, expansive work of exegesis in the single life of Christ.

In addition to offering a continental parallel to Middle English scripture, Gerson's paradigm invites us to examine Wycliffite lives of Christ as theological exercises. Although comprehensive close translation is the most widely discussed form of Wycliffite scripture, we know they valued and produced other forms as well: for example, Fiona Somerset has shown how Wycliffites employed biblical summary to draw attention to particular themes, while Jennifer Illig has shown how frequently scripture is interpolated in the Wycliffite sermon cycle.[6] Rather than question whether *Oon of Foure* could really be Wycliffite on account of its form, we should ask how harmonization could serve distinctly Wycliffite aims. What unites the gospels in the Wycliffite Bible, the *Glossed Gospels*, and *Oon of Foure* is a dedication to comprehensiveness. The makers of the *Glossed Gospels* omit nothing from their biblical source, instead adding more material for the reader to digest along with the basic text. Whereas most late-medieval gospel harmonies abridge or excise parts of Christ's life, *Oon of Foure* harmonizes all distinct episodes from the four gospels into one coherent account. I argue that this interest in comprehensiveness is not simply a sign of the writers' ideology, an endpoint that indicates the presence of Wycliffism, but also a textual strategy employed with a specific theological aim: to bridge the gap between the text of the gospels and the transcendent divine Word they represent.

According to Wyclif, the material texts of the gospels are lower-order representations of the eternal Book of Life, or "Christ the Truth."[7] From this perspective, the gospels present an especially perplexing hermeneutical situation. Christ is both the subject of the *vita*—a historical person whose life story seems subject to the limitations of memory and textual transmission—as well as the interpretive key for eliciting that *vita's* meaning and the transcendent Truth to which it points. As Ian Levy writes, "Christ is himself the Second Person of the Trinity, the Word of God and source of all truth." But, he goes on to say, Christ is also an incarnate person, whose life "becomes the standard of sanctity borne out in humble service that is the essential disposition needed for properly grasping the meaning of scripture."[8] The gospels should teach readers the historical life of Jesus and, in so doing, reveal the Eternal Truth signified in these books and the whole of scripture.[9] Given this complex theology, Wycliffite translators likely aspired to do more than simply spread the plain text of scripture to lay readers. To represent Christ as the alpha and the omega—the unified source and full plentitude of meaning—translators embraced commentary and harmonization.[10] Such textual strategies that add to or rearrange scripture do not mark these lives of Christ as non-Wycliffite; rather, they reflect a Wycliffite Christology that conceived of Christ as historical person, hermeneutic guide, and divine Truth.

Before considering how each life of Christ attempts to bridge the gap between the text of the gospels and the transcendent divine Word they represent, I should articulate more fully the evidence that *Oon of Foure* and the *Glossed Gospels* belong to a common corpus of Wycliffite biblical writing. First, *Oon of Foure* often appears alongside Wycliffite Bible translation. In most cases, Middle English epistles follow the gospel harmony to form a more complete New Testament.[11] Glasgow University MS General 223, for example, has the Catholic epistles after *Oon of Foure*, but it differs from most manuscripts in that it also contains Wycliffite treatises on the basic elements of the faith. In Cambridge, St. John's College MS G. 25, *Oon of Foure* excerpts accompany a Wycliffite translation of Apocalypse as well as two polemical sermons.[12] Second, the *Glossed Gospels* and *Oon of Foure* share a common prologue. Although the prologues to the *Glossed Gospels* differ across manuscripts, the same introduction to the glossed version of Matthew in Oxford, Bodleian Library MS Laud Misc. 235 also prefaces *Oon of Foure* in four manuscripts.[13] This text introduces readers to Augustine's rule of charity and Tyconius's seven rules for scriptural interpretation. Since the same content from Augustine's *De doctrina christiana* appears in the General Prologue to the Wycliffite Bible as well, we might regard this material as standard guidance for readers of Wycliffite translation.[14] A third connection between the two texts has emerged from

Paul Martin Smith's study of how each renders its Latin original. Smith argues that the translations in the *Glossed Gospels* and *Oon of Foure* "are linked through common vocabulary and idiom" and surmises that the gospel harmony translation may have influenced some revised Early Version manuscripts of the Wycliffite Bible.[15] Since *Oon of Foure* derives from Clement of Llanthony's *Unum ex Quattuor*, not the Vulgate, its translation will naturally differ from that in the *Glossed Gospels*, but it seems the translators of each text employed similar methods. Finally, a fourth potential connection—admittedly one that remains hypothetical—is the two texts' association with Greyfriars at Oxford. Anne Hudson has argued that the producers of the Wycliffite Bible, as well as of the *Glossed Gospels* and three other early Wycliffite projects, may have borrowed the scholarly materials they needed from the Oxford Franciscans.[16] Since the Greyfriars library included a copy of the Latin harmony from which *Oon of Foure* was made, it seems plausible that the same group produced this translation as produced the plain text of the gospels and its glossed versions.[17]

While we do not have definitive proof that *Oon of Foure* is Wycliffite, the bulk of our evidence points in that direction. Exploring what roles these contrasting lives of Christ played within the program of Wycliffite biblical translation strengthens our sense of their interconnection and helps us move beyond questions of affiliation to better understand their intellectual and devotional aims. My analysis will show that in the *Glossed Gospels* and *Oon of Foure*, comprehensively translating the gospels facilitates distinct but interrelated goals: namely, to show the simultaneous expansive meaning and fundamental unity of scripture. Together, glossed gospels and gospel harmonies attempt to convey scripture's metaphysics.

OPENING UP THE LIFE OF CHRIST

The *Glossed Gospels* may not fit our conventional expectations for a life of Christ. Modeled on and often translating Aquinas's *Catena aurea*, the *Glossed Gospels* appear more academic than devotional, elucidating short passages of scripture with a catalogue of authoritative interpretations.[18] But at their core are the oldest *vitae Christi*, the four gospels, which the makers of the *Glossed Gospels* highlight through differentiated text size or underlining.[19] The commentary that follows each short scriptural passage elucidates multiple meanings, guiding readers beyond the surface of the text to what the compilers regarded as the intended meaning of the divine author. We know well that by the later Middle Ages theologians often equated this intended meaning with the literal sense.[20] Far from reducing scripture to one simplistic level of meaning (like modern literalism), this conception of the literal sense characterizes multiple, often figurative meanings as integral to the text. It asserts that scripture is always more than what the basic text immediately communicates. From this perspective, the commentary in the *Glossed Gospels* opens up the life of Christ for readers so that they can see the profuse significations of a single story or image.[21]

Representing the full text of all four gospels with a catalogue of authoritative interpretations impresses upon readers the expansiveness of the life of Christ. The gospels' precise words matter because each word gives rise to potentially limitless meaning. An example from the Beatitudes in Matthew's gospel illustrates this phenomenon. After quoting Matthew 5:9—"Blessid be peisible men, for þei schulen be clepid þe sones of God"— the compilers offer the following commentary on the concept of being peaceful:

> *Peisible*: þei bén peisible whiche maken first pees in her herte, aftirward bitwixe briþeren discordinge. For what profitiþ it þat oþere men be pesid bi þee whanne batels of vices ben in þi soule. Ierom here. Þei ben peisible in hem silf whiche dressen alle stryngis of her wille, and maken hem suget to resoun, þat þe soule be suget to his souereyn þat is God and alle þe lowere þingis of þe soule be suget to resoun and þe spirit. Þe soule may not comaunde to his lower partis if it is not suget to God. And þis is pees þat is ȝouun in erþe to men of good wille. Austin here . . . Not oneli þei ben pesible whiche reconcelen enmyes in to pees but also þei þat ben vnmyndeful of yuels, and þei louen pees. Þat pees is blessid which is set in þe herte, not in wordis. Þei þat reconcelen oþere mennis enmyes and ben neuere reconcelid of herte to her owne enmyes ben scorneris of pees, not loueris of pees. Crisostom here.[22]

Readings from both Jerome and pseudo-Chrysostom seize on the most intuitive meaning—reconciling disputes among individuals—and insist that the text invokes another form of peacemaking as well, peace within the heart. While all three commentators address making peace within the self, they do so in differing ways that expand and deepen the concept. Jerome's comments refer to a battle of vices, while Augustine gives a more elaborate account of ordering the self: a peacemaker subjects the soul to God generally and the will to reason specifically. Pseudo-Chrysostom's gloss reminds readers that words alone are insufficient, that living peace-fully requires love, especially of one's enemies. Together, these varied inter-pretations characterize even small units of text as polyvalent and show how devout readers unfolded their meaning across space and time.[23]

Although this style of glossing appears academic, prologues accompa-nying the glosses ascribe to them practical purposes. There is no standard preface to the *Glossed Gospels,* yet most prologues characterize the gospels as exemplary texts that show their readers how to live.[24] For example, the prologue to Matthew in British Library MS Add. 41175 states that "oure Lord Iesu Crist, veri god and veri man, tauȝte in his owne persoone, and comaundide hise apostlis and disciplis to preche it to alle maner men. And whoeuer bileueþ þe gospel and kepiþ it in his liyf schal gete remyssioun of alle hise synnes."[25] Here, the gospel is not so much the written record of Jesus's life but his manner of living, the "standard of sanctity" to which Levy refers. Just as the author suggests that the reader should not only be-lieve but keep, or adhere, to that life, he later refers to the gospel as "þe riȝt weie to heuene," a path to salvation for not only the learned but also "lewid men and sympli-lettrid prestis."[26] The prologue to Matthew in Laud Misc. 235 also describes the gospel as a rule to which readers should adhere, but in this case it is described as a remedy for the spiritually sick. The author encourages readers to "leyin to oure seke peple þe plastre of holy writ." After coming to know the life of Christ with the interpretations of theo-logical "doctours," readers may heal others by making them "knowe and amende her yuel lyuynge and acord wiþ holy writ, byfore þat þei of þis lyf gon."[27] According to these prologues, the *Glossed Gospels* convey what many lives of Christ aim to convey: the ultimate exemplar for Christian living embodied in the historical life of Jesus.

But why would comprehension of that exemplary life require a catalog of exegesis? Glosses to Luke 14:12–14 offer one example of how this activity unfolds the life of Christ in ways both intellectual and practical. The fol-lowing excerpt from Cambridge University Library MS Kk.2.9 expounds upon the moment when Jesus instructs guests at a Pharisee's house to in-vite the poor, crippled, blind, and lame to their banquets:

Þerfore he þat clepiþ pore men to þe feest shal resseyue mede in tyme to coming. He þat clepiþ frendis, briþeren, and riche men resseyueþ his mede here. But also if he doþ þis for good bi ensaumple of þe sones of blessid Iob, as oþere offices of broþeres loue, he þat comaundide rewardiþ he þat clepiþ to þe feest. Glotouns eþer lecchoures for wildenesse shal be punyschid bi euere lastyng peyne in tyme to coming. *Bede here.* ¶ But þou seist a pore man is vnclene and ful of filþis, waysche þou hym and make hym to sitte wiþ þee at þe boord. If he haþ filþi cloþis ȝyue þou a clene cloþ to hym. Crist neyȝeþ to þee bi hym and þou spekist veyn þingis. *Crisostom.* ¶ Þerfore dispise þou not men liggyng, as if þei ben no þing worþ. Þenke what þei ben and þou shalt fynde þe preeciouste of hem. Þei han þe ymage of þe sauyour, þei ben eiris of godis to coming, þei ben keie bereris of þe rewme of heuen accusers and sufficient excusers, not spekyng but bi holdun of þe iuge. *Gregory Nycene.* ¶ Þerfore it bicomeþ to resseyue pore men in solers [upper chambers] aboue. If þis plesiþ not, at þe leest resseyue þou Crist byneþe, where þi werk beestis and seruauntis ben. At þe leest, a pore man be maad keper of þi dore. For where almis is, þe deuel dar not entre. Þouȝ þou sittist not wiþ hem, sende messis to hem fro þi boord. *Crisostom.* ¶ Gostly he þat eschewiþ veynglorie clepiþ to gostly feeste pore men, þat is vnkunnyng men to make hem riche, feble, þat is men hauyng sik conciens for to hele hem, crokid, þat is men bowun away fro resoun, þat þei make riȝt weies, blynde, þat is hem þat wanten þe siȝt of treuþe þat þei se verey liȝt þei mowen not ȝelde to þee, þat is, þei kunnen not brynge forþ answere. *Origen.*[28]

The layout of the text, which I emulate in this modern transcription, demarcates a number of distinct interpretations for one relatively straightforward behavioral instruction. Just this small section contains five strands of commentary from four different exegetes, both complicating the text's meaning and applying it to daily life. Interpretations attributed to Chrysostom and Gregory of Nyssa address material poverty and physical disability, while simultaneously reminding readers of Jesus' association with the poor: Such guests may be unclean or unable to walk but what one does for them, one does for God as well.[29] Yet the gloss attributed to Origen clarifies that Jesus's instruction can apply to the spiritually poor or lame as well. Understood figuratively, Luke 14:13 could encourage one to teach the unlearned, counsel sinners to repent, or show reason and right belief to those who misunderstand the truth. All readings are presented as valid, all implied by the life of Christ. At the same time that the glosses show the gospel's multiple meanings, they also encourage readers to enact its lessons. The glosses attributed to Chrysostom are exceedingly practical: if your poor guests are dirty, wash them. If having poor people at your table makes you uncomfortable, at least welcome them among your servants or your animals. The *Glossed Gospels*, therefore, impress upon their readers that the life of Christ is bigger than any basic narrative. Yet expansion of that narrative does not necessarily make the gospels esoteric or the sole purview of academics. Their meaning is multiple *and* actionable.

In addition to encouraging practical social actions, the *Glossed Gospels* model how to read, so that audiences may responsibly discover meanings that go beyond the basic text. As the previous passages demonstrate, the glosses insist upon multiple meanings without privileging one reading over another.[30] Nonetheless, readers should not mistake the glosses' variety for uncontrolled dispersion or fragmentation. An expansive text does not mean that the gospel can mean anything for anyone. An epilogue attached to the Matthew gloss in Laud Misc. 235 offers three reasons for why these particular interpretations should be believed: The first reason is their combined antiquity and authority, which the author phrases as their "oldenesse and holynesse"; the second is the exegetes' great knowledge of holy scripture along with the church's long acceptance of their interpretations, "approuynge her bookis for goode and trewe." The third reason for these exegetes' inclusion, which the epilogue author refers to as the most important, is their perceived embodiment of scripture: "for þei acordiden so myche wiþ holy writ and resoun in spekynge and lyuynge, and weren euere meke and redy to be amendid if ony man coude fynde defaute by holy writ or resoun in her writynge."[31] With this criterion, we return to the idea that Christ is both the subject of the text and the key to its interpretation. Good living, after the model and teachings of Christ, is crucial to being a good reader of the *vita Christi*. While this reasoning may appear problematically circular, we could conceive of it as spiraling. The meanings that emanate from the text maintain an ongoing connection to a unifying truth that grounds all right interpretation.

I will return to the idea of unity grounding multiplicity later in this essay, but there remains more to say about the correspondence between authoritative interpretation and devout living. The epilogue's contention that these exegetes embodied the life of Christ in word and deed recommends the same paradigm to its readers. Living humbly like Christ is the starting point for comprehending the gospel and measuring that comprehension. The *Glossed Gospels*, therefore, represent both the text and the interpretive community as open, in the sense that if one reads like a saint, one can further expound the life of Christ. To read like a saint means understanding a given passage of scripture as Augustine, Ambrose, or Bede did, while also manifesting the same charitable disposition attributed to these figures and ultimately to Christ. The range of authorities cited within the glosses offers evidence that saintly readers can be found in any historical period. Although the prologues assert that only the oldest authorities are included, the prologue in Laud Misc. 235 still names Bernard of Clairvaux, Peter Lombard, and Robert Grosseteste among these most ancient exegetes. Within the glosses, one can also find reference to Ranulph Higden, Peraldus, Johannes Halgrinus of Abbeville, and even an anonymous figure who is said to have preached recently in Oxford.[32] The community of saintly readers, then, can be found across the life of the church and remains open for contemporary readers to join. Likewise, the meaning emerging from the gospels is not fixed but expands as readers who live like Christ seek the gospels' application to their own time. A glossed life of Christ, therefore, implies that through devout reading, the words of scripture will ever more fully, but never sufficiently, express the divine Word.

SHOWING UNITY IN MULTIPLICITY

The *Glossed Gospels* gesture toward the divine person of Christ by insisting that the text contains untold layers of meaning. What prevents this multiplicity from being so dispersed and varied that it becomes meaningless is the idea that the divine Word is also single or unified. Harmony, as Gerson argues, is the necessary complement to the generative, expansive movement of glosses. Although *Oon of Foure* occupies a marginal position in the study of medieval English religiosity, the text was anything but marginal to late medieval culture. The gospel harmony genre has a long history stretching back to the second century and enjoyed broad popularity in the fourteenth and fifteenth centuries.[33] In addition to English works like the Pepysian gospel harmony and the various Middle English translations of the pseudo-Bonaventuran *Meditationes vitae Christi,* we can look to contemporary continental texts, including vernacularizations of Tatian's *Diatessaron* or Ludolph of Saxony's *Life of Christ,* for evidence of the genre's popularity.[34] The Middle English *Oon of Foure* survives in fifteen manuscripts dating to circa 1400 and after, and its twelfth-century source, Clement of Llanthony's *Unum ex Quattuor,* survives in a similar number of copies.[35] Although there is some precedent for using gospel harmonies within liturgical contexts,[36] we have ampler evidence of their theological function: harmonization acts out the assertion that all parts of scripture can be integrated into one coherent Truth. The most influential theological treatise outlining this principle is Augustine's *De consensu Evangelistarum,* which provided guiding principles for both Clement of Llanthony's and Gerson's gospel harmonies. Responding to those who impugned the truth of the gospel on account of its disparate witnesses, Augustine explores the four books' concordance "with the view of seeing how self-consistent they are, and how truly in harmony with each other."[37]

It is easiest to conceive of harmonization episodically: the four evangelists recount different aspects of Jesus's life, and a harmonized version can give these distinct narratives a single chronology. In the first chapters of *Oon of Foure,* this is the predominant task. John's attestation that the Word was with God in the beginning comes first, grounding the life of Christ in the Trinity and locating the son's role in creation. From there, the *vita* moves to the nativity and weaves together episodes from Matthew's and Luke's gospels. Yet narratives of Jesus's ministry and passion frequently describe the same event; therefore, the harmony generally follows Matthew's narrative while adding unique elements from Mark, Luke, or John. Because Clement of Llanthony favored comprehensiveness over brevity, he includes both versions of similar events like the Sermon on the Mount (Matthew 5–7) and the Sermon on the Plain (Luke 6). Jesus comes down from the mountain and delivers a similar sermon to a new audience. Yet where multiple gospels recount the same event, Clement harmonizes scripture at the sentence level, integrating specific words from one gospel that another lacks. We can see this phenomenon in *Oon of Foure*'s account of the Last Supper:

[Mt. 26:26] Forsoþe hem soupinge, Ihesu toc bred and [Lk. 22:19] dide þankingis [Mt. 26:26] and blissede and brac and ȝaf to hise disciplys and seide, "Take ȝee and eteþ. Þis is my body [Lk. 22:19–20] þat shal ben bitaken for 3ou. Do 3ee þis þing in to my commemoracioun." In liic maner, also he taking þe kuppe aftir þat he soupide [Mt. 26:27] dide þankingis and 3af to hem and seide, "Drinke 3ee alle of þis." [Mk. 14:23] And þei drunken alle þerof. And he seide to hem, "Forsoþe þis is my blod of þe newe testament þat shal be shed out for manye [Mt. 26:28–29] in to remysseoun of synnes. Treuli I seie to 3ou þat I shal not drinken fro þis tyme of þis generacioun of þe vyne til in to þat dai whan I shal drinke it newe wiþ 3ou in þe rewme of my fadir."[38]

The harmony presents this institution of the words of consecration with reference to three of the four gospels, changing sources to integrate phrases as small as Luke's "dide þankingis" or Mark's affirmation that after Jesus instructs all to drink, "þei drunken alle þerof." Inclusion of such small discrepant phrases reflects the belief that all parts belong to the same whole and can be reconciled with one another to convey one coherent life.

Oon of Foure, therefore, has an explicitly theological aim in that it demonstrates the fundamental unity of scripture. But like the *Glossed Gospels*, this translation was more than an academic exercise. A prologue appearing in four manuscripts describes the gospel as a rule by which readers should live:[39]

Cristyn men owen to trauel myche ne3t and day about þe tixt of holy writ and nameli þe gospel in here moder-tunge, siþen Iesu Crist, verri God and man, tau3te þis gospel wiþ his blessed mouþ, and kepte it in his lijf, and for kepynge and halowynge þerof he schedde his precius blod, and 3af it wryten bi his foure gospelleris, Matheu, Mark, Luyk and Jon, þat eche man schulde reule his lif þerbi.[40]

The gospel is a mode of living, preached and enacted by Jesus, that the evangelists recorded to guide others to the same holy life. Elsewhere, I have argued that a harmonized version of the gospels makes the life of Christ easier to emulate. Placing the events of the four gospels into a coherent order creates a singular exemplar that aims, at least, to eliminate contradictions and ambiguities from the life of Christ for those who seek to follow it.[41] Yet if *Oon of Foure* emerges from a context of Wycliffite translation, living the gospel is inextricably linked to comprehending the gospel. In the harmony, readers find the gospel embodied in the historical life of Jesus, an incarnation of the transcendent Word. Likewise, when readers embody the gospel themselves, they better perceive the eternal Book of Christ to which individual scriptural books attest. The unity of harmony inspires and grounds their inquiry into a larger truth of Christ.

HARMONIZATION: A WYCLIFFITE FORM OF GLOSSING

The final piece of evidence that these contrasting lives of Christ did complementary work within a common Wycliffite culture of biblical translation is the Wycliffite affinity for harmonization. Aside from *Oon of Foure*, Wycliffite harmonies remain relatively unknown, in part due to their manuscript contexts, where they appear alongside better-known yet still unedited texts. What Michael Kuczynski has called a Wycliffite *catena* of Psalms certainly falls into this category. Huntington Library MS HM 501 is a scriptural miscellany that includes excerpts from *Oon of Foure* as well as three different versions of the Psalms.[42] Kuczynski refers to the most abbreviated Psalter as a *catena* to emphasize the network of associations that link different excerpts. He writes that this collection of 142 verses from 23 Psalms is "drawn from across the Psalter and reassembled out of their regular order but with a consistent sense."[43] Essentially, the compiler abridged and harmonized the Psalter around the particular themes of spiritual poverty and divine wrath. If we look closely at other *Oon of Foure* manuscripts that include Wycliffite biblical translation, more examples of harmonization emerge. In Oxford, Bodleian Library MS Bodley 771, *Oon of Foure* and its apparatus are followed by what Smith describes as "select passages from the Old and New Testaments."[44] Indeed, it is on account of these translations that the manuscript appears in lists of "Wycliffite Bibles." Yet they consist of scriptural excerpts arranged in an order different from their traditional biblical sequence, often according to theme. A passage on pride, for example, combines excerpts from Isaiah, Proverbs, Ecclesiasticus, and Job within two columns of text.[45] Similarly, the copy of *Oon of Foure* in British Library MS Royal 17 C. xxxiii is followed by "selected passages from the Wycliffite translations of the Old and New Testaments."[46] Here too, one finds harmonized excerpts, grouped together thematically to demonstrate the many attestations to a particular doctrine throughout scripture.

Additional evidence for Wycliffite interest in harmony comes from within the *Glossed Gospels* themselves, further suggesting that glossing and harmonization were related translation strategies. While Anne Hudson and Henry Hargreaves each discuss the topical passages that appear throughout the *Glossed Gospels*, they focus on the additional sources featured in these sections rather than how the style of commentary changes to a form of harmonization.[47] Topical passages offer sustained commentary on a relevant contemporary issue, whether sacramental (like confession or the Eucharist), ecclesial (on the office of the priesthood or the keys to the kingdom), or moral (on homicide, humility, or avarice). The compiler of the glosses in York Minster MS XVI.D.2 draws attention to these passages most explicitly, offering a list near the end of the manuscript, but they can be found across most exemplars.[48] Breaking from the normal pattern modeled on the *Catena aurea*, in these sections the compilers combine scriptural references—often from the Old Testament or other parts of the New Testament—with canon law and sometimes more recent exegetical authorities to endorse or condemn a particular practice. The following excerpt from a topical passage on confession combines a reference to the Psalter with three different sections of Luke's gospel:[49]

> *Dauiþ seiþ*, knoulech ʒe to þe lord for he is good, for his merci is wiþouten ende. Efte, God we schulen knoulech to þee. We schulen knoulech, and inwardli we schulen clepe þi name and we schulen telle þi meruels. And eft, for þe þouʒt of a man schal knoulech to þee, and þe relikis of þouʒt schulen make a feeste dai to þee. *Crist seiþ* of Marie Mawdelen þat was ful of seuene deuelis, þat is alle synnes, as Gregory expowneþ in xxxiiii omeli þat many synnes ben forʒouen to hir, for sche louyde myche. And he seide to hir aftirward, þi feiþ haþ maad þee saaf. Go þou in pees. As Luyk witnessiþ in þe vii and viii c°. And here in xvii c° of Luyk, *Crist seiþ* to þe Samaritan clensid bifore or he cam to prestis, rise þou and go, for þi feiþ haþ made þee saaf. And eft *Crist seiþ* to þe womman in flux of blood, þi feiþ haþ maad þee saaf, in þe viii c° of Luyk. *Crist seiþ* in þe gospel, Luyk viii c°, I wole merci and not sacrifice.[50]

Throughout most of the glosses, commentary follows short excerpts of scripture; in the topical sections, scriptural lemmata disappear. Instead, the section begins with the invocation of a biblical authority: "Dauiþ seiþ, knoulech ʒe to þe lord," or as you can see four times in this short selection, "Crist seiþ." The compiler will still cite traditional authorities, like Gregory the Great in this example, but these now complement abundant references to particular gospel passages or other books of scripture. With this distinct style of commentary, the creators of the *Glossed Gospels* harmonize scriptural quotations from across the biblical canon, making an argument about its coherence and its clarity on the topic of confession. If all scripture attests to one unified truth, then other scriptural passages are as good a tool for expounding scripture's meaning as ancient exegesis.

When we widen our investigations to encompass more than close translation of full scriptural books, we find that Wycliffites avidly harmonized and glossed scripture. But this does not mean that Wycliffites created lives of Christ just like their contemporaries. In contrast with works like *Cursor Mundi*, the *South English Ministry and Passion,* or the *Stanzaic Life of Christ,* Wycliffites do not gloss the harmonized life of Christ. Unlike these abridgements, they endeavored to omit nothing, suggesting that every bit of text bears witness to an integrated, transcendent truth. Consequently, demonstrating unity and multiplicity via two separate texts may be a practical matter; the long Luke commentary alone fills 298 folios of text in double columns. Maintaining separate demonstrations of unity and multiplicity, however, may also prevent these *vitae Christi* from displacing the four gospels. Wycliffites represented the life of Christ in three primary ways: as the plain text of the four gospels, as a glossed version of one or more individual gospels, and as gospel harmony. Although I have explored the latter two, the first remains the predominant Wycliffite form of representation. The plain text of all four gospels survives in twenty full Bibles, ninety-three complete New Testaments, and at least twenty-six manuscripts with only parts of the New Testament.[51] In re-forming the life of Christ, Wycliffite writers made more explicit what readers should glean from the evangelists' texts, inviting them to join a community of saintly readers, embody Jesus's ethics, and in these ways to reach greater intellection of God. They are, fundamentally, Wycliffite theological exercises—at once intellectual and pragmatic—that attempt to bridge the distance between word and Word, historical life and divine Person.

APPENDIX: MANUSCRIPTS OF THE *GLOSSED GOSPELS*
AND *OON OF FOURE*

Glossed Gospels

Cambridge, Fitzwilliam Museum McClean 133 (sixteenth-century copy of Laud Misc. 235)

Cambridge, Trinity College B.1.38 (short gloss on Matthew and short gloss on John)

Cambridge, University Library ff.6.31 (miscellany with excerpts from Matthew gloss)

Cambridge, University Library Ii.6.55 (miscellany with excerpts from John gloss)

Cambridge, University Library MS Kk.2.9 (long gloss on Luke)

Edinburgh, National Library 6124 (bifolium with excerpts of Matthew gloss)

London, British Library MS Additional 28026 (long gloss on Matthew)

London, British Library MS Additional 41175 (short gloss on Matthew)

Longleat House, Wiltshire, Marquess of Bath MS 5 (some marginal annotations)

New Haven, Yale Beinecke (olim Keio), Takamiya 31 (some marginal annotations)

Oxford, Bodleian Library MS Bodley 143 (short gloss on Luke)

Oxford, Bodleian Library MS Bodley 243 (short gloss on Luke and short gloss on John)

Oxford, Bodleian Library MS Laud Misc. 235 (intermediate gloss on Matthew)

York Minster XVI.D.2 (glosses to the dominical gospels)

Oon of Foure

Cambridge, Peterborough Cathedral MS 8

Cambridge, St. John's College MS G.25 (extracts only)

Dublin, Sir John Glavin (incomplete)

Glasgow, University MS General 223

London, British Library MS Arundel 254

London, British Library MS Harley 1862

London, British Library MS Harley 6333

London, British Library MS Royal 17 D.viii

London, British Library MS Royal 17 C.xxxiii

New York, Columbia University MS Plimpton 268

Oxford, Bodleian Library MS Bodley 481

Oxford, Bodleian Library MS Bodley 771

Oxford, Bodleian Library MS Bodley 978

Oxford, Christ Church College MS Allestree L.41

San Marino, Huntington Library MS HM 501 (extracts only)

NOTES

1. Standard descriptions of the Wycliffite Bible note that an early version carefully reproduced Latin syntax while the later version was more idiomatic. I refer to both as close translation, agreeing with David Lawton that the two strategies present "a choice not between literal and free translation but between two understandings or types of literal translation." See Lawton, "Englishing the Bible, 1066–1549," in *The Cambridge History of Medieval English Literature*, ed. David Wallace (Cambridge: Cambridge University Press, 1999), 470.

2. Anne Hudson states that "early critics," namely Forshall and Madden and Margaret Deanesly, thought *Oon of Foure* was Wycliffite, but she finds it unlikely that Wycliffites would create a gospel harmony, since they valued "the precise words of scripture." *The Premature Reformation: Wycliffite Texts and Lollard History* (Oxford: Clarendon Press, 1988), 267. In more recent scholarship, Mishtooni Bose also doubts the harmony's affiliation with Wycliffism, citing Ralph Hanna's study of earlier biblical translation in one copy, yet Hanna himself calls the harmony "possibly Lollard." See Bose, "Reversing the Life of Christ: Dissent, Orthodoxy, and Affectivity in Late Medieval England," in *The Pseudo-Bonaventuran Lives of Christ: Exploring the Middle English Tradition*, ed. Ian Johnson and Allan F. Westphall (Turnhout, Belgium: Brepols, 2013), 67 and Hanna, *London Literature, 1300–1380* (Cambridge: Cambridge University Press, 2005), 307. In contrast, Paul Martin Smith has argued the harmony is Wycliffite and Elizabeth Schirmer has included *Oon of Foure* in a canon of Lollard biblical translation. See Smith, "An Edition of Parts I–V of the Wycliffite Translation of Clement of Llanthony's Latin Gospel Harmony *Unum ex Quattor* known as *Oon of Foure*," 2 vols. (PhD diss., University of Southampton, 1985), and Schirmer, "Canon Wars and Outlier Manuscripts: Gospel Harmony in the Lollard Controversy," *Huntington Library Quarterly* 73, no. 1 (2010): 1–36.

3. Hudson claims that the *Glossed Gospels* were "founded on a structure of *displayed* adherence to the central Western orthodox tradition" in her extensive study of *Glossed Gospels* manuscripts and sources: *Doctors in English: A Study of the Wycliffite Gospel Commentaries* (Liverpool: Liverpool University Press, 2015), cxxxviii. In *The Premature Reformation*, she asserts that the compilers simply "impart[ed] basic instruction on biblical texts in a dispassionate and almost pedantically correct form" (258). Henry Hargreaves similarly describes the *Glossed Gospels* as uncontroversial, asserting that they contain "the most obvious works to choose for anyone wanting to compile an orthodox commentary on the gospels in the fourteenth century." See Hargreaves, "Popularising Biblical Scholarship: The Role of the Wycliffite *Glossed Gospels*," in *The Bible and Medieval Culture*, ed. Willem Lourdaux and Daniël Verhelst (Leuven, Netherlands: Leuven University Press, 1979), 183.

4. This translated excerpt of Gerson's preface comes from Marijke H. De Lang, "Jean Gerson's Harmony of the Gospels (1420)," *Nederlandsch Archief voor*

Kerkgeschiedenis 71, no. 1 (1991): 46. The Latin text states "quoniam habet omnis varietas ad unum vel pauca reduci. Quid erit illud unum vel paucum convenientius accipiendum quam evangelium?" See Jean Gerson, "Monotesaron," in *L'oeuvre Doctrinale (423–491)*, ed. Palémon Glorieux, vol. 9 of *Oeuvres Complètes* (Paris: Desclée, 1973), 246.

5. Marc Vial describes Gerson's principle as "die Einheit und Vielfalt des Wortes Gottes [the unity and diversity of God's word]" and suggests it was drawn from Bonaventure's writings. See Vial, "Zur Funktion des *Monotessaron* des Johannes Gerson," in *Evangelienharmonien des Mittelalters*, ed. Christoph Burger, A. A. den Hollander, and Ulrich Schmid (Assen, Netherlands: Royal Van Gorcum, 2004), 56 and 64.

6. See Fiona Somerset, *Feeling Like Saints: Lollard Writings after Wyclif* (Ithaca, NY: Cornell University Press, 2014), 166–202 and Jennifer Illig, "Through a Lens of Likeness: Reading *English Wycliffite Sermons* in Light of Contemporary Sermon Texts" (PhD diss., Fordham University, 2014), 85–92.

7. On Wyclif's equation of the Book of Life with Christ, see Ian Christopher Levy, *Holy Scripture and the Quest for Authority at the End of the Middle Ages* (Notre Dame, IN: University of Notre Dame Press, 2012), 62–65. Levy also attributes a similar view to Henry of Ghent, Nicholas of Lyra, and Jan Hus (4, 9, and 155).

8. Levy, *Holy Scripture*, 65.

9. According to Christopher Ocker, late medieval theologians attributed to scripture a more uniform purpose than their predecessors. For what he describes as "the theologian's conviction that biblical teaching taken as a whole had a single purpose and a single subject," see Ocker, *Biblical Poetics Before Humanism and Reformation* (Cambridge: Cambridge University Press, 2002), 24–29.

10. Kantik Ghosh suggests the possibility of Wycliffites embracing commentary and harmony in his description of Wycliffites "thinking in alternatives" about biblical hermeneutics. Ghosh discusses passages of the Wycliffite sermon cycle that attribute a "sentential unity" to all scripture as well as passages that refer to an exegetical tradition that explicates scripture's complexity and multiple meanings. The former, Ghosh remarks, "would go some way towards explaining the otherwise unlikely Lollard involvement with *Oon of Foure*." See *The Wycliffite Heresy: Authority and the Interpretation of Texts* (Cambridge: Cambridge University Press, 2002), 121–130, 244n22.

11. In six *Oon of Foure* manuscripts, additional Wycliffite translations of scripture follow the harmony. This includes Glasgow, University MS General 223; London, British Library MS Royal 17 C.xxxiii, MS Harley 6333, and MS Arundel 254; and Oxford, Bodleian Library MS Bodley 771 and Bodley 978. Additionally, in San Marino, Huntington Library MS HM 501, excerpts from *Oon of Foure* are combined with later version Wycliffite Bible translations to form a composite life of Christ. The ninth item in a biblical miscellany, this life of Christ starts with the nativity from *Oon of Foure* and ends with the harmony's passion and

resurrection narratives. Between these two sections are most of the Sermon on the Mount (Matthew 4:23–5:48), the healing of the centurion's servant (Matthew 8:2–12), and the raising of Lazarus (John 12:1–13:1). For a brief description of the *vita* and a table of contents for HM 501, see Schirmer, "Canon Wars," 25–27, but note that the entry for fols. 133–134v contains a typo, stating John 1–13:1 where it should read 12–13:1.

12. The Apocalypse translation contains commentary. The two sermons are "Vae octuplex" and "Of Ministers in the Church." For more on Cambridge, St. John's College MS G. 25, see Hanna, *London Literature*, 307–308.

13. The relevant manuscripts are Oxford, Christ Church College MS Allestree L. 41, Harley 6333, Arundel 254, and Glasgow General 223. The version in Laud Misc. 235 is considerably longer than the prologue in the *Oon of Foure* manuscripts. The additional text explains the sources used in the *Glossed Gospels* and, taking a polemical turn, warns against three enemies of the church: simoniacal priests, false religious, and those who prevent others from knowing scripture. For the full text, see Mary Dove, ed., *The Earliest Advocates of the English Bible: The Texts of the Medieval Debate* (Exeter, England: University of Exeter Press, 2010), 174–179.

14. See chap. 12 of the General Prologue in Dove, *Earliest Advocates*, 63–70.

15. "Early Version" (EV) translations of the Wycliffite Bible vary considerably from one another on account of revisions. The *Glossed Gospels* translations belong to a group of EV manuscripts known as the V-group. Paul Smith, "Could the Gospel Harmony *Oon of Foure* Represent an Intermediate Version of the Wycliffite Bible?," *Studia Neophilologica* 80 (2008): 162, 166.

16. Hudson suggests that the Wycliffite sermon cycle, the related *Floretum* and *Rosarium*, and the Wycliffite version of Rolle's Psalter commentary belong to the same translation program as the comprehensive Bible translation and the *Glossed Gospels*. For her argument that the materials needed to make these texts came from the Oxford Franciscans, see Anne Hudson, "Five Problems in Wycliffite Texts and a Suggestion," *Medium Aevum* 80, no. 2 (2011): 310–316.

17. For a list of books known to have been in the Greyfriars library, see K. W. Humphreys, ed., *The Friars' Libraries* (London: British Library, 1990), 224–229.

18. For a detailed account of the *Glossed Gospels* sources, see Hudson, *Doctors in English*, liii–cxvi. For a shorter summary, see *Premature Reformation*, 252–254 and Hargreaves, "Popularising Biblical Scholarship," 182–183.

19. Based on the differentiation of scripture and gloss, as well as the clear delineation of sources, Rita Copeland posits that the glosses could have facilitated lay education within Lollard conventicles. See Copeland, *Pedagogy, Intellectuals, and Dissent in the Later Middle Ages: Lollardy and Ideas of Learning* (Cambridge: Cambridge University Press, 2001), 130–140.

20. On the expansion of the literal sense, see Levy, *Holy Scripture*, 11–23, and Ocker, *Biblical Poetics*, 71–111.

21. This kind of systematic glossing is not unique among Middle English

texts. Commentaries on Matthew, Mark, and Luke, all written in a northern dialect, survive in three fourteenth- and fifteenth-century manuscripts. Unlike the *Glossed Gospels*, they include a Latin text of the gospels as well as a Middle English translation. For a description of their sources and methods, as well as the text of their prologues, see A. B. Kraebel, "Middle English Gospel Glosses and the Translation of Exegetical Authority," *Traditio* 69 (2014): 87–123.

22. British Library MS Add. 41175, fol. 13rb. To show the greatest number of exegetes within a small space, I have omitted one additional interpretation from Augustine.

23. For a description of the Bible in the late Middle Ages as an "evolving text," see Christopher Ocker, "The Bible in the Fifteenth Century," in *Christianity in Western Europe c. 1100–c. 1500*, ed. Miri Rubin and Walter Simons, vol. 4 of *The Cambridge History of Christianity* (Cambridge: Cambridge University Press, 2009), 480.

24. Unique prologues appear before short and intermediate Matthew, short Luke, and short John. All prologues are available in Dove, *Earliest Advocates*.

25. Ibid., 172.

26. Ibid.

27. Ibid., 178.

28. Cambridge, University Library MS Kk.2.9, fol. 168vb–169ra.

29. Compare Matthew 25:35–40.

30. Kraebel characterizes the independence of each commentary strand in the *Glossed Gospels* as a point of contrast between Wycliffite exegesis and the northern Middle English commentaries. With reference to the Matthew commentary in particular, Kraebel writes that glosses from Aquinas's *Catena aurea* are "sewn into a continuous text, held together by the vernacular author's elaborations and additions" ("Middle English Gospel Glosses," 97).

31. Dove, *Earliest Advocates*, 180.

32. Add. 41175, fol. 147vb.

33. The earliest known gospel harmony is Tatian's *Diatessaron*, which dates from the mid-second century. For the history of this harmony, see William L. Petersen, *Tatian's Diatessaron: Its Creation, Dissemination, Significance, and History in Scholarship* (Leiden, Netherlands: Brill, 1994).

34. Sabrina Corbellini, for example, has studied Venetian and Tuscan translations of the *Diatessaron* that date from the mid-fourteenth century to the third quarter of the fifteenth century. See Corbellini, "Retelling the Bible in Medieval Italy: The Case of the Italian Gospel Harmonies," in *Retelling the Bible: Literary, Historical, and Social Contexts*, ed. Lucie Doležalová and Tamás Visi (Frankfurt am Main: Peter Lang, 2011), 213–244. Ludolph of Saxony's fourteenth-century Latin *Life of Christ* was translated into six European vernaculars, including Dutch, Italian, French, Spanish, and Portuguese in addition to German. See John J. Ryan, "Historical Thinking in Ludolph of Saxony's *Life of Christ*," *Journal of Medieval and Renaissance Studies* 12, no. 1 (1982): 67.

35. Richard Sharpe lists fourteen extant copies and refers to six other copies attested to among the collections of British medieval libraries. See Sharpe, ed., *A Handlist of the Latin Writers of Great Britain and Ireland before 1540* (Turnhout, Belgium: Brepols, 1997), 87–88.

36. A translation of Tatian's *Diatessaron* served as the standard version of the gospels in Syria through the fifth century. See Petersen, *Tatian's Diatessaron*, 38. With regard to late medieval harmonies, a number of *Oon of Foure* manuscripts contain liturgical calendars or marginal notations indicating the relevant liturgical occasion for a given passage.

37. Saint Augustine, "The Harmony of the Gospels," in *Nicene and Post-Nicene Fathers* vol. 6, ed. Philip Schaff (Peabody, MA: Hendrickson, 1994), 102.

38. Harley 1862, fol. 64vb. I have added the source citations. Although Clement's text includes such indications of source embedded within the text, copies of *Oon of Foure* name the relevant sources in the margins at the beginning of a given section.

39. The prologue appears in four manuscripts: British Library MS Harley 6333, British Library MS Arundel 254, Glasgow University MS General 223, and Cambridge University Library Peterborough Cathedral MS 8. It also appears in Cambridge, University Library MS Ii.6.26, a collection of tracts defending biblical translation.

40. Dove, *Earliest Advocates*, 103–104.

41. Mary Raschko, "*Oon of Foure*: Harmonizing Wycliffite and Pseudo-Bonaventuran Approaches to the Life of Christ," in *The Pseudo-Bonaventuran Lives of Christ: Exploring the Middle English Tradition*, ed. Ian Johnson and Allan F. Westphall (Turnhout, Belgium: Brepols, 2013), 353–357.

42. On the manuscript's various Psalters, see Michael P. Kuczynski, "An Unpublished Lollard Psalms *Catena* in Huntington Library MS HM 501," *Journal of the Early Book Society* 13 (2010): 95–138.

43. Kuczynski, "Unpublished Lollard Psalms," 111.

44. Smith, "Edition of Parts I–V," 1:xvii. The relevant text appears on fols. 80–118v.

45. Bodley 771, fol. 114vb–115rb.

46. Smith, "Edition of Parts I–V," 1:xxiii. The relevant text appears on fols. 226–316v.

47. Although Hudson's analysis primarily pertains to the introduction of new authorities, in reference to one topic, she describes the integration of commentary from other *Glossed Gospels* manuscripts, showing how the compiler combined commentary on Luke 12, Matthew 6, Matthew 5, Luke 14, Luke 18, and Matthew 25 to explicate a passage from Luke 11. In another instance, she refers to "a long string of biblical references." See *Doctors in English*, xcix–c. For Hargreaves on the topics, see "Popularising Biblical Scholarship," 183–189.

48. In addition to York Minster XVI.D.2, topics can be found in British Library MS Add. 28026 and MS Add. 41175, Cambridge, University Library MS

Kk.2.9, and Oxford, Bodleian Library MS Bodley 243. In Bodley 143, the topic on confession has been removed by the excision of one folio and the erasure of the neighboring verso and recto pages.

49. The line attributed to David is Psalm 106.1.

50. York Minster MS XVI.D.2, fol. 185ra; italics mine.

51. These numbers are based on Mary Dove's index in *The First English Bible: The Text and Context of the Wycliffite Versions* (Cambridge: Cambridge University Press, 2007), 281–306.

CONTRIBUTORS

MISHTOONI BOSE, Christ Church, University of Oxford

LUIGI CAMPI, Università degli Studi di Torino

PAVLÍNA CERMANOVÁ, The Centre for Medieval Studies at Charles University and the Academy of Sciences of the Czech Republic

LOUISA Z. FOROUGHI, Center for Medieval Studies, Fordham University

J. PATRICK HORNBECK II, Fordham University

JENNIFER ILLIG, Mount St. Mary's Abbey

KATHLEEN E. KENNEDY, Pennsylvania State University—Brandywine

IAN CHRISTOPHER LEVY, Providence College

OTA PAVLÍČEK, Institute of Philosophy of the Czech Academy of Sciences

MARY RASCHKO, Whitman College

FIONA SOMERSET, Department of English, University of Connecticut

PAVEL SOUKUP, Filosofický ústav Akademie věd České republiky, v.v.i. (Institute of Philosophy of the Czech Academy of Sciences)

MICHAEL VAN DUSSEN, McGill University

JOHN VAN ENGEN, University of Notre Dame

INDEX

FORDHAM SERIES IN MEDIEVAL STUDIES
Mary C. Erler and Franklin T. Harkins, series editors

Ronald B. Begley and Joseph W. Koterski, S.J. (eds.), *Medieval Education*
Teodolinda Barolini and H. Wayne Storey (eds.), *Dante for the New Millennium*
Richard F. Gyug (ed.), *Medieval Cultures in Contact*
Seeta Chaganti (ed.), *Medieval Poetics and Social Practice: Responding to the Work of Penn R. Szittya*
Devorah Schoenfeld, *Isaac on Jewish and Christian Altars: Polemic and Exegesis in Rashi and the "Glossa Ordinaria"*
Martin Chase, S.J. (ed.), *Eddic, Skaldic, and Beyond: Poetic Variety in Medieval Iceland and Norway*
Felice Lifshitz, *Religious Women in Early Carolingian Francia: A Study of Manuscript Transmission and Monastic Culture*
Sam Zeno Conedera, S.J., *Ecclesiastical Knights: The Military Orders in Castile, 1150–1330*
J. Patrick Hornbeck II and Michael Van Dussen (eds.), *Europe After Wyclif*